Poland's Threatening Other

Poland's Threatening Other

The Image of the Jew from 1880 to the Present

Joanna Beata Michlic

UNIVERSITY OF NEBRASKA PRESS
LINCOLN AND LONDON

Sections of chapters 4 and 6
were previously published
in
"Anti-Jewish Violence in Poland,
1918–1939
and
1945–1949,"
Polin 13 (2000): 34–61.

Set in Garamond and Futura by Bob Reitz.
Designed by R. W. Boeche.

Library of Congress Cataloging-in-
Publication Data
Michlic, Joanna B.
Poland's threatening other:
the image of the Jew from 1880 to
the present / Joanna Beata Michlic.
p.   cm.
Includes bibliographical references and index.
ISBN-13: 978-0-8032-3240-2 (hardcover: alk. paper)
ISBN-10: 0-8032-3240-3 (hardcover: alk. paper)
ISBN-13: 978-0-8032-2079-9 (paperback: alk. paper)
1. Jews—Persecutions—Poland—History.
2. Antisemitism—Poland—History.
3. Poland—Politics and government.
4. Nationalism—Poland.
5. Jews—Poland—Public opinion.
6. Public opinion—Poland.
7. Poland—Ethnic relations.
I. Title.
DS135.P6M465   2006
305.892'4043809—dc22
2005031549

This book is dedicated to the memory of
Jacek Kuroń (1934–2004),
a remarkable post-1945 Polish politician and intellectual
who throughout his entire career,
before and after 1989,
condemned not only anti-Semitic actions but also anti-Jewish sentiments
and was dedicated to creating
a civic and pluralistic Poland for all citizens,
and to the memory of my cousin
Zbyszek S.

Contents

Preface

As I began to write this book in the middle of the 1990s, some people advised me not to pursue the subject. One such advice giver was the late Lidia Ciołkoszowa, a culturally assimilated Polish-Jewish woman and a well-known figure in the Polish émigré circle in London. Although Mrs. Ciołkoszowa was acutely aware of the complexities of the problem due to her own experiences in interwar Poland, she saw the issue of Polish anti-Semitism as a painful subject and exploring it as opening a Pandora's box.

In the past Polish scholars felt constrained from undertaking scholarly examination of the nature of anti-Jewish prejudices for fear of harming the good name of Poland by revealing "dark aspects" of Polish treatment of national and cultural minorities. Furthermore, many Polish scholars for a long time rejected the notion of Polish anti-Semitism as an important political, social, and cultural phenomenon in the history of modern Poland. They omitted and minimalized its presence and impact on political culture, Polish-Jewish relations, and the experience of the Jewish community and rationalized it as a phenomenon rooted in objective grounds such as the size of the Jewish community and its intrinsic qualities. This approach persists in post-1989 ethnonationalistic historiography.

At the same time, in some Jewish writings and some corners of popular Jewish memory Polish anti-Semitism has functioned as a mythologized phenomenon. It has acquired the characteristics of a unique and ahistorical phenomenon, either assessed as incomparable to other forms of antiminority prejudice and other manifestations of anti-Semitism in Europe or wrongly and simplistically equated with Nazi anti-Semitic genocidal ideology and practice. These two different sets of assumptions constitute the main obstacles to scholarly analysis of the subject.

This book offers a new reading of the history of Polish anti-Semitism. In it I analyze the nature and impact of anti-Jewish prejudice on modern Polish society and culture. Specifically this book traces the history of the concept of the Jew as the threatening other and its role in the formation and development of modern Polish national identity based on the matrix of exclusivist ethnic nationalism.

In its various shades and intensities exclusivist ethnic nationalism had the upper hand over inclusive civic nationalism in Polish political culture and society throughout the late nineteenth century and the greater part of the twentieth. Only in the aftermath of the political transformation of 1989 has Polish civic nationalism gradually begun to gain the upper hand over its counterpart. As civic nationalism and the culture of pluralism have become more assertive and influential, some Polish scholars have begun to unearth and critically examine the legacy of Polish anti-Semitism and other antiminority prejudices. This book belongs to this new school of critical inquiry into the nature of anti-Jewish prejudice.

In the course of my researching and writing this work numerous colleagues, friends, and institutions offered me their generous support in many ways. The list is long, and here I can only mention a few. My first thanks must go to John D. Klier and Anthony D. Smith for their constructive criticism and advice and their moral support in what can now be viewed as the formative stage of the book—the writing of my doctoral dissertation. I owe a particular debt of gratitude to Antony Polonsky for his wisdom, encouragement, support, and sound suggestions in the final stages of writing. I would also like to thank John Hutchinson, Andrzej Paczkowski, Shimon Redlich, Timothy Snyder, Michael Steinlauf, and Jerzy Tomaszewski for useful suggestions and Hanna and Leon Volovici and Tony Coren for their encouragement. Finally a special note of thanks goes to Ruth Abrams, my editor, with whom I spent enjoyable moments discussing linguistic and other matters in Somerville, Massachusetts, and to the editors at the University of Nebraska Press for walking me through the steps necessary to turn this into a book.

I would also like to thank *Polin* for permitting me to reproduce material.

Abbreviations

AB Extraordinary Peace-Bringing Action (Ausserodentliche Befriedungungsaktion)

AK Home Army (Armia Krajowa)

AL People's Army (Armia Ludowa)

AWS Solidarity Electoral Alliance (Akcja Wyborcza Solidarność)

CKZP Central Committee of Jews in Poland (Centralny Komitet Żydów w Polsce)

FOP Front for the Rebirth of Poland (Front Odrodzenia Polski)

GG General Government (Generalna Gubernia)

GL People's Guard (Gwardia Ludowa)

IPN Institute for National Memory (Instytut Pamięci Narodowej)

KOR Committee to Defend Workers (Komitet Obrony Robotników)

KPP Communist Party of Poland (Komunistyczna Partii Polski)

KPRP Communist Workers' Party of Poland (Komunistyczna Partia Robotnicza Polski)

LPR League of Polish Families (Liga Polskich Rodzin)

MSW Ministry of Foreign Affairs (Ministerstwo Spraw Zagranicznych)

MWP All-Polish Youth (Młodzież Wszechpolska)

NPR National Workers' Party (Narodowa Partia Robotnicza)

NSZ National Armed Forces (Narodowe Siły Zbrojne)

ONR National Radical Camp (Obóz Narodowo-Radykalny)

OWP Camp for a Greater Poland (Obóz Wielkiej Polski)

OZN or OZON Camp of National Unity (Obóz Zjednoczenia Narodowego)

PAP Polish Press Agency (Polska Agencja Prasowa)

PiS Law and Justice (Prawo i Sprawiedliwość)

PKWN Polish Committee of National Liberation (Polski Komitet
Wyzwolenia Narodowego)

PPR   Polish Workers' Party (Polska Partia Robotnicza)

PPS   Polish Socialist Party (Polska Partia Socjalistyczna)

PPS-WRN Freedom-Equality-Independence Party (Partia
Socjalistyczna-Wolność-Równość-Niepodległość)

PSKL Polish Catholic and People's Union (Polskie Stronnictwo
Katolicko-Ludowe)

PSL   Polish Peasant Party (Polskie Stronnictwo Ludowe)

PZPR Polish United Workers' Party (Polska Zjednoczona Partia
Robotnicza)

SD   Democratic Party (Stronnictwo Demokratyczne)

SL   Peasant Party (Stronnictwo Ludowe)

SN   National Democrats (Narodowi Demokraci)

SP   Labor Party (Stronnictwo Pracy)

TON   Association for National Education (Towarzystwo Oświaty
Narodowej)

TRJN Temporary Government of National Unity (Tymczasowy
Rząd Jedności Narodowej)

UB   Secret Police (Urząd Bezpieczeństwa)

UOP   Bureau of State Defense (Urząd Obrony Państwa)

WiN   Freedom and Independence (Wolność i Niepodległość)

ZBOWiD Union of Fighters for Freedom and Democracy (Związek
Bojowników o Wolność i Demokrację)

ZSCH Union of Peasants Party (Związek Stronnictwa Chłopskiego)

ZSP   Union of Polish Syndicalists (Związek Polskich
Syndykalistów)

1. Introduction

The Concept of the Jew as the Threatening Other
and Modern Nation Building in Poland

This book is a synthetic study of the nature and significance of modern Polish anti-Jewish tropes, which first arose in the post-1864 period among conservative, traditionalist, and Roman Catholic circles. In the 1880s the core ethnonationalist Polish movement National Democracy (Narodowa Demokracja) introduced anti-Jewish images and stereotypes into the discourse of national politics. The National Democracy movement made anti-Jewish ideas a major part of its ideology. Through the National Democrats anti-Jewish tropes became a powerful emotive tool for nation building, based on a vision of Poland that excluded Jews and lacked tolerance of the cultural and religious diversity represented by other minorities.[1] These anti-Jewish idioms, as the National Democrats transformed them, had their strongest political and social influence in interwar Poland (1918–39), particularly in the post-1935 period, and continued to influence Polish political culture, attitudes, and behavior toward Jews during both World War II (1939–45), when Poland was occupied by two totalitarian regimes, Nazi Germany (1939–45) and the Soviet Union (1939–41), and the postwar Communist period (1945–89). In Communist Poland anti-Jewish idioms were part of the language and imagery of the anti-Zionist campaign of 1968–69, which resulted in the forced exile of the majority of the remaining post-1945 Polish Jewry. The Communist regime employed the same anti-Jewish rhetoric in the 1970s and 1980s against its political opposition: the Committee for the Defense of the Workers (Komitet Obrony Robotników, KOR) and the first Solidarity movement (Solidarność). Finally, anti-Semitic tropes reemerged openly in the anti-Communist camp, particularly in the right-wing sections of the Solidarity movement and in the so-called Closed Catholic Church, during the political and economic transformation of Poland

in 1989 and 1990, which led to Poland's regaining full sovereignty. Yet in the
new post-Communist Poland important groups of public intellectuals, politicians, and Roman Catholic laypersons and clergy representing the Open Catholic Church have critically discussed, powerfully challenged, and rejected these
recurrent anti-Jewish cultural images as never before.[2] Nonelites, particularly
youth engaged in activities such as Colorful Tolerance (Kolorowa Tolerancja)
and affiliated with organizations such as the Wrocław-based scholarly circle
of students called Hope-Hope (Hatikva-Nadzieja), have also taken part in the
open examination and rejection of anti-Jewish tropes.[3]

The process of challenging and deconstructing anti-Jewish idioms and images is part and parcel of another post-1989 process, which can be thought
of as the rebuilding of Poland on the model of civic nationalism, which does
not define Polishness in a narrow ethno-national sense. Moreover, this model
treats with respect the variety of minority cultures and faiths that have existed
and still do in the Polish territories, along with their memories. Cultivating
respect for the memories of minorities is particularly important in the Polish
case, given the fact that contemporary Poland is one of the world's most ethnically homogenous nation-states, with national, ethnic, and religious minorities
accounting for only approximately 4 percent of the population.[4] Upon his
appointment on 24 August 1989 as Poland's first non-Communist prime minister, Tadeusz Mazowiecki (1927–) articulated his desire to rebuild the post-1989
Polish nation on the model of civic nationalism and a culture of pluralism. In
one of his parliamentary speeches in 1989 Mazowiecki, a politician and writer
representing the liberal Catholic intelligentsia in the first Solidarity movement,
stated: "The Polish state cannot be an ideological or religious state. It has to
be a state in which no citizen will experience discrimination or be treated in
a privileged way because of his ideological convictions. . . . The government
wishes to cooperate with the Roman Catholic Church and all other denominations in Poland. . . . Poland is a homeland not only of Poles. We live in this
land together with representatives of other 'national groups.' The government
wishes that they would see themselves as a part of Poland and would cultivate
their languages and their cultures, and thus enrich our common society."[5]

One good illustration of the close link between challenging anti-Jewish
idioms and rebuilding Poland on the model of civic nationalism is the new
language being used in reference to Jews past and present by leading politicians
such as Aleksander Kwaśniewski, former president of Poland; representatives
of state institutions such as Leon Kieres, former chairman of the Institute of

National Memory (Instytut Pamięci Narodowej, ipn); and representatives of important social and religious institutions such as Father Adam Boniecki, the editor in chief of *Tygodnik Powszechny*, a leading social and cultural weekly of the Open Catholic Church.[6] Their descriptions of Jews as "Polish Jews," "our cocitizens," and "costewards of this land" reflect the inclusion of Jews in the realm of Polishness and the firm rejection of an ethno-nationalist vision of Poland in which there is only room for a single culture and a single faith, ethnic Polish and Roman Catholic. Another important illustration of this link is the affirmation of regret for sufferings inflicted upon Polish Jews by members of the ethnic Polish community, voiced by public intellectuals such as Jan Tomasz Gross, Maria Janion, the late Father Stanisław Musiał, Hanna Świda-Ziemba, and Joanna Tokarska-Bakir, among others.[7] Memories of suffering inflicted upon others, described by certain American scholars as "dangerous . . . because they call the community to alter ancient evils," are important to the contemporary civic and pluralist model of Poland and its advocates.[8] Such memories do not exist in the ethno-nationalist vision of Poland, which preserves only the memory of suffering received.

Aims and Approach

In Polish history attitudes toward Jews and other minorities have constituted a litmus test of democracy, which is embodied in the concept of modern civic nationalism. The presence of anti-Jewish idioms in Polish cultural and political life, in contrast, can be seen as one of the chief markers of the modern Polish ethno-nationalism that began in the late nineteenth century as a manifestation of the wider European phenomenon of exclusivist ethno-linguistic or integral nationalism.[9] The key underlying assumption of this book is that in order to fully grasp the nature, continuity, and longevity of Polish anti-Jewish representations and their significance, one has to take into account their role in the process of Polish nation building. In the late nineteenth century and the first half of the twentieth ethno-nationalism became the dominant model in the formation of modern Polish national identity.[10] During this period, in the painful struggle over the vision of Poland and its people, ethno-nationalism gained the upper hand over modern Polish civic nationalism. The latter form of nationalism was most clearly pronounced in Józef Piłsudski's model of a federalist Poland in the interwar period, which traced its cultural roots to Jagiellonian Poland (Rzeczpospolita Obojga Narodów). Many champions of civic and pluralistic Poland in the post-Communist era have "rediscovered" the cultural traditions of Jagiellonian Poland and view them as a historical heritage on which a new civic and pluralistic Polish society might be based, constituting an alternative to the ethno-nationalist model of society.[11] Their turning to the heritage of a premodern multiethnic and multicultural Polish state indicates the importance of a distinctive past in reshaping contemporary Polish national identity. It is a manifestation of the reselection, recombination, and recodification of previously existing symbols and values.

Although major theories of nationalism generally take for granted the "other" in the formation of national identity and nationalism, scholars from various fields have recently turned their attention to the problem of the "other" evaluated as a rival, adversary, or enemy and the formation of modern national self-identity.[12] Drawing on Fredrick Barth's classic theory of ethnicity, sociologist Anna Triandafyllidou argues that the external or internal "threatening other" is an important part of the process of the formation and reevaluation of national identity and that in some cases an imagined "threatening other" can be as important in influencing the self-conception of the nation as an actual "threatening other."[13] Polish scholars of various disciplines—sociology, the history of Polish literature, and social history—have long argued that the division between "ourselves" (swoi) and "the other" (obcy) is an important feature of modern Polish collective self-identification and memory.[14] Jan Stanisław Bystroń and Aleksander Hertz conducted the first major sociological studies of the division between "us" and "them" and Polish national identity in the interwar period. Both scholars concentrated on discussing the impact of the "other" on pre-1939 Polish national identity and voiced criticism of the division between "us"—ethnic Poles—and "them"—other groups dwelling in Poland.[15] Their criticism of the role of the "other" in political culture focuses on moral issues rather than empirical matters. These scholars were, in particular, critical of the use of the "other" (evaluated as a "threatening other") in political culture for the purpose of increasing national awareness and cohesion, a phenomenon that they witnessed in daily life in interwar Poland.[16] In spite of strong normative judgment, their sociological analyses remain valuable for the study of the other in Polish society.

Historical literature on Polish (ethno)-nationalism hardly discusses the use of anti-Jewish cultural representations as fundamental to the process of the formation of national identity. Rather, it takes one of two general approaches, representing two opposite normative positions. The first approach, which deplores and rejects ethno-nationalism, recognizes anti-Semitism as a key aspect of the doctrine of the National Democracy movement and its offshoot radical organizations. However, it tends to ignore the broader cultural origins and scope of ethno-nationalist thinking, the impact of National Democracy on modern political culture and society at large.[17] The second approach, which to varying degrees endorses the ethno-nationalist vision of Poland advocated by the National Democracy movement, tends either to neutralize the role of anti-Semitism as a key concept in the doctrine of National Democracy or to endorse it, using it to explain anti-Jewish practices and policies.[18]

A few Polish scholars have indicated the importance of anti-Jewish tropes in the formation of modern Polish national identity based on the matrix of ethno-nationalism, though they do not conduct a detailed empirical analysis of the problem. In her article "The Question of the Assimilation of Jews in the Polish Kingdom (1864–1897): An Interpretive Essay" Alina Cała, a social historian of modern Jewish history, suggests that "anti-Semitism strengthened the role of the Jew (or rather his myth) as a determinant of Polish national consciousness. Whole social groups discovered their national allegiance as an offshoot of the feeling of separateness from the Jews. . . . It could be said metaphorically that they entered the national *sacrum*, although in this sphere they most often took on the character of the devil. The Jewish question became an integral part of the Polish complex."[19]

The issue of shaping Polish national identity and the identification of the Jew as the archetype of everything defined as "not-Polish" or "anti-Polish" is also indirectly indicated by Michael Steinlauf, an American scholar of Eastern European Jewish culture and society. In his pioneering book on the memory of the Holocaust in post-1945 Poland he argues that the concept of national conflict between Jews and Poles gave Polish anti-Semitism a unique logic that made it different from other European anti-Semitic movements.[20] Steinlauf makes a persuasive case for the longevity, persistence, and centrality of the concept of national conflict between Jews and Poles in Polish anti-Semitism, though not for its uniqueness. Recent sociological studies show evidence for Steinlauf's assertions about the persistence of Polish anti-Semitic ideas, demonstrating that "remnants" of the long-lasting effect of the polarization of Poles and Jews on the collective self-definition of Poles were still detectable in the late 1980s and early 1990s. For example, according to a survey conducted in Poland in May 1992, Jews were still viewed as competitors in a moral-cultural sense.[21] Polish social historian Marcin Kula surveyed a social group representing the so-called philosemitic voice, condemning anti-Semitic discourse in the 1980s and 1990s, and found within this group a widespread "silent assumption" that

Jews, even those most assimilated into Polish culture, failed to be the same as ethnic Poles, constituting a lesser category of citizens.[22]

Though culturally assimilated Polish Jews and Jewish converts to Roman Catholicism played an important role in the development of modern Polish "high culture" and in democratic political trends, Poles have historically considered them not entirely Polish. This has been true since the nineteenth century. This problem resulted from two interrelated cultural trends: the majority of Polish Jews maintained a strong moral-cultural identity, and large segments of Polish elites perceived Jews as a "proto-nation" or "a nation culturally incompatible" with a Polish nation. German and Russian nationalist discourse also influenced Polish ethno-nationalist discourse. The exclusionary ethno-nationalist position toward assimilated Polish Jews and Jews of Polish origin was particularly acute in interwar Poland, when anti-Semites conducted intense yet unsuccessful attempts to exclude these two social groups from playing any role in Polish culture. In his memoirs Richard Pipes, an American scholar of Russian and Soviet history who was born and grew up in interwar Poland, also reflects on this problem: "The population at large was imbued with a hostility towards Jews, instilled in it over centuries by the Catholic Church. It was not racial anti-Semitism but it was only slightly less painful since it could be averted only by renouncing one's own religion and one's own people, and even then, in Polish eyes, one never quite got rid of one's Jewishness."[23]

The presence of anti-Jewish traditions in post-1945 Poland has sometimes been referred to as "anti-Semitism without Jews." The reoccurrence of anti-Jewish discourse in the public sphere in the late 1980s and early 1990s was particularly puzzling to many scholars and observers both in Poland and abroad since it occurred in a social environment in which Jews constituted a numerically insignificant portion of the population.[24] In the aftermath of the forced exile of thirty thousand individuals in 1968–69 the remaining Jewish community is now estimated at between five thousand and twenty thousand individuals in a population of close to forty million.[25] Some scholars describe the persistence of such phenomena as "anti-Jewish paranoia," an obsession with Jewish omnipresence and omnipotence.[26] Attempting to explain the recurrence of anti-Jewish sentiment in the 1980s and early 1990s, Marcin Kula attributes it to the heritage of the interwar period, claiming that such beliefs and sentiments have a self-reproducing character.[27] Jolanta Ambrosiewicz-Jacobs and Anna Maria Orla-Bukowska draw similar conclusions in "After the

Fall: Attitudes towards Jews in Post-1989 Poland": "What has once entered the cultural subconscious cannot easily be removed."[28]

Both Polish and foreign scholars have begun to reexamine and reevaluate Polish anti-Semitism in the last decade as they have gained free access to archives in Poland and other East European countries. The new historians of this subject have tended to treat historical periods such as the interwar period, World War II (WWII), and the Communist and post-Communist periods separately. Many of the essential new historical works on the subject are descriptive in nature, mainly concerned with the discussion of anti-Semitic policies and practices in a particular period and locality and not with the beliefs behind such policies and practices. This book is a pioneering study of the duration of anti-Jewish idioms over a long time span, bringing together the pre-1939, wartime, and post-1945 periods to show the long-term impact of anti-Jewish beliefs on Polish political culture and identity and on Polish Jews.

Various scholars, including historians, sociologists, and literary historians, have asserted the continuity of anti-Jewish themes in discourse about the Polish nation, though they do not analyze this continuity.[29] In her important book *Neutralizing Memory: The Jew in Contemporary Poland*, which examines the image of the Jew in the political culture of the 1980s, Polish-born scholar Irena Irwin-Zarecka argues that both more radical ethno-nationalist discourse and mainstream Polish intellectual discussions are based on the subtle premise that the Jews, as an unassimilated ethno-cultural collectivity, constitute a problem within Polish society and that there has always been incompatibility between Polish and Jewish interests: "[The Jew as a problem] has enjoyed wide currency over the last years, its grip on the structure of discourse about things Jewish in Poland extend[ing] beyond the realm of the generally expected. . . . The notion that Jews constitute a problem by their very presence is one of the core premises of any analysis of the 'Jewish question,' past and present."[30]

In his important study of Roman Catholicism in Poland, *Próba rozmowy*, Michał Jagiełło, the writer and former deputy minister of culture and the arts (1989–97), also suggests the peculiar continuity of anti-Jewish traditions, which he calls a "chronic disease" (przewlekła choroba).[31] Perhaps Frank Golczewski, a historian based in Germany, has voiced the most striking, albeit indirect view of the importance of examining the actual impact of anti-Jewish themes on modern Polish national discourse. In his article "Anti-Semitic Literature in Poland before the First World War" he states: "Playing down the anti-Jewish theme in Polish political thinking limits our understanding of some crucial aspects of Polish history. Twentieth-century anti-Semitic measures were explained merely as peculiar peripheral acts of unimportant personalities, although these phenomena were in fact a response to a quite important tradition in Polish political thought. At whatever point you look at modern Polish history, a specific 'Judeocentrism' (not always the same as anti-Semitism) can be observed—most of all in the National Democrats, but in other political groups as well."[32]

I argue that by pursuing an analysis of anti-Jewish idioms over a lengthy chronological span one can demonstrate their power, persistence, and consequences while detailing their modifications, transformations, and discontinuities. Through such an analysis one can expand interpretive horizons in the field of Polish-Jewish relations, modern Polish anti-Semitism, and nationalism. So far, in all these three areas anti-Jewish idioms have been underresearched; this is why I have dedicated this work to their analysis.[33]

I recognize that one reason for such a lack of research is that historians who focus on an agent-based narrative approach attach little value to the study of historical agents' beliefs and ideas, especially over a long-range chronological span. As a result this school of writing, despite its many virtues, fails to explain the persistence and coherence of ideas, traditions, social beliefs, and national mythologies and their impact on societies. This school of historiography not only attaches little value to the examination of the nature and dynamics of social perceptions and beliefs but also focuses scant attention on the more general issue of the constraining and shaping role of culture. Still, some historians, such as Omer Bartov, have in recent years raised the issue of the importance of the study of prejudice and fundamental perceptions and beliefs in order to illuminate the ways in which societies relate to the minority groups in their midst. This is the position that constitutes the departure point of this book.[34]

The three main objectives of this book are analyzing the structure and dynamics of anti-Jewish idioms over a long time period; providing an explanation for their continuity, regardless of the size of the Jewish population or the actual presence of Jews in post-1939 Poland; and discussing their social and political functions. Regarding the latter objective I focus on four main processes in which, I argue, the anti-Jewish idiom played an essential and irreducible role:

> 1. Raising national awareness and cohesion and raising political and social mobilization. This process began in the late preindependence period (1880–1918) and was particularly intensified in the ethno-nationalist po-

litical discourse of the post-independence period (1918–39). Attempts at similarly raising national cohesion and political and social mobilization were also cynically made by ethno-nationalist sections of the Communist regime, particularly in 1968–69 and the early 1980s. Such strategies were also used by various right-wing ethno-nationalists of the anti-Communist camp in the post-1989 period.

2. Rationalizing what scholarly literature on nationalism calls the project of purifying a nation-state from a minority, which can take on various forms.[35] The first and mildest form is assimilation, which aims at the establishment of a homogenous society in which members of a minority abandon their traditions, culture, and language in favor of the traditions, culture, and language of the dominant nation. The core Polish ethno-nationalists, the National Democrats, most consistently and firmly advocated this position in relation to Slavic minorities such as Ukrainians and Belorussians, but not in relation to Jews. The second form is separation, aimed at keeping a minority in a position of social and political inferiority. This position was contemplated by various ethno-nationalists in the late nineteenth century and also in the interwar period but did not constitute a major approach to solving the "Jewish question." It was mainly treated as a measure for preserving what was defined by ethno-nationalists as the authenticity and purity of ethnic Polish morale and culture and as a first step toward Jewish mass emigration. The third form is emigration and forced emigration, which aim at physically removing a minority from the polity. This was the main position advocated by Polish ethno-nationalists, particularly in the interwar period, when their project of Jewish mass emigration from Poland gained a high level of political and social acceptability and popularity. However, this position was only realized by the Polish ethno-nationalist Communist regime in 1968–69, when it was implemented against the remaining post-1945 Jewish community. The anti-Jewish idiom provided a rationale for removing Jews from the Polish polity and for their separation from the ethnic Polish community. The final form of purification is genocide, which aims at the physical elimination of a minority.[36] The latter is generally confined only to those cases where ethnic nationalism is strongly intertwined with biological racism and produces policies that lead to the dehumanization of a minority, as in the case of Nazi Germany. With the exception of some radical individuals during the interwar period, core Polish ethno-nationalist elites did not advocate genocide of Jews or of any other minority. It is also important to bear in mind that the exclusion of Jews from the realm of the Polish nation-state is a complex problem. It was not the Polish ethno-nationalists who realized the goal of excluding Jews, but the German occupiers of Poland in World War II.

3. Inciting, rationalizing, and justifying anti-Jewish violence. Historical literature still lacks comparative studies of anti-Jewish violence in interwar, wartime, and early post-1945 Poland, as well as a typology of this violence, which could serve as a point of departure for such comparative analysis. In this book I do not argue for a monocausal explanatory approach to anti-Jewish violence. Nevertheless, I argue that anti-Jewish idioms, particularly those presenting the Jew as a threat to the political, social, and physical well-being of ethnic Poles, are an essential and irreducible factor in explaining anti-Jewish violence between 1918 and 1948.

4. Delegitimizing political opponents and rival groups. This process is the most long-lasting and still survives in contemporary Poland among right-wing nationalistic groups and in popular culture—among football fans, for example. In general in this process (historically and contemporarily) the term *Jew* does not necessarily refer to actual Jews or persons of Jewish origin; Jewish identity, in fact, can be irrelevant to labeling individuals, movements, and groups as Jewish. Instead, the term *Jew* simply connotes an abstract and strongly negative meaning; it represents all values and qualities that are seen as strongly negative and antinational. Thus *Jew* functions as a term of political and social abuse.

This book mainly focuses on the presence of a variety of anti-Jewish ideas of different intensities among ethno-nationalist elites over a long period and does not analyze in detail the impact of these ideas on society at large. Research into the latter is urgently needed, albeit difficult to conduct in respect to the pre-1939 historical period because of a lack of comprehensive data. My general position on the impact of anti-Jewish idioms on society at large is that it is possible to infer from elite usage of such idioms that the segments of wider society that supported them also believed in them. The popularity of particular political and social groups and their programs, and the number of anti-Jewish publications such as books and newspapers in circulation, are also good indicators of the acceptability of anti-Jewish idioms within society at large. For example, as I discuss in chapter 3, almost the entire Catholic press in interwar Poland disseminated anti-Jewish ideas in milder or stronger form, depending on the profile of each particular paper. This means that the Catholic press to various degrees shaped perceptions of Jews among its readers and that these readers, those exposed to the Catholic press on a regular basis, were influenced by the papers' presentation of social facts.

My other general position in respect to political and cultural elites acting in an ethno-nationalized society is that it is implausible to view them as existing outside of their communities. Elites are both generally constrained by the ideas of the communities into which they have been socialized and are also likely to be inspired by them. For example, Michael Steinlauf discusses such phenomena in his study of the memory of the Holocaust in postwar Poland, where he convincingly argues that the perception of the Holocaust among Communist elites was shaped by nonelites' perception of the event.[37] In my own analysis of the approaches of a significant group of professional historians who strongly criticized Jan T. Gross's *Neighbors*, focused on the massacre of Jedwabne Jews by the local Polish community on 10 July 1941, I found the common use of anti-Jewish idioms identical to those that persisted in collective memory in post-1945 Poland.[38] Therefore I argue that there is a need for further research on the relationship between ideas and sentiments advocated by ethno-nationalist elites and their presence within society at large. It appears that in the Polish case this relationship may be more of a dynamic and two-way process rather than a static one. This is not to say that anti-Jewish idioms cannot become marginal or disappear from mainstream political culture. They can indeed become insignificant in mainstream political culture. What is needed for such a process to be realized is the presence of a more assertive domestic culture of civic and pluralistic nationalism and the pressure of international Western opinion. These two conditions can be found in post-Communist Poland, and their effects on the mainstream political scene have been felt in the post-1995 period.

This book is not a general history of Polish-Jewish relations and Polish nationalism, nor is it a study of the Roman Catholic Church and the State per se, nor of changing class and social relations, nor of the representations of Jews among elites advocating the civic model of a Polish nation-state. A broader study of Polish civic nationalism and its perspectives on Jewish and other minorities over a long time period is definitely needed. This book does briefly touch upon a comparative examination of the images and representations of other minorities in Poland within the culture of ethno-nationalism; thorough research into this subject is also needed. Finally, this work does not discuss internal affairs of the Jewish community and its full response to anti-Jewish idioms. The sample of responses of members of the Jewish community to such idioms, presented in this work, demonstrates that many of them had a clear understanding of the political culture of Polish exclusivist ethno-nationalism. There is also a need for further research on this subject, as well as on the impact of anti-Jewish idioms on the identity of Polish Jews, their sense of Jewishness and Polishness over a long time period.

This book intentionally does not investigate Jews as social actors to any great extent. It challenges Polish historical literature dedicated to the discussion of Polish anti-Semitism and the "dark aspects" of Polish-Jewish relations in the twentieth century that portrays both areas as the result of objective contextual factors. Frequently Polish historians of this school attribute anti-Semitism to Jews, citing Jewish overpopulation, the excessive concentration of Jews in commerce and manufacturing, the lack of Jewish enthusiasm for Polish independence, and an overrepresentation of Jews in Communist circles. This perspective totally fails to explain the continuity of anti-Semitic attitudes and actions in post-1939 Poland, in which the social and economic position of Jews had dramatically changed. I argue that such an understanding of these ostensibly "objective" circumstances has actually been conditioned by a set of prejudicial preconceptions about Jews and their relations to Polish society, which as a rule encouraged Polish elites to interpret specific situations in a way that invariably cast both Jewish behavior and qualities in an unfavorable light. Ethno-nationalism has conditioned many Polish historians of anti-Semitism to themselves see in the Jew the harmful alien, the harmful other to Polish society, who cannot be included within the definition of a Pole.

Irwin-Zarecka was perhaps the first scholar to describe the implicit anti-Semitism in the majority of post-1945 Polish historical literature. She states that some post-1945 historical works simply present the core ethno-nationalist version of Polish history, in which the National Democratic representation of the Polish Jew appears as a perfectly objective historical fact. She views such phenomena as particularly troubling because of historians' role as the guardians of official memory in forging public opinion and knowledge about the national past: "What is troubling is not their presence [images of 'Jewish crimes'] in the writings of the nationalistic Right, but their prominent position within what appear as perfectly objective historical studies."[39]

Jerzy Tomaszewski, a Polish historian, also observes that in the post-1945 period historians have either denied the problem of anti-Semitism or omitted it, or have tended to define it as an external phenomenon created by a "foreign hand": "I am constantly surprised to read opinions of serious people who suggest that there had in fact been no anti-Semitism in Polish society after WWII, or that it turned out to be only a transient phenomenon, provoked, what is more, by external forces."[40]

There is no doubt that such historiography has continued in the post-1989 period both in Poland and also among Polish historians abroad. [41] One of its main characteristics is the argument that the conflict between Poles and Jews is between two roughly equal groups and that however the Poles may have wronged the Jews, the Jews have committed equal or even greater wrongs against the Poles. Thus this approach simply marginalizes, omits, and denies the importance of modern Polish anti-Semitism and instead contains to varying degrees and intensities anti-Jewish idioms. Given the persistence of such an approach one can fully understand the actual importance of Gross's *Neighbors*, first published in Polish in May 2000. [42] *Neighbors* is the book that most powerfully challenges the historical literature based on the ethno-nationalist model of Poland. I discuss the debate over Gross's *Neighbors* in the final chapter of the book, considering it in the context of the new body of critical Polish history writing of the last two decades, which boldly discusses various aspects of modern Polish anti-Semitism without omission, marginalization, or denial. This constitutes a departure from the dominant paradigm of historical writing in the post-1945 period, which uncritically presented an ethno-nationalist vision of Poland, demonstrating that a civic and pluralistic perspective on Poland and its people has also entered post-1989 Polish historiography.

This book also opposes an attitude that can be found in popular collective Jewish memory that presents Polish anti-Semitism as "unique" or "uniquely extreme," as equal to or "even more severe" than Nazi anti-Semitism, with its full-scale genocidal solution to the "Jewish question." This view is deplorable and should be challenged through education; it only results in the "mythologization" of modern Polish anti-Semitism and is counterproductive to its understanding and explanation. At the same time I recognize that the origins of this Jewish view of Polish culture are complex, predating World War II, going back to the alarming news about the situation of Polish Jewry in Poland in the aftermath of World War I (WWI). The news brought by some Jewish survivors from Poland who had personally experienced or witnessed extreme hostility on the part of some ethnic Poles before and during WWII solidified this view in the Jewish community. [43] Based in personal anger and painful emotional reactions to actual anti-Jewish attitudes and actions, these views were verbalized in harsh, exaggerated, and unjust statements about Poles and Poland in general. Without a proper understanding of the personal traumatic nature of such survivors' statements, some Western media and writers in the 1960s, 1970s, and 1980s used them to portray Poland's overall relations with Polish Jews in WWII. [44] By conflating Polish anti-Semitism in WWII with the Holocaust, they have reinforced and disseminated the mythologized representation of Polish anti-Semitism as unique and equal in its impact to the Nazi genocide of European Jewry and promulgated the ahistorical and false notion that the Germans chose Poland as the center for their genocidal practices because of Polish anti-Semitism. Various postwar anti-Jewish actions, including the wave of early postwar anti-Jewish violence in 1945–47 and the "Zionist purge" of 1968–69, made such views more convincing, especially since the latter took place at a time when Western Germany had already embarked on the process of coming to terms with its "dark past." Polish political and cultural elites between 1945 and the 1980s, both in Poland and in émigré circles in the free world, failed to acknowledge the damaging consequences of modern Polish anti-Semitism and frequently minimalized it or omitted it from discussions of Polish history and culture. This resistance to acknowledging its reality also contributed to maintaining the myth of a uniquely virulent Polish anti-Semitism.

At the same time it must be recognized that the majority of leading Israeli scholars of the Holocaust, such as Yehuda Bauer, and pioneering historians of Polish-Jewish relations during World War II, such as David Engel, Israel Gutman, and Shmuel Krakowski, reject the Polish-uniqueness argument and maintain a clear qualitative distinction between the behavior of the ethnic Polish population toward Jews in WWII and the treatment of Jews by the Nazi state. [45] Paradoxically the limited use of this approach in scholarly writings is also confirmed by the contemporary anti-Semitic Web site of one radical Catholic Polish organization, whose ideological heritage lies in the National Democracy movement's radical offshoot movement of the interwar period. [46] Among the leading foreign "anti-Polish Jewish" authors listed on the main page of this site are Leon Uris, a writer; Rabbi H. M. Shonfeld; and O. Pinkus, a Jewish survivor. However, antipolonism, defined as the state of being under Jewish influence, is attributed to many Poles, including the late Pope John Paul II (Jan Wojtyła, 1920–2005).

One also has to acknowledge that the mindset equating Poles with Nazi Germans cannot be viewed as the only one that exists in popular Jewish memory of Poland or one that cannot be modified and changed by encounters with individual Poles and familiarity with the history of Poland and Polish Jewry. Its absence from public reactions of world Jewish organizations to the 10 July 2001 commemorations of the sixtieth anniversary of the murder of

Jedwabne Jews can be seen as a good example of the limited impact of this mindset.[47] Among Jewish survivors from Poland and their families who have harsh negative memories of Poles and Poland, such views may also change through contact with individual Poles, as Oren Rudavsky shows movingly in his documentary film *Hiding and Seeking*.[48] Therefore I also reject the perspective that equates postwar anti-Polish stereotyping by Jews with the anti-Jewish idioms that are part of modern Polish ethno-nationalist political culture and memory. This equation, sometimes made by well-meaning authors, ignores the qualitative differences between the two phenomena. Such authors do not contextualize these two phenomena historically and thus produce ahistorical, naive conclusions that in fact tend to minimize the scope and social impact of modern Polish anti-Semitism.[49] Anti-Polish stereotyping in Jewish popular memory is a subject that, as convincingly argued by the scholar Zvi Gitelman, still awaits careful identification and examination.[50] My tentative proposition here is that this stereotyping basically constitutes a reaction to the negative experience of Jews in modern Poland. This reaction takes on the form of biased and unjustified expressions and overgeneralizations. However, such stereotyping does not constitute an important and irreducible element of Jewish national identity and nationalism either in Israel or in the Jewish Diaspora, whereas anti-Jewish idioms constitute an important element of modern Polish ethno-nationalism and ethno-national identity, which have only recently begun undergoing modification.

This book is written from the liberal position of recognition of the rights of a minority to the maintenance of its ethno-cultural makeup and of recognition of such a minority as an integral part of the national community defined in the civic and pluralist sense.[51]

My approach in this book represents a type of holistic sociohistorical analysis, rather than traditional history writing, focusing on an agent-based narrative. I apply theoretical insights in sociohistorical analysis, which is synthetic in nature and therefore uses a large selection of primary and secondary sources. At the heart of my analysis is the ethno-nationalist representation of the Jew as the harmful alien/threatening other to Poland and its people. In the literature on anti-Judaism and anti-Semitism various scholars, such as Roger I. Moore, Frank Felsenstein, and Saul Friedländer, apply the terms *other*, *threatening other*, and *enemy within* in their analyses of perceptions of Jews by different social agents in both premodern and modern societies.[52]

Looking at examples of the image of the Jew as the threatening other in modern societies I recognize that such a perception is not limited to nations shaped on the matrix of ethnic nationalism with weak civic elements but may also be found in nations based on civic nationalism with some ethnic elements, such as pre-1945 France. Nevertheless, the general position taken here is that the longevity of such an image, and its damaging impact on Jews and the political culture of the dominant nation, are usually much stronger in nations that are characterized by strong ethnic nationalist tendencies, rather than in nations in which ethnic nationalist tendencies are mitigated by more assertive civic and pluralistic nationalism. When exclusivist and homogenizing attitudes mingle with ethno-nationalism, the repercussions for Jews and other minorities categorized as a threat can be most severe.[53] Given the scope and longevity of the negative image of the Jew in societies under various historical and sociopolitical conditions, one can also argue that Jews represent a special case of a minority evaluated in such a way.[54]

I treat the representation of the Jew as the harmful other as a myth constructed by ethno-nationalist elites. I primarily understand a myth to refer to a socially constructed belief that is experienced as a social truth. In the recent literature on national mythology scholars like George Schöpflin argue that myths constitute an important cultural force within a nation and a way of delimiting knowledge about reality.[55] What matters in a myth is its emotional content, which may be biased and formed on a prejudicial perception, not on historically validated truth. According to Schöpflin, if the message conveyed in a national myth is primarily incongruent with reality, then such a myth can be damaging for all the segments of national community that believe in it.[56]

In terms of its structure the myth consists of a network of concepts and themes usually expressed in a narrative form. The basic concept on which the ethno-nationalist representation of the Jew is based is the notion of the Jew as the other whose qualities and social actions stand in opposition to the qualities and social actions of ethnic Poles. This representation assesses Jewish actions and qualities as antagonistic to the political, social, economic, and cultural (religious) well-being of ethnic Poles; thus the Jew and the Pole are incompatible with each other. Such a concept can be viewed as Judeocentric because it defines Polishness as an identity that stands in opposition to Jewishness: "the Pole is everything that the Jew is not." Some historians view this perspective as the result of the failure of the historical attempt to assimilate Jews into the Polish moral/cultural code, initially advocated by some Enlightenment thinkers at the end of the eighteenth century.

The representation of the Jew as the threatening other contains various general themes, such as political, social, cultural (religious), and economic threat; the damage that the Jews have already caused and may cause in the future to the Polish state and its people; the international Jewish plot to undermine the Polish national essence; and the Jew as a universal culprit, also hindering the development of other Christian nations. Any representation of the Jew that contains one such theme or more constitutes an anti-Semitic idiom. Some of these themes indicate that one myth can be interrelated with other national myths. I argue, for example, that the representation of the Jew as the harmful alien to Poland is closely linked with the national myth of the suffering and decline of Poland, advocated by core ethno-nationalists. Here the Jew is seen as responsible for the eighteenth-century partitions of Poland; twentieth-century wars and invasions, such as the Polish-Soviet War of 1920; the Communist takeover of 1945–48; the weak development of an ethnic Polish bourgeoisie in the nineteenth century; all social and economic problems of the interwar period, including unemployment within the large social group made up of peasants; and the social and economic weaknesses of the Communist system. The latter view was expressed by ethno-nationalist Communist elites in 1968–69.

The themes and narratives of any myth, including this one, can be expressed in more or less elaborated and intensified form and can undergo addition and expansion as well as deletion and substitution.[57] Moreover, a myth's individual narratives may contradict or overlap each other, although this does not necessarily affect the myth in terms of its persistence and emotive power. This is exactly the case with the representation of the Jew as a threat to the Polish nation, in which, for example, the narrative of the Jew as Communist comfortably coexists with the narrative of the Jew as Western capitalist and carrier of Western liberalism—two narratives that constantly appeared in ethno-nationalist discourse in interwar Poland.

Myths are also characterized by their adaptability to different historical and sociopolitical contexts and by their functional vitality.[58] Their role is usually polyfunctional—myths can act as a source of information, in this case information about Polish Jews and their history, and as a means of explaining and interpreting events taking place in a nation, in this case disastrous political, social, and economic developments in Polish history. Besides these two functions, the myth of the Jew as the harmful other played a specific role in ethno-nationalist political culture, providing rationalization and justification for the purification of a Polish nation from Jews, raising national cohesion and awareness, and discrediting political opponents. It also played an important role in anti-Jewish violence.

In clarifying my own perspective on the general reasons for the emergence of the representation of a minority as a national threat, I mainly draw on Leonard W. Doob's classic *Patriotism and Nationalism: Their Psychological Foundations* and Aleksander Hertz's *The Jews in Polish Culture*, both published in 1964. I also draw on Hertz's earlier article "Insiders against Outsiders," published in Polish in 1934, and James Aho's *The Thing of Darkness: A Sociology of the Enemy.*[59]

Doob's and Hertz's conceptualizations of the other are similar. Both define the other as a psychosocial category that is historically conditioned and manifested in different forms and intensities. Both also recognize that the notion of the other can be a powerful driving force in modern society.

How does the other become the threatening/harmful other—the enemy of the nation? Both Doob and Hertz argue that the evaluation of an out-group as the threatening other may be independent of the group's qualities and activities per se, but instead may be dependent on the process of its evaluation by an in-group, which in turn may be prejudiced. This perspective stands in sharp opposition to the claim that the perception of an out-group as an enemy is rooted in the group's inherent qualities and activities, a claim that is frequently applied in studies of middleman minorities—of which Jews are a good example. According to the scholar Walter Zenner, the latter perspective may be rooted, in some cases, in anti-middleman sentiments and stereotypes, even though in other cases it may be rooted in the actions of minorities.[60]

Hertz and Aho also emphasize that the mythologization of the other as the enemy can continue regardless of the actual social position and numerical size of the mythologized other.[61] Once a social construction of an adversary has been assembled and accepted as social truth, it can be difficult to deconstruct it.[62] I argue that historical analysis of the development of the representation of the Jew as the harmful other in Poland in the post-1939 period confirms the validity of such a position.

Why do nations need the threatening other? This question has occupied many scholars since the early twentieth century, beginning with the social scientist William G. Sumner.[63] His concept of the use of the other as a means to raise national cohesion remains important and has been used and elaborated by other scholars.[64] Both Doob and Hertz are in agreement with Sumner's proposition that the other provides an effective spur for in-group cohesion.

Doob stresses that raising cohesiveness is especially important when the nation goes through social, political, and economic crises.[65] In such times as a war, occupation of the state by a foreign power, or continuous economic and social crises, "scapegoating" is always on the rise. It makes the nation feel good about itself, as blame for experienced misfortunes is transferred to the out-group, which may not in fact be responsible for the crisis. Doob also notes that in such situations "scapegoating" not only increases national cohesion but also makes the nation feel superior to the group perceived as the other.[66] Scapegoating of Jews for social, political, cultural, and economic problems by Polish ethno-nationalist political elites in the postindependence period from 1918 to 1939 and also by ethno-nationalist Communist elites in the post-1945 period can be seen as a good illustration of such a phenomenon.

Doob's and Hertz's positions reveal that historical and sociopolitical conditions are an important underlying factor in the development of the propensity to represent a minority as a national threat. A nation that has experienced a wave of political, social, or economic crises shows a greater tendency to refer to the threatening other than does a nation undergoing stable development. Undoubtedly the memory of the various wars that Poland fought during the seventeenth and eighteenth centuries, and Poland's partitions and the subsequent fragmentation and deep divisions within a society existing under three separate political and cultural spheres of influence between 1795 and 1918, can be seen as an essential factor contributing to the development and popularity of the ethno-nationalist model of Poland, which excluded Jews and did not tolerate the multicultural and religious diversity of other groups that also lived in the Polish territories.

In *The Jews in Polish Culture* Hertz also provides another reason why some minorities are evaluated as the alien-enemy. According to him, such an evaluation can be related to the fact that the out-group may be viewed as the carrier and representative of new values that are feared by the in-group, the dominant nation, which may be uncertain of its own system of values: "Human communities in a state of deep inner conflict, uncertain of their own values and disturbed by their own weakness, regarded with all the greater alarm those who might introduce new values threatening the old. Whether those aliens really bore some new and different values was given no thought. Alien-enemies, bearers of corruption, were seen everywhere."[67]

This proposition also can be useful in explaining the persistence of modern anti-Jewish idioms in post-1864 Poland. Historical analysis reveals that by the

end of the nineteenth century Jews were associated with the ethos of moder-
nity, Western liberalism, secularism, capitalism, and the ethos of socialism and
Communism. A large segment of traditional Polish conservative and Roman
Catholic elites of noble origin perceived all these currents and their values as
non-Polish or anti-Polish. Thus the Jew came to be the embodiment of anti-
Polishness.

Hertz also argues that in some circumstances the more the other absorbs
the cultural values of the in-group, the more it is perceived as the threatening other. He states, "Anti-Semitism assumed its most acute forms when
the assimilation of Jews to non-Jews, speaking objectively, had become an
unquestionable fact."[68] Historical analysis of ethno-nationalist perceptions of
culturally assimilated Jews, who had a strong or even total self-identification as
Poles, as a group polluting Polish culture in the interwar period also confirms
the historical validity of such a proposition. This tendency continued to be
evident in the work of a group of ethno-nationalist artists during WWII, such
as the poet Tadeusz Gajcy, and in the opinions expressed by ethno-nationalist
Communist elites, particularly in 1968–69.

Terminology, Sources, and Structure

In my discussion of nationalism I use the concepts of ethnic and civic nationalism that are widely used in Anglo-Saxon scholarly literature on nationalism,
rather than adhering to continental European notions of nationalism, which
provide a much narrower definition of nationalism as a certain right-wing
ideology and movement. I am fully aware of interesting theoretical literature
that questions the existence of civic nationalism altogether but do not find it
relevant to the subject under analysis.[69] At the same time I reject the idea that
there is no profound difference between civic and pluralistic and ethnic nationalism and that there is thus no difference between an "open-door" concept of
citizenship, such as exists in the United States, and the concept of belonging
to a nation, which was dominant in modern Poland and other East European
countries before 1989. I see the concept of the "multivocalness" of all societies,
which claims that all societies are equivalent and that all national cultures,
containing a mixture of ethnic and civic components, are roughly the same,
as an interesting theoretical proposition, representing a current intellectual
trend of evolving global culture, but one that, in fact, is questionable in terms
of explaining the history and legacies of ethnic nationalism and prejudicial
attitudes toward Jews and other minorities in post-1864 Poland.[70]

Following Anthony D. Smith's definition I refer to ethno-nationalism as an ideology and movement according to which national membership lies in genealogy and in a common vernacular culture and history.[71] The principles of ethnic nationalism stand in sharp contrast to the principles of territorial civic nationalism. In the latter the main criteria lie in a territory, a common legal code, and a common public culture for all citizens, whereas in the ethno-nationalist world-view ethnicity equals nation and is seen as the main constituting element of the state: "Vernacular cultures, notably language and customs, are more highly prized than legal equality, and popular mobilization more than citizenship. . . . In place of a civic, mass culture, ethnic nationalisms extol native history and a more circumscribed ethnic culture."[72]

In my opinion the application of the Anglo-Saxon typology of nationalism can be helpful in clarifying the broader impact of exclusivist ethnic nationalism on Polish political culture and society as a whole. Historical and social studies that apply the narrower continental definition of nationalism ignore the extent to which ethnic nationalism, with its anti-Jewish idioms, influenced modern national discourse and interethnic relations in the post-1864 period.[73]

I also use the concept of the ethno-nationalization of the state, which Rogers Brubaker first introduced in his article "Nationalizing States in the Old 'New Europe'—and the New."[74] According to Brubaker, ethnic nationalization is a grand-scale project that ethno-nationalist elites pursued in the postindependence period.[75] Ethnic nationalization includes areas of politics, economy, and culture and can vary greatly from one state to another, depending on the position of ethno-nationalists within the state and the spread of their doctrine within the populace. From Brubaker's definition, which I find useful in the analysis of Polish ethnic-nationalist attitudes and policies toward Jews, it is clear that there is one main conviction behind all forms of ethnic nationalization—the view that the nation has experienced unfair treatment and been weakened by other ethnic and national groups in the past.[76] The claim of mistreatment refers to the entire socioeconomic and cultural development of the nation. Therefore ethno-nationalists claim that they have the right to exclude any minorities that have in their judgment contaminated the nation and are a bearer of nonnational values that might divide the nation-state and weaken its national essence once again. In other words, ethno-nationalists see themselves as guardians of the nation who have a duty to purify it from all alien elements perceived as threatening. Brubaker also suggests that ethnic nationalization after a nation-state has achieved independence has a much more diffuse character than it does during a preindependence phase. This is true of Polish nationalism in interwar Poland, as well as in ethno-nationalist Communist Poland during the late 1960s. Brubaker states: "Consequently, it is harder to pinpoint what is specifically 'nationalist' about politics in such states. In such settings, nationalism becomes an 'aspect' of politics, embracing both formal policies and informal practices and existing both within and outside the state."[77]

This book draws on archival materials, document collections, parliamentary speeches, political programs, newspapers of various periods, memoirs, other printed and unprinted sources, and scholarly publications. Its aim is to provide a "global picture" of the development and impact of the representation of the Jew as the threatening other in its historical context, based on both my own research and the work of other scholars, particularly the findings of more recent historical literature and theoretical works on nationalism and the notion of the "other."

The book is divided into eight chapters. This introductory chapter explores general aspects of modern Polish anti-Semitism based on the matrix of modern Polish ethno-nationalism and introduces the theoretical concepts that underlie the book's sociohistorical analysis—such as the importance of the threatening other in the ideology of exclusivist ethno-nationalism and the historical and psychosocial reasons for and nature of the emergence of the other in national discourse. Chapters 2 and 3 constitute historical introductions, discussing the development and social functions of the representation of the Jew as the threatening other, from the notion's emergence in the post-1864 period until 1918 and between 1918 and 1939. In chapter 2 the pre-1880 period is discussed. Chapter 4 provides a careful analysis of the role of the representation of the Jew as the threatening other in the initialization, rationalization, and justification of anti-Jewish violence during the interwar period. Chapter 5 explores this representation in German-occupied Poland in WWII, from 1939 to 1945. This, in fact, is a central chapter of the book because it investigates the continuity of anti-Semitic idioms in a radically different sociopolitical context, in which Polish Jews were subjugated to the genocide masterminded by an external social agent—the Nazi occupier. In this chapter attention is focused on the presence of such representation in political discourse among ethno-nationalist underground elites and its impact on the processes of witnessing the Nazi extermination of Jews and Polish rescue activities and on instances of anti-Jewish violence, particularly during the summer of 1941. Chapter 6 analyzes the development of anti-Jewish idioms in the early postwar period (1945–49) among anti-Communist political elites and their emergence within the Communist political movement, along with their role in anti-Jewish violence of the period. Chapter 7 explores the development of such idioms and their use by ethno-nationalist Communist elites of 1967–89. It defines the Zionist purge of 1968–69 as the final realization of the ethno-nationalists' main goal of excluding Jews from the realm of the Polish nation-state. Chapter 8 examines the continuity and modification of such discourse between 1989 and 2002, as well as the new intellectual discourse aimed at challenging and deconstructing anti-Jewish representations past and present. It also assesses to what extent the model of Polishness that embraces every culture and faith has succeeded in replacing the backward-looking ethno-nationalist vision of Polishness, intolerant of multiethnic and multicultural diversity and instead advocating a single culture and religion.

2. The Representation of the Jew as the Threatening Other

A Historical Introduction, Part I

What is this "Jewish question" of which you constantly speak? You cannot deny us the right to live; all animals have the right to live, and we are, after all, human beings. A solution has to be found, since to kill us all is unthinkable. When we try to engage in agriculture, you say, "The Jews are taking over our land." When we obtain qualifications in medicine, law, and administration, you say, "The Jews are crowding us out." Confined to commerce one in a thousand among us creates a successful business thanks to his frugality, resourcefulness, and willingness to take risks. You then loudly proclaim, "The Jews are corrupters and exploiters." We convert to your religion and traditions in order to integrate better into society. Do you accept us then? You call us "converts." Thus we lose our place in our community while you do not accept us. Finally, when in civic institutions we wish to serve the country that has nurtured and brought us up with our abilities and our resources, then you tell us: "We do not want you here. Go away! All you do is trade and exploit." In the light of all this, in God's name, it is hard to talk about brotherly love or even logic.

Kazimierz Zalewski, *Górą nasi. Komedia w pięciu aktach*

The Crystallization and Development of the Image, 1880s–1918

The myth of the Jew as the harmful other in all aspects of Polish national existence emerged in the post-1864 period—an era that saw the loss of enthusiasm for the insurrectionary romantic traditions of the first half the nineteenth century and witnessed the full-scale encounter of Polish society with modernity. The final development of the myth occurred in the late preindependence period, between the 1880s and 1918, when the exclusivist ethnic type of modern Polish political nationalism was full-fledged. The simultaneous development of these two phenomena was no coincidence. After all, the myth constituted both an intrinsic element and a product of Polish nation building, based on a matrix of exclusivist ethnic nationalism. In fact, without the doctrine of exclusivist ethno-nationalism the belief in the Jew as a threat to the Polish nation could not have been transformed into the powerful and long-lived representation it has been.

From its crystallization the myth was a manifestation of exclusivist tendencies in political and social thought. It was first found in the political and literary writings of radical conservative and Catholic intelligentsia of noble origin, the pauperized aristocracy, and the ethnic Polish bourgeoisie. Their anti-Jewish writings predated the emergence of the core political movement and ideology of modern Polish ethno-nationalism, National Democracy.

In singling out the Jew as the chief enemy of Poland and its people, the Polish integral nationalists were acting no differently from similar contemporary French, German, Hungarian, and Romanian groups.[1] Indeed, some Polish writers engaged in constructing the image of the Jew as a national threat drew on French, German, and Russian anti-Jewish literature.[2] In terms of the content of the myth, analogous major themes and narratives can be found in other European versions of the Jew as an enemy of the nation. In terms of the dynamics of the myth and its impact on political and popular culture and on majority relations with the Jewish community, in each case anti-Semitism developed in a way unique to its particular historical and sociocultural context.[3]

In Polish territories the development of the myth occurred at a time when the issue of national survival, continuity, and character became strongly intertwined with the issue of the modernization of society. In the post-1864 period Poles could no longer escape the encounter with modernity. Major social and economic upheavals in Polish society led to growing urbanization and the rise of a nascent proletariat class. Modern Polish political movements and parties emerged in all three partitioned zones. These developments also affected the Jewish community. The encounter with modernity led to the emergence of a secularized Jewish intelligentsia and a nascent Jewish proletariat. Ideas of Jewish socialism and above all Jewish nationalism penetrated the traditional Orthodox community and engaged many young Jews.[4]

Recent historical literature takes one of three major approaches to the rise and early development of modern Polish anti-Semitism. The first approach explains it as a phenomenon rooted in social, political, and economic processes of the stateless Polish society of the late nineteenth and early twentieth centuries. Historians taking this approach identify the roots of Polish anti-Semitism in

Polish fear and frustration after more than a century of foreign rule and "the sense of threat and political, cultural and economic inadequacies strongly felt by the underdeveloped Polish middle classes, the inefficient bourgeoisie and pauperized intelligentsia."[5]

The second approach identifies the roots of modern anti-Semitism in the demographic, social, and political developments occurring within Polish Jewry. This approach has been the most dominant in the discussion of the rise of modern anti-Semitism in Polish historiography. As a rule it is based on the premise of interpreting the "imagining" of the Polish nation in an ethnic sense, not in a civic sense. In some cases it endorses the "mild" ethno-nationalist perception of the Jews as a group whose actions and qualities prevented ethnic Poles from proper social and economic development.[6] These historians view developments of the Jewish community in Polish lands in the nineteenth century, such as the arrival of Jews from Russia in the Russian partitioned zone, as a series of unfortunate events. As part of this approach the following causes are given for the development of anti-Semitism: the large increase of the Jewish urban population in both the Russian and the Austrian partitioned zones in the late nineteenth century, the rise of modern political socialist (Bund) and nationalist (Zionist) movements, and the slow and limited cultural assimilation of the Jewish community.

The third, and most sophisticated, approach combines the first and the second. It identifies various developments within both the ethnic Polish and the Jewish communities as major factors behind the rise of modern anti-Semitism. Thus anti-Semitism is presented as an unfortunate outcome of a combination of objective social, cultural, and economic aspects of Polish society in the late nineteenth and early twentieth centuries.[7] Historian Theodore R. Weeks, for example, states the following: "During the post-1905 crisis, on the other hand, we must take into account the feelings of defeat, vulnerability, and political isolation that obsessed the Poles in those days. Also, we must remember that Polish national identity came under broad attack by the Russian authorities throughout this period, and at the same time the Poles witnessed a flourishing of Jewish culture in both Yiddish and Hebrew and the birth and rapid growth of Zionism and other autonomous Jewish national movements. This does not, of course, justify the increase in Polish anti-Semitism on the eve of the First World War, but it may help to explain it."[8]

Regardless of the differences among them, the three approaches implicitly assume the inevitability of the rise of modern Polish anti-Semitism. Leaving aside the notion of inevitability, which cannot be dismissed as irrelevant, what is missing even from the most sophisticated third approach is an inquiry into Polish national culture, particularly perceptions of the other in political and social thought, as an important factor in the rise and development of modern Polish anti-Semitism. The social belief in the notion of the Jew as the harmful other must be central to any such inquiry because it was important in discussions of the reality and future of a Polish nation in political and social writings of the late nineteenth and early twentieth centuries. An increasing segment of Polish elites took up the idea of the Jew as the harmful other: Catholics, radical conservative groups, and representatives of the young National Democracy and the peasant movement. At the same time Polish liberals and moderate conservatives and the leaders of the newly established Polish Socialist Party (PPS) rejected and criticized anti-Jewish stereotyping.[9] The most important post-1863 school of Polish social thought, that of the Warsaw Positivists, condemned and rejected anti-Jewish beliefs, at least until the first decade of the twentieth century.[10]

Such a situation raises a set of questions: Was the belief in the Jew as the harmful enemy of the Polish nation congruent with reality? Was it based on a prejudiced perception of Jews rooted in a particular cultural paradigm? Or was it the result of a particular fusion of prejudiced views and some aspects of reality? How did the belief influence evaluation of the qualities and actions of the Jewish community? Was its emergence inevitable, and if so how can it be explained? Where do its roots come from, and what is its significance?

The emergence of the belief is a sign of the failure to integrate the Jewish community in Polish lands. This failure cannot be explained without looking closely at the historical development of the Polish nation and nationalism and the concepts of the inclusiveness and exclusiveness of the Jewish community prior to and after 1863. The relations between earlier forms of anti-Jewish prejudice and the post-1864 myth of the Jew as a malign threat must also be examined in order to establish whether any of the earlier anti-Jewish concepts were referred to, reworked, and incorporated by modern anti-Jewish writers.

The Jewish Presence before 1864

In premodern Poland, as everywhere in Western Christendom, the position of Jews had a dual character. On the one hand, Jews had a recognized position guaranteed by charters and performed some occupations that were crucial to the functioning of premodern society, such as trading, banking and money lending, and minting. At the same time they were a pariah group espousing a despised religion, tolerated only to demonstrate the truth of Christianity.

The origins of Polish Jewry are mired in obscurity.[11] According to available evidence, the first contact between Jews and Poles dates back to the tenth and eleventh centuries. The earliest permanent Jewish settlements in the first Polish Kingdom occurred in the twelfth century.[12] At the beginning the Polish Kingdom consisted of an ethnically uniform state with boundaries that were closely similar to those of post-1945 Poland. Its first royal rulers came from the Piast dynasty (996–1370). The last Piast ruler, Kazimierz III, Wielki (Casimir III) (1333–70), known as Casimir the Great, was, in contemporary terms, a talented, visionary, and efficient "state modernizer." He can be credited not only with the development of an impressive number of new towns and castles built of brick and stone but also with major reforms of the legal, administrative, and fiscal system.[13] He was also the first monarch under whose rule Poland began to transform itself into a premodern multiethnic and multireligious society—his 1349 conquest of Red-Ruthenia, with its local Eastern Slavic population, is an example of the nature of this transformation. Another important development in building this multiethnic and multireligious society centered on the charters of rights extended to the Armenian and Jewish communities. Casimir the Great granted a separate law to the Armenian community and invited Jews from Western Europe to settle down in the country.[14] He saw in the Jewish community a social group that was experienced in commerce and trade, two important areas of the economy that the medieval Polish state urgently needed to develop.

Casimir the Great is known as the medieval Polish king most favorably disposed toward Jewish settlement in Polish territories. He ratified the charter of rights granted in 1264 to the Jews of Wielkopolska (Great Poland) by Bolesław Pobożny (Bolesław the Pious) and implemented it in the entire Polish Kingdom. This charter of rights became one of the main documents determining the legal and social status of the Jewish community up to the partitions of the state in the late eighteenth century.[15]

One of the first major critics of Casimir's decision to invite Jews into Poland and grant them extensive rights and privileges was the famous fifteenth-century historical chronicler Jan Długosz (1415–80). Długosz's perceptions of Jews conformed to the negative image presented in the teachings of the medieval Roman Catholic Church, which saw in the Jews a group that was to be tolerated in an inferior position in order to demonstrate the truth of

Christianity. [16] Much later in the nineteenth century some modern critics of Casimir's decision to invite Jews into Poland used this historical fact to elaborate the modern representation of the Jew as a national enemy. They would interpret Casimir's decision as the beginning of the "Jewish disaster" that had subsequently befallen the Polish state and its people. In their eyes the arrival of Jewish communities in Poland under the rule of Casimir the Great was the result of the monarch's misguided actions. They also saw the extension of privileges to the Jewish communities of Poland as stemming from Jewish trickery of the Polish king. [17]

The Jewish community in Poland continued to grow during the fifteenth and sixteenth centuries, with fifty thousand individuals living there by the sixteenth century. [18] During this period major political, social, and economic changes occurred in the Polish Kingdom. By then the state was ruled by the second royal dynasty, that of the Jagiellonians (1386–1572), which was Lithuanian in origin. [19] Under the Jagiellonian dynasty the state's boundaries dramatically expanded. The Union of Lublin on 1 July 1569 united the Polish Kingdom and the Grand Duchy of Lithuania and brought the duchy's heartland, known at present as Belorussia, and the vast, rich lands of the Ukraine under the Polish crown. As a result the country became the second-largest state in Europe. The Polish-Lithuanian Commonwealth (Rzeczpospolita Obojga Narodów) enjoyed a high profile on the political map of Europe and experienced great economic growth and prosperity. The latter was achieved as a result of two interrelated developments in which Jews played an important role: the colonization of the Ukraine and the commonwealth's taking on a leading role in the international grain trade. [20] Sixteenth-century Poland, as the saying goes, "became the granary of Europe."

The achievements of the Jagiellonian state were not confined to the economic sphere. The European trends of humanism, the Renaissance, and the Reformation brought about dynamic cultural developments in the arts and literature: for example, authors such as Jan Kochanowski (1530–84), the most eminent Slavic poet until the beginning of the nineteenth century, created works of great artistic merit. [21] As a result the Jagiellonian period came to be assessed as the Golden Age of Polish history, coinciding with the Golden Age in the history of Polish Jews. [22] As recorded in various documents of the sixteenth century, the Jewish community came to perceive the Polish-Lithuanian Commonwealth as their home, relatively free of the persecution to which other European Jewish communities had been exposed since the eleventh century. [23]

The last Jagiellonian monarch, Zygmunt August (Sigismund August) (1548–72), granted Polish Jewry unique communal autonomy in religious and legal matters (the *kahal* system), and the national Council of Jews of Four Lands (Va'ad arba aratsot) was established. [24] The latter institution functioned as an internal bicameral parliament until the second decade of the eighteenth century. Gershon Hundert describes the institutional structure of Polish Jews as the most sophisticated in European Jewish history, the manifestation of a positive and secure identity with a distinctive moral-cultural code. [25] The character of the Polish state no doubt fostered the development of such an assertive Jewish identity.

The premodern Polish state was a polity in which, until the seventeenth century, "others"—meaning nonethnic Poles—were treated in an inclusive way. The historian Andrzej Zamoyski defines this period in Polish history as an attempt to "[build] utopia on earth." [26] Some features atypical of other European states characterized Polish society and fostered inclusiveness. The supposed majority population—ethnic Poles—did not constitute a demographic majority in either the ethnic or the religious sense. Ethnic Poles, whose language, customs, and cultural mores had fully developed by the end of the sixteenth century, constituted approximately 40 percent of the entire population, estimated at ten million inhabitants. [27] The size of the ethnic Polish community would not change dramatically in the next two centuries and would reach an estimated 60 percent by the eighteenth century. The Slavic populations of the eastern part of the commonwealth, Lithuanians and other Baltic ethnic groups, Germans, Jews, Armenians, Tatars, Italians, and Scots together represented the demographic majority. Religious denominations such as the Orthodox, Uniate (Greek Orthodox), and Armenian Churches; Judaism; Karaism; Islam; and different strands of Protestantism—Calvinism, Lutheranism, and Arianism—also represented together the demographic majority. Roman Catholics, members of what was by the seventeenth century seen as the main religion of ethnic Poles, constituted the demographic minority. Even after the successful Counter-Reformation of the seventeenth century, which resulted in the expulsion of Arians from the state and the re-Catholicization of the Protestant nobility, Roman Catholics still constituted less than 50 percent of the population. [28]

The multireligious and multiethnic diversity of the premodern Polish state prompted Gershon Hundert to question the use of the term *minority* in assessing the position of the Jewish community in the Polish-Lithuanian Commonwealth. [29] Hundert suggests that Salo Wittmayer Baron's classic general observation about the favorable status of Jews in states of multiple nationality applies exactly to the position of Jews in premodern Poland. [30] This is no doubt a correct and important conclusion. However, when we look at perceptions of the Jewish community by different sections of premodern Christian society, the situation appears more complex than it does at the level of the status of Jews vis-à-vis the premodern Polish state.

Various historical records show that despite the spiritual and physical distance between Jews and Christians, sixteenth-century Polish Jewry interacted in a variety of ways, on both economic and social levels, with different sections of society, divided into estates. [31] The estate with which Jews developed close economic ties was the *szlachta* (the estate of the nobility), which was also characterized by unique features not found in other premodern European states. With the extinction of the Jagiellonian dynasty in 1572, unlike in other European premodern states where political power was concentrated in the monarch, Poland became the Republic of Nobility (Rzeczpospolita Szlachecka). All legislative power was shifted to the gentry, which in effect became, to use scholar Elie Kedourie's term, the Polish state. [32] The nobility, regardless of its internal religious and social diversity, was the only estate that held the status of the Polish political nation, and this situation did not change, except for some amendments concerning the political rights of barefoot *szlachta* (*gołota*), during the era of state reforms masterminded in the second half of the eighteenth century by the last king of Poland, Stanisław August Poniatowski (1732–98). [33] The gentry was also much more numerous in Poland than elsewhere in Europe. The available data for the end of the eighteenth century shows that it constituted at least 6 percent of the total population, versus 3 percent in Great Britain, 0.7 percent in France, 2 percent in Russia, and 4 percent in Hungary. [34]

Polish Jews forged an alliance with the nobility, called by Moshe Rosman a marriage of convenience that "nonetheless grant[ed] the Jews the power to pursue their economic and political interest." [35] This marriage of convenience benefited both parties. For the nobility, forbidden by the laws of 1505, 1538, and 1550 to engage in industry and commerce, under penalty of losing their rights and privileges, Jews performed vital economic functions from which the nobility profited. [36] Jews were merchants and craftspeople. They were also the main administrators of noble estates, engaged in collecting taxes and tolls. They held *arendy* (leases) on mills and on the manufacture and distribution of liquor and malt, economic activities that were the monopoly of noble owners.[37] The latter type of lease, known as "propination" rights, became the most common type of *arenda* in eastern parts of the commonwealth in the eighteenth century.

The close economic ties between Jews and the nobility, particularly magnates, became for the first time a subject of criticism in the turbulent seventeenth century. The Roman Catholic burgher class, whose trading rights were curtailed by the nobility, began to blame Jews for the lack of a strong urban economy in the state, rather than the nobility, who had the political power to hold back the development of towns. They held Jews responsible for corrupting nobles and for the lack of concern of many nobles for the situation of the state. Thus the economic role of Jews was seen not only as harming one particular group but also as leading to the increasing impoverishment of the entire population: "You tricked the nobility and rich magnates. And now suddenly you have impoverished all our estates."[38]

Burgher plebeian writers, who were influenced by the teachings of the Roman Catholic Church, introduced a new quality to anti-Jewish representations of the medieval Christian Church. The emphasis in their writing, as Baron points out, was on "the purported misdeeds and crimes of contemporary Jewry in their relations with Christians and not on the theological differences between Judaism and Christianity, which constituted the main feature of the early medieval anti-Jewish works."[39] The titles of major anti-Jewish works, written or commissioned by burghers, illustrate this change—for example, Przecław Majewski's *Żydowskie okrucieństwa, mordy i zabobony* (Jewish Cruelties, Murders, and Superstitions), published originally in 1589 and republished in 1636; Aleksander Hubicki's *Żydowskie okrucieństwa nad najświętszym sakramentem i dziadkami chrześcijańskimi* (Jewish Cruelty over the Holy Host and Christian Folk), published in 1602; Sebastian Miczyński's *Zwierciadło Korony Polskiej, urazy ciężkie i utrapienie wielkie, które ponosi od żydów, wyrażające . . .* (The Heavy Injuries and Great Worries Inflicted by the Jews on the Mirror of the Polish Crown), published in 1618; and Sebastian Śleszkowski's *Odkrycie zdrad żydowskich* (The Discovery of Jewish Betrayal), published in 1621.[40]

In her book on the concept of the Polish nation and society in Polish plebeian literature of the seventeenth century Urszula Augustyniak gives examples of Jews being described as social parasites, as "insects eating Poland from within," as spies for foreign entities, and as "God's plague" threatening the economy of the burghers.[41] Burgher writers praised the expulsion of the Jews from Spain in the fifteenth century and the contemporary Russian policy of excluding Jews from the Russian state: "Moscow is wiser. . . . She neither stands a Jew nor a foreigner." [42] They also described the small group of Jews who had converted to Catholicism as outsiders who could not be trusted. [43] A plebeian proverb of the time warns that "a converted Jew like a domesticated wolf is a two-faced friend." [44] Thus the nascent idea of the exclusion of Jews and other heretics from the state was formulated in this genre of Polish writings. These premodern exclusionary ideas had their roots in Roman Catholic preaching about the Jews and in mistrust of newcomers, particularly in the religious community. According to Magdalena Teter, exclusionary attitudes toward converted Jews originated in the Jesuit order, which refused to accept descendents of Jews as members in the sixteenth century. [45] In Poland the Chełmno Synod of 1745 implemented a discriminatory practice toward Jewish converts, defining them, along with Protestants and Schismatics, as unfit to enjoy the rights of full Catholics. The issue of the exclusion of converted Jews from the community of Roman Catholics, as will be discussed later in the chapter, would reemerge in some writings of the nineteenth century. It would also become an aspect of the writings of a small group of radical Catholic integral nationalists in interwar Poland.

The Polish historian Janusz Tazbir emphasizes that the anti-Jewish image of the seventeenth century was the outcome of a combination of economic tensions and rivalry and growing xenophobia and ethnocentrism among the Roman Catholic population. [46] According to him, xenophobia and ethnocentrism were intrinsic cultural aspects of the successful Counter-Reformation in the Polish-Lithuanian Commonwealth in the seventeenth century. One of the main achievements of the Counter-Reformation was the emergence of the idea of a fusion between Polishness and Catholicism. The most powerful symbol of this fusion was the crowning of the Virgin Mary as queen of Poland after the victory over the Swedes in 1655, at the Paulinian Monastery at the Jasna Góra in Częstochowa. [47]

The series of wars fought throughout almost the entire seventeenth century—with Russia (1612, 1617–18), Sweden (1626–29, 1655–60), the Ottoman Empire (1672–73), and the Cossacks (1648)—fostered the development of xenophobia and ethnocentrism. The facts that none of the foreign powers with which Poland fought was Roman Catholic, but either Orthodox (Russia) or Protestant (Sweden) or Muslim (the Ottoman Empire), and that the second war with Protestant Sweden, the Deluge (1655–60), was fought in the heartland of Poland, not in its borderlands, also fostered the new negative evaluation of internal others.[48] As a result for the first time such others living in the Polish state came to be treated with suspicion. Until that time different religious and ethnic groups had been treated in an inclusive way, the character of society predominantly open. In the seventeenth century, however, premodern Polish society gradually became what can be called closed. Increasing intolerance and exclusiveness emerging in that century and continuing into the eighteenth were eventually, as argued by Magda Teter, to become part and parcel of modern Polish nationalism.[49]

The post-1864 myth of the Jew as the enemy of the nation was not a simple continuation of the seventeenth-century negative representation of the Jew. There were major qualitative differences between the two representations. The seventeenth century's negative representation of the Jew was rooted in Roman Catholic teaching, with its contempt for Jews and its portrayal of them as a pariah people. Negative perceptions of Jews were also aggravated by broader xenophobic and ethnocentric reactions toward various internal others, which emerged as a result of historical developments in the seventeenth century. In this premodern society the concept of a Polish political nation carried a completely different meaning than does the modern concept of nationhood.

Still, to some ethno-nationalist writers of the late nineteenth and early twentieth centuries the ideas presented in the seventeenth-century burghers' writings were a source of inspiration. These writers discovered in the burgher texts a vision of Polish society that was similar to their own vision of a Polish nation. They cited this genre as a reliable historical source of information—as a firsthand account of Jewish harm in premodern Poland. The nineteenth-century ethno-nationalists viewed these seventeenth-century burgher plebeians as one of the two estates in premodern Poland that, unlike the nobility, showed concern for the Polish national interest. In the eyes of the modern integral nationalist writers the burghers' objections to the presence of Jews in the state and to their leading role in the state economy made them wise "fathers" of the nation, who "should be followed and imitated."[50] Some modern ethno-nationalist writers also praised the premodern Roman Catholic clergy. They called the clergy true defenders of the Polish nation against the Jewish invasion: "In premodern Poland anti-Jewish activities were guided by the Roman Catholic Church, which knew well the Jewish soul and Jewish goals. The Church warned Polish society against the destructive activities of the Jews and was in charge of fighting against the Jewish invasion."[51] These writers overlooked the important role the Roman Catholic Church played in the economic integration of the Jewish community, particularly in the seventeenth and eighteenth centuries.[52] In their evaluation of the Church's position on the Jews they focused exclusively on the Church's anti-Jewish writings, sermons, and legislation, and not on its economic entanglement with the Jewish community.

Until recently historians of premodern Polish Jewry overlooked expressions of anti-Jewish attitudes by sections of the eighteenth-century Polish population.[53] The eighteenth century, however, proved to be even more turbulent and destructive for Polish society than the seventeenth had been.[54] During its first three decades nearly complete chaos ruled over the commonwealth. The country was subjugated to a stream of Cossack revolts in the Ukraine and to another war with Sweden, the Northern War (1700–1721), in which the Swedish Army once again marched across the country causing destruction and famine. In this period the state experienced a political crisis in which neighboring powers began to intervene.[55] Nevertheless, after the election of King Stanisław August Poniatowski on 6 September 1764 important intellectual trends aimed at introducing political and social reforms developed that brought about some positive, albeit short-term fruits.

Concerning the Jewish community, two opposing trends emerged during the second half of the eighteenth century. Under the influence of the philosophy of the Enlightenment, as in other parts of Europe, Polish reformers made important efforts at transforming Jews from members of a religious community into citizens. On the other hand, negative representations of Jews intensified in political debates.

As in previous centuries the main eighteenth-century critics of the Jewish community came from the underdeveloped ethnic Polish burgher estate and the Catholic clergy. However, these critics were joined by a growing number of nobles.[56] In the case of the nobility most of the critical voices came from its growing pauperized segment (*gołota*), which, unlike the large landowners, could not see in the Jews indispensable administrators of estates.[57] Instead, like the burgher class landless nobles saw in Jews skillful economic competitors. Their views were also colored by Roman Catholic teachings. The fact that Jesuits were in charge of the education of several generations of *szlachta*, from the triumph of the Counter-Reformation in the seventeenth century until the middle of the eighteenth, had an impact on the thinking of nobles.[58]

The eighteenth-century Roman Catholic clergy, as in the previous century, disseminated the image of Jews both as a pariah group espousing a religion that was false and harmful to Christianity and as harmful to the contemporary Christian community.[59] The clergy defined the Jewish threat in cultural, economic, religious, and physical terms. The clergy spread the blood libel, presenting Jews as a threat to the physical life of Christians—as a group that in order to fulfill their religious rituals needed to use Christian blood. This belief, which was widespread all over medieval Europe, had its roots in medieval Christian superstitions and was expressed in accusations of child murder and host desecration. It was still popular in eighteenth-century Poland despite the fact that the Apostolic See had already condemned blood-libel accusations.[60] According to a recent study, there were eighty-one accusations and court cases of ritual murder in Poland between 1547 and 1787, sixteen in the sixteenth century, thirty-three in the seventeenth century, and thirty-two in the eighteenth century.[61]

The Polish Catholic Church disseminated accusations of Jewish ritual murder of Christians, particularly Christian children, in various forms: in the Church's iconography, in sermons, and in books. One of the most striking examples of iconography from the eighteenth century depicting Jews engaged in ritual murder is the painting in the cathedral in the city of Sandomierz, in southeastern Poland.[62] This painting was commissioned in 1710 by Stefan Żuchowski (1666–1716), a well-known clergyman who held various important positions in the state, such as commissioner for Jewish affairs and secretary to the first Saxon king, August II, who ruled in Poland between 1697 and 1733.[63]

A good example of a book depicting ritual murder is *Złość żydowska* (Jewish Malice), written by the priest Gaudent Pikulski. This work was published in 1758 and republished twice in a new revised edition in 1760.[64] Perhaps one of the most striking articulations of the accusation of ritual murder is the eighteenth-century slogan "Freedom cannot exist without *liberum veto*, nor can Jewish matzo exist without Christian blood," coined by the rural priest Jędrzej Kitowicz, the author of a popular book about life under the last Saxon king, August III (1733–63). The comparison of ritual murder to *liberum veto*, which was a real parliamentary practice, reveals the extent to which a prejudiced way of thinking about Jews based on nonrational assumptions acquired the status of a social truth among Roman Catholic clergy in the premodern period. These beliefs were both powerful and persistent; Roman Catholic clergymen continued to espouse them until the first half of the twentieth century. In the early post-1945 period blood-libel imagery was an important part of the representation of the Jew as the enemy of the Polish nation and in that representation was to play an important role in inciting anti-Jewish violence.

A body of political and social writings published in the second half of the eighteenth century blamed the Jewish community for all contemporary political, social, and economic ills experienced by the state and its Christian population. As in the previous century Christian burghers accused the Jewish community of hindering the Polish urban economy and blamed Jews for the nobility's negative attitude toward commerce. The reasoning behind the latter belief can be summarized as follows: Jews, whose main occupation was commerce, were the most contemptible nation in the world; therefore the commerce they conducted was also worthy only of contempt, and this explains the general repulsion toward commerce in Poland.[65] This naive explanation completely ignores the cultural tendency among Polish nobles, as among nobles in other countries, to regard commerce as a "low" profession.[66]

Christian burgher writers also blamed Jews for the materialism and egoism of the nobility, particularly of the magnates. In this accusation the Jew appears as a negative influence on the character of the members of the Polish political nation. In this narrative a noble who associates with a Jew loses social virtues and instead acquires social vices. Eighteenth-century anti-Jewish writers also blamed Jews for political corruption and treason; financial fraud; and the impoverishment of towns, industry, and villages. All of these negative developments actually occurred in eighteenth-century Poland, but Jews had no real control over them, either as a community or as individuals.

Some writers also blamed Jews for the spread of alcoholism among the Polish peasantry. Alcoholism, which became a social problem in the eighteenth-century Polish village, had many social, cultural, and psychological causes. One of the background factors behind the emergence of this social problem lay in the major shift in the state economy—the international trade in grain lost its importance in the early eighteenth century and was superseded by the domestic production and trade of alcoholic beverages. The *szlachta* dominated this economic sector; they owned the distilleries.[67] Jews were the innkeepers of taverns, which sold alcoholic beverages to peasants—the main consumers of such beverages in rural areas, often going into debt over the purchase of drink.[68] One well-known burgher writer complained:

> The noble will complain that the Polish peasant is a terrible drunkard, yet every noble will establish five or six taverns in each of his villages or towns, as a net for trapping that peasant. He then puts it in the hands of the most competent Jews he can find, those who will pay him the most, which is to

say, those who will be most effective in deceiving the peasants and inducing them to drinking. . . . The Jews' cheating and skinning from the peasant his last cent impedes his farming, so that instead of enriching the country, he destroys it and prepares your downfall. . . . Besides the unlawful slavery of our farmer, the Jews are the second great cause of his lack of industriousness, of his ignorance, of his drunkenness, and of his poverty. It is only the peasants who bear the burden of having to clothe and feed several hundred thousand Jews.[69]

In the negative evaluation of peasants' alcoholism the Jewish innkeeper, not the noble, became the main focus of criticism; the Jew was perceived as the source of peasants' misery and vices. As in other eighteenth-century accusations the Jew is portrayed as the cunning harmful other wanting to destroy the Christian population. Thus the concept of seeking social justice for the peasants for the first time came to be intertwined with anti-Jewish prejudice. Such phenomena would persist in the modern period, in the ethno-nationalist way of thinking about solving social problems.

The prejudicial nature of the negative evaluation of the Jewish innkeeper can be easily uncovered by comparing it with the typical portrayal of the Christian innkeeper, who because of his Christian faith allegedly held different attitudes toward peasants and therefore did not cause alcoholism and misery among the peasantry. The falsity of this argument was exposed by the middle of the nineteenth century. By then the number of Jewish innkeepers in villages had been drastically reduced through legislation introduced in the Russian partitioned zone in the second and third decades of the nineteenth century.[70] Still, alcoholism among peasants, instead of decreasing, increased, possibly due to improvements in the methods of producing alcoholic beverages. However, as Artur Eisenbach notes: "In the fifth decade of the nineteenth century after almost a complete disappearance of Jews from this area of *folwark* [agricultural economy], a myth about the destructive role of the Jewish innkeeper was still in circulation both in the country and in émigré circles. The publicists from the Polish political conservative and central camps used this myth in polemics against the emancipation of Jews."[71] This phenomenon suggests the persistence of anti-Jewish concepts over a long period and the lack of critical inquiry into them.

The modern post-1863 belief in the Jew as an enemy of the Polish nation was not a linear continuation of eighteenth-century negative representations. Rather, clergy and bourgeois anti-Jewish writers created a particular pattern of thinking about Jews in the late eighteenth century that influenced Polish culture into the nineteenth and even twentieth centuries. There is a striking similarity between the eighteenth-century anti-Jewish polemicists' strategy of making the Jewish community a scapegoat for all the misfortunes of the Polish Christian population and state and the late nineteenth- and early twentieth-century integral nationalists' strategy of making the Jewish community a scapegoat for all national disasters and problems. In terms of the language and expressions that modern Polish anti-Semites used to describe the Jew, some similarities can be found with the language and expressions used by eighteenth-century anti-Jewish writers.

In eighteenth-century terms describing the Jewish community acquired a strong connotation of dirt and pollution. Such expressions as "harmful locusts," "the Jews poison the air with their stink," and "the Jews rot the air of towns" are good examples of this phenomenon. These expressions were circulated in publications of significant importance. For example, the burgher-class Stanisław Staszic (1755–1826), one of the leading figures of the Polish Enlightenment, in one of his major and most influential works, *Przestrogi dla Polski* (Admonishments for Poland), published in 1790, categorized the Jews as locusts destroying Polish towns and villages: "Jews are the summer and winter locust plague of our country. These two species of creatures accelerate the flow of money, facilitate the transformation of wealth, impoverish industrious people, lay waste the most fertile fields, fill villages with want, and infect the air with putrefaction. The Jewish race impoverishes our villages and infects our cities with rot."[72]

These expressions indicate the emergence of the nascent concept of the Jew as a spoiler and polluter of the urban and rural landscape, a concept that was an important element of later ethno-nationalist negative descriptions of the traditional Jewish community in small towns and villages.

According to Mary Douglas, the concept of the polluter is applied to social groups whose function within society gives them much greater importance than is reflected in their status and influence.[73] This observation is applicable to the situation of the Jewish community in the eighteenth-century Polish-Lithuanian Commonwealth. Though Polish Jewry in 1765 formed only 5.35 percent of the population of the commonwealth, estimated at between 12.3 and 14 million individuals, Jews were extremely active in various areas of the state economy. This situation was even noted by foreign visitors to the country in the eighteenth and nineteenth centuries.[74] One noted: "They seemed, indeed, the only people who were in a state of activity, exercising almost all professions, and engaged in every branch of trade; millers, whitesmiths, saddlers, drivers, innkeepers, and sometimes even as farmers. Their constant bustle makes them appear more abundant in number than they really are."[75]

At the same time their status within society did not reflect their economic importance. On the social level they were a separate corporate estate that neither constituted a part of the burgher estate nor enjoyed civic rights like the burgher and peasant estates. Still, various attempts at incorporating Polish Jews into the burgher class—the middle class—and making them citizens were debated in the Polish parliament in February 1775 and during the famous Four-Year Parliament (1788–92), which culminated in the constitution of 3 May 1791.[76] King Stanisław August Poniatowski and a group of enlightened nobles such as Tadeusz Czacki, Mateusz Butrymowicz, Jacek Jezierski, and Józef Pawlikowski, among others, advocated a variety of reforms of the social, occupational, and political status of the Jewish community.[77] These status reforms were also supported by a group of Jews such as Zalkind Hourwitz and Salomon Polonus, who were representatives of the Jewish Enlightenment—the Haskalah movement in Poland.[78]

Polish debates about the position of Jews in society were, like similar debates in Western and Central European countries, a first phase in the emancipation process of European Jewry.[79] In the Western and Central European models this phase of emancipation was a manifestation of changes in the idea of a nation, brought about by the birth of modern concepts of nationalism and the nation-state. This nationalism was characterized by a strong homogenizing tendency on the part of the state, a tendency that was seen as necessary in molding a modern nation out of different social classes. However, in the case of Poland the attempts at reforming the social and political status of Jews were not realized before the final partitioning of the state in 1795. Due to strong opposition from the burgher class, which also erupted into minor anti-Jewish disturbances in the spring of 1790, Jews were not incorporated into the nascent middle class.

Neither was the political emancipation of Polish Jewry, like the emancipation of the peasants, achieved at that time. Hundert differentiates among three reasons for the failure to grant Jews citizenship: opposition from the burghers; "the refusal of *szlachta* to 'countenance any diminution of their authority over their own holdings'[;] and the conservatism of the Jewish representatives involved in the debates, who wished to retain some of their corporate system and privileges."[80]

According to Eisenbach, the Jewish representatives in the debates, having lived in Poland for centuries, saw themselves as an integral part of the burgher estate (the third estate), in spite of religious and ethno-cultural differences. A large section of the Jewish middle class shared this perception in the nineteenth and twentieth centuries. [81] Therefore during the debates in the Polish parliament the representatives of this group consistently claimed that their cultural distinctiveness was compatible with loyalty to the Polish monarch and state. A small Haskalah movement within the Polish Jewry, like everywhere else in Western and Central Europe, supported the program of acculturation. [82] It was from this latter group that, on the eve of the last partition in 1795, Jewish fighters for the Polish cause emerged; they fought in the Kościuszko insurrectionary movement of 1794 and later in the legions of Henryk Dąbrowski. [83]

The position of representatives of the conservative Jewish majority stood in sharp contrast to the proposals of Polish Reformers. Stanisław Staszic, mentioned above, was a Reformer who in 1808 was elected president of the Society of the Friends of Learning in Warsaw, the future Polish Academy of Sciences. Staszic advocated forcible assimilation of Jews into Polish mores and customs and the Polish language as the only means of guaranteeing harmonious existence between them and ethnic Poles and as a prerequisite for granting Jews some civic rights, but not full equality. Staszic's proposal is an example of an inclusionary model based on a strong idea of the homogenization of society, which manifested itself in the proposal of extensive assimilation of Jews into Polish culture, not atypical of that era. [84] Staszic's proposal also implied the rise of a nascent idea of antagonism between Poles and Jews. This antagonism found its expression in phrases such as "the [Jewish] state within a state" and "the [Jewish] nation within a nation," which came to be commonly used by ethno-nationalists in the nineteenth and twentieth centuries. Undoubtedly the structure of the premodern Jewish community contributed to the development of this perception. However, the idea of the Jew as harmful other that Staszic himself espoused in his writing contributed to the emergence of the concept of antagonism between Poles and Jews. Staszic believed that premodern Polish Jewry, with its ethno-cultural composition and activities, was responsible for the antagonism. Staszic's views are an example of what the historian Andrzej Walicki defines as the crystallization of the nascent concept of an ethnic type of modern Polish national identity that arose at the end of the Enlightenment period. [85]

Interestingly the notion of antagonism did not seem to apply to other ethno-cultural minorities in the pre-1795 Polish state. One reason for this was the difference in visibility between the Jewish community and other ethno-cultural groups vis-à-vis the ethnic Roman Catholic Polish population. Polish Jews were a "visible" strong ethno-cultural group because of their prominent role in the state economy, their maintenance of a distinctive moral-cultural identity, and their internal institutions, whereas other ethno-cultural groups appeared "less visible" in an economic and cultural sense. The large Slavic groups and the Lithuanian community in the northeastern and eastern parts of the commonwealth had not yet fully developed collective identities. In the case of smaller ethno-cultural groups, such as the Polish Armenian and Muslim Tatar communities, they had acquired a level of "invisibility" by the end of the eighteenth century. These groups underwent extensive cultural polonization during the seventeenth and eighteenth centuries, beginning in the period of the Counter-Reformation. In the process of polonization both groups lost the use of their respective languages in daily life, which did not happen to premodern Polish Jews, whose main language remained Yiddish.[86] The communal life of the Armenians had also disintegrated by the end of the eighteenth century, whereas such a process did not take place in the case of Polish Jews, despite the abolition of the Council of Four Lands in 1764.[87] This also suggests that the appearance of the nascent concept of antagonism between Poles and Jews can be explained by a negative evaluation of the otherness of Jews. It is in this context that the ethno-cultural distinctiveness of premodern Polish Jewry can be seen as one of the factors contributing to what Zienkowska and Hundert identify as the emergence of the duality of Poles and Jews.[88] Still, by the end of the eighteenth century Polish Jewry constituted and was perceived as an intrinsic part of the Polish social landscape. The dominant concept of a Polish nation was that of a nation of nobles in the political sense, and the dominant concept of a Polish state was that of Jagiellonian Poland, encompassing all the pre-1772 territories with all their populations.

The year 1795 marked the final, third partition of the premodern Polish state by its three expanding neighbors: the Russian and Austrian Empires and the Prussian state. From 1795 until 1918 Poland, in the words of nineteenth-century British intellectual Lord Acton, "was a nation demanding to be united in a State—a soul, as it were, wandering in search of a body in which to begin life over again."[89] The issue of regaining sovereignty and the territories of the pre-1772 Polish-Lithuanian Commonwealth was a major preoccupation of Polish political and cultural elites during the first six decades of the nineteenth century. Discussions about nationhood and the lost state were accompanied by various insurrectionary activities and uprisings in all three partitioned zones in the first half of the nineteenth century.[90] The two most important national uprisings, of November 1830–31 and of January 1863–64, occurred in the Russian-occupied zone, which contained the largest and most central parts of the First Polish Republic, including the capital, Warsaw.[91] The insurrectionary movement of the early 1860s that culminated in the Uprising of 1863–64 was the last serious attempt in the nineteenth century at restoring the Polish-Lithuanian Commonwealth.[92] The division of the insurrectionary national emblem into three parts, symbolizing the Crown (Poland), Lithuania, and the Ukraine, was one of many manifestations of the desire to restore the premodern state.[93] Romanticism was the ideology and movement in which the spirit of these Polish political discussions and uprisings was shaped.

There is no doubt that, according to the ethos of Polish liberal and idealistic romantic nationalism, Jews constituted an intrinsic part of Polish society and of a future independent Polish nation-state. For example, this ethos can be found in two important contemporary representations of Polish Jews created by the imminent national romantic bard Adam Mickiewicz (1799–1855). Mickiewicz created the image of the traditional Jewish innkeeper Jankiel, "the honest Jew who loved our country like a patriot true," in the well-known national poem "Pan Tadeusz" (1834), and the image of Israel as the Older Brother whose fate would be forever intertwined with that of Poland—without free Poland there is no free Jewry—in *Księgi narodu i pielgrzymstwa polskiego* (Books of the Polish Nation and Pilgrimage) (1832).[94]

The same ethos was demonstrated in the numerous patriotic manifestations of 1861 and 1862 in Warsaw, in which Poles and Jews participated together as one united political force against the Russian oppressor. Some of these manifestations were immediately documented in literary works. The late romantic poet Cyprian Kamil Norwid (1821–83), in the poem "Żydowie polscy" (Polish Jews), written in 1861, praised the solidarity of Jews with Poles in the manifestation of 8 April 1861, during which Michał Landy, a young Jewish gymnasium student, took up a cross from a wounded priest and was immediately killed by a Russian soldier: "Then once again the Maccabee stood. Not in ambiguous anxiety with the Pole on a Warsaw Pavement."[95]

The inclusive ethos was also reflected in political proclamations promising the abolition of all distinctions between Jews and other citizens. The first such proclamation, entitled "To Our Israelite Brothers," was issued on 23 February

1846 by the leaders of the very short-lived Polish uprising at the Free City of Cracow. [96] In the 1840s similar proclamations were supported by Polish revolutionaries in the grand duchy of Posen and Galicia and were enacted by the revolutionary parliaments in both Prussia and Galicia. [97] Similar appeals were issued during the insurrectionary movement of the early 1860s, a period that came to symbolize the historical moment of "Polish-Jewish brotherhood" against the Russian oppressor. [98]

In his recent study Brian Porter makes a sweeping assertion about the position of Jews within stateless Polish society in the first half of the nineteenth century: "Polish nationalism in the period from 1830 to 1863 became more inclusive than it ever had been before and perhaps ever would be again. The most striking example can be seen in the unparalleled openness Polish nationalists showed toward the Jews around mid-century. . . . One could still be a judeophobe, but it was becoming increasingly difficult to be a judeophobic nationalist." [99]

Porter's evaluation of the romantic liberal nationalism of the mid-1850s as an inclusive ideology toward Polish Jewry and other ethno-cultural groups is definitely correct. However, his evaluation of Polish romantic nationalism as a uniformly inclusive and liberal force is questionable. Polish romanticism was not a monolithic national movement that expressed only one single set of positive attitudes toward Jews, without any significant judeophobic elements concerning the position of Jews within Polish society or any influence of an ethnic component.

Polish romantic nationalism, like German nationalism, was not a uniform force guided only by liberal and idealistic notions. [100] In fact, the movement and ideology were not free of certain paradoxes concerning the concept of a Polish nation. As observed by the literary historian Irena Grudzińska-Gross, ethnic origin was of great importance to many members of the Polish political émigré community (Wielka Emigracja) in Paris, which became the main center of political life after the failed uprising of November 1830–31:

> The correspondence of the Poles and emigrants gives a totally different impression. The national issue is constantly and comprehensively discussed here. And the fact that someone is of Lithuanian, Mazurian, or Jewish origin is treated as very important in the evaluation of the person under discussion: his character, his points of view, and his actions. Discussions about the Jewish origin of Mickiewicz poisoned the atmosphere of the "Polish streets" of Paris. Although from the outside the Polish émigré community might have

appeared as a monolithic body, from the inside the community was divided into a huge number of tribes fighting with each other. In France such a phenomenon was to emerge approximately thirty years later.[101]

The leading scholar of Polish nationalism, Andrzej Walicki, and the literary historian Stanisław Eile also take into account the paradoxes of the romantic era. They argue that despite advocacy of the liberal romantic ethos encompassed in the slogan "your freedom and ours" (za naszą wolność i waszą), the Polish romantic period also contributed to fostering the idea of an ethnic Polish nation with a particular set of values.[102]

In the first half of the nineteenth century the majority of political and cultural elites, both in exile and in the partitioned country, were still of noble origin. This situation also played an important role in attitudes toward nationhood and national values.[103] There is no doubt that the concept of a political nation, despite the often declared wish to include the *lud* (commoners, the people, peasants), to a large degree still drew on the tradition of the Polish-Lithuanian Commonwealth and embraced only those who were nobles. The phrase "Gente Ruthenus (vel Lithuanus), natione Polonus" continued to be important in defining belonging to the Polish nation. At the same time the gentry had basically already been polonized culturally and linguistically, and its significant segments saw in Catholicism, conservatism, traditionalism, and the idyllic rural life the key markers of Polish national (cultural) identity.[104] The same segments of the nobility were inclined to perceive new Western trends such as capitalism, industrialization, and urbanization as doctrines with values that somehow, in their eyes, stood in opposition to Polishness. In turn the latter phenomenon had some impact on the way these segments of the nobility, particularly in the kingdom of Poland, perceived the Jewish bourgeoisie. Expatriate nobles often had mixed reactions toward wealthy Warsaw Jews who acted as the forerunners of modernization, involved in building the banking and trading system and bringing railways to the Russian partitioned zone.[105] Although these negative reactions may be attributed to the fact that the Jewish bourgeoisie was associated with Russian rule, the cultural Judeocentric element behind the negative attitudes also should be considered. Patriotic Polish nobles did not express such ambivalent reactions toward the German bourgeoisie and the new German colonists who were also involved in economic modernization and who, in contrast to the Jewish community, enjoyed full political and civic rights in the kingdom of Poland.[106] On occasion the conservative nobles would widen their negative reactions toward Jewish entrepreneurs to include Poles who worked for Jewish employers. For example, the family of journalist Józef Ignacy Kraszewski (1812–87) accused him of having served Jewish capital in an earlier stage of his career, when he left *Gazeta Warszawska* for *Gazeta Codzienna*, which was owned by Ludwik Kronenberg, one of the major Jewish entrepreneurs committed to the Polish cause.[107]

Gazeta Warszawska, first published in 1801, is a good example of an important mid-nineteenth-century conservative daily that disseminated negative representations of Jews as a group harmful to Christian society. These representations constituted to a great degree the continuation of negative images of Jews formulated in the late eighteenth century. The *Gazeta* launched the so-called Jewish war in 1859, a series of vicious attacks, full of invective, on the successful Jewish bourgeoisie.[108] The leaders of the National Democracy movement praised the *Gazeta* later in the century as the first forum for Polish integral nationalism, considering it a predecessor of their movement: "[The *Gazeta Warszawska*] was the leading national paper that advocated the preservation of Polish national culture, fought against the Jewish influence, and warned against the German threat long before the birth of Roman Dmowski."[109]

Artur Eisenbach's study *Wobec kwestii żydowskiej* is an important historical analysis of attitudes toward Polish Jewry in the first half of the nineteenth century. In it Eisenbach shows that important émigrés displayed anti-Jewish perceptions. Among conservative and right-wing émigré circles, and also among segments of the nobility in the partitioned country—landowners, the aristocracy, and the Roman Catholic clergy—it was common to perceive Jews as not belonging to Polish society.[110] Such anti-Jewish perceptions and attitudes did not undermine the inclusive ethos of liberal and democratic romantic Polish nationalism but constituted a parallel undercurrent.

Various representations of Jews as harmful aliens within Christian society were, as argued by Eisenbach, transmitted from one generation of the nobility to the next.[111] Importantly they were influential both in the evaluation of the role of Jews in society and as potential members of a future political nation and in the evaluation of Jews as potential members of the Polish insurrectionary forces. The latter was, for example, clearly visible during the Uprising of November 1830, whose leaders were split on the issue of drafting Jewish volunteers into the National Guard. Those against accepting Jews into the Guard invariably questioned their commitment to the national cause and looked upon them with mistrust or disdain, absent in the drafting of other groups, such as Tatar volunteers.[112]

Some pre-1864 negative representations of Jews were later incorporated into the modern representation of the Jew as the harmful alien. The most important among them is the perception of Jews as an alien force that does not constitute a part of the Polish middle class but instead causes damage to the Polish economy. Individuals like Stanisław Staszic, Andrzej Zamoyski, and Wincenty Korwin-Krasiński, among others, expressed such ideas.[113] Of course in contrast, others, like Wawrzyniec Surowiecki, Jan Pawlikowski, and Jan L. Żukowski, members of a democratic left-wing political group, argued that Jews played an important positive role in the economy and perceived them as an intrinsic part of Polish society who should be granted civic rights unconditionally.[114]

Another negative perception of Jews in the first half of the nineteenth century that was influential in later periods was the image of the Jewish convert who, despite his conversion to Christianity, cannot be entirely trusted as a Pole. This was a manifestation of the implicit influence of ethnicity on the thinking of some segments of the conservative and ultra-conservative political and cultural elite. Such representations were used in the evaluation of first- and second-generation Frankists, originally an offshoot of an eighteenth-century Jewish mystical movement that emerged in the territory of the Polish-Lithuanian Commonwealth.[115] By the first two decades of the nineteenth century the first and second generations of Frankists had become Roman Catholic nobles who produced a number of prominent thinkers and military figures committed to the Polish cause. Another group of converts that anti-Jewish writers similarly mistrusted were former members of the Polish Haskalah movement, who in the course of the first two decades of the nineteenth century had also converted to Roman Catholicism. Negative representations of the Jewish convert can be found in works such as Wincenty Korwin-Krasiński's pamphlet *Uwagi o żydach* (Notes about Jews)(1818); the anonymous pamphlet *O żydach i judaizmie* (About Jews and Judaism), published in Siedlce (1820); and the well-known national drama *Nieboska komedia* (*The Un-divine Comedy*) (1835), written by the son of Wincenty Korwin-Krasiński, Zygmunt Krasiński (1812–59).[116] Nationalists began to use this image in political discussions during the 1830s, 1840s, and 1850s as a strategy to criticize rivals. For example, the well-known writer Julian Ursyn Niemcewicz (1758–1841), who after the Uprising of November 1830 joined democratic Polish circles in Paris, suggested that converts such as Jan Czyński (1801–67) could not commit to the Polish cause as well as ethnic Poles: "Can Jews love Poland more than Poles?"[117]

Niemcewicz was also an author of another important idea that late nineteenth-century anti-Semites incorporated into the modern representation of the Jew as the harmful alien, with the slogan "Judeo-Polonia." In 1858 the pamphlet *Rok 3333 czyli Sen niesłychany* (The Year 3333; or, An Incredible Dream), which he had written three decades before, appeared in *Przegląd Poznański* . The pamphlet contains a vision of a future Warsaw becoming a Jewish city and being renamed Moszkopolis.[118] To readers at the time of publication this pamphlet was humorous, but by the late nineteenth century and the beginning of the twentieth the work was frequently circulated and introduced as a warning foreseeing the tragic future of a Poland transformed into Judeo-Polonia. In the anonymous edition of 1913 the pamphlet's introduction describes it as a warning against the "dangerous alien who slowly digs a grave for Poles." In 1932 the writer Roman Brandstaetter called this pamphlet "the most malicious pamphlet about Jewry written in Polish literature."[119]

The size of the Jewish community played a role in the evaluation of Jews as a physical threat to Poles and the creation of the doomsday vision of Poland being transformed into "Judeo-Polonia." According to the available data, in the nineteenth century the highest concentration of both ethnic Polish and Jewish populations was in the Russian partitioned zone, and the lowest concentration of both populations was in the Prussian partitioned zone. By the end of the nineteenth century the number of Jews living in the Russian partitioned zone was 1,271,000, or 14 percent of the entire population; in the Austrian partitioned zone it was 800,000, or 10 percent; and in the Prussian partitioned zone it was 50,000, or 2 percent.[120] As in previous centuries Jews mostly lived in towns. For example, in 1865 there were 5,336,100 individuals in the kingdom of Poland, of whom 1,415 000 (26.5 percent) lived in urban areas. The Jewish population included 719,100 individuals, of whom 657,900 (91.5 percent) resided in cities and towns; Jews constituted 46.5 percent of the urban population. In 1865 in Warsaw 74,078 Jews constituted 31.4 percent of the population.[121] However, the size of the Jewish community was not the only essential factor in the creation of the anti-Jewish myth of Jews as capable in the future of physically swallowing the ethnic Polish community, which began to circulate in the mid–nineteenth century. The Jewish community was not the only group whose size was increasing in the nineteenth century. For example, the ethnic Polish community in the Russian zone had increased from

1,000,000 in 1870 to 1,450,000 by 1900.[122] A combination of factors, such as the difficulty of seeing Jews as a part of the Polish middle class, the perception of Jews and their activities as alien and harmful to Christian society, and the size of the urban Jewish populations, together contributed to often alarming forecasts about the emergence of Judeo-Polonia.[123]

One of the central features of nineteenth-century Polish-Jewish history was the failure of the politics of the integration of Jews into Polish lands.[124] This failure had many causes, including the rule of foreign powers over Polish territories, the weakness of the middle class and of middle-class values in Polish society, the prevalence of anti-middle-class thinking common among the Polish nobility and intelligentsia, the size and conservatism of Polish Jewry, and the strength of anti-Jewish attitudes and perceptions on both governmental and popular levels.

In general the integration of Jews was most successful in Prussian Poland, where most anti-Jewish restrictions were lifted in 1848. However, in the second half of the nineteenth century, when the conflict between the Polish majority and the German government, committed to the Germanization of the area, escalated, the majority of the Jews fled the region. In Galicia Jews achieved civil equality in 1868; the Polish nobility, which gained control over the province in the early 1860s, accepted the granting of full legal equality under pressure from Vienna. In the Russian zone, the kingdom of Poland, the Jews achieved civil equality in 1862. The viceroy of the Russian-controlled civil government, the Polish Margrave Aleksander Wielopolski (1803–77), to whom is ascribed the controversial saying "One can do something for the Poles, but with the Poles never" (Dla Polaków można coś zrobić z Polakami nigdy), issued the Emancipatory Act on the eve of the outbreak of the Uprising of January 1863–64.[125] A segment of the conservative and Catholic Polish press reacted to this legislation negatively, perceiving the civic equality of Jews not only as an economic threat but also as an insult directed at Catholic culture and as a disaster in terms of the national interest of Poles.[126]

After Russia crushed the January Uprising in 1864 the highly influential Warsaw Positivists, members of a social and political school of thought, came to support the integration of Jews into Polish society. The writer Aleksander Świętochowski (1849–1938) led the group; he was known as the "pope" of the Warsaw Positivists.[127] The Positivists advocated a program of "organic work" and emphasized the importance of the cultural and economic progress of society instead of insurrection. They viewed society as an organism into which all social classes ought to be integrated in a harmonious manner. They saw in the industrial Western European countries with a strong bourgeoisie the model for modern Polish society. For this reason they were critical of the nobility's prejudicial attitudes toward industry and commerce. In the 1870s, 1880s, and 1890s the Positivists were vehement supporters of including Jews in Polish society and granting them (as individuals) equal rights. [128] Therefore during this period many Positivist writers, such as Aleksander Świętochowski, Bolesław Prus (1847–1912), Eliza Orzeszkowa (1841–1910), and Klemens Junosza-Szaniawski (1849–98), created positive and sympathetic images of Jews. They expressed fierce criticism of the anti-Jewish atmosphere and anti-Jewish events such as the pogrom against Warsaw Jews of 25–27 December 1881, which shocked Warsaw Jews and the city's intelligentsia. [129] Some Positivists, like Bolesław Prus and Klemens Junosza-Szaniawski, were brilliant analysts of the predicament of Jews in society and the emergence of intensified anti-Jewish discourse in the 1880s. As one of the characters in Prus's novel *Lalka* eloquently puts it: "Wrong to be a Jew, wrong to be a convert. . . . Night is falling, a night in which everything looks gray and ambiguous." [130]

A similar view was expressed by Junosza-Szaniawski in his novel *Nasi żydzi w miasteczkach i na wsiach*:

> Regarding the "Jewish question," public opinion goes round and round in a magic circle and cannot find a way out. The unenlightened Jew in his dirty gabardine cloth who exploits and poisons the peasants with vodka we call a scoundrel—and for him we have contempt. The Jew who has left his backward community, taken off his dirty gabardine, and accepted European education and desires to work in a productive way we call an arrogant trickster—and for him we also have contempt. Finally, the Jew who has ceased to be a Jew, has cut off his links with his tribe, has converted to Christianity, and has entered our society, him we call the *meches* [convert]—and for him we also have contempt. [131]

However, from the late 1890s the views of Warsaw Positivists on Jews also came to gradually change. For example, the writer Prus became more critical of the Jewish community: "The Jews in Galicia [the Austrian partitioned zone] constitute one tenth of the entire population. They are characterized by poverty, ignorance, separatism, and harmfulness toward the rest of the inhabitants. Therefore the people feel resentment towards them." [132]

In the first three decades of the twentieth century some Warsaw Positivists came to perceive Jews in a manner similar to that of the group of anti-Jewish writers whose attitudes they had earlier severely criticized.[133] A case in point is Świętochowski, who by the second decade of the twentieth century came close to sharing the opinions of the main political movement of core ethno-nationalists, the National Democrats.[134]

This dramatic change in the Warsaw Positivists' perception of Jews is multifaceted. By the 1890s the members of the circle began to view capitalism mainly in negative terms—they developed a growing revulsion against the excesses and injustices of capitalist practices in the late nineteenth century. Thus their previous vision of a Poland modeled on the Western capitalist system was heavily shaken if not undermined. The emergence of the "new Jewish politics," as manifested in the Bundist, Folkist, and Zionist movements, with assertive autonomist claims, also contributed heavily to the Positivists' shift in their view of Jews as potential members of Polish society.[135] The Positivists' radical departure from the concept of Jews as an intrinsic part of Polish society to the concept of Jews as a harmful alien group may have sprung from their advocacy of an unrealistic model of integration. Świętochowski and other Positivists advocated Jewish assimilation in the 1880s, by which notion they understood that Jews would abandon all markers of their distinctive moral-cultural code, not only language and dress but also morality and religion. According to the leading scholar of Positivism, the late Stanisław Blejwas, Świętochowski was, for example, convinced in 1882—one year after the outbreak of violent anti-Jewish disturbances in Warsaw—that such assimilation of Jews into Polish culture would put an end to anti-Semitism.[136] Świętochowski wrote, "If today Jews with all their separateness disappeared, tomorrow the anti-Semitic movement would be reduced to the farts of ultramontane nobles."[137]

The Positivists were deeply and unrealistically disappointed by the fact that the majority of the Orthodox Jewish community did not give up or intend to give up their moral-cultural identity. At first they thought that the environment should be blamed for the lack of modern education and the "regressive aspects" of the life of Orthodox Jews, but seeing that Jews were not eager to jettison their religion and culture, the Positivists decided that Jews themselves were to blame for anti-Semitism.[138] Acculturation to Polish culture among Orthodox Jews was particularly slow in the Russian partitioned zone, where the Jewish Orthodox community kept to itself. This was the result of strong Jewish religious conservatism and of the Russian government's introduction of an intensive policy of Russification in the educational system in the aftermath of the Uprising of 1863–64. Many Jews in the north of the kingdom of Poland who were inclined to assimilate began to speak Russian rather than Polish.[139] In any case the Positivists' program of integration through total assimilation (*spolszczenie/przepolszczenie*), which they put forward in the 1880s, was neither realistic in the conditions of nineteenth-century stateless Poland nor based on acceptance of cultural difference. The Warsaw Positivists took a position marked by strong homogenizing tendencies and low acceptance of internal cultural diversity. This homogenizing tendency was a characteristic that the Warsaw Positivists shared with contemporary German liberals.[140]

Still, some contemporary Polish writers understood the paradoxes of the Warsaw Positivists' vision of integration and were critical of what the historian Benjamin Nathans calls "a Faustian bargain of emancipation in return for assimilation."[141] For example, in a work entitled *Antysemityzm i kwestia żydowska* (Anti-Semitism and the "Jewish Question"), published in 1907, the little-known author Adam Boryna questioned the concept of the total assimilation of Jews:

> Treating the "Jewish question" without prejudice and without illusion, first of all we have to abandon our hopes for the expansion of the assimilation of the Jews in the name of moral principles. . . . This principle cannot be regarded as noncontroversial and infallible because it would be very hard to deny the Jews the right to cultivate their national distinctiveness. In fact, if we consequently follow such a principle to its logical conclusion it would mean that we ourselves would have to demand from our own emigrants [ethnic Poles] total assimilation into the nations among whom they dwell. Thus their moral duty would be to abandon their Polishness and to assimilate into the American or Brazilian nations.[142]

The Emergence of the Full-Fledged Myth between the 1880s and 1918

The emergence of the belief in the Jew as the harmful alien can be chronologically located with a fair degree of precision, because it was manifested in both vocabulary and argumentation in a distinct body of literary and journalistic works from the early 1880s. In this writing it is possible to observe a substantial increase in the use of descriptions such as "enemy" (wróg) and "foreigner" (obcokrajowiec) to describe the Jews as a collectivity. The earlier eighteenth-century concept of the Jew as a polluter and spoiler of the country is used in this literature in the context of discourse about the organic body of the Polish nation and those elements that cause harm to it. Thus Jews are portrayed as a kind of sickness, a social, economic, and cultural disease that the Polish nation had been enduring for a long time. In the words of Cracow conservative Stanisław Koźmian: " 'The Jewish question' in Poland is like gout, we cannot get rid of it, but we have to make sure that it causes us a minimum of discomfort."[143]

Such descriptions as "swamp" (bagno), "disgusting locusts" (szarańcza podła), "filthy insects" (plugawe robactwo), "weeds" (chwasty), "Jewish plague" (plaga żydowska), and "enslavement by Jews" (niewola żydowska) constituted the basic late nineteenth-century vocabulary regarding the Jewish presence.[144] In this literature there is a radicalization of opinions in terms of contemplating solutions to the situation, expressed more in the language and tone of some of the writings than in the proposal of any specific resolutions: "Like a medical doctor curing a human being, the state has the right and duty to use radical measures for the well-being of the national organism. In the last resort the state has the right to cut that part of the body that is affected by gout because if one part of the body suffers the entire body is affected."[145]

Common arguments found in this new anti-Jewish discourse include the following: First, Jews were not suited for integration into the Polish nation because they were culturally and ethnically alien and were furthermore an older and more powerful people than the Poles. Second, alone among the ethnocultural groups inhabiting the Polish territories, Jews constituted a unique case, one that had in the past and could yet have in the future a disastrous impact on the Polish state and Polish national "well-being." In fact, they were permanently engaged in the process of the judaization (*zażydzenie*) of the Polish universe, including its territory, economy, language, customs, and traditions. Jews were also traitors to the Polish national cause as they frequently represented foreign interests, especially those of the chief external Polish enemies, the Germans and the Russians. Jews were carriers of anti-Polish doctrines, values, and norms such as free-thinking Western liberalism, socialism, and Communism.[146] Poland was an innocent and suffering victim of the Jewish invasion. Finally, Poles should defend themselves in a more organized and effective way so as to show Jews that they were the true and sole owners of Poland and that, in fact, Jews were not suited to reside among Poles but should look for a homeland elsewhere. In such argumentation the Jew was always characterized as the perpetrator vis-à-vis the Pole as the victim, and as a threat to all aspects of national life.

Complex and highly emotionally charged narratives based on this argumentation came to be woven into the fully elaborated myth of the Jew as the harmful alien. Mythmakers coming from different social groups, such as the pauperized nobility, the intelligentsia of noble origin, and the new growing ethnic Polish bourgeoisie, constructed these narratives. By profession they were journalists, writers, lawyers, pedagogues, politicians, and Catholic priests.[147] They made up the first school of ethno-nationalist thinkers of different varieties and intensities preceding the emergence of the National Democracy movement. Although none of these thinkers were leading intellectuals of the late nineteenth century, their ideas influenced and corresponded with the way of thinking of substantial segments of radical, conservative, right-wing elites and significant sections of the Roman Catholic Church. As Andrzej Jaszczuk and Alina Cała have argued, post-1864 anti-Semitic idioms spread from conservative Catholic circles into the intelligentsia and to the national and peasant movements, gaining significant popularity among these circles.[148] These conservative Catholic circles were an important social force, not an isolated, marginal social movement. A flourishing printing industry facilitated the dissemination of anti-Jewish idioms on a significant scale among a growing literate segment of society.

What most of these mythmakers had in common was their claim to represent and defend both national and Catholic interests, which by that time had become irreversibly intertwined. By the nineteenth century the fusion of Catholicism and Polish ethno-cultural identity was a historical fact rooted in the nascent seventeenth-century concept of the Roman Catholic Church as the guardian of the Polish nation and the depository of national traditions.[149] In the nineteenth century this fusion was intensified by the prominent role of the Roman Catholic clergy, especially its lower ranks, in national uprisings and activities aimed at the preservation of Polish language and culture and by the fact that the Prussian and Russian states were advancing Protestant and Orthodox interests.

Among the first and most influential mythmakers of the late preindependence period four very different authors deserve to be discussed: Jan Jeleński, Teodor Jeske-Choiński, Andrzej J. Niemojewski, and Father Marian Morawski. Jan Jeleński (1845–1909), a conservative Catholic and self-made businessman, came from a family of the pauperized nobility. He propagated the myth of the Jew as the harmful alien to the Polish nation with his own populist press. His weekly *Rola* (Soil), which was first published in 1883 and remained in circulation for the next thirty years, was the main forum for his views. Interestingly this weekly successfully competed for Roman Catholic readers with another radical conservative paper organ, *Niwa*, renamed *Niwa Polska* in

1898. In the latter similar, albeit somewhat less aggressive and extreme opinions about Jews were disseminated, particularly by one contributor, a bitter rival of Jeleński, the priest Ignacy Charczewski. [150] Jeleński set up another weekly, *Dziennik Dla Wszystkich* (News for Everybody), in 1905. He also wrote separate pamphlets and created a network of libraries with collections of anti-Jewish works. [151] Jeleński can be considered the first writer in the post-1863 period to suggest that in the best interests of Poles Jews should first be isolated and then should leave all Polish territories through emigration. He can also be regarded as the propagator of such popular catchphrases as "Do not buy at Jewish shops" (Nie kupuj u żyda), "Be aware of the Jew" (Strzeź się żyda), and "Bread for our own people" (Chleb dla swoich). After the social revolution of 1905, which swept through the cities of the Russian partitioned zone, Jeleński also accused Jews of causing social unrest. In his pamphlet entitled *Wrogom własnej ojczyzny* (To the Enemies of Their Own Homeland) he categorized Jews and socialists as the "killers" of Poland and voiced his support for the National Democracy movement. According to him, "all honest and just" Poles should "support this party." [152]

Teodor Jeske-Choiński (1854–1920) was an ex-Positivist turned conservative. Jeske-Choiński, a Pole of German ethnic origin, was a more sophisticated exponent of anti-Jewish themes than Jeleński was. His works were aimed at a more educated stratum of Polish society than were Jeleński's publications. In the 1880s and 1890s he wrote for various conservative papers, including Jeleński's radical conservative *Rola*. [153] He later also wrote for the Jesuit *Przegląd Powszechny* (Common Review), which was representative of the middle-of-the-road Catholic press, not its radical segment. His most important work, *Poznaj żyda* (Let's Get to Know the Jew), published in 1912, can be viewed as containing the most elaborate single contemporary representation of the belief in the Jew as a national Polish enemy. It includes a number of key anti-Semitic tropes: the Jew as responsible for all past and present Polish misfortunes and weaknesses; the Jew as a threat to all aspects of Polish life; and the Jew as the "internal plague," the polluter of Poland, who alone had the power to prevent a future rebirth of the Polish state.

In the same work Jeske-Choiński also provides an elaborate rationalization and justification of anti-Semitism as national self-defense. The characterization of anti-Semitism as national self-defense was to play a crucial role in the development of anti-Jewish violence, its initiation, rationalization, and justification. Although this type of anti-Semitism was not limited only to Poland, but was present in all other European countries of the late nineteenth century, in the Polish case it persisted for an unusually long time. It is present in discourse about Jews even in the post-1945 period, particularly the rationalization of anti-Jewish violence and other aspects of the "dark past" of Polish-Jewish relations. According to this explanation, the Jew himself was to blame for the emergence of anti-Semitism and for those anti-Semitic activities directed against him:

> Anti-Semitism is simply a form of self-defense by Christians against the active hatred directed against them by Jews. Anti-Semitism will cease to exist when the Jew finally understands that living in someone else's home means learning how to be an acceptable guest and how neither to aspire to the role of the host nor to harm the host. . . . After all, our Christian culture is humanitarian. . . .
>
> The self-defense of Christian nations against Jews is not only desirable but is also a duty dictated by the instinct for self-preservation. At present, as in no other period of time, fulfilling this duty is so urgent because Jews, having been granted equality, are powerful and dangerous on an incredible scale just as they were before the destruction of the Temple. . . . Self-defense has to be both material and spiritual. It is important not only to defend the material culture and the right to exist but also to defend the Christian soul, which has been poisoned by the Jewish press, and to defend the Christian conscience, which has been mocked by Jewish cynicism and commercial shrewdness. . . . All this is of primary relevance to us Poles, of whom the Jews have come to be particularly fond, so particularly in fact that we are on the verge of suffocation. . . . [The Jews speak thus:] "If you do not allow us to establish a 'Judeo-Polonia state' and a nation of 'Judeo-Polish people,' we will strangle you."[154]

The third major anti-Jewish writer was Andrzej J. Niemojewski (1864–1921). Niemojewski was an ex-socialist and freethinker, and there were important differences between his world-view and those of Jeleński and Jeske-Choiński. In contrast to these two writers, who looked to Western European anti-Semitic discourse for inspiration, Niemojewski fashioned his anti-Jewish writings after the work of various anti-Jewish Russian and Lithuanian writers, the Judeophobes, who categorized the Jewish religion as the source of all social evil.[155] He was also fiercely anticlerical, an attitude that gained him a reputation as the *enfant terrible* of the Polish intelligentsia. In the major work *Skład i Pochód Armji Piątego Zaboru* (The Structure and March of the Army of the Fifth Partition [of Poland]), published in 1911, Niemojewski called the Jews the fifth partitioning power of Poland. (He saw the Roman Catholic clergy as the fourth partitioning power.) He also propagated belief in the Jew as the national enemy in the press organ *Myśl Niepodległa* (Independent Thought), which he set up in 1906, and in a series of lectures published as booklets, including *Dusza żydowska w świetle Talmudu* (The Jewish Soul in the Mirror of the Talmud) and *Etyka Talmudu* (The Ethics of the Talmud). In the latter work he provided an explanation for why anti-Semitism should be treated as an important and necessary ideology. According to Niemojewski, there is an irreconcilable dichotomy between the Jewish and Polish cultures and between the ethnic if not racial characteristics of the two groups: "Polish Democracy and Patriotism in relation to Judaism and Semitism is like culture and civilization in relation to slavery and despotism. It is also like rationalism and free thought in relation to revelation and dogmatism. Thus to be a Polish Democrat means to be the enemy of Jewishness, in other words, to be an anti-Semite."[156]

Father Marian Morawski (1845–1901) was a professor of philosophy at the Jagiellonian University. He was also the editor of the Jesuit monthly *Przegląd Powszechny*, whose first issue appeared in 1884.[157] In February 1896 he published the article "Asemityzm" (Asemitism), an important instance of the "mild" use of the image of the Jew as a national threat. In "Asemityzm" Morawski both condemned violence against the Jews and advocated separatism from the Jews, whom he viewed as the enemies of both Christianity and the Polish nation.[158] Morawski understood separatism as an economic and moral strategy that the Poles had to take up in defense against the Jewish force. By the moral strategy of separating Poles from Jews Morawski understood an enforced policy of social and cultural separatism, including exclusion of Jews from social clubs. According to Morawski, Polish youth should also be isolated from the presence and influence of Jews. Morawski's article was well-received in nonradical Catholic circles. The article was reprinted in *Niwa Polska* in 1898.[159]

The contemporary Ukrainian critic Iwan Franko (1856–1916), himself not free of anti-Jewish perceptions, who wrote for the Polish cultural journal *Tydzień*, was the first discerning critic of Morawski's concept of asemitism.[160] He noted: "The most appropriate conclusion from his [Morawski's] argumentation is wishful thinking that the Jews should go to Hell. . . . He does not like the incitement to violence, the crowds and the noise. He is too sensitive and too well-educated to support such things. . . . Father Morawski does not demand the abandonment of equal civil rights for Jews, but at the same time accepts that perhaps in the future one would have to adopt such radical measures. He opposes special legislation against the Jews, but at the same time demands legislation formulated in such a way that would prevent Jewish abuses."[161]

The historian Andrzej Jaszczuk calls Morawski's asemitism another form of anti-Semitism.[162] The scholar Michał Jagiełło convincingly argues that Morawski's position represents what he calls a softer version of anti-Semitism—"ułagodzony antysemityzm"—which stood in opposition to the hardcore anti-Semitism—"twardy antysemityzm"—disseminated in papers such as Jeleński's *Rola*.[163] At the same time Jagiełło recognizes that Morawski's representation of Jews was based on his belief in Jews as a harmful alien group constituting a national threat. The problem of nonviolent anti-Semitism/asemitism recurred in the interwar period, by then expressed by the phrase "cultural anti-Semitism" (antysemityzm kulturalny). Although "cultural anti-Semitism," like asemitism, opposed the use of anti-Jewish violence, it contributed to the spread of the perception of Jews as a national threat, because this was its premise. Jagiełło was the first Polish scholar to acknowledge this common premise of the two forms of anti-Semitism. The impact of cultural anti-Semitism on Polish society in the late nineteenth century and the first half of the twentieth bears further investigation.

On the whole, in the 1880s and 1890s many radical conservative newspapers, and the Catholic press with some rare exceptions, disseminated the image of the Jew as the enemy of the Poles and Christianity.[164] Among the papers that propagated this image were those like the extreme *Rola*, which advocated taking radical anti-Jewish measures, and those like the middle-of-the-road Catholic *Przegląd Powszechny*, which opposed anti-Jewish violence. The image was also propagated in second- and third-class literary works, whereas the liberal press and liberal authors in all three partitioned zones did not use or disseminate this image of the Jew.[165]

The Myth and the National Democracy Movement

In the 1890s the representation of the Jew as a national threat entered the realm of modern Polish politics. Anti-Semitic rhetoric and imagery began to appear with varying degrees of importance and intensity in the political press and in the programs of two out of the three major political movements that crystallized during the last decade of the nineteenth century—the National Democrats and the peasant movement. The political press and programs of the third major political movement, the Polish Socialist Party (Polska Partia Socjalistyczna, PPS), founded in Paris in November 1892, were free of the representation of Jews as a harmful alien group.[166] The PPS's unquestionable leader between 1892 and 1918, Józef Piłsudski (1867–1935), the future marshal of the Second Republic, who had a strong attachment to the traditions of Jagiellonian Poland, saw Jews as an integral part of Polish society.[167] Piłsudski maintained that the solution to the "Jewish question" was intricately linked with Poland's regaining its independence, a position drawing on Mickiewicz's romantic vision of the union between Poland and Israel, the Older Brother. These two ideas constituted the foundation of Piłsudski's approach toward Jewry at least from 1894.[168] Despite the presence of two contradictory attitudes toward cultural assimilation and Jewish minority rights within the PPS after the emergence of Jewish "new politics" in the 1890s, the PPS supported the concept of equal rights for all citizens of a future Poland regardless of their religion or ethnic background.[169]

In contrast, the National Democrat movement was the core exponent of ethnic Polish nationalism in its integral form. The Union of Social Democrats (Stronnictwo Narodowo-Demokratyczne) was set up by Roman Dmowski (1864–1939) on 1 April 1897 and later was commonly referred to as the National Democracy movement or Endecja. Its forerunner was the National League (Narodowa Liga), set up in Warsaw in 1893.[170] For the National Democracy movement, one of the fastest-growing political movements of the time, the myth of the Jew as a national enemy became an important ideological element, and its politicians, activists, and supporters subsequently developed the most explicit, elaborate, and aggressive narratives and themes of the myth.

From the outset National Democracy rejected the actuality of premodern multiethnic Jagiellonian Poland and instead advocated the concept of a "powerful Poland" (Polska mocarstwowa) that would resemble the model of a homogenous ethnically and culturally Piast Poland.[171] Although at the beginning of its political activity Endecja's three founding fathers, Jan L. Popławski (1854–1908), Zygmunt Balicki (1858–1916), and Roman Dmowski, were members of illegal political organizations like the academic Union of Polish Youth (Związek Młodzieży Polskiej), known as Zet, in which socialists were also active, it became completely clear that there was a huge discrepancy between the ethnonationalist vision of a future independent Poland and Polish nation and the socialist vision, and that cooperation between these two political camps was out of the question.[172]

Although the National Democratic movement was initially small, it grew rapidly in all three partitioned zones. This was particularly visible in the variety of publications released by the National Democracy movement and the

National League, including separate papers for youth, intelligentsia, and the peasantry, as well as papers directed at the émigré Polish communities in France and the United States.[173] Another illustration of the rapid growth and increasing popularity of the movement was the development of the Association for National Education (Towarzystwo Oświaty Narodowej, TON), founded in 1899 in the Russian partitioned zone. In 1904 TON included six thousand members, mostly teachers of peasant background, and its supporters were estimated at another twelve thousand.[174] By the end of the first decade of the twentieth century the movement had gained support among all social groups in all three partitioned zones and came to be seen as the political force representing the interests of ethnic Poles.[175] The remarkable success of National Democracy was clear to some contemporary observers. In the words of a key Polish literary critic, the acculturated Jew Wilhelm Feldman, "The National Democrats [were] not a party but a clearly defined moral-political movement powerful throughout the whole of Poland."[176]

Barbara Toruńczyk provides a very important and convincing explanation for the remarkable growth of National Democracy that is too often ignored in the literature on the movement.[177] According to her, the party's strategy for reaching the masses and expanding its membership was based on identifying and grasping the dominant values and modes of thinking represented by prominent political and cultural movements, including conservative, traditionalist, and Catholic groups, and assimilating these values and modes into the National Democratic political program. Toruńczyk calls this process a revolution in the way of thinking of the proclaimed secular elites of National Democracy, its inner circle.[178] This process no doubt constituted a paradox, given the fact that during the late preindependence period the relationship between National Democracy and the Roman Catholic Church was not yet smooth but based on what can be called a struggle over the supremacy of values—national versus Catholic.[179] Yet National Democracy's assimilation of the sentiments and values of the Catholic and conservative traditions is a good illustration of the importance of the reuse and adoption of the existing stock of moral and cultural sentiments in the realm of politics.[180]

The concept of the Jew as the harmful alien other constituted one of the major aspects of the thinking among significant segments of conservative and Catholic elites in post-1864. Not only did the National Democrats capture and elaborate on this concept, but they made it a focal point of their ideology.[181] They transferred it to the level of modern national politics, and in this new form they delivered it back to society. Without that transfer the concept of the Jew as a national threat could not have become so powerful, potent, and long-lived. The National Democrats used this concept as a powerful political tool in the process of molding a modern Polish nation-to-be—the most urgent process of the preindependence period. They used it as a tool in raising national cohesiveness among ethnic Poles of different social classes with conflicting social and economic interests.[182]

Not every social class within Polish society had a fully developed Polish national awareness in the first decade of the twentieth century. The nobility, the intelligentsia of noble origin, and the bourgeoisie had a strong national awareness, but the peasantry, the largest social group, constituting approximately 75 percent of the population, was characterized by a weak sense of national awareness and a strong sense of local identity.[183] A significant segment of the peasantry associated the concept of Polishness with the nobility and the serfdom system and therefore feared it. This was the result of a historical legacy, one shaped by the *szlachta*.[184] The theoreticians and politicians of the National Democracy movement were severely critical of the *szlachta* but could not discard this social group as an unimportant unit of the Polish nation. Thus in such a social context the notion of the Jew as a national threat came as a useful tool for unifying otherwise conflicting social groups and raising the national awareness of the least nationally conscious groups.

The National Democrats applied the representation of the Jew as a national threat in the process of selecting components of culture identified as authentically Polish vis-à-vis components evaluated as anti-Polish. In the post-1864 reality the representation of the Jew as the carrier of anti-Polish values such as free thinking, anti-Christian values, Western liberalism, socialism, and Communism was already in existence, and the National Democrats captured, elaborated on, and inserted this representation into party doctrine.[185] They used stereotypes about Jews to prescribe a model of national culture, what should constitute this culture and what should be excluded from it.[186] Individuals, as well as political and social groups that were exponents of values categorized by the National Democrats as anti-Polish, were evaluated as suffering from uncritical "Judeophilism" (Judofilstwo) and being in the service of Jews.[187]

The fact that the National Democratic movement employed the image of the Jew as a national threat as the core element of its ideology differentiated it from the emerging peasant movement, which, like Endecja, became a party with mass support.[188] This is not to say that some peasant parties, like the

Union of Peasants Party (Związek Stronnictwa Chłopskiego, ZSCH), founded in 1893 in Galicia, and some ideologues of the peasant movement, like Father Stanisław Stojałowski, the leader of the Christian-Peasant Party (Stronnictwo Chrześcijańsko-Ludowe), also founded in Galicia in 1896, did not use the concept of the Jew as a national threat in a radical way.[189] As convincingly argued by the scholar Kai Struve, Father Stojałowski used anti-Semitic images as one of the central elements of his party's program. The concept of Jews as an alien and harmful group that should be eradicated from Galician villages also served him as a tool for the political mobilization of a significant number of Galician peasants for whom the Jew had previously simply represented an intrinsic element of their daily life—a feature of the local landscape.[190] The immediate result of Stojałowski's propaganda was the anti-Jewish riots in Central Galicia in 1898.

The main Peasant Party (Stronnictwo Ludowe, SL), which Bolesław Wysłouch founded in 1895 in Galicia, dealt differently with Jews. The concept of the Jew as the harmful alien was more an underlying than a central concept of SL's ideology.[191] The SL used anti-Semitic language and images less frequently and in a more moderate way. SL's members opposed radical violent measures against Jews because, they insisted, anti-Jewish violence led to social disorder and death among peasants: "It is well-known also that the *ludowscy* [SL followers] do not like Jews and that we try hard to stop their abuses. But we are doing so in a proper, responsible, and legal manner. We call for boycotting the tavern: the tavern keeper will leave without force if he no longer has anything to do in the village. Do not buy from a Jew, do not sell him anything, and do not borrow from him. Let us take the trade in our hands and found banks, and let us organize the wage work ourselves. Then even the worst Jew will no longer be able to harm us, and we will get rid of him without violence and misery."[192] However, the SL endorsed the concept of the removal of Jews—the Orthodox Jewish masses—from Polish soil in the party's program of 1903, the same year that the Peasant Party changed its name to the Polish Peasant Party (Polskie Stronnictwo Ludowe, PSL). The fusion of peasant and ethno-national politics continued into the interwar period.[193]

Importantly the Jew was not the only other representing a national threat to National Democrats. Their anti-German position also played an important role in their ideology. However, there was a qualitative difference between their anti-Jewish and their anti-German positions. In the latter case the perception of Germans as the other was based on long historical experiences going back to the medieval period—the time of the first German invasions into the Polish territories—and was reinforced by the more recent experience of the harsh discriminatory German policy "Drang nach Osten"—the forced Germanization of ethnic Poles in the Prussian (German) partitioned zone, a policy first introduced by Bismarck, first chancellor of the united German state (1871).[194] At the same time the politicians of the National Democracy movement, like Dmowski, admired the German nation for its success in ruthlessly advancing German interests.[195] By contrast the National Democrats based their representation of Jews as the internal enemy on various prejudicial views regarding the place and role of Jews in Polish society.

Comparing the images of Germans to those of Jews, we can also see that the former were definitely more static and limited in content, as reality obviated any need for elaborate mythologized stories. Importantly, in contrast to Jews, Germans who lived in Polish territories were not perceived as a national threat in either a political or a cultural sense. This perspective would be reflected in Polish treatment of the German minority in interwar Poland, where the principles of marginalization and tit for tat were generally advocated by Polish ethno-nationalists, who viewed the German minority through the perspective of relations between the Second Republic and the Weimar Republic and subsequently the Third Reich.[196]

The National Democrats saw in Slavic groups like Ukrainians and Lithuanians societies that were inferior culturally to the Polish nation and therefore should be absorbed into the Polish nation through the process of strong cultural assimilation. The Polish nation, representing higher cultural standards than other Slavic nations, had a right and a duty to promote its civilized mission as far as it was possible.[197] Dmowski also saw Russians as culturally inferior to Poles.[198]

In contrast, in the eyes of Dmowski Jews represented a culture and civilization that was older than the Polish nation. Jewish culture and civilization were totally different from Christian civilization. Therefore Jews were a powerful threat who could only hinder the development and progress of the Polish nation. There is no doubt that the perception of the Jew as always aiming to undermine the Polish national cause was reinforced by the demands of secular Jewish movements, both Zionist and socialist, for equal rights and communal minority rights.[199] The National Democrats saw Zionist claims as an immediate threat to the young Polish nation and believed that the only correct reply to the Zionist position was to mobilize Poles against both Zionist groups and the Orthodox Jewish masses.[200] This view was incidentally also that of Positivists like Prus and Świętochowski.[201]

Some scholars view 1905—a year of political and social revolution sweeping throughout late imperial Russia and the Russian partitioned zone—as the year of the transformation of Polish ethno-nationalism into a fully mature, integral ideology and movement. By the end of 1905 the National Democracy movement was functioning openly in all three partitioned zones.[202] In 1905 the National Democrats intensified their use of the concept of conflict between Jewish and Polish economic interests and between the moral-cultural codes of the two communities. From 1905 onward the National Democracy movement's appeals to ethnic Poles for a national awakening (*przebudzenie Polaków*) consistently stressed these two types of conflicts.[203] The party intensified these appeals in the aftermath of the fourth Russian State Duma (parliament) election of 1912. In that election the PPS, greatly aided by the Jewish vote, defeated the National Democrats, who had headed the Polish Circle (Polskie Koło) in the Russian parliament since 1907.[204] Although Eugeniusz Jagiełło was a relatively unknown PPS candidate, it was widely recognized that he was "the only Christian [on the electoral list] that was not an anti-Semite," and this fact definitely contributed to his victory over Endecja's candidate, Roman Dmowski.[205]

In the aftermath of the election Dmowski proclaimed a social and economic boycott of the Jewish population in the Russian partitioned zone and urged Poles to unite and rise against their internal enemy. The key slogan "Do not buy at Jewish shops" (Nie kupuj u żyda) was put forward as a "national commandment" (nakaz narodowy). The National Democratic press praised Poles who supported the boycott for being truly patriotic and Catholic and accused the segments of the Polish population that did not approve of the boycott of violating "the most holy national principle."[206]

The damaging impact of the practice of social mobilization based on the concept of conflict and threat was correctly analyzed two decades later by one of the most discerning critics of integral Polish nationalism, Ludwik Oberlaender. In the Polish-language Zionist journal *Miesięcznik żydowski* (The Jewish Monthly) Oberlaender stated, "The ideology of anti-Semitism, constructed and used by Dmowski as a means of awakening 'creative powers' within the ethnic Polish community, has arrested the development of these powers over a long period of time, and is subsequently developing into a separate phenomenon."[207]

The discussion of the role of National Democracy in disseminating the representation of the Jew as the harmful alien cannot be complete without a brief look at the legacy of Dmowski. In Dmowski's writing we find the full range of the narratives and themes of this representation. Dmowski is generally recognized as the founder of modern Polish integral nationalism and its leading practitioner. During World War I (1914–18) he also became a statesman for the Polish cause whose position exceeded in importance his earlier role as the leader of his political party. Dmowski, a biologist by training and fluent in English, was, like many Europeans of his time, influenced by Social Darwinism. His ideas, as Antony Polonsky argues, constituted "a variant of the intellectual current represented by people like Enrico Corradini, Vilfredo Pareto and Gustave Le Bon."[208]

Dmowski may be regarded as the Polish Edouard Drumont (1844–1917), the influential French anti-Semite of the same period.[209] In Polish historiography, however, there is a tendency to underplay the central role of anti-Jewish ideas in Dmowski's political thought.[210] Walicki recently pointed to the flaws of this analysis, which, as he argues, leads to misunderstanding the core doctrine of Polish integral nationalism. Walicki insists that the anti-Jewish position was an intrinsic structural aspect of Dmowski's doctrine of Polish national identity.[211] Alvin M. Fountain, Dmowski's biographer, suggests that the earliest evidence of Dmowski's negative evaluation of Jews as harmful aliens goes back to his high school days and is recorded in one of his essays written as a reply to a Jewish member of the clandestine youth club Watchtower (Strażnica).[212]

In his first major and most popular work, the so-called Bible of modern Polish nationalism, *Myśli nowoczesnego Polaka* (Thoughts of a Modern Pole), which was first published in 1902, Dmowski elaborated on the theme of the Jew as the cause of all past and present misfortunes and weaknesses of the Polish nation—including the lack of a strong ethnic Polish bourgeoisie—a position strongly modeled on the beliefs of the eighteenth-century burgher thinker Stanisław Staszic: "Because of the Jews Poland remained a nation of nobles down to the middle of the nineteenth century and even longer as it is to a certain degree today. If they had not existed, a part of the Polish people would have organized itself to perform the social functions that they fulfilled and would have emerged as a rival force to the nobility as a third estate that has played such an important role in the development of European societies and has become the principal force in modern social life."[213]

He also introduced the theme of the Jew as a threat to the present and future

Polish nation and provided a carefully constructed explanation as to why Jews could not be considered a part of the Polish nation-to-be. Here a sense of fear of the other, intertwined with a sense of inferiority and superiority toward the other, becomes apparent:

> We have to come alive and expand our existence [as a nation] in all aspects. Our aim should be to become a strong nation, one that cannot be defeated. Where we can we should civilize foreign elements and expand our potential by absorbing these elements into our nation. Not only do we have a right to do so, but this is also our duty. . . . Our national organism should absorb only those [foreign elements] that are capable of assimilating, elements that should serve to expand our growth and collective potential—a category Jews do not fall into. Their distinctive individuality that developed over hundreds of years does not allow us to assimilate the majority of them into our nation because our nation is too young and our national character not yet fully formed. In fact, it is the Jews who are in a better position to assimilate our majority into their culture and even to assimilate a part of us in a physical sense. [The other reason we cannot assimilate them] lies in the character of their race, which has never lived in the way in which a society of our type has lived. [The Jews] have far too many characteristics that are alien to our moral code and that would play a destructive role in our lives. Mingling with the majority of them would lead to our destruction: the young and creative elements on which the foundation of our future existence depends would be dissolved by the Jewish elements.[214]

Dmowski also seemed to believe that the expulsion of the Jews from the Polish territories would put an end to all the troubles experienced by the country. He was inspired in his program for the purification of Jews from Poland by the medieval Spanish policy of the expulsion of the Jews: "All Poland's troubles are the result of centuries of Jewish invasion. If we want to be a great independent nation, we must get rid of the Jews as the Spaniards did in the fifteenth century."[215]

In *Kwestia żydowska, cześć I: Separatyzm Żydów i jego źródła* (The Jewish Question Part I: Separatism in the Case of the Jews and Its Source), published in 1909, Dmowski divided the Jewish community into two parts—the first and larger section composed of Jews who were either religious or secular, both socialist and Zionist, and the second and smaller group composed of culturally assimilated Jews. Dmowski evaluated the whole of the first group as a hostile camp that had consciously "embarked on a battle" with the Polish nation, while the second group of assimilated Jews he criticized for failing to transform themselves into "proper, rightful Poles." Their Polishness, according to Dmowski, was shabby, weak, and untrustworthy. In contrast, their Jewishness was transparent. Furthermore, they dared to force Jewish ideas and values upon Polish society: "With the fast-growing numbers of Jewish intelligentsia, the number of assimilated Jews has been expanding but has been losing its quality. This great production of assimilated Jews has shown signs characteristic of mass production, namely superficial and shallow aspects. The number of Poles of Jewish origin has increased enormously, but they have been shabby, second-rate Poles. . . . This intelligentsia has created its own Jewish sphere with a separate soul and separate attitude. Moreover, it has felt its power growing, and therefore it has come to desire to force its own values and aspirations upon Polish society."[216]

In *Upadek myśli konserwatywnej w Polsce* (The Fall of Conservative Thought in Poland), first published in 1914, Dmowski restated his previous position on assimilated Jews. According to him, the major tragedies and biggest mistakes of the nineteenth century were the program of the cultural assimilation of Jews advocated in the post-1864 period and the decision of Count Aleksander Wielopolski, conservative head of the Polish administration, to grant Jews civic rights.[217] For Dmowski the assimilated Jew was a revolutionary—the representative of characteristics incompatible with Polish conservative traditions. The culturally assimilated Jew, like the Orthodox Jew, constituted a force directed against the Polish nation, its traditions and values. Antagonism and incompatibility existed between Poles and Jews in a cultural, ethnic, and racial sense. Thus Jews as a collectivity were the enemy of both Polish society and the Christian religion: "The Jew cannot represent traditional aspects of European society, even when he insists on adopting such traditions. The entire tradition of European society is alien to the Jew. Furthermore, it stands in opposition to all the values with which the Jewish soul converged during long centuries. The Jew despises the entire history of European people. He hates their religion and looks at their social hierarchy as a system that he can destroy and next take over. His instinct leads him toward action aiming at the destruction of European respect for tradition and of European attachment to religion."[218]

Characteristically Dmowski insisted that his outlook on Jews was shaped not by prejudice, but by concerns over the fate of Poland: "In spite of everything, I can honestly say that I do not feel hatred toward the Jews. And in general I am not guided in politics by hatred. I only care about Poland and its well-being and regard it as my duty not to allow anyone to cause my country any harm."[219]

Thus Dmowski, like Jeske-Choiński, suggested, first, that there were "objective grounds" for considering Jews as harmful aliens and, second, that Jews themselves were responsible for their being categorized as the enemy. This explanation of anti-Semitism shows that the National Democrats were convinced that the Polish national community, among all other European Christian nations, was the one most threatened by Jews because of the size of the Jewish community and its moral-cultural makeup. Therefore in their eyes self-defense against this "enormous threat" was primarily a necessity and could not be evaluated as morally and socially wrong. Such convictions also guided the National Democrats and their supporters in the post-1918 period and penetrated intellectual discourse.

Thus at the end of "the long nineteenth century," when the "dream" of Poland regaining its independence was coming closer to realization, social belief in the Jew as the chief internal enemy emerged as an answer to all significant questions about the troubling aspects of social, political, and economic life. Its central role in the ideology of the integralist nationalist camp continued during the postindependence period (1918–39). The interwar period was a turning point in terms of further development of this social construction and its impact on political culture, Polish society at large, and Polish-Jewish relations.

3. The Myth of the Jew as the Threatening Other in Interwar Poland, 1918–39

A Historical Introduction, Part II

There is very little knowledge of Jews and Jewish matters in Poland today. In this respect the Polish soul and mentality are full of prejudice and bias, the entire attitude based on "magical thinking": the most hideous, stupid, and outrageous ideas are accepted as truth without being questioned. . . . Thus it is too easy to make generalizations about Jewish matters without seeing the diversity of Jewish life and to use the Jewish issue for the purpose of political demagoguery. . . . Indeed, Dmowski's methods reveal just how easily this can be done.

Ludwik Oberlaender, "Ruchy nacjonalistyczne a antysemityzm"

Introduction

The Polish Second Republic (Druga Rzeczpospolita), which emerged after 130 years of foreign rule, was the largest state in East-Central Europe, with a population of over twenty-seven million. Its ethnic composition resembled that of the prepartition First Republic: ethnic Poles constituted approximately 65 percent of the entire population; Ukrainians, the largest minority, 16 percent; Jews 10 percent; Belorussians 6 percent; and ethnic Germans 3 percent. Approximately 65 percent of the entire population declared affiliation with the Roman Catholic denomination.[1]

Britain and France (the Entente powers) supported the reemergence of the Polish state, which they and others viewed as an example of the triumph of the national principle. In Poland itself Poles welcomed independence with euphoria. Many shared great expectations that this new state would quickly develop into a highly modernized European nation with a stable political and economic system.[2] The new Polish constitution of 1921 (Konstytucja Marcowa), modeled on the constitution of the Third French Republic, was an expression of a commitment to Western European liberal democracy. It guaranteed equal rights for all Polish citizens, irrespective of religion and nationality. Articles 110 and 111 of the constitution guaranteed minorities equal treatment under the law and the right to establish and maintain their own religious, cultural, and educational institutions.[3] Therefore expectations that the new Poland would develop along the model of civic nationalism, aimed at creating a pluralistic society and respecting cultural differences, were also high. However, exclusionary Polish ethno-nationalism prevented the fulfillment of these expectations. Poland was not exceptional in this respect, but rather exemplified the direction of a large part of continental Europe.

The period between 1918 and 1922 had already signaled that the rebuilding of Poland on the model of civic nationalism would be difficult. The first two and a half years of independence were a turbulent period of struggle for the frontiers of the new state. The country only took the form it held for most of the interwar period in March 1922, when the Wilno (Vilnius) region, conquered by the Polish Army in 1920 in a military mission ordered by Józef Piłsudski, was finally incorporated into Poland.[4] The struggle for the eastern frontier in some sense symbolized the struggle between two opposite concepts of Poland: the Poland of Roman Dmowski, which represented the model of integral nationalism, and the Poland of Józef Piłsudski, which represented the model of civic nationalism. Concerning the issue of Polish borders, the latter vision was that of a federalist Polish state linked to the independent states of the Ukraine, Belorussia, and Lithuania. In his efforts at building such a state Piłsudski, who was at the time both head of state and commander in chief, mounted an offense in April 1920 against the newly created state of Bolshevik Russia. The Polish-Soviet War of 1920 ended in August of the same year at the Battle of Warsaw, which was known as the "miracle on the Vistula." The National Democratic camp harshly criticized this military operation as "a rash event" and even as criminal folly.

Dmowski's vision of Poland did not include any federalist alliance with the Ukraine, Belorussia, and Lithuania. In fact, Dmowski was openly hostile to the legacy of the premodern multiethnic Jagiellonian state to which Piłsudski was attached. Dmowski's vision of Poland was of a monoreligious and mono-cultural united state. His vision of the eastern border endorsed only those areas with populations that would be easily assimilated into the Polish nation. Dmowski's vision triumphed in the agreement reached with Soviet Russia in the Treaty of Riga of 18 March 1921. Dmowski also triumphed over Piłsudski in domestic political affairs. Between the first parliamentary election in 1922 and Piłsudski's coup d'état of May 1926 the National Democracy party, in coalition with other right-wing political parties, dominated the parliament.

In the aftermath of Piłsudski's successful coup d'état of 1926 the so-called Sanacja, which originated in the Independent Camp (Obóz Niepodległoś-ciowy), headed by Piłsudski, took over the government and remained in power until the outbreak of World War II.[5] However, this new political development did not lead to a decline in the significant influence of National Democracy on political culture. Paradoxically certain political developments of the 1930s led to endorsement of the Endeks' vision of Poland by political movements and parties that otherwise stood in ideological opposition to the National Democracy movement.

In the parliamentary election of 1930, which was marked by considerable fraud, Sanacja gained 46.8 percent of the available seats and on forming the government became independent of political opponents. The same year the National Democracy party became the main opposition party, representing 12.7 percent of the seats in parliament.[6] Both the National Democracy party and left-wing political parties opposed the Sanacja government.[7] However, after Piłsudski's death in May 1935 deep changes occurred within the Sanacja movement, bringing its prominent right-wing section ideologically closer to the National Democrats. The Camp of National Unity (Obóz Zjednoczenia Narodowego, OZN or OZON), established in February 1937 from the right-wing section of Sanacja, the most radical group within the government, attempted to merge Piłsudski's independence ethos with that of the National Democrats.[8] From the outset OZN, headed by Colonel Adam Koc (1891–1969) and under the patronage of the president of state, Ignacy Mościcki (1867–1946), and Marshal Edward Rydz-Śmigły (1886–1942), openly endorsed the core ethno-nationalist position on the desired vision of the Polish nation.[9] Such a move to the right can be explained by two factors. First, the Sanacja government without Piłsudski was weak and lacked political cohesion. Therefore the right wing of the Sanacja movement opted to exploit anti-Jewish sentiment as a means of gaining stability and greater influence among the various parties representing the political right. Second, there was a generational shift of political elites, which led to a radicalization of politics in the early 1930s. The so-called generation of 1918, a generation of individuals like Colonel Koc who had been born in the 1890s and entered the political scene approximately in 1918, began gradually to replace the previous generations of politicians who had been born between the 1860s and 1880s. They were more radical in terms of the formulation of political programs and their actualization. [10] This change of elites was a widespread phenomenon. In the National Democratic movement the so-called young (*młodzi*), concentrated in the National Radical Camp (Obóz Narodowo-Radykalny, ONR), rebelled against the old (*starzy*). [11] The "young" of the National Democracy movement demanded more radical measures to realize the ethno-nationalist vision of Poland. They saw the generation of the "old," except for Dmowski, as too ineffective, too moderate. Thus the attempt at total realization of the ethno-nationalization of the state, its institutions, policies, and practices, came to be the driving force of state politics. Those who opposed that goal found themselves in the minority.

Of course the struggle against the process of the ethno-nationalization of Poland began in the early years of independence. The civic vision of Poland, advocated by Marshal Piłsudski and the PPS and supported by the liberal intelligentsia, strongly clashed with the vision of Poland represented by the National Democracy party. In the early 1920s the ethno-nationalization forcefully advocated by the National Democracy movement was manifested in the exclusion of Jews from employment in the public sector, from obtaining licenses to operate businesses in government-sponsored sections of the economy, and from obtaining any considerable government bank credits. [12] Jews were also rarely employed in non-Jewish factories. Peasants replaced Jewish workers in the various branches of industry over which the state established a monopoly, such as the tobacco industry. [13]

Another important early indication that the model of civic Poland would encounter severe obstacles in its realization was the reaction in Poland to the Minorities Treaty. This treaty was part of the Versailles Peace Agreement. Although Poland was the first among eight newly created states of East-Central and Eastern Europe to sign the Minorities Treaty on 28 July 1919, as Salo Wittmayer Baron argues, it did so under tremendous pressure from the Entente Powers. [14] For Dmowski, who was one of the two signatories, this was an embarrassing event that led him to develop the conviction that Western democracies were dominated by Jewish influences. [15] It is undeniable that representatives of American, Western, and Eastern European Jews played an important role in drafting and securing the Minorities Treaty. It is also undeniable that American and Western Jewish representatives like Louis Marshall (1856–1929) and Julian Mack (1866–1943), and their Eastern European counterparts like Nachum Sokolow (1859–1936) and Leo Motzkin (1867–1933), were divided on the issue of granting East European Jewry communal rights.[16] The former group advocated support for individual rights modeled on the rights of Western European Jewry, whereas the latter insisted on granting communal rights to Eastern European Jewry. However, for Dmowski such varied positions on the rights of Jews were of no relevance. He interpreted the demand for Jewish rights on the individual or the communitarian level as an attempt to create a Polish-Jewish state in Poland. In his proposed vision of the emerging Polish nation there was room for neither "Poles of Mosaic faith" nor a Jewish community with a claim to communal rights to an autonomous culture and language. In his eyes only those of the "Polish race," namely ethnic Poles and those groups perceived as assimilable to the Polish nation, qualified for Polish citizenship. A Pole had to prove that he had not been Jewish for three generations.[17]

In the aftermath of Versailles right-wing parties, like the Christian Alliance of National Unity (Chrześcijański Związek Jedności Narodowej), and the political center, represented by the psl "Piast" group and the National Workers' Party (Narodowa Partia Robotnicza, npr), had a strong negative reaction to the Minorities Treaty, which revealed the strength of the ethno-nationalist vision of Poland at the time. Ethno-nationalists of various shades and degrees found the Minorities Treaty hard to stomach.[18] They understood the Minorities Treaty as a "humiliating enforced treaty" and as an act of invasion into the domestic policies of the new state. In particular they viewed Jewish minority rights as an "insult" and "attempted crime" against the Polish state and its people.[19] In National Democracy circles Western and Polish Jewry was frequently held responsible for Poland being forced to sign the Minorities Treaty. Such an interpretation survived the treaty itself: Foreign Minister Józef Beck (1894–1944) renounced the treaty in September 1934.[20]

Some historians have underplayed the role of the National Democrats in shaping interwar political culture on the grounds that this party did not succeed in forming a single government in the interwar period and that its role declined after its early success in gaining one-third of all 444 seats in the first parliamentary election, of November 1922.[21] Such a position views National Democrats only from the perspective of electoral or parliamentary success and failure. It totally ignores National Democracy as a movement with remarkable political and social influence, promulgating a vision of the Polish nation that other right-wing and center-right-wing parties, the institution of the Roman Catholic Church, and the post-1935 Sanacja government came to endorse to various degrees. Evidence of the influence of the National Democracy movement on political culture is provided by the level of acceptance of its anti-Jewish perspective by a significant segment of otherwise ideologically diverse political parties and organizations, the Roman Catholic Church, and segments of the nonelite. This was particularly clear in the second half of the 1930s.[22] Comparing political anti-Semitism in interwar Germany and Poland, William Hagen discerningly observes that "at the ideological level, the antisemitic slogans and pronouncements of the right-wing radicals, the Catholic Church and the post-Piłsudski regime had become by 1939 'almost interchangeable.'"[23]

In the late 1930s both the OZN, one of the most influential political groups in the post-1935 government, and National Democracy constituted mass movements. OZN had one hundred thousand members in 1938, while the National Democracy movement could claim approximately two hundred thousand members in 1939, meaning that its membership was higher than the membership of the main Polish Peasant Party and the PPS combined.[24] The extent to which ethno-nationalism was endorsed by the OZN can be illustrated in a number of different ways. One of the most striking examples of extreme ethno-nationalism gaining the upper hand in the OZN was the group's increasing ineptitude in handling the issue of national minorities' cultural rights.[25] Though Poles generally considered Ukrainians and Belorussians part of the same Slavic family as Poles, in the late 1930s the OZN began a policy of forced cultural assimilation of these two groups, a policy that before 1935 had been mainly advocated by the National Democrats.[26] The Polish government forced closures of Orthodox churches and Belorussian schools in the heavily Belorussian northeastern territories, and the Polish Army destroyed Orthodox churches in heavily Ukrainian Wołyń, in southeastern Poland.[27] Jews were the only large minority in Poland without any irredentist territorial aspirations, but the OZN nevertheless endorsed the ethno-nationalist project of reducing Polish Jewry through emigration.

Another illustration of the extent to which the OZN endorsed ethno-nationalist views is the fact that some OZN members, such as its first leader, Colonel Koc, had close personal links with members of radical offshoot organizations of National Democracy, such as ONR-Falanga. For example, in June 1937 Colonel Koc became head of the youth movement called the Union of Young Poland (Związek Młodej Polski), which originated in ONR-Falanga circles.[28] In 1938 Colonel Koc was appointed a senator on behalf of the OZN. The leadership of the OZN was transferred to Gen. Stanisław Skwarczyński (1888–1981).[29] As a rule membership in the OZN was limited to ethnic Poles of Christian faith.

The ozn excluded Jews, even those considered Polish patriots who had given great service to their country. Such exclusion was a manifestation of ethnonationalist practice on the organizational level.

Many historians have also underestimated the impact of the National Democracy movement on society at large on the grounds that this political movement did not "produce any great minds." This view originated in liberal intelligentsia circles in the pre-1939 period.[30] It is true that National Democracy failed to extend its influence over the high culture of interwar Poland; members of the liberal intelligentsia were the main creators and disseminators of this culture. One of the intelligentsia's main forums was the literary and cultural journal *Wiadomości Literackie* (Literary News) (1924–39), edited by the Jewish convert Mieczysław Grydzewski (1894–1970). *Wiadomości Literackie* strongly opposed the vision of Poland and Polish culture advocated by the National Democrats. The Endeks labeled it a Jewish journal.

However, this is not to say that National Democracy did not have influence on various sections of society. In fact, it penetrated almost all different sections of the emerging ethnic Polish middle class—the class on which the modern Polish nation was built. This fact was even noticeable to foreign observers. In 1939 Joel Cang, the British adviser to Neville Laski, wrote "that it is safe to say that almost the whole of the newly created middle class in Poland is in principle anti-Jewish and Endek in outlook."[31] Although the National Democracy movement did not manage to conquer Polish villages because of the existence of a strong peasant movement, it enjoyed a large following among prosperous farmers, academic youth, and individuals like Maurycy Zamoyski (1871–1937), the largest landowner in interwar Poland.

One of the most popular explanations of anti-Semitism in interwar Poland was that it had objective causes, namely the size and peculiar economic structure of the Jewish community. This explanation was common in political and intellectual discourse of the interwar period and was repeated in later periods.[32] It is commonly encountered in post-1945 Polish historiography of the interwar period.[33] A recent example is Olaf Bergman's *Narodowa Demokracja wobec problematyki żydowskiej w latach 1918–1929* (The Treatment of the Jewish Problem by National Democrats 1918–1929), in which the author pairs critical analysis of National Democracy with an uncritical reading that espouses National Democratic views. Such a fusion of ideas produces contradictory and inevitably unsatisfactory historical interpretation.[34] Ezra Mendelsohn challenges

such an approach in his article "Interwar Poland: Good or Bad for the Jews?":
"No one can deny that the large number of Polish Jews and their peculiar
economic structure and role in the Polish economy had influenced attitudes
toward them, just as no one can deny that Polish backwardness must be taken
into account in any effort to understand the Polish state's Jewish policy. But
it is surely misleading to assume that the condition of Polish Jewry and the
backwardness of the Polish state rendered inevitable the state's policies and
society's attitudes toward the Jewish minority." [35] Mendelsohn points to the
peculiar qualities of anti-Semitic attitudes in interwar Poland. He claims that
pre-1939 anti-Semitism "was not at all the same as anti-Ukrainian or anti-
German feelings" and that "it had much deeper and more emotional roots." [36]

There is no doubt that a large minority group can be seen as a burden by
a young state like interwar Poland, emerging from a long period of stateless
existence and troubled by deep economic and social problems. There is also no
doubt that the size, qualities, and actions of a minority group can contribute to
the rise of negative images among segments of the majority group. However,
in the case of the ethno-nationalists in interwar Poland it was not the size
of the Jewish population or its cultural qualities or actions that caused anti-
Semitism; rather, anti-Semitism stemmed from ethno-nationalists' view of the
size, qualities, and actions of Jews. Their premise was the concept of the Jew as
the chief harmful alien in the political, cultural/religious, social, and economic
sense. This premise, already in use in the late preindependence period, made
them view Jews differently from other minorities.

As a result Polish Jewry, unlike any other minority, was at the center of
ethno-nationalist attention and was placed in the limelight of any debate
concerning the state and its people. During the interwar period, as in the
pre-1918 period, National Democrats declared that Jews were in a state of
war with the true owners of the Polish state, ethnic Poles. The aim of such
rhetoric was to create an atmosphere of social panic and anti-Jewish hostility,
particularly among the poor and uneducated masses and youths. Judging by
their involvement in outbreaks of anti-Jewish violence in the interwar period,
these were the social groups most susceptible to the intense and emotionally
charged National Democratic propaganda.

Throughout the 1920s National Democrats also accused Polish Jews of damaging the interests and image of the Polish state and nation in the international
arena. They voiced these accusations despite the fact that, as Gershon Bacon
has shown, Polish Jews refrained from petitioning the League of Nations with

their grievances.[37] In comparison with the number of petitions made by ethnic German and Ukrainian citizens of Poland in the 1920s, Jews exercised the right to petition on a miniscule scale. Even though some Jewish communities in the borderline regions had not considered themselves potential Polish citizens in the period before and immediately after 1918, various Jewish political organizations based in Poland, from the Bundists to the Zionists, pledged loyalty to the Polish state in the aftermath of Poland's regaining independence.[38] In the case of Agudas Yisrael, which was the main Orthodox political party, the pledge of loyalty was based on the Talmudic principle "Dina de Malkhuta Dina" (The Law of the State Is Law), which was also exercised in the pre-1795 period.[39] Despite these explicit declarations of loyalty from Jewish organizations, National Democrats targeted Jews as "the main villains" acting against the interests of Poland and dishonoring its good name. The plausible explanation for such accusations is that they were based on the representation of Jews as the most harmful resident aliens.

Nevertheless, among Polish political and cultural elites influential sectors opposed and condemned both anti-Jewish violence and the perception of Jews as the enemy of Poland and ethnic Poles. Among such groups were the PPS and the Democratic Party (Stronnictwo Demokratyczne, SD), the small breakaway left wing of Sanacja, established in the late 1930s as a reaction to the rapprochement of post-1935 Sanacja with National Democracy.[40] There were also political and social organizations whose members largely adhered to the PPS and Democratic Party ethos, such as the Association of Polish Teachers (Związek Nauczycielstwa Polskiego) and the Democratic Clubs (Kluby Demokratyczne). The left wing of the Polish Peasant Party–Liberation (Polskie Stronnictwo Ludowe–Wyzwolenie) also opposed anti-Jewish violence and other anti-Semitic actions.[41] Well-known individuals who opposed anti-Jewish perceptions and violence included intellectuals who held progressive, liberal views such as Tadeusz Kotarbiński (1886–1981), a philosopher at the University of Warsaw; Mieczysław Michałowicz (1876–1965), director of the Children's Clinic at the University of Warsaw; and Ryszard Ganszyniec, a professor at the University of Jan Kazimierz in L'viv (Lwów).[42] Kotarbiński and Michałowicz were among contributors to a 116-page book entitled *Polacy o Żydach* (Poles about Jews), published in 1937, an important collection of mainly liberal, socialist, and Communist voices condemning anti-Semitism.[43] Interestingly the only voice in this book representing religious authority belonged to Grzegorz (Hryhorij) Chomyszyn (1867–1947), bishop of the Uniate

Church in Poland, who was later killed by the Soviets. [44] In the National Democratic press political parties, social organizations, and individuals who opposed anti-Semitism were as a rule labeled as traitors of the Polish nation and servants of the Jews. Such individuals were commonly referred to as "shabbes goys" (szabejsgoje), "Jewish servants" (żydowskie pachołki), and "Jewish uncles" (żydowscy wujkowie). [45]

The Image and Minority Rights

The image of the Jew as the harmful alien who does not belong in the Polish nation was manifested in political attitudes toward the concepts of equal rights and the cultural autonomy of Jews. Many politicians viewed Jewish equality as a privilege granted Jews, and many thought of Jewish cultural autonomy as a threat if not an insult to Poles. A year after the March Constitution of 1921 became the binding law of the state, Apolinary Hartglas, the Zionist journalist, reflected upon this phenomenon. In his political pamphlet *Żółta łata* (The Yellow Patch) Hartglas noted similarities between contemporary perceptions of equal rights for Jews and perceptions of such rights present in the discourse of the Four-Year Parliament (1788–92). He also noted a clear discrepancy between official endorsement of the concept of equal rights and its practice: "A few advocates of Jewish equal rights state that all legal restrictions should be abolished in order to speed up the integration of Jews into Polish society. A much larger group claims that even equality granted on paper should be made conditional on the level of cultural assimilation of Jews into the Polish [ethnic] nation. At the same time it is clear to them that three million Polish Jews cannot and do not wish to be assimilated in such a way. Overall there is a lack of support for true equal rights for Jews." [46]

In February 1939 Moshe Sneh (Kleinbaum) (1909–72), the last chief leader of the Zionist movement in Poland in the late 1930s, made similar observations about the attitudes of Polish politicians regarding equal rights for Jews: "From a formal point of view the Jews were citizens enjoying equal rights; in reality they are treated as a 'foreign and harmful element.' It is in the nature of life to destroy all things that are untrue, founded on fiction and on an internal lie. There will therefore have to come a radical change in the attitude of the Polish government to the Jews: for good or for ill, as true citizens or as 'pernicious aliens.' One way or the other." [47]

Prominent Polish politicians considered the concept of equal rights a Jewish attempt to gain special privileges. This suggests that Hartglas was correct in observing the persistence of the old way of thinking about Jews. In their parliamentary speeches politicians either explicitly referred to equal rights for Jews in such a way or alluded to it. [48] A case in point were the speeches of Wincenty Witos (1874–1945), the unquestionable leader of the moderate wing of the peasant movement and three-time prime minister in the interwar period. On 17 October 1923, as the newly appointed prime minister, he indicated that Jews had a privileged status within Polish society: "Here with full responsibility, I must say that Polish society in general is, in many areas, still a long way from possessing what the Jews in Poland possess. Constitutional rights apply to everyone equally, and if the honorable deputy [the Zionist MP, Dr. Leon Reich] were to review all the areas of life and objectively draw the necessary conclusions, he would arrive at the conviction that Poland ranks first in Europe in tolerance; it is a country where Jews, above all others, fare best." [49]

Another prominent political figure, General Władysław Sikorski (1881–1943), short-term prime minister from 1922 through the first half of 1923 and prime-minister-to-be during World War II, expressed a similar position. In his parliamentary speech of 19 January 1923 Sikorski indicated that the government viewed Jewish demands for equal rights as a struggle for privileges and that, in fact, equal rights for Jews might even be suspended in the future: "The Jewish minority undoubtedly believes that the rights which Poland has voluntarily granted it will be safeguarded by the government. But a note of warning is necessary, because too often the defense of its justified interests has been turned by the Jewish side into a struggle for privilege." [50]

References to equal rights as a Jewish attempt to gain privileges was featured in the political programs of various right-wing and center-right political parties, such as the center-right NPR, established in May 1920. [51] Karol Popiel led the NPR, which was popular among sections of the lower middle class and the working class. In 1937 the NPR merged with the Christian Democratic Party to form the Labor Party (Stronnictwo Pracy, SP). The latter was one of the most influential political parties in WWII. The party platform read: "The NPR does not recognize Jews as a separate national minority and denies their jargon [Yiddish] the right to be considered an official language. . . . In its recognition of the equal rights and duties of all citizens of the Polish State, the NPR opposes all sorts of attempts to gain privileges by the Jewish community at the expense of the Christian population, namely, attempts at receiving rights and attempts at abstaining from fulfilling their duties toward the State." [52]

The political program of the Polish Catholic and People's Union (Polskie

Stronnictwo Katolicko-Ludowe, pskl), a small Christian Democratic party, expressed a similar approach to equal rights for Jews:

> Regarding the Jewish masses of several millions, pskl upholds the ground of traditional Polish religious toleration, which is guaranteed by the Constitution on the grounds of social and civic justice. However, the party is not going to tolerate the privileged position of Jews in any aspect of life. . . . Our point of view is that there are definitely too many Jews in Poland and that their influence on our life is generally negative and harmful, and that the saturation of Polish cities with Jews also causes poverty among Jews themselves. pskl wholeheartedly supports the emigration of Jews from Poland to other countries and will defend the Polish state from the new Jewish invasion from the East, although we grant Jews equal rights with other citizens and condemn anti-Jewish excesses on the part of irresponsible elements. However, we will not allow the Jews to create a state within a state and will concentrate all our efforts against Jewish parties acting against the Polish state and its sovereignty. [53]

These examples show that there was a positive correlation between the representation of the Jew as the harmful alien and a negative approach to the concept of equal rights for Jews. Such an approach was voiced by ethnonationalists of various parties, not only by National Democrats.

The representation of the Jew as the harmful alien was found in various forms in the right-wing segments of the peasant movement and the Christian Democrats, significant segments of the conservative and monarchist movements, and many other smaller right-wing and center-right political parties. It was also found in a small anticlerical political group, advocating Panslavism and integral nationalism, named after its paper, *Zadruga*. [54]

Władysław Studnicki (1867–1953) of the conservative movement is a good example of an influential, albeit controversial politician who used the representation of the Jew as the harmful alien in a form similar to the fully elaborated version voiced by National Democracy. For example, in his work *Sprawa polsko-żydowska* (The Polish-Jewish Issue) Studnicki categorized Jews as "parasites on the healthy branch of the Polish tree" and blamed them for the disintegration of premodern Poland. [55] A good example of the relatively early spread of the ethno-nationalist perspective on Jews among politicians of the right-wing Sanacja is the case of mp Bogusław Miedziński (1891–1972). In February 1934 Miedziński, who served during WWI in Piłsudski's Legions, made a controversial speech during a session of the parliamentary Budget

Commission. In his speech Miedziński stated that he was personally affronted that three million Jews lived in Poland and that Polish cities were occupied by huge Jewish masses; everyone, he said, would prefer all of them to be gone.[56] His remarks, which caused a high degree of embarrassment to the Sanacja government, still at the time supportive of the inclusion of Jews in the Polish state, received unprecedented applause from the National Democratic MPs.

The PPS was the only major political party to reject the representation of the Jew as the harmful alien throughout the interwar period. However, in the late 1930s within the PPS there were some members susceptible to the ethno-national perspective, such as Jan M. Borski, an assimilated Jew. In his pamphlet *Sprawa żydowska a socjalizm: Polemika z Bundem* (The Jewish Issue and Socialism: Polemics with the Bund), published in 1937 by the official PPS publishing house, Robotnik (The Worker), Borski categorized Jews as spiritually and emotionally alien to Poles and called for the emigration of Jews from Poland. Borski's pamphlet was primarily a reaction to his party's recognition of the principle of minority rights for Jews, and influential PPS politicians criticized it strongly. Borski's was not a representative PPS view but an example of the impact of the ethno-nationalist vision of Poland on individuals, including assimilated Polish Jews.[57]

In the post-1935 period the impact of such negative representations of Jews on the policies and practices of the state intensified. The Sanacja government actively embarked on curtailing the equal rights of Jews. The first anti-Jewish and also anti-Muslim Tatar legislation, introduced in 1936, restricted ritual slaughter (*shekhita*).[58] This legislation, which greatly affected the urban Jewish population, was the only legislation openly and explicitly introduced as anti-Jewish. In other cases the main strategy of the government was to introduce bills that formally looked as though they would affect all citizens and thus could not be categorized as discriminating against the Jewish minority.[59] This was the case with the Law of 31 March 1938, concerning taking away Polish citizenship from Polish citizens living abroad, introduced by Wiktor Tomir Drymmer, director of the Consular Section of the Ministry of Foreign Affairs (MSW) and a former member of Piłsudski's Legions. As Jerzy Tomaszewski has argued, although the official explanation for the introduction of this legislation did not mention Jews at all, it was primarily directed at them.[60] Its aim was to prevent Jews from returning to Poland and thus to strip them of Polish citizenship. The use of this strategy confirms the thesis of Rogers Brubaker about the diffuse nature of some ethno-nationalist practices in the postindependence period.[61]

In 1934 the Sanacja government signed a ten-year nonaggression pact with Nazi Germany. The Nazi introduction of anti-Jewish legislation between 1933 and 1935 made a significant impression on the National Democracy party and on some members of the right-wing section of Sanacja, but the post-1935 government did not implement discriminatory legislation against Jews similar to Nazi anti-Jewish legislation. [62] However, some MPs from the OZN drafted such anti-Jewish legislation, and parliament discussed it. In May 1938 the Supreme OZN Council adopted a thirteen-paragraph resolution on the "Jewish question" in which representation of the Jew as the chief harmful other served as a rationale for the proposal of mass emigration of Jews from Poland. This proposal, as indicated earlier, was supported by a significant number of political parties and endorsed by the government. [63]

The Image within the Roman Catholic Church

Recent research on anti-Semitism in interwar Poland reveals the extent to which the Roman Catholic Church absorbed and disseminated the representation of the Jew as the harmful alien. This anti-Jewish position was manifested in a variety of forms in almost the entire Roman Catholic press and among both the lower and upper ranks of Catholic clergy. [64] Michał Jagiełło and Dariusz Libionka argue that even monthlies such as *Prąd* (Trend) and *Odrodzenie* (Rebirth), two main journals of the Catholic academic youth movement Odrodzenie, published in Lublin, were not entirely free from "mild" and even "strong" representations of Jews as harmful aliens. [65] Although the Odrodzenie movement strongly opposed the anti-Jewish violence that National Democracy and its offshoot radical organizations orchestrated, it treated Jews in a totally different way from other ethno-cultural groups living in Poland. Odrodzenie viewed Ukrainians and Belorussians as communities at a lower level of civilization that Polish nation should culturally assimilate. In contrast, Odrodzenie viewed Jews as a destructive social, economic, and cultural power within the Polish nation and as an enemy of Christianity and the Christian ethos. Therefore there was no place for them in the Polish nation-state. The Odrodzenie movement advocated this position regarding Jews and Slavic minorities, basically similar to Dmowski's approach toward nonethnic Poles, in their ideological Declaration of 1923:

> We must and we are entitled, thanks to our cultural superiority, to influ-
> ence our nonethnic Polish citizens [współobywateli nie-Polaków]. We must
> integrate them into the Polish nation by means of assimilating them into

the cultural ethos of our civilization. However, we have to take a totally different approach toward the "Jewish power." Because of their ethics and their imperialistic goals the Jews have forced us to take a different approach toward them. Our duty is to fight against the Jewish goal of destroying the material, spiritual, and national achievement of Poland. Our duty is to organize positive action toward the enrichment of our Christian heritage, to nationalize [unarodowienie] our industry and commerce, and to spread among Poles the awareness of their separate identity and their unity and of exclusive rights to the Second Polish Republic.[66]

A former leading member of Odrodzenie, Stefan Świeżawski, recently acknowledged past prejudice in the movement. In his interview entitled "Plantacja Ducha Świetego," published in *Apokryf*, the cultural supplement of *Tygodnik Powszechny*, Świeżawski stated that "Odrodzenie as an organization opposed all racist and anti-Semitic tendencies, but among my closest friends from the movement there were some whose views about the Jews were no different from the views of the members of the All-Polish Youth [Młodzież Wszechpolska]."[67] This exemplifies the scope of Judeocentric and anti-Jewish traditions in Catholicism in interwar Poland. The Catholic monthly journals *Prąd* and *Odrodzenie* are the predecessors of the contemporary *Tygodnik Powszechny* (Common Weekly), a journal of the progressive Catholic intelligentsia in post-1945 Poland, which since the late 1980s has played a crucial role in the critical analysis of anti-Semitism and the "dark past" of Polish-Jewish relations. Whatever other former Odrodzenie members now concentrated around *Tygodnik Powszechny* may have thought in the past, this journal has shown itself capable of critical analysis and intellectual and moral condemnation of the anti-Jewish aspect of the organization's heritage.

The Roman Catholic Church had a major impact on shaping the attitudes of the Roman Catholic population, particularly its largest segment, the peasantry.[68] As in the late preindependence period the peasantry constituted approximately three-quarters of the entire population in post-1918 Poland.[69] The Church was a powerful institution with its own press. In fact, Catholic publications constituted 23 percent of all Polish periodicals published in the interwar period.[70] Next to Sunday sermons and daily services the press was the main medium of communication between the Church and its literate folk.

The Catholic press was characterized by dynamic and competitive development and a fair-sized readership. The daily Franciscan *Mały Dziennik* (Small Daily, 1935–39) is perhaps one of the best illustrations of such dynamism. Its first issue appeared in the summer of 1935 with 8,000 copies. By the end of the same year the paper was printing an unprecedented 140,650 copies.[71] *Mały Dziennik* was designed as an affordable popular paper for the Catholic masses and as such enjoyed remarkable success. This was one of the most radical anti-Jewish Catholic papers, and its chief editor, Father Marian Wójcik, was known for having close ties with National Democracy and its offshoot radical organizations. *Mały Dziennik*, directed at an unsophisticated reader, regularly published simple stories of the individual lives of Catholic Poles. As a rule in such stories the Jew was always made responsible for the hardship and misery of their lives. The Jew was the perpetrator, and the Pole the long-suffering victim. The titles of the stories themselves express such an image of the Jew: "How the Jew Was Stealing Money from the Treasury and at the Same Time Was Poisoning the Goys" (26 June 1936); "Terrible Conditions in the Jewish Factory" (28 June 1935); and "Jewish Educators Poison Our Children with the Venom of Hatred and Atheism" (25 June 1935).[72]

Next to such stories *Mały Dziennik* ran rhymes and poems in a form resembling prayers, also representing the Jew as harmful alien. This type of writing also can be found in Catholic papers that were not as radically anti-Jewish as *Mały Dziennik*. For example, the monthly Jesuit *Przegląd Powszechny*, which was directed at educated and sophisticated readers, published the following poem, entitled "A myśmy . . . ślepi!" (Yet We Are Blind!), in December 1922:

> Jewry is contaminating Poland thoroughly:
> It scandalizes the young, destroys the unity of the common people.
> By means of the atheistic press it poisons the spirit,
> Incites to evil, provokes, divides.
> . . . .
> A terrible gangrene has infiltrated our body
> Yet we . . . are blind[.]
> The Jews have gained control of Polish business,
> As though we are imbeciles,
> And they cheat, extort, and steal. . . .[73]

The image of the Jew as the enemy of the Polish nation and Christianity was one of the main features of the Catholic press in the interwar period, disseminated either in a milder or a stronger version, depending on the ideological profile of the periodical. This indicates the extent to which the Roman Catholic population was exposed through the religious medium to the exclusivist ethnonationalist perspective. We can infer from this that significant segments of the population absorbed the representation of the Jew as the harmful alien to varying degrees. One of the more recent studies of local Jewish history in northern Poland shows that even in Pomorze (Pomerania), where Jews constituted less than 0.7 percent of the population in the interwar period, local society was "bombarded" with publications disseminating the belief in the Jew as the harmful alien.[74]

Despite some major earlier ideological and ethical disagreements the Roman Catholic Church and the National Democracy party became mutually supportive of each other in the post-1918 period. This was the result of an emerging agreement between the two on the issue of the moral leadership of the Polish nation. In its political program of October 1919 National Democracy recognized the Roman Catholic Church as the moral authority and chief educator of the Polish nation. In 1927 Dmowski published a brochure, *Kościół, Naród i Państwo* (Church, Nation, and State), in which he proclaimed his party's adherence and loyalty to the Catholic ethos. He also emphasized the importance of the role of the Church in the state, expressed in the concept of the "Katolickie państwo narodu polskiego" (Catholic state of the Polish nation). The brochure was well received in Church circles.

In exchange for recognizing the Church's moral leadership National Democracy enjoyed significant support among the Catholic clergy. The clergy's lower and higher ranks, including bishops and archbishops, were active members of National Democracy, along with its offshoot radical organizations.[75] For example, in the pre-1926 period bishops represented National Democracy in both the lower and the upper house of the parliament. Clergymen also ran the party's Department of Catholic Propaganda.[76] In the Łomża region, where during WWII a wave of extreme anti-Jewish violence occurred in the summer of 1941, Stanisław Łukomski, bishop of the Łomża diocese, and the majority of local priests were supporters of the National Democracy movement.[77] The Catholic press expressed support for Dmowski's party in statements such as the following: "healthy nationalism . . . is a natural supporter of Catholicism. Catholics have a duty to nurture nationalism."[78]

The relationship between the Roman Catholic Church and National Democracy in interwar Poland is an example of the strong fusion of integral ethno-nationalism and religion. This fusion resulted in two intertwined phenomena, which continued to persist in the post-1939 period: strong Catholic ethno-nationalism and strong ethno-nationalist Catholicism. This situation had a particularly negative impact on Jews, viewed as the harmful alien to both the Polish nation and Christianity.

National Democracy used religion to justify its programs and policies toward Jews. National Democrats referred to Catholicism as a strategy of dissociating their party's position from that of the Nazis. A good illustration of this strategy is present in the article "Katolicyzm, rasizm i sprawa żydowska" (Catholicism, Racism, and the Jewish Question), published in the chief theoretical paper of National Democracy, *Myśl Narodowa* (National Thought), on 15 December 1935: "Our ideology is older than Hitler's ideology. . . . In our treatment of Jews we never found ourselves in conflict with the Church. . . . We are not racists. . . . Our main goal is to serve the nation. There is no conflict between our nationalism and Catholicism. We define the Jews as the enemy of our nation and as a foreign element, which has caused the degeneration of European culture and civilization. . . . The battle of the Polish nation with the Jews does not stand in conflict with the Roman Catholic Church but in fact serves its interest."[79]

This type of reasoning, which clearly involved a high level of rationalization of the myth of the Jew as the enemy of the Polish nation, allowed National Democracy and its offshoot radical organizations that were fascist in nature to dismiss completely any similarities between their views on Polish Jews and radical right-wing German representations of Jews as the chief threatening other to the German nation.[80] The National Democrats insisted that their perspective was not based on racist grounds like the Nazi one, but was rooted in concerns over the fate of the Polish nation, a notion that emerged in the preindependence period in Jeske-Choiński's and Dmowski's writings. Thus they once again convinced themselves that the anti-Semitism they advocated represented an exceptional case—totally different from other anti-Semitic ideologies of the time.

At the same time, in some radical ethno-nationalist publications like the Catholic *Mały Dziennik* there are examples of approval of Nazi anti-Jewish policies and actions and portrayals of Jews as perpetrators vis-à-vis Germans. An article published in *Mały Dziennik* on 11–12 November 1938 states the following: "The news about the death of vom Rath brought fire into three synagogues in Berlin. The mad Jews have not satisfied themselves with the blood of a third-grade clerk." In this article the assassination of the German diplomat Ernst vom Rath by a young Polish Jew, Hershel Grynszpan, on 7 November 1938 in Paris is treated as Jewish savagery ("żydowskie rozbestwienie"). This article also minimalizes the criminal nature of the anti-Jewish violence known as Kristallnacht that erupted in Germany in the aftermath of this assassination by juxtaposing it with the alleged collective crimes of Jews in Bolshevik Russia: "Of course Jewry would prefer to spread throughout the world the system that it has already introduced in Bolshevik Russia and instead of shooting third-grade clerks would prefer shooting great men without punishment."[81]

Even those Polish ethno-nationalists who opposed the use of anti-Jewish violence as a means of "solving the Jewish question" in interwar Poland failed to question anti-Jewish stereotypes. While they could recognize that anti-Jewish violence was socially undesirable and morally wrong, they entirely rejected the possibility of their own views being prejudiced and false. This shows the power of ethno-nationalist ways of thinking. Perhaps one of the most striking illustrations of this is the official declaration of ozn's program, written by Colonel Koc: "With regard to the Jewish population our position is this: we value too highly the standard and content of our cultural life and the public peace, law, and order that no state can dispense with to approve acts of license or brutal anti-Jewish reactions that hurt the prestige and dignity of a great nation. On the other hand, the instinct for cultural self-defense is understandable, and the tendency of Polish society to economic independence is natural."[82]

The ozn's declaration was published in the majority of daily papers in late February 1937. Characteristically it addressed the Jewish community separately, under the subtitle "Sprawa żydowska—samoobrona kulturalna i gospodarcza" (The Jewish Question—Cultural and Economic Self-Defense). Jews were omitted from the section dedicated to "Minorities" and from the section dedicated to the "Polish Middle Class." The absence of Jews from both these sections points to the level of their exclusion from the fabric of Polish society in the ozn's vision of Poland. Their exclusion from the middle class is particularly striking because the Jewish population in interwar Poland was mainly urban. Three-quarters of all Polish Jews lived in towns in 1931, making up one-quarter of the population in towns with over twenty thousand inhabitants and nearly 30 percent in towns with fewer than twenty thousand.[83] Most Jews belonged to the lower middle class, with an estimated two million belonging to the petty bourgeoisie. Approximately one hundred thousand Jews were wealthy bourgeoisie, seven hundred thousand were working class, and three hundred thousand were professionals and members of the intelligentsia.[84]

Development of the Image

As in the late preindependence era, during the interwar period the representation of the Jew as the harmful alien proved to be versatile and multifaceted. Its main theme, of the destructive nature of the Jews, already fully developed by 1918, intensified in free independent Poland. The National Democrats and other ethno-nationalists skillfully adapted this representation of the Jew to contemporary political, social, and economic conditions. Every event and development in the interwar period was incorporated into the narrative of the destructiveness of the Jews. For example, Jews were even made responsible for the surplus emigration of the largest Polish social group, the peasants, who were leaving Poland in search of a better life. Ethno-nationalist papers of various kinds frequently stressed that "eight million Poles are forced to live outside their homeland, while four million Jews occupy Poland," and that "Polish peasants, instead of emigrating to foreign countries in search of bread and work, should find such bread and work in towns and cities in their homeland. We demand that this happen in the name of simple justice."[85]

Between 1918 and 1939 the constantly repeated main themes were similar to those of the late preindependence period: the Jews were the greatest enemy of the Polish religion, Catholicism, and of its moral-cultural code; the Jews were behind freemasonry and wanted to rule over the Polish state; the Jews were the exponents of international finance harmful to the Polish economy; the Jews were moral degenerates who had a demoralizing effect on the Polish culture and people; the Jews were the inventors and propagators of free thinking, liberalism, socialism, Communism, and Bolshevism—ideologies alien and harmful to the Polish national cause; and the Jews conspired with other enemies of Poland against her.[86]

The fact that some of these themes contradicted each other was of no significance to their disseminators. In some cases various themes were used separately in order to cope with a specific challenge, such as opposing Communism, socialism, and free thinking. Yet on the whole many themes were simultaneously emphasized. For example, the image of the Jew as a Communist was frequently accompanied by the image of the Jew as a cultural and moral degenerate whose mind was occupied with pornography, moral dirt, and filth. A good illustration of such a combination is the well-known letter of May 1936 by Cardinal August Hlond (1881–1948), the long-serving primate of Poland between 1926 and 1948: "It is a fact that Jews oppose the Catholic Church, are steeped in free thinking, and represent the avant-garde of the atheist movement, the Bolshevik movement, and subversive action. The Jews have a disastrous effect on morality, and their publishing houses dispense pornography. It is true that the Jews commit fraud and usury and deal in white slavery. It is true that in schools the influence of the Jewish youth upon the Catholic youth is generally evil."[87]

Judeo-Bolshevism (żydo-bolszewizm) and Judeo-Communism (żydoko-muna) were the most frequently propagated themes of the Jew as the threatening other in the interwar period. Ethno-nationalists continued to disseminate these themes in a way that seems to show they were divorced from reality.[88] The triumph of the Bolshevik Revolution in November 1917 and the subsequent establishment of the first Communist state—Soviet Russia—raised widespread fear of Communism, which was not limited to Poland but also prominent in other European states such as the Weimar Republic, where Communist revolts erupted between 1919 and 1923 in various localities.[89] The fear of Communism was widely accompanied by its identification with Jews. This identification was partly caused by the sudden appearance of Jews in positions of power where they had never been seen before and was reinforced by the *Protocols of the Elders of Zion*, a Russian forgery that accused Jews of seeking, through devious means, total reign over Christian society.[90] The Polish ethno-nationalist press frequently described the Soviet political system as a Judeo-Bolshevik political threat endangering the existence of Poland and other European nations. Even before the beginning of the Polish-Soviet War of 1920, in which the Soviets constituted a real immediate threat to the Polish state, the Soviet Army entering the central Polish territories in the summer of 1920, ethno-nationalists had already begun to describe Bolshevism in the press as a Jewish conspiracy aimed at oppressing the Russian people and conquering the entire world.[91]

In his small booklet *O Żydach wiadomości pożyteczne* (Useful News about the Jews) Stanisław Rybarkiewicz claimed that Jews had masterminded the Bolshevik Revolution and oppressed the Russian people. This genre of writing often cast the Russians as victims of the Communist revolution.[92]

As a tool for evaluating political threats and providing "knowledge" about Jews, Judeo-Communism persisted in right-wing nationalistic and Catholic discourse long after the real danger of Communism was gone in interwar Poland.[93] By the second half of the 1920s the Communist political movement had ceased to represent any real political power in Poland. Though there had been danger of a Communist rebellion in the northeastern and southeastern parts of Poland between 1918 and 1920, by the second half of the 1920s Communists had lost all their popular following.[94]

In the 1920s and 1930s ethno-nationalist writers interwove contemporary events with the theme of Judeo-Communism. This was the case with the Polish-Soviet War of 1920. Although this war ended in a Polish victory, the "Miracle on the Vistula," this historical event was used to reinforce the credibility of Judeo-Bolshevism. Ethno-nationalist writers insisted that the Polish-Soviet War of 1920 exposed the Jews as harmful aliens within the Polish state. The writing of Reverend Stanisław Trzeciak, perhaps the most prolific radical, aggressive propagator of the representation of the Jew as the harmful alien, is a good example of such a position. In his article "W obliczu grozy" (Facing Danger), published in March 1937 in the radical right-wing Catholic paper *Pro Christo*, Trzeciak stated: "The Jews betrayed the Polish Army. They did not participate in the defense of Lwów. They constituted 99 percent of those who acted against the Polish state during the Soviet-Polish War of 1920. Ninety-eight or 100 percent of Jews are Communist revolutionaries."[95]

Second- and third-class writers, members of the academic community and journalists, stressed the notion of the Jewish origin and nature of Communism. In his small brochure *U źródeł antysemityzmu* (The Sources of Anti-Semitism) Waldemar Olszewski claimed that Jews were the driving force behind Communism. He also insisted that anti-Semitism was the outcome of "odious Jewish behavior and Jewish characteristics," not of anti-Jewish prejudice.[96] In his book *Chłop a państwo narodowe* (A Peasant and the National State) Karol Stojanowski, a professor at the University of Poznań and a member of National Democracy, insisted that only his party was capable of victory over Judeo-Communism and that the Russian people were the victims of Judeo-Communism.[97]

In the 1930s, in right-wing nationalistic and Catholic circles, the intensification of the theme of Judeo-Communism developed in parallel to the intensification of general anti-Communist discourse. In this discourse Communism was defined as an ideology and movement that was totally alien to the spiritual European Christian ethos, Polish nationalism, and Polish statehood. For example, in 1936 the Komitet Prasy Młodych (Youth Press Committee) was set up in order to fight Communism and promote Polish nationalism, which was understood as being in opposition to Communism.[98] The committee consisted of a group of journalists representing fifteen various newspapers, ranging from the radical right wing, to the center-right wing, to the conservative and Catholic press. Colonel Koc wrote the ozn's Ideological Declaration of February 1937, in which he perpetuated this idea of the opposition between Communism and Polish nationalism, declaring: "We reject Communism and revolutionary methods. . . . Communism in ideas, methods, and aims is totally alien to the Polish spirit [duch polski]. A Communist Poland would cease to be Poland."[99]

The Communists in interwar Poland supported a nonnational agenda and saw in the newly reemerged bourgeois Poland an enemy of the working class and Marxist revolution. This helped the ethno-nationalists to define Communism as an ideology with an anti-Polish ethos and as a primarily anti-Polish movement. The fact that the Communist Party of Poland (Komunistyczna Partia Polski, KPP) was subordinate to the Comintern, based in Moscow, also contributed to the popular interwar evaluation of the KPP as a party that advocated a political ideology antithetical to the ethos of Polish workers.[100] The emergence of internal divisions about the national issue, which crystallized among the leaders of the KPP in the 1920s, was of no significance to the ethno-nationalists' definition of all Communists as an anti-Polish political group.[101]

The KPP was set up on 16 December 1918 under the original name the Workers' Party of Poland (Komunistyczna Partia Robotnicza Polski, KPRP). At the beginning it numbered between eight thousand and ten thousand members. Throughout its entire existence, until 1938, the KPP was an illegal political organization; its members were frequently arrested, and strict police surveillance was kept over KPP activities.[102] The KPP constituted the chief party among pro-Soviet parties in interwar Poland. In ethno-nationalist circles the KPP was labeled not only as an anti-Polish party because of its ideological declarations and critical position on the political system of the reemerged Polish state but also as a Judeo-Communist party composed of and supported by Jews.[103] This latter definition of the KPP, common among right-wing ethno-nationalist and Catholic circles, was expressed in the popular slogan "Not every Communist is a Jew, but every Jew is a Communist."[104] Was the notion of Judeo-Communism accurate in the case of the KPP and its supporters? Or was it a manifestation of a prejudicial position on the Jewish community that defined it as ideologically, politically, and spiritually alien to Polish nationalism and the Polish nation?

Various studies of the membership profile of the KPP show that it did indeed include a high number of nonethnic Poles, namely Jews, Belorussians, and Ukrainians. Most minority KPP members were attracted to the party by its consistent policy opposing discrimination. However, the KPP was not essentially a Jewish party supported by Polish Jews, nor a Ukrainian or Belorussian party, but a radical political organization whose membership was multiethnic and mostly composed of workers. On average Jews constituted between one-third and one-fourth of the whole Communist movement. They played an important role in the leadership of the KPP, given their high level of education.[105] The social background of Jewish Communists was different from that of other Communists: they usually came from the middle class, whereas other members of the party usually came from a working-class or peasant background. Polish historian Antoni Czubiński gives an estimate of 40 percent for Jewish membership of the KPP in the 1920s and stresses that Ukrainians and Belorussians also made up a high percentage of the party's membership at the time.[106] According to Jaff Schatz, the highest number of Jewish members in the entire Communist movement in the 1930s is estimated at approximately ten thousand individuals. Taking into account the fact that Polish Jews numbered approximately three million during the same period, we can clearly see that only a very small segment of the Jewish community was attracted to Communism. Even if one takes into account the significant Communist victory in the parliamentary elections of 1928, and the fact that two-fifths of all votes cast for the Communist movement at that time were Jewish, this would still indicate that only 5 percent of the entire Jewish community were supporters of Communism.[107] Schatz's conclusions are similar to those of a more recent study by Jeffrey S. Kopstein and Jason Wittenberg. Based on careful statistical analysis of the membership of the KPP, examining declared religious affiliation in the census of 1928, Kopstein and Wittenberg conclude that only 7 percent of Jewish voters supported Communism in the parliamentary election of the same year: "Our research has shown that the idea of the Jewish Communist is a myth at the mass level. Roughly 93 percent of Jewish voters supported non-Communist parties in 1928, and only around 7 percent of the Communists' electoral support came from Jews."[108] In the 1930s the KPP began to gain more supporters among the working class due to the severe political, social, and economic crisis, but support for the Party among Jews did not appear to change. According to Antoni Czubiński, during the crisis of the early 1930s 70 percent of KPP members were ethnic Poles, between 22 and 26 percent were Jews, and 3 percent were Ukrainians.[109] Thus the theme of Judeo-Communism, intertwined with the definition of Communism understood as an anti-Polish ideology, was a prejudicial belief belonging to the larger theme of the Jewish conspiracy. This theme came to play an important role in Polish-Jewish relations in World War II and during the postwar period.

The theme of the Jewish conspiracy against Poland was not limited only to one external enemy, namely the Soviet state, but also referred to an older external enemy, Germany. In the case of the Soviet Union ethno-nationalists like the Endeks portrayed Jews as both the creators and chief executors of the external threat. In the case of Germany ethno-nationalists portrayed Jews as overzealous executors of anti-Polish policies. National Democrat writers continued to describe Jews this way even in the aftermath of the establishment of the Nazi government in Germany in January 1933. Roman Dmowski even claimed that Hitler, like previous heads of the German (Prussian) state, might use Jews in order to destroy Poland and that therefore it would not be expedient for him to destroy the German Jews. In Dmowski's book *Przewrót* (Change), first published in 1934, he wrote:

> Concerning the German ambition to the East [ruling over Poland] it is important to remember that Prussian politicians, beginning with Frederick the Great, have always employed the Jews. The Jews have been their most precious tools. In the eighteenth century the Jews served as the main agents of the demoralization and corruption of the Prussian parliament and acted as brokers and spies for the Prussians. Later they constituted the pillar of Prussian power in occupied Polish territories. All of them publicly announced their identification with Germany. They were also keen to participate in the Germanization [of the Poles], in which they were even more insolent than the Germans themselves. . . .
>
> The Jews also constituted the forerunners of German culture in Polish territories partitioned by Austria and Russia. The entire Jewish population without exception served in the German Army when it entered the Congress Kingdom [the Russian partitioned zone] many years ago [during World War I].
>
> If Poland did not have so many Jews the partition of Poland would never have happened and Prussian Eastern policy would not have been so triumphant.
>
> [The Germans] are now advocating the same Prussian policy toward the East. Therefore they have to go hand in hand with the Jews—there is no other option. If the Germans go with the Jews against Poland they cannot therefore destroy the Jews in Germany.[110]

Dmowski also published the novel *Dziedzictwo* (Inheritance) under the pen name Kazimierz Wybranowski.[111] The novel, first published in parts in *Gazeta Warszawska*, is an example of the use of similarly aggressive and radical anti-Semitic idioms.

Political, Social, and Cultural Functions of the Image

Ethno-nationalists used the image of the Jew as the enemy of the Polish nation for different purposes. On the level of national discourse the image was intended to raise the collective cohesiveness of Poles and provide a simplistic explanation for the nation's past and present failures—in essence suggesting that Poland would be a great and prosperous nation if not for the presence of Jews, who as ungrateful guests had mistreated the host nation since their first settlement in Poland: "The Jews have a heart like a stone for a country that hosts them."[112]

This type of reasoning intensified at times of social, political, and economic crisis. The interwar period in Poland was rife with such crises. For example, the first formative years of the Second Polish Republic of 1918–20 were a period of finalizing international agreements over state borders, culminating in the Polish-Soviet War of 1920. Between 1929 and the early 1930s Poland underwent a period of major financial and economic crisis during the Great Depression. The depression gravely affected the Polish economy, which even before 1929 had a low production index of 116.4.[113] Between 1936 and 1939 Polish society experienced a period of intense social and economic tensions.

Polish ethno-nationalists explained every social problem the state experienced in the interwar period with the representation of Jews as the most powerful threat to the Polish nation. This scapegoating promised illusionary simple and quick solutions. For example, the National Democratic solution to the problem of the modernization of villages and towns throughout the 1930s, which the Sanacja government absorbed and advocated in the post-1935 period, was Jewish emigration. Exclusivist ethno-nationalist thinking constituted the base of projects for solving labor-market and housing problems. According to such logic the Jews were villains who took from ethnic Poles everything that by right should belong to them. The ethno-nationalists saw the peasants as the "soil of the country," an integral part of the Polish people with a right to employment. They saw Polish Jews simply as an alien element whose presence constituted an obstacle to the development of Poles. Therefore the Jews had no right to keep their occupations and properties.

This type of thinking had a significant impact on Polish society in the interwar period and beyond. These arguments effectively blocked any rational inquiry into the real reasons behind the slow modernization of the newly reestablished state and high unemployment among peasants and part of the working class. Interwar Poland was predominantly agricultural, with a surplus rural population estimated at as high as 4.5 million in the 1930s. Poland's industrial development was slow because of a lack of capital and the difficult process of integrating an economy inherited from the three partitioned zones.[114]

Of course in the Polish liberal and left-wing press many voices opposed such ethno-nationalist solutions to economic and social problems. For example, in the book *Polacy o Żydach* Kazimiera Muszałówna included a chapter entitled "Antysemityzm—wróg Polski" (Anti-Semitism—the Enemy of Poland) in which she ridiculed and condemned the logic of ethno-nationalist argumentation: "Only an uneducated, politically unsophisticated, poor man confused by long unemployment could believe in the idea that dismissing one hundred Jewish workers would generate jobs for one hundred Polish workers and that such a proposal applied to the entire Jewish population would bring about a happy ending to the economic crisis and result in the disappearance of all economic difficulties in the country."[115]

The representatives of Polish Jews in the parliament were also often engaged in polemics against this ethno-nationalist approach to the economy, identifying its lack of logic and sophistication.[116] For example, MP Emil Sommerstein (1883–1957), chairman of the Jewish parliamentary circle between 1938 and 1939 and chairman of the Central Committee of Jews in Poland in the early postwar period (1944–46), exposed the poverty of ethno-nationalist policies of employment in a speech in parliament on 17 February 1938:

> And the issue of the ennoblement of market stalls! Gentlemen, you want to solve the unemployment of five or perhaps seven million peasants by getting rid of the Jewish market stalls. How many market stalls exist in Poland? I do not know if the honorable MP Mr. Marchlewski knows the figure. There are 70,000 market stalls in total in all of Poland; 25,000 are located in the central provinces; 17,000 in the eastern provinces; 14,500 in the southern provinces; and 15,000 in the western provinces. Gentlemen, you have to admit that among the 15,000 market stalls in the western provinces there are no Jewish owners. In the other provinces many market stalls are also owned by Christians. Therefore we are talking here about approximately 40,000 Jewish market stalls, which [according to you] are the source of economic problems, particularly the unemployment of landless peasants and others. . . .
> In my opinion the moral principle of the program of rebuilding economic life, about which Mr. Minister spoke, should follow "do not use force; do not build economic life, to speak mildly, on dishonesty, unfair competition and demonstrations." But you gentlemen wish to simplify the issue in the following way: let the Jews build the factories with their own financial means.

However, no blue-collar [Żyd-robotnik] or white-collar [Żyd-urzędnik] Jew or Jewish commercial trader should dare to work in them. . . . This is an over-simplified approach that cannot last long. Therefore we are not afraid of the program of the nationalization [unarodowienie, or ethno-nationalization] of commerce. . . . Finally, I would like to remind Mr. Minister [Antoni Roman] that he is minister of industry and commerce of the Polish state and not just minister of industry and commerce of one nationality [ethnic Poles].[117]

The National Democrats also used the image of the Jew as the enemy to assert legitimacy and authority, simultaneously discrediting political rivals who were not necessarily of ethnic Jewish origin. This strategy can be traced back to the late preindependence period. For example, Jeleński castigated as Jewish the entire section of society that did not subscribe to his paper *Rola*.[118] Traces of this strategy can also be found in the pre-1918 writings of Dmowski. In 1903 Dmowski implicitly criticized his main political rival, Piłsudski, by asking how a man who was such an honest and good Pole could be a member of a socialist party. According to Dmowski, who did not seem to make distinctions among different strands of Polish socialist parties, socialism aimed at the "destruction of Polishness." He described the members of the socialist movement "as a psychological type who is alien to our civilized society, and whose otherness is rooted in their race, which is different from ours, and in degeneration." Furthermore, according to him, socialists could be divided into three categories: Jews who transformed socialism into a "doctrine full of nihilism and hatred toward Christianity and Christian ethics and civilization"; individuals to whom national traditions were alien because of their upbringing; and "the revolutionary type who would rebel against any social structure."[119]

In the post-1918 period Marshal Piłsudski was a target of similar and even more aggressive labeling. One of the publications of National Democracy portrayed Piłsudski as a politician favored by the enemies of Poland—Jews, Germans, and Ukrainians. Piłsudski was a man who had "betrayed the nation" because the enemies of ethnic Poles had supported him. In his book *Sprawa Skrudlika* (The Skrudlik Affair) Mieczysław Skrudlik, a former member of Piłsudski's Legions who joined the National Democracy movement, claimed that he left Piłsudski's Independence Camp because of the Jews and converted Jews who were among its members. He claimed that Piłsudski was the protec-tor of "Judeo-Polonia."[120]

As in the preindependence period, the PPS was the political party that came under constant attack for being a Jewish party run by Jews and those who served Jewish interests. [121] In 1938 the National Democrats published a brochure entitled *PPS wrogiem ludu pracującego i sługa żydowskiego kapitału* (The PPS: The Enemy of the Working Class and the Servant of Jewish Capitalism). In it they accused the PPS of being the enemy of the working class and the product of a Jewish belief system. The brochure portrayed socialism as the enemy of Christianity, the Polish state, the nation, and the individual family.[122]

In the early 1930s, during the intensified political struggle between National Democracy and the government, the National Democrats accused the ruling Sanacja government of representing Jewish interests above those of ethnic Poles. Discrediting political rivals by labeling them as Jews was a common political strategy, even manifested in mutual accusations between rival extreme ethno-nationalist organizations, newspapers, and politicians.[123] The most well-known case was the labeling of Wojciech Wasiutyński (1910–94) as a Jew. Wasiutyński was a leading young activist of the radical ethno-nationalist organization ONR-Falanga. He came from a family with a strong Endek tradition; his father, Bogdan Wasiutyński (1882–1940), was a close associate of Dmowski. Bogdan Wasiutyński, a senator, was also the author of the anti-Semitic book *Odżydzanie miast and miasteczek* (The Dejudaizaition of Towns and Cities). In 1936 another young radical, Aleksander Heinrich, accused Wojciech Wasiutyński of having a Jewish grandparent on the maternal side—the painter Józef Buchbinder. He sold the story to the liberal *Wiadomości Literackie*. Wojciech Wasiutyński filed a libel suit against the editors of *Wiadomości Literackie* for publishing the story. Instead he insisted that his grandfather was the illegitimate son of a nobleman, Jan Zembrzuski.[124] The case of Wasiutyński reveals the instrumental nature of the practice of labeling political opponents as Jews.

Purification of the Polish Nation-State, Culture, and "Soul"

One of the most powerful narratives of the representation of the Jew as the harmful alien was that of the Jew as a polluter of the Polish nation and Polish territories. This narrative provided the prime rationale and justification for the project of the purification of the Polish nation from the physical presence of Jews and from Jewish spiritual and cultural influence. The presence of these ideas in Polish culture served to marginalize Polish Jewry by questioning their social belonging and thus making them unwanted outsiders in society.

Though ethno-nationalists propagated negative images of all Jews, they distinguished among the traditional Orthodox community, more culturally assimilated Jews, and ethnically mixed people. They perceived traditional Orthodox Jewry as a polluter of the Polish economy and the Polish geographical landscape—cities and villages—and characterized highly acculturated and assimilated Polish Jews and ethnically mixed individuals as polluters of Polish culture: arts, theater, cinema, science, and education. Ethno-nationalists saw assimilated Polish Jews and ethnically mixed individuals as more harmful to ethnic Poles than the numerically larger group of traditional Orthodox Jewry. After all, they had penetrated what the ethno-nationalists viewed as the "soul" of the nation because of their involvement in and contributions to culture; traditional Orthodox Jews, on the other hand, did not leave a mark on the "soul" of the Polish nation since they maintained their own separate culture: "We consider those who are of mixed-ethnic origin—the Polako-Żydzi, or Żydo-Polacy—as the most damaging element in our society. We consider them extremely harmful because they spread poison into Polish culture. We shall not change our view on this matter; we have to defend ourselves from them."[125]

Ethno-nationalist anti-Semites believed the physical departure of the Jewish Orthodox community from the Polish state would mark an end to the pollution of the rural and urban landscapes. In the case of assimilated Jews ethno-nationalists were not satisfied that their physical departure would be sufficient to purify the "soul" of the nation. The culture itself would have to be cleansed of their influence. The project of the ethno-nationalization of Polish culture was never realized, although voices in its support were raised not only during the interwar period but also in later periods. Polish high culture rejected the calls of ethno-nationalization and the exclusion of the contributions of all minorities.

Though most ethno-nationalists did not concern themselves with this issue, members of the most radical ethno-nationalist Roman Catholic circles viewed Jewish converts to Catholicism as polluters—of a very dangerous type—because of the level of their potential and actual "infiltration" of the core ethnic Polish community through marriage, thus spoiling the biological purity of the ethnic Polish group. These circles embraced the medieval Spanish concept of purity of blood (*limpieza de sangre*), first applied by the Spanish Inquisition toward new Christians (Conversos). This approach was clearly racial.[126] These religious anti-Semites denied Jewish converts membership in the Roman Catholic community in Poland; converts were only allocated a somewhat precarious place in an abstract Catholic community.[127] The Marian Order monthly *Pro Christo* and the weekly *Kultura* (Culture), published by the Central Institute of Catholic Action, along with well-known public figures such as the ultraconservative journalist and politician Stanisław Mackiewicz-Cat (1896–1966) and the writer Zofia Kossak-Szczucka (1890–1968), a leading member of Catholic Action (Akcja Katolicka), were outspoken representatives of this extreme racial position. [128] On 27 September 1936 Kossak-Szczucka proclaimed in *Kultura* that Jews were both physically and mentally "a race apart" and that therefore marriage with a Jew led to degeneration not only of the children born out of such a union but also of the fourth generation: "Jews are so terribly alien to us, alien and unpleasant, that they are a race apart. They irritate us and all their traits grate against our sensibilities. Their oriental impetuosity, argumentativeness, specific mode of thought, the set of their eyes, the shape of their ears, the winking of their eyelids, the line of their lips, everything. In families of mixed blood we detect the traces of these features to the third or the fourth generation and beyond." [129]

Although Catholicism was one of the chief markers of Polish national identity, in the eyes of extreme exclusivist ethno-nationalists the conversion of Jews to Catholicism did not automatically mean their inclusion in the Polish nation. Racial anti-Semites perceived Jewish converts to Catholicism as a separate group, different from both ethnic Poles and Jews, a dangerous polluter, threatening the very biological essence of ethnic Poles and their future. Perhaps one of the most striking examples of the damaging influence of exclusionary racial thinking on individuals in this period was the case of the convert and Roman Catholic priest Tadeusz Puder. On 3 July 1938 Puder was physically attacked by Rafał Michalski, a young radical, in the Church of St. Jacek in Warsaw. [130]

Examples of exclusionary attitudes toward converted Jews can be found not only in the more radical papers like ONR-Falanga's *Prosto z mostu* but also in more moderate papers like *Przegląd Katolicki* and *Ateneum Kapłańskie*. These three newspapers treated converted Jews as an unfortunate group that should have its own separate church. Converts were perceived neither as Poles, because of their ethnicity, nor as members of the Roman Catholic community. Some authors in *Ateneum Kapłańskie* deliberated the question of converted Jews' potential ability to build bridges between Christians and Jews. Even to this they saw two major obstacles. The first was degeneration of faith among the already converted, a situation caused by their separateness within the Christian community: "After the conversion they are left to themselves, without any care, which is needed in order to strengthen their faith. As a result their faith quickly becomes degenerated and old ways of life and traditions take over." [131]

The second obstacle was the rise of Jewish nationalism, which had turned the Jews away from Christianity and in fact, authors stressed, made them into a zealous enemy of Christian nations: "Today we cannot talk about the assimilation of Jews by Baptism. . . . Extreme Zionism has transformed the Jews into the enemy of Christian nations. It took them away from the possibility of 'seeing light' and thus prepared the basis for sowing anti-Semitism."[132] Ethno-nationalists of one stripe or another objected to the inclusion in Polish society of any kind of Jew, even those who had assimilated or converted. Unlike other minorities—Slavic groups and Germans—neither acculturation nor complete polonization constituted a guarantee of the inclusion of Jews in the Polish nation.[133]

National Democracy created a persistent image in Polish popular culture of the assimilated Jew as a cause of the degeneration or even destruction of all cultural institutions, such as theater, cinema, cabaret, and the film and radio industries. They portrayed Jews as polluters of music, the arts, the vernacular Polish language, and Polish literature. Ethno-nationalist writers called the Jewish presence in the arts a spiritual disease (*schorzenie duchowe*) and an abomination (*żydowskie paskudztwo*). The Endeks' zealous desire to purify the national language and literature from alien elements closely resembles the trend advocated in late nineteenth-century France by Charles Maurras (1868–1952).[134] The Endeks insisted that Polish-Jewish artists who wrote in the Polish language were not creating Polish literature but simply using the Polish language as a "technical medium" for their works. The Endeks categorized works in Polish by Jews as intrinsically alien to Polish spirituality: "Tuwim does not write Polish poetry; he only uses the Polish language. His poetry does not represent the spirit of Juliusz Słowacki, but that of Heinrich Heine . . . the soul of a merchant and Jewish poet."[135]

This position was widely circulated in various papers. *Myśl Narodowa* had a special column entitled "Na Widowni" (On Display), which was almost entirely dedicated to fighting the influences of "Judeo-Polish culture." The chief writers of this column were Stanisław Pieńkowski, Jan Rembieliński, and Zygmunt Wasilewski.[136] The writers and poets who came under their attack constituted a very diverse group both literarily and socially, but this did not stop their critics from seeing them as a uniform group of polluters. Among the most frequently attacked were Julian Tuwim (1894–1953), Józef Wittlin (1896–1976), Marian Hemar (1901–72), Roman Brandstaetter (1906–87), and Janusz Korczak (1878–1942).[137] The historian Marceli Handelsman (1882–1945), the founder of the Historical Institute at the University of Warsaw and a main interwar specialist on political history, became a target of similar attacks.[138]

In addition to their attacks on individual Jewish writers and intellectuals, the Endeks attacked the entire Polish-Jewish cultural milieu for poisoning the minds of writers and artists of ethnic Polish origin who were either professionally associated with Jews or influenced by their works. They saw both actual Jewish literary works and Jewish cultural and intellectual influence on Poles as a threat to Polish culture:

> The Jews also inscribe the slogans of demoralization and destruction on their fighting banner. This is how they influence our literature, arts, and music. . . . Although the Jewish contribution to our literature has no value, they use their influence on Polish writers. They infect them with certain ideas and Jewish principles, and lately such phenomena are on the rise. I will cite one small example. Recently a Pole, Dr. Falkowski, published a textbook for primary school in which the idea of God and the Fatherland is not mentioned on purpose; in the book for children there is not one word about God and the Fatherland! Next a Jew, Korczak-Goldszmit, a Jewish educator, writes books for Poles on how to love a child. This man knows well the psychology of a Jewish child and approaches the subject from the point of view of Jewish pedagogy. Thus he dares to force his ideas on Polish mothers and Polish educators.[139]

There were anti-Semitic attacks on Polish artists who were associated professionally with Jewish colleagues, portraying such artists as polluters of Polish culture as well. Ethno-nationalists accused the literary group Skamander, which included poets like Antoni Słonimski (1895–1976), Julian Tuwim, Kazimierz Wierzyński (1894–1969), and Jerzy Iwaszkiewicz (1894–1980), of being "Bolsheviks," "moral perverts," and "pathological erotomaniacs." On 13 March 1921 *Kurier Warszawski* (The Warsaw Courier) wrote the following description of Skamander's literary program: "The Jews want to destroy the national ethos, logic, faith, and all aesthetic values. . . . The new poetry is nothing more than a Jewish conspiracy . . . rooted in Bolshevism."[140]

Achieving both ethnic and cultural sameness, one of the main markers of ethno-nationalist cultural projects, was one of the main goals of National Democracy and its radical offshoot organizations.[141] The Roman Catholic clergy were also obsessed with the purity of "the souls" of "Polak-Catholics" and therefore were constantly engaged in instructing Poles how "to feel, think, and act." National Democracy and the Catholic clergy were generally unsatisfied with the state of morals and spirituality in society. They wanted to conduct a moral and spiritual revolution that would bring about one uniform desirable way of life: conservative, traditional, and Catholic in character. They perceived Jews as the chief obstacles to the realization of their project, as the embodiment of alien values and traditions and the cause of all the imperfections, weaknesses, and shortcomings of ethnic Poles. In fact, radical ethno-nationalists insisted that the presence of the Jewish community caused a sense of confusion about identity among (ethnic) Poles. The mere presence of Jews was allegedly responsible for polluting the mentality and soul of ethnic Poles and was preventing them from "breathing in the Polish spirit," in short, from becoming "better Poles." [142] Anti-Semites advocated dejudaization as the necessary method of "improving an ethnic Pole," of helping him to rediscover his real identity: "Dejudaization of the press and radio and dejudaization of the Polish mentality are as vital as dejudaization of commerce, crafts, and industry. In fact, work on the rebirth of the soul of the Nation should start with dejudaization of the Polish mentality because there is no possibility of dejudaization of Poland without dejudaization of the Polish mentality. The true Polish national and Catholic press can play an enormous role in this process. However, we need to free ourselves from Jewish influence, from the Jews and from the 'white' Jews [biali Żydzi, Poles who cooperate with Jews]." [143] Another writer asked:

> Do we retain a sense of who we are? At first glance everything looks all right; we have our own state, we rule according to our own will, we live in normal conditions under which we can develop our national civilization on the material and spiritual levels. However, . . . let's look at some figures: 42.5 percent of all of European Jewry lives in the borders of Poland, we have approximately 4 million Jews. . . . Still the figures do not constitute the core of the matter. . . . After all, the existence of "national minorities" is not something unusual and cannot provide a reason for despair. The truly tragic fact is that Jewish businessmen and industrialists have replaced Us, the Poles. . . . Another truly terrible fact is that . . . Jewish writers and journalists write for us and that Jewish teachers educate our youth. . . . Such a sick and humiliating system cannot continue, neither in a great nation such as we are nor in a simple nation. We have to regain our national character in its entirety, we have to regain a sense of our identity—this is the most urgent task awaiting the entire community. . . . Our paper begins by publishing list of questions on "How to Nationalize Polish Life." We have no doubt that we will be able to throw light on how to realize the great and necessary task of the dejudaization of Poland in the fastest and most efficient way. [144]

Adam Heydel (1899–1941), a well-known liberal economist affiliated with the moderate sector of Endecja, similarly claimed that Jews who were active in culture polluted both the Polish culture and Polish cities and were like an unstoppable flood.[145]

This type of reasoning reveals the deep insecurities of the core ethno-nationalists about Polish identity and culture, as well as their authoritarian tendencies. In their argumentation (ethnic) Polish identity emerges vis-à-vis Jewish identity as a weak category that could be easily manipulated and modified. In order to regain national strength and rediscover a true sense of identity Poles had to be isolated from Jews. The Pole could not be a complete Pole in the presence of the Jew because the Jew did not allow him to maintain confidence in his identity. Ethno-nationalists defined Polish national identity as Catholicism, traditionalism, and conservatism, but, more important to them, in opposition to Jewish identity. The Pole was everything that the Jew was not, and vice versa. National Democracy used this rather peculiar model of self-definition as a powerful tool for raising national awareness among the large uneducated rural population in the interwar period. As Alina Cała has shown in her book on the image of the Jew in Polish folk culture in the 1970s, the impact of National Democracy's negative images of Polish Jewry persisted in Polish life long after 1939.[146]

Projects of Separation and Emigration

Ethno-nationalists regarded the concept of social and cultural separateness, first advocated in the late nineteenth century by the Jesuit Marian Morawski, as a necessary step toward the purification of the Polish nation from the Jewish polluter. In the interwar period National Democracy and its offshoot radical organizations, along with more mainstream conservative and center-right-wing political groups, advocated separation of the two communities in the areas of culture and the education of the youth and in the professions where Jews were prominent. In interwar Poland 56 percent of doctors in private practice and 33.5 percent of lawyers, notary publics, and legal advisors were Jewish. The ethno-nationalist desire for separation was often expressed in slogans: "Jewish arts for Jews and Polish arts for Poles."[147] "Jewish doctors for Jewish patients, Jewish lawyers for Jewish clients."[148] "National tragedy—Jewish teachers in Polish schools."[149]

Although ethno-nationalists failed to achieve a substantial separation between Poles and acculturated Polish Jews within the realm of Polish culture, they succeeded in achieving separation in some professional organizations. For example, in the late 1930s the so-called Aryan paragraph was introduced by the Union of Architects of the Second Polish Republic, the Union of Medical Doctors of Poland, and the Polish Lawyers' Association. [150] Each professional organization cited economic reasons, particularly the troubled labor market, as an explanation for introducing the anti-Jewish measure. Thus an exclusivist ethno-nationalist position on the state economy was realized: Jews had to be excluded from professional organizations in order to allow Poles to reach their full economic potential.

In some cases the exclusivist ethno-nationalist position concerning the separation of the two peoples was not based on economic, social, and cultural grounds alone, but also contained a racial component, perhaps most apparent in demands for the separation of Jewish youth from Polish youth in schools, children's organizations, and other educational institutions. The need for the separation of Polish and Jewish children and youths was voiced in various publications. For example, in the pseudoscholarly work *Poziom intelektualny młodzieży polskiej i żydowskiej w naszych gimnazjach* (Intellectual Abilities of Polish and Jewish Youths in Polish High Schools) Professor Ludwik Jaxa-Bykowski, who was to become an important figure in the higher education system set up by the Polish Underground during WWII, demanded the separation of Jewish and Polish children on both ethno-cultural and racial grounds. Jaxa-Bykowski claimed that contact between Jewish and Polish youths led to the degeneration of intellectual abilities among the latter and that the Jewish biological and ethno-cultural makeup constituted a threat to the Polish intellect and mental health. [151] At the same time he stressed that youths from Slavic minorities did not exert any damaging impact on ethnic Polish youths. Jaxa-Bykowski's position reveals the extent to which clear racial ideas shaped the thinking of Polish ethno-nationalists.

The ethno-nationalists wanted to purify the territory of Poland from Jews by mass emigration; they viewed this as essential if Poles were to attain full development. Thus mass emigration of Jews became the ultimate goal of all ethno-nationalists. The perception of the Jew as the chief harmful alien provided a rationale for the emigration project and was expressed in various ethno-nationalist writings. In the political program of 1938 the newly set up center-right Labor Party declared:

[In Poland] "the Jewish issue" has a separate and more extreme ramification. The well-being of our nation and of our Polish state has been harmed to a great extent by the oversized Jewish population and its social and territorial spread. More important, the moral distinctiveness and political and social trends within the Jewish community are seriously damaging to our economic, cultural, and moral interest. The solution to this extremely urgent issue primarily lies in support of [ethnic] Polish economic and cultural development, . . . the modification of the capitalist system, . . . [and] the development of Polish industries, businesses, and free professions. . . . The Polish government and society at large should cooperate in the implementation of the mass emigration of the Jews. Such legislation will provide the fastest nationalization of Polish political, economic, social, and cultural life.[152]

Father Stanisław Trzeciak, one of the most radical ethno-nationalists, expressed similar views. In *W obliczu grozy. Dwa przeciwne światy* (Facing the Impending Storm: Two Contradictory Worlds) Trzeciak wrote: "The harm that has been caused to the Polish nation by granting equal rights to the Jews must be repaired. In the first instance civic rights have to be removed from the Jews, and next they themselves have to be removed from Poland. These are indispensable requirements if Poland is to remain Poland and to free itself from economic captivity and the destructive intellectual influence of the Jewish world. It is high time that these incredible historical mistakes were reversed and that resolutions were made regarding all the harm the Jews have caused Poland. The most important enemy is the enemy within."[153]

The former statement clearly represents a more moderate version of the myth of the Jew as the harmful other, while the latter represents a more aggressive version. Political programs generally expressed a more moderate version of the myth than did newspapers, journals, and other writings.

By the middle of the 1930s, with the exception of the PPS, the Democratic Party, the left wing of Sanacja, the KPP, and other small left-wing socialist parties, a majority of political elites advocated the concept of the emigration of Jews from Poland. Of course one has to acknowledge that among the more prominent parties and political groups there was no uniform policy or program for actual implementation of the project of Jewish emigration.[154] Some political parties and politicians had a more detailed program for the potential realization of Jewish emigration than others did. Some political groups, such as the post-1935 Sanacja government, opted for cooperation with Zionist organizations in order to speed up the emigration process and insisted that Jewish emigration was also a positive way of solving poverty among the Jewish community. Center-right-wing political parties and politicians proposed plans for the gradual emigration of Jews, while extreme ethno-nationalist organizations demanded their total and instant removal. As a rule the political party that propagated the most aggressive and elaborated myth of the Jew as the harmful other proposed the most radical measures for how to implement emigration and speed up its process. For example, the National Radical Camp, ONR, advocated instantly stripping Polish Jews of all their civic rights and not permitting them to take any of their financial assets abroad. According to the ONR, Jewish financial assets and properties belonged to the Poles from whom they had been originally stolen. [155] In its political program of April 1935 the ONR explicitly expressed such a position: "A Jew cannot be a citizen of the Polish state. Until the time of the completion of the mass emigration of Jews from Poland, the Jew should be given the status of 'attached person' to the state. . . . The Jews are the ones that must emigrate from Poland—not the Polish workers and peasants. Dejudaization of Polish towns and cities is a necessary requirement for the healthy development of the national economy." [156]

Characteristically the main objective of ethno-nationalists was, first, to achieve the polonization of cities and towns where the Jewish minority, a traditionally strongly urbanized group, constituted an average of between 30 and 40 percent. Second, their objective was to achieve the polonization of commerce and industry, areas in which Polish Jews were traditionally active and for which Polish nobility and peasants had shown little inclination or aptitude in previous periods. [157] One can suggest that the inevitable process of the modernization of Polish society, which took place in the interwar period, led to the intensified quest for the removal of the Polish Jews, who were one of the main original agents of the modernization of Polish society in the nineteenth century.

Unsurprisingly the process of targeting Jews as a group obliged to leave Poland for the good of the host nation was rationalized to a high degree. Most Polish politicians in the 1930s insisted that the grounds for Jewish emigration were "objective"—meaning economic and demographic—and therefore could not be categorized as prejudice. However, these "objective grounds" were basically a form of camouflage for anti-Jewish prejudice. In many writings such camouflage was unsuccessful and revealed the prevalent perception of the Jew as the alien polluter of the Polish state and the nation. A good example of such a phenomenon is *Sprawa polsko-żydowska*, written by the prominent conservative politician Władysław Studnicki.

In this work Studnicki proposed a detailed plan for the gradual emigration of one hundred thousand Jews a year, which, according to him, would lead to the dejudaization of Poland within thirty years. Unlike the more radical exclusivist ethno-nationalist politicians, Studnicki insisted that Jews were entitled to take their financial assets with them. He also suggested that Poland should hold a protectorate over Palestine, to which Polish Jews were supposed to emigrate en masse. Although Studnicki insisted that his advocacy of the emigration of Jews from Poland was based not on hatred but on statistics, his work contains references that directly point to the use of anti-Semitic idioms, such as "dejudaization of Poland," "the Jews as the Polish misfortune," and "the Jews as parasites on the healthy branch of the Polish tree."[158] The case of Studnicki reveals both the extent to which belief in the Jew as the harmful alien was rationalized by large segments of the political elite and the lack of understanding on their part of the nature of their prejudicial beliefs.

The project of emigration was perceived as a just means of disposing of Jews and as compatible with the Catholic ethos. With the exception of a small group of extreme exclusivist ethno-nationalists who proposed a more radical form of disposing of the Jews by force, the majority of Polish ethno-nationalist political elites and the Catholic Church insisted that they "did not wish to harm the Jews, but simply wanted them to leave Poland." Their ideological world-view prevented them from recognizing that the removal from Jews of the right to Polish citizenship could be classified as an unlawful, unjust, and prejudicial practice.[159]

In the post-1935 period, as earlier indicated, the Sanacja government endorsed the project of Jewish emigration. One can argue that one of the background reasons for the implementation of this program was the Polish state's failure to conduct necessary agrarian reforms. Powerful landowners, who constituted an important pressure group in interwar Poland, opposed such reforms. Therefore in the project of replacing the urban Jewish population with the peasant population the government also saw an easy way of solving the social and economic problems of the country.

In the historiography of the Polish Jewry of interwar Poland various scholars have discussed the impact of Polish (ethno-)nationalism on the Jewish community, writing opposite historical interpretations.[160] Celia Heller, in her book *On the Edge of Destruction*, argues that the period between the two world wars was a rehearsal for the Holocaust. Polish actions had by 1939 pushed the Jews to "the edge of destruction," and it only remained for the Nazis to complete what they had begun. There is little doubt that her thesis was created in the shadow of the Holocaust by someone who was personally affected by it. In his article "Political Anti-Semitism in Interwar Germany and Poland" William Hagen expresses a more accurate, subtle, and complex view. According to him, "prior to and independent of wartime mass murder, the central and eastern European Jews—despite their indubitable cultural and religious vitality—faced the threat . . . of the dissolution of their collective and communal existence." [161]

No doubt contradictions were part and parcel of the lives of minorities in Poland and other countries in Eastern Europe between the two world wars. By the end of 1939 integral nationalists had destroyed the "dream" of Polishness, which would mean preserving and respecting every culture and every faith of all Polish citizens. The vision of a monoreligious and monocultural Poland appeared to triumph. Still, there were political and social organizations and individuals who remained committed to the ideal of the civic and pluralistic model of the Polish nation.

4. The Myth and Anti-Jewish Violence between 1918 and 1939

Instigation, Rationalization, and Justification of Violence

Hatred is carrying over from the street to the school bench. It is flooding the entire country. It will encounter no dams, nor will it encounter any breakers that would direct this storm—which arose not from agitation but from poverty—into channels that are useful, creative, and constructive.

Ksawery Pruszyński, "Przytyk i stragan"

Introduction

Scholars of the history of nationalism recognize exclusivist ethno-nationalism as one of the main factors that strains the bonds that sustain civility in ethnically mixed societies. This type of nationalism has frequently led to interethnic tensions and eruptions of violence, which in turn have led to flows of refugees and asylum seekers from minorities threatened by such violence.[1]

The ethno-nationalism of the National Democracy party, with its elaborated representation of the Jew as the enemy of Poland and its people, was one of the main factors behind various anti-Jewish hostilities that occurred in interwar Poland. There were also other factors behind hostilities, including economic greed and a desire to plunder and cause physical and moral injuries.

Anti-Jewish hostilities included inflicting damage on Jewish properties—private homes, shops, institutions, and synagogues; slander; physical harassment; and assaults on and murders of individuals and groups. The myth of the Jew as a national threat constituted a premise for the legitimization of anti-Jewish violence as national self-defense. Such legitimization progressed in four main stages: first, mandating and justifying anti-Jewish violence; second, paying tribute to the perpetrators of such violence as national heroes; third, shifting the responsibility for such violence onto its victims; and finally, minimizing the unethical and criminal nature of such violence. This pattern of legitimizing anti-Jewish violence continued into later periods of Polish history.[2]

The historical literature about anti-Jewish violence in interwar Poland has been growing in the last two decades. Historians have published historical sources regarding the most acute cases of anti-Jewish hostilities, such as the killings of Jews by Polish military units in Pińsk on 5 April 1919, in Lida on 16 and 17 April, and in Vilnius (Wilno) on 19 April 1919.[3] Another selection of documents was published about violence against Jews in the peasant riots in Małopolska in May 1919; materials about the Przytyk pogrom of 9 March 1936 were also made available.[4] In the last fifteen years several historians have published new historical studies of anti-Jewish violence in Poland. Most of these works are descriptive, discussing the events of either a particular wave of violence or a single riot, such as the Przytyk pogrom, or anti-Jewish rioting at universities.[5] Some of these works focus on the causes of anti-Jewish violence; Frank Golczewski's *Polnisch-Jüdische Beziehungen 1881–1922* examines the role of anti-Semitism in the Polish Army's violence against Jews in the eastern territories in the early postwar period (1918–20).[6] William Hagen shifts the focus from description of anti-Jewish violence to interpretive analysis of ethnic violence's meanings and messages in its perpetrators' eyes. In his article "The Moral Economy of Popular Violence: The Pogrom in Lwów, November 1918" he concludes that anti-Jewish violence had multiple lines of development and that the perception of cultural outsiders played a salient role in the way the violence was rationalized by its perpetrators.[7]

One of the features of this new historical literature is that it includes Polish historians such as Jolanta Żyndul and Monika Natkowska among its contributors. This is a recent development. Before the 1980s Polish historians minimized or completely omitted the subject of anti-Jewish hostilities in historical works published both in Communist Poland and abroad.[8] When they did discuss the anti-Jewish violence of the interwar period, they presented it as a result of "objective social and economic conditions." Even more recently this latter approach has reemerged. One of its most intellectually disturbing examples is Piotr Gontarczyk's *Pogrom? Zajścia polsko-żydowskie w Przytyku 9 marca 1936 r. Mity, Fakty, Dokumenty*, in which the author interprets the anti-Jewish violence in Przytyk as a "zero-sum game" between Poles and Jews.[9] Gontarczyk implies that the local Jews carried the responsibility for the outburst of anti-Jewish violence; they were guilty because a group of them embarked on active defense of their community. Gontarczyk's work represents a highly rationalized version of the ethno-nationalist approach, legitimizing anti-Jewish violence as national self-defense, based on the perception of Jews not as a group included in the Polish nation but as an "alien and harmful nation." This position was common among core ethno-nationalist circles in interwar Poland and acted as one of the main factors behind the outbursts of anti-Jewish hostilities.

Historical Background of the Violence

It is possible to differentiate among four major waves of anti-Jewish violence that swept interwar Poland, each characterized by specific historical and social conditions and developments. The first wave, in 1918–20, was rooted in the process of the formation of the new Polish nation-state and military fighting over the eastern border with the Bolsheviks. The second, in 1930–33, was based primarily at universities. The third, and the least researched, was linked to the emergence of the National Radical Camp in 1934. The last, in 1935–37, was the most widespread and severe, involving university students and other sections of the civilian population.[10]

The first wave of violence began in 1918 during the Polish-Ukrainian War (1918–19) over the southeastern territories. In these attacks 230 Jews died, a relatively large number. One of the first and worst instances of anti-Jewish violence was the Lwów pogrom, which occurred in the last week of November 1918.[11] In three days 72 Jews were murdered and 443 others injured. The chief perpetrators of these murders were soldiers and officers of the so-called Blue Army (Błękitna Armia), set up in France in 1917 by General Józef Haller (1873–1960), and lawless civilians. Another instance of severe anti-Jewish violence occurred on 5 April 1919 in Pińsk, where 35 Jews, including women and children, were executed on the order of a commander of the local Polish military garrison.[12] Similar instances of violence conducted by Polish military units took place in Lublin, Lida, Wilno, and a number of other towns and villages in the southeastern and northeastern territories.[13]

A separate wave of anti-Jewish violence also occurred in the spring of 1919 in Małopolska (lesser Poland, west Galicia) in villages such as Niebylec, where riots occurred on 28 April 1919; Strzyżów, where riots occurred on 21 April 1919; and Baranów, where riots occurred on 5 May 1919. These riots were part of a peasant social revolt that had erupted that spring.[14] The worst case in this wave of violence took place in Kolbuszowa, Rzeszów district, on 6 May 1919, resulting in eight dead and one hundred injured.[15]

The second major wave broke out at universities during the first term of the academic year 1930–31 and again during the same term of the following two academic years.[16] During this phase anti-Jewish riots were frequently intertwined with demonstrations against the Sanacja government, which was portrayed by National Democracy as representing Jewish interests.[17] Student organizations such as All-Polish Youth (Młodzież Wszechpolska, MWP) and the Youth Movement of the Camp for a Greater Poland (Ruch Młodych Obozu Wielkiej Polski) advocated violence against Jewish students. National Democracy founded MWP in 1922, and the Camp for a Greater Poland (OWP), a more extreme organization founded at the end of 1926, set up its youth movement in early 1927. The national government of Poland banned both the youth movement of the OWP and the OWP itself in early 1933 on the grounds that they posed a threat to the stability of the state.[18]

Brotherly Help (Bratnia Pomoc) was another student social organization whose members were involved in anti-Jewish hostilities at various universities. According to available data, approximately 60 percent of all registered students at universities were members of Brotherly Help associations in 1930. All-Polish Youth and the youth movement of the OWP controlled Brotherly Help associations at most universities. The only exception was the Jagiellonian University in Cracow, where membership of the student self-help association was open to Jewish students.[19] In some cities gymnasium students joined university students in anti-Jewish hostilities. The Scout movement was also heavily influenced by National Democracy.[20]

Ethno-nationalist views enjoyed a significant level of popularity among sections of university youth.[21] Student organizations run and controlled by National Democracy and the OWP regarded anti-Jewish actions as a way to put pressure on the government to introduce a policy of "numerus clausus." "Numerus clausus" was a discriminatory policy aimed at limiting the number of Polish-Jewish students at Polish universities and other institutions of higher education. It was condemned by Jewish students, a substantial section of leading Polish intellectuals and liberal intelligentsia, and the international academic community.[22]

A third wave of anti-Jewish violence on campus began in the spring of 1934, initiated by the newly formed National Radical Camp (ONR), which had replaced the disbanded OWP. The ONR orchestrated anti-Jewish violence in April, May, and the first half of June.[23] The extremely violent nature of these riots prompted the leaders of the Jewish community to begin talks on setting up an organization to monitor anti-Jewish events in the country.[24] Given the explicitly fascist position and militant nature of the ONR, on 12 May 1934 the Ministry of Interior Affairs had to issue special directives against the hostilities. In July of the same year the Sanacja government, alarmed by the ONR's strong anti-Sanacja stance and its extreme violent position toward Jews, made the ONR illegal. However, this action did not put an end to the activities of the ONR since many of its members were also members of the legal National Democracy party.

The fourth wave of anti-Jewish hostilities occurred between 1935 and 1937 amid sharply increasing popular support for the ethno-nationalization of the Polish state during the second half of the 1930s.[25] Once again violence broke out at the universities, where All-Polish Youth and the ONR intensified the campaign for "ghetto benches" for Jewish students. The activists and supporters of this campaign were easily identifiable by a green ribbon pinned to their jackets. The campaign for "ghetto benches" aimed at the segregation of Polish and Jewish students at universities and other institutions of higher education. All-Polish Youth and the ONR saw the "ghetto bench" system as the first step on the road to forcing Jewish students to leave universities in Poland. In the late 1930s the academic youth of National Democracy and the ONR also started to demand the introduction of a policy of "numerus nullus," aimed at the complete "dejudaization" of all Polish institutions of higher education. Leading representatives of the Jewish community, such as Izaak Rubinsztein, condemned the policy of "ghetto benches." In his speech of 21 February 1936 in the parliament Rubinsztein stated: "And now students wish to separate themselves from Jews and demand separate benches. The Almighty God has kept us together on the same land throughout the ages, and now they refuse to sit with us on the same benches. Since we live together on the same land, we should sit together on the same benches."[26]

The extreme ethno-nationalists won the campaign for "ghetto benches" in 1937 after the Sanacja government granted universities the power to regulate the seating of Polish and Jewish students, arguing that such a measure would bring an end to violent disturbances and guarantee the maintenance of peace on campuses. However, violence continued to take place after "ghetto benches" were introduced, and in some cases there was even an escalation of violence, resulting in the individual murders of Jewish students.[27] In many universities radical right-wing students used physical force to move Jewish students to the "segregated sections" of lecture halls. The majority of Jewish students refused to accept the new system of seating on the grounds that it violated their civil rights. A significant number of Polish university professors and democratic student organizations condemned the policy of "ghetto benches." The student groups who opposed segregating Jews were diverse, including Imperial Thought (Myśl Mocarstwowa), a conservative student organization close to the left-wing Sanacja; Academic Civic Youth (Akademicka Młodzież Państwowa), a left-wing Sanacja organization; the PPS; and international academic groups.[28]

Outside the universities local sections of National Democracy instigated anti-Jewish violence in 150 towns and villages. The most frequent rioting took place in central Poland, where the Jewish community was highly concentrated. However, violence erupted in other parts of the country regardless of the size of the Jewish population living in any particular area. For example, in Silesia, where Jews constituted just 1.7 percent of the population, attacks also took place.[29]

The widespread eruption of violence between 1935 and 1937 was a direct result of the newly intensified anti-Jewish campaign launched by National Democracy and the ONR in 1935. These political parties looked on violence as a viable and indeed indispensable tool of "speeding" the process of the emigration of Jews from Poland and thus reaching their ultimate goal: the "dejudaization of the Polish state" (odżydzanie Polski). On 15 November 1935 one of leading papers of National Democracy, the *Warszawski Dziennik Narodowy*, called for the expulsion of Jews from the capital, Warsaw. The paper insisted that such expulsion would mark a first major step toward the complete "dejudaization" of Poland.[30] The National Democracy party did not seem to view anti-Jewish violence as a tool for the physical destruction of the Jewish community. Its main aim was to make the daily life of Polish Jews so odious and unbearable (*obrzydzanie*) that they would be "persuaded" to emigrate "voluntarily." It was also meant to warn Jews that Poles were no longer willing to tolerate their presence within the Polish nation-state. Between 1935 and 1937 an estimated two thousand Jews were injured and between twenty and thirty killed.[31] Two Jews were killed in Grodno on 5 June 1936 and in Przytyk on 9 March 1936. Among the highest number of individuals killed in one riot by civilians were five dead in Odrzywół on 20 and 27 November 1935.

The two most common forms of violence directed against Jews in interwar Poland were smashing windows and plundering shops and private homes, and beating up inhabitants of villages and towns, students at universities, and commuters on trains. At certain times on some of the suburban lines in Warsaw, such as Warsaw-Otwock, the police had to set up extra patrols in order to protect Jewish travelers.[32] Less common were the burning of Jewish shops, the bombing of Jewish institutions and synagogues, and throwing harmful chemicals at Jews in the street.[33]

The Destructive Language of the Myth

Polish ethno-nationalists deployed the myth of the Jew as the harmful alien in both political propaganda and popular culture, using a highly emotive vocabulary—primitive, vulgar, and aggressive. The National Democrats and the ONR described the threatening Jewish other using words that expressed a high level of animosity and hostility, referring to the Jewish "menace," "horde," "curse," "flood," and "tribe of parasites." Even the term *Jew* itself came to have negative connotations. This was reinforced by phrases stressing struggle, battle, and even war against Jews. Examples from two interwar monthly journals, the student monthly *Alma Mater* and the Catholic *Pro Christo*, use these expressions in a typical way: "the struggle against the Jews is a national duty";[34] "the struggle against the Jews is also a struggle against the Communist gangrene that is spreading around the country; it is a struggle for our true independence";[35] "our existence is dependent on how we fight the Jews step by step."[36]

In the political propaganda of National Democracy, the OWP, the ONR, and All-Polish Youth of the 1930s anti-Jewish language was recurrent and violent. The "struggle against the Jews" (walka z Żydami) became the key slogan of the core ethno-nationalist press, including a whole range of student, social, cultural, Catholic, and tabloid papers. The purpose of using such expressions was to portray Polish-Jewish relations as a zero-sum conflict in which the Polish ethnic community had to take action to defend itself against control and destruction by Jews. The extent to which the wider population absorbed this anti-Jewish vocabulary is difficult to establish, owing to the lack of data and a viable methodology. At the very least the section of society that actively took part in anti-Jewish violence had absorbed the messages in this language, since there was a high level of social mobilization. Some of the riots organized by National Democracy attracted substantial crowds. The largest numbered fifteen thousand people participating in anti-Jewish hostilities in Częstochowa on 19 June 1937.[37]

The readers of the core ethno-nationalist press and literature were also exposed to anti-Jewish vocabulary. Since this body of writing constituted a large part of all publications in interwar Poland, the degree of absorption and level of popularity of such anti-Jewish propaganda cannot be seen as marginal.[38] A look at the circulations of the anti-Semitic tabloid newspapers that constituted the most extreme part of the core ethno-nationalist press shows that even these papers had a good-sized readership. In 1938 alone the circulation of such papers exceeded one hundred thousand in a single circulation, equaling that of all weeklies dedicated to social and literary issues published in Poland at the time. Two of the extreme anti-Jewish weeklies, *Pod pręgierz* (Under the Ban) and *Samoobrona Narodu* (Self-Defense of the Nation), each reached a circulation of more than twenty-five thousand for a single issue the same year.[39]

The same anti-Jewish language was employed in popular books about Jews. Ethno-nationalist journals and newspaper advertised the so-called Jewish Expert Library (Biblioteka Żydoznawcza), consisting of books by prominent anti-Semitic authors such as Stanisław Trzeciak, Marian Morawski, and Henryk Rolicki (whose real name was Tadeusz Gluziński). An entire genre of "expert" books on Jews with anti-Semitic content was directed at both the more sophisticated and the popular market.[40] For example, *Alma Mater*, directed at Catholic academic youth, ran a special column entitled "Co czytać?" (Books to Read) in which anti-Jewish and anti-Communist works were highly recommended. The popular newspaper *Mały Dziennik* published similar columns, and *Pro Christo* published a list of recommended books on Jews entitled "Literatura Żydoznawcza" (Literature on the Subject of Jews).

The National Democracy party and All-Polish Youth organized lectures, seminars, and discussions that used the same violently anti-Semitic language as their newspapers, journals, and books. These events were significant propagators of ethnic hatred, and cases of spontaneous attacks on individual Jews after such events were reported in the Jewish and Polish press. Among the more extreme examples was the knife attack by Jan Antczak on three Jewish men in Łódź in January 1937, which took place after a lecture given by the priest Stanisław Trzeciak. Two of the men were badly injured, and the other died.[41]

The representation of the Jew as a harmful enemy aiming at the destruction of the Polish nation created in the segments of society most susceptible to ethno-nationalist propaganda what is described in sociological literature as a "moral panic."[42] All the elements of "moral panic" can be detected in the pattern of behavior of the perpetrators and supporters of anti-Jewish violence in interwar Poland. There was concern over the behavior of Jews, allegedly causing harm to the political, economic, social, and cultural development of ethnic Poles. Second, there were wildly exaggerated claims about the peril of this threat—such as the destruction of the Polish nation. Third, there was consensus on the threat posed by Jews. Fourth, there was an increased level of hostility toward Jews. Fifth, there were outbursts of volatility directed at Jews. And finally, there was a sense of self-righteousness in justifying anti-Jewish violence as national self-defense.

Violence as National Self-Defense

The perpetrators of anti-Jewish violence in interwar Poland and their supporters legitimized it as national self-defense. At the root of such legitimization lay the myth of the Jew as the chief harmful other. To understand how anti-Jewish violence was justified as national self-defense, one has to look at the ethno-nationalist use of prominent themes in Polish national mythology: those of victimhood and of unjust treatment by others. For obvious historical reasons such themes had been important in Polish national mythology since at least the partition of the First Polish Republic in the second half of the eighteenth century. As in many other national mythologies a central message in Polish national culture is that Poles are always the victims and others are the oppressors of the Polish nation. The ethno-nationalist version of national history intertwined the theme of Polish victimhood with the myth of the Jew as the dangerous and sinister oppressor of the Polish nation. This interpretation stressed that Poles had been consistently marginalized and thwarted by Jews, relegated to the position of a minority in their own country. This myth emphasized Jewish ingratitude to their Polish hosts, who had allowed Jews to settle in Polish territory at times when other states in Europe had expelled them. Finally, this myth legitimated the necessity of Poles "fighting back" in order to regain their rightful position in their country.

The tendency to legitimize anti-Jewish violence as national self-defense was first found in the speech and actions of officers and soldiers of the Haller and Wielkopolska (Great Poland) Armies in the eastern territories between 1918 and 1919. In general these officers and soldiers shared the convictions that the Jews as a collectivity were the enemy of the Polish nation-state and that they collaborated with other enemies—the Bolsheviks, the Ukrainians, and the Lithuanians. The chief accusation made against Jews was of Bolshevism, and many units and individuals in these armies treated all Jews as Communists, despite the evident political diversity within Jewish communities and their traditional religious character.[43]

This strong belief that all Jews were Bolsheviks and therefore subversive resulted in the murder of seventy-two Jews in Lwów between 22 and 24 November 1918, while thirty-five were killed in Pińsk on 5 April 1919. Similar hostilities, albeit resulting in fewer casualties, took place in other towns. Some soldiers and officers, even of high rank, were extremely brutal toward members of the Jewish population not only during the riots but also in their aftermath. For example, in Lida, which was entered by the Polish Army in April 1919, soldiers under the command of General Dąbrowski stopped several elderly Jews on 11 June and cut off their beards with swords and knives. [44] The wartime situation also increased aggression and hostility toward Jews as an internal enemy because of the widely publicized myth that all Polish Jews were Communists in league with Poland's external enemy Soviet Russia. [45] Robberies constituted one element of the attacks on the Jewish population. Arthur L. Goodhart, a captain in the U.S. Army who was a member of the American commission headed by Henry Morgenthau to investigate the violence, reported in his 1920 book that soldiers stole boots even from the dead. [46]

The massacres and other hostilities caused an uproar in the Polish parliament, where Ignacy Daszyński (1866–1936), one of the leaders of the PPS, demanded an end to the violence of the army, whose members he referred to as "hooligans in uniform." [47] These condemnations, however, did not stop the soldiers, officers, and heads of the armies from believing that they acted in national self-defense during the riots and in their aftermath. In his written reply to the speaker of the parliament of 2 July 1919 General Józef Leśniewski, minister of war, defended the anti-Jewish violence of the Polish units in Lida on the grounds that the Polish Army had the right to kill their adversaries. In his justification of the riots he referred to Jews as a Communist or Communist-minded community that was disloyal to Poland and therefore deserved to be punished:

> Others were killed because Communist-minded Jews fought in the battles on the side of the Bolsheviks. Several people of this type died during the military clashes: others were killed by the Polish soldiers who rushed into the town. The latter, when they come across armed civilians, who shoot the soldiers and whom the soldiers suspect of being their enemies, would naturally kill their adversaries, real or imagined, out of [a] sense of self-preservation. Additionally, it should be mentioned that our soldiers were outraged by the discovery of corpses of our soldiers who had been taken prison[er] by the Bolsheviks the day before. The prisoners were murdered in the most barbaric manner under conditions that suggest the local Jews were involved. [48]

In his private memoirs Lieutenant Antoni Jakubowski wrote about the Lwów killings in even more emotional language: "The Jewish perfidy was even bigger than the Ukrainian one. . . . The Jews were rightly punished. The whole suburb had to be pacified by military action."[49] These statements suggest that National Democracy, with its anti-Jewish views, enjoyed support among officers and soldiers of the Haller and Wielkopolska Armies. The PPS's leading journal, *Robotnik* (A Worker), openly discussed the popularity of National Democratic views within the Polish military. Most contributors to *Robotnik* raised the issue of total unequivocal condemnation of anti-Jewish riots. In his correspondence from Lwów of 19 December 1918 Roman Halny, one of the PPS journalists, wrote:

> Robbery, damage to properties estimated at millions zlotys is nothing in comparison to the most cruel side of the event—the mass murder of innocent victims. The mass murder is a stain on our honor and a disgrace to the flag that flies over Polish Lwów. Hiding these events will not lead to anything good. Such a strategy can only cause damage to the Polish cause. . . . Let's not hide the truth behind lies. . . . We have to speak the truth in a loud voice and punish those who were involved in the mass murder. . . . The view that only bandits released from prison and hooligans were responsible for the riots, presented in the National Democratic press, will not lead to anything good. It is beyond a doubt that soldiers of Polish military units took part in these shameful events and that the pogroms were caused by "bandits"—not just those who were released from prison but those who should go to prison.[50]

Halny's position on national shame and honor meant that the entire truth about the riots should be disclosed and that nothing should be hidden under the carpet. The majority of Polish politicians, however, when talking with representatives of foreign states and international organizations who were shocked by the news of the treatment of Jews by the Polish military, generally either minimized anti-Jewish hostilities and attributed them to "hooligans in the army" or spoke about the "foreign powers responsible for them" or even denied them. This was the case not only with politicians from National Democracy but also with politicians who were committed to a civic model of Poland and opposed anti-Semitism. For example, in his response to a protest against anti-Jewish violence in Galicia voiced by the Swedish Social Democrats in the summer of 1919 Daszyński insisted that Austrians had masterminded the violence.[51] Goodhart, who accompanied the American commission to investigate the violence, wrote about a similar response from Professor Szymon Aszkenazy

(1866?–1935), an assimilated Polish Jew born into an Orthodox family who became an acclaimed interwar Polish historian. Aszkenazy, who held a very rare high position as a Jew, acting as an official Polish representative at the League of Nations between 1920 and 1923, claimed, as reported by Goodhart, that "only a small proportion of the Poles were really nationalists" and that nationalism "both on the part of Poles and also Jews was a temporary result of the war."[52]

Responses of individuals like Daszyński and Aszkenazy can be explained away as politically naive. They can also be seen as an attempt on their part to save national honor, which was supposed to be achieved by presenting Poland in the best light to the international world, even if such a presentation differed from reality, a phenomenon that was to continue in the post-1939 period.[53] Such official responses were met with skepticism on the part of the representatives of Western Jewry, who were well informed about the hostilities. Jews in Western Europe, many of whom had been exposed positively to the idea of the Polish state on the eve of Poland's regaining its independence, began to lose sympathy for Poland as a result of the news about the anti-Jewish hostilities conducted in the eastern territories between 1918 and 1920.[54] They were critical of the Polish government's inaction in the face of the riots and organized demonstrations against violence and various events in support of Eastern European Jews. National Democracy interpreted the organized reactions of Western Jewry, particularly American Jews, as an affront and as interference in Polish domestic affairs, to be termed as "antipolonism." This understanding of "antipolonism" continued to develop in various Polish political circles in the post-1939 period.

The legitimization of anti-Jewish hostilities as national self-defense can also be found in the peasant social rebellion in Małopolska in April and May 1919. Records of the investigation reveal that members of National Democracy justified the peasants' violence against Jews on the grounds that Jews constituted a political threat to the nation. For example, Desydery Ostrowski, headmaster of a local high school and leader of the local section of National Democracy, stated in the autumn of 1919: "In my opinion the Jewish menace is one that is hostile to us, and socialism—also hostile to us—is supported mainly by the Jews. During the war we saw the Jews as they betrayed us and supported the Germans."[55]

The National Democrats also used national self-defense as grounds for the anti-Jewish student riots of the 1930s. In the aftermath of the first major

rioting the Supreme Council of National Democracy passed a resolution on
22 November 1931 stating:

> The number of Jews in this country and their strong position in its economic
> life, which has only strengthened under the present government, are threat-
> ening our economic future. Their destructive influence on the population's
> morals and on national spiritual life, and their hostile attitude toward the
> Polish raison d'être, prove that the rightful aim of Polish national politics has
> to be opposition to the Jewish Threat. Therefore the Supreme Council sees
> in the latest student "events" a sign of the battle for Polishness and proof that
> the majority of Polish youths are highly patriotic. This for us is reassurance
> that the political and cultural future of our Homeland will be secured and
> that the State will become a national [ethno-national] one.[56]

Adam Doboszyński, the chief instigator of the "march on Myślenice" (marsz
na Myślenice) of 22 and 23 June 1936 and a member of the National Democracy
party, also used national self-defense as his justification. Under Doboszyński's
command 150 people terrorized the local Jewish community and destroyed all
its material goods. The Myślenice police could not stop the attack because
they were disarmed by Doboszyński's men. In the aftermath Doboszyński
was proclaimed a national hero in National Democracy circles and was later
appointed to the position of vice-chairman of the party. It is worth adding
that after his return to Poland in 1946 Doboszyński was placed in charge of
restructuring the executive council of the party.[57]

The perpetrators of the Przytyk pogrom expressed the same idea—that their
actions were defending the Polish state—through their lawyers during the trial
in June 1936. According to the historian Joshua Rothenberg:

> The Endek lawyers acting for the Polish defendants repeatedly attacked not
> only the Jewish defendants, but the Jewish people as a whole. One of their
> most frequent accusations was that most Jews were Communists and that the
> Jewish defendants were either Communists or were manipulated by Commu-
> nists. The Jewish religion was also attacked. The question of the right of Jews
> to remain in Poland was raised on numerous occasions.
>
>   According to several Jewish newspaper correspondents, the Polish defen-
> dants, and even more so the witnesses, conducted themselves defiantly, like
> heroes to whom the future of Poland was entrusted.[58]

The sentences of the Przytyk defendants exemplified the common tendency
to be more lenient toward ethnic Poles participating in anti-Jewish riots than
toward Jewish codefendants. Fourteen Jews and forty-two Poles were brought

to trial in the district court in Radom, the trial ending on 26 June. A Jew named Leska, who was accused of killing a Pole, Wieśniak, was sentenced to eight years in prison; two other Jews were sentenced to five and six years respectively for shooting at farmers. Four Poles accused of killing a Jewish couple, the Minkowskis, were acquitted because of an alleged lack of evidence. In addition, three Jews and eighteen Poles were acquitted. Eight Jews received six- to ten-month prison sentences, and twenty-two Poles received six months to a year in prison. [59] Although Jews and left-wing political and social organizations such as the PPS protested the sentences, those of the Poles were not revised, except for a few, which were slightly increased. In such cases the judicial institution gave a clear impression of minimizing the criminal nature of interethnic violence, thereby making such violence socially acceptable. Żyndul suggests that some judges saw ideological reasons, such as acting in national self-defense, as extenuating circumstances. [60] This indicates that such judges were themselves supporters of National Democracy or felt obliged to support the National Democratic position on anti-Jewish violence.

In the wake of specific riots or violent incidents perpetrators and their lawyers and journalists representing the ethno-nationalist press shifted responsibility for anti-Jewish violence onto Jews. For example, *Mały Dziennik* reported from the trial concerning the Grodno riot of June 1935, which erupted after the funeral of a Pole killed by two Jews over a personal matter: "If the Jews of Grodno had condemned the murder of Kuszcza [the surname of the dead Pole] and had joined in the funeral procession, the excesses would not have taken place. Immediately after the murder of Kuszcza a story was circulated that the murder was committed over a woman at a dancing hall. The Jews themselves are responsible for the excesses. The streets on which the funeral procession took place and where an angry wave of people was walking were crowded during the evening hours. Therefore it was difficult to see and to judge what people were doing. . . . Testimonies of Jewish witnesses should therefore be dismissed." [61]

Perpetrators and supporters of physical violence shifted responsibility for anti-Jewish violence onto Jews, but so did some political groups and social institutions that in principle condemned the use of physical violence. This included the Roman Catholic Church. The most salient examples are the responses to the Przytyk pogrom by Primate August Hlond, Archbishop Adam Sapieha of Cracow (1867–1951), and the Catholic Press Agency and the response of Cardinal Aleksander Kakowski (1862–1938) to a delegation of rabbis in June 1934. In the aftermath of the Przytyk pogrom Cardinal Hlond and Archbishop Sapieha issued similar pastoral letters. [62] These letters contained a general statement condemning physical violence and an endorsement of an economic boycott of Jews. The letters accused the Jewish community of atheism, Bolshevism, corruption, and dissemination of pornography. Those parts of the letters dedicated to the condemnation of violence are short and written in vague terms, whereas their criticism of Jews is direct and explicit. The Polish-Jewish press received these letters as statements that could only contribute to an increase in interethnic hostility.

The response of the Catholic Press Agency (Katolicka Agencja Prasowa) to the Przytyk pogrom raised even more controversy. As in the case of the pastoral letters, its statement contained a message condemning the physical attacks against Jews but at the same time demanded the cultural separation of the Polish majority from the Jews and the social and economic emancipation of the ethnic Polish population. [63]

Finally, when a delegation of rabbis from the Union of Rabbis of the Polish Republic (Związek Rabinów Rzeczypospolitej) visited Cardinal Kakowski on 7 June 1934 and asked him to influence the National Democracy youth movement not to orchestrate anti-Jewish disturbances, his response was full of contradictions. On the one hand, he entirely condemned anti-Jewish riots; on the other hand, he spoke about Jewish provocation and charged the Jewish community with the crimes of insulting Christian feelings, spreading atheism, and supporting Communism. [64] The Polish Church responded to anti-Jewish violence by condemning it on the grounds of a long Christian tradition of protecting Jews from violence, going back to the earliest Christian councils and popes, while at the same time blaming Jews for causing anti-Jewish incidents. [65]

Responses to anti-Jewish violence by the post-1935 Sanacja government were similar to those of the Church. On the one hand, the leaders of the OZN condemned incidents of anti-Jewish violence as socially destabilizing occurrences that led to slander of the good name of Poland and the nation. On the other hand, they insisted on the right of the Polish nation to self-defense against Jews. The latter view is expressed in the well-known statement of 4 June 1936 made in the parliament by Prime Minister Felicjan Sławoj-Składkowski (1885–1962): "Economic struggle, certainly yes, but without inflicting harm." [66] All these cases provide good evidence that certain individuals and organizations that condemned anti-Jewish violence perceived Jews as the threatening other in much the same way as did individuals and organizations that advocated and perpetrated violence. Within their circles condemnation of anti-Jewish violence was never absolute; most authors shifted at least some responsibility for anti-Jewish violence onto the Jewish minority.

Wiktor Alter (1890–1941), one of the leaders of the Bund, the Jewish Socialist Party, observed similarities between National Democratic perceptions of Jews and those of organizations and parties that advocated nonviolence. In his work *Antysemityzm gospodarczy w świetle cyfr* (Anti-Semitism in the Light of Statistics) he referred to the former group as "zoological anti-Semites" (zoologiczni antysemici), while he called the latter "cultural anti-Semites" (kulturalni antysemici): "The National Democracy party goes straight to the point: we hate the Jews and do not wish to know them. . . . They hate Jews in an obsessive and paranoid way. . . . Therefore it is not surprising that this blind hatred . . . is manifested in attacks on women, children, and the elderly. . . .'Cultural anti-Semites' (primarily supporters of Sanacja and the Peasant Party) condemn such excesses. They disagree with the means—the use of violence. However, they agree with the content of the Endek message, with the 'dejudaization' of Poland, and justify the 'dejudaization' on economic grounds."[67]

Controversial responses to anti-Jewish violence can also be found among some members of the cultural elite, such as the father of Polish Positivism, Świętochowski. In his statement of 16 April 1937 Świętochowski stated that anti-Jewish violence was "natural and understandable" because of the size and moral-cultural makeup of Jews. This represents a drastic change in his views, radically different from those he held in the 1880s.[68] Świętochowski also criticized liberals for condemning anti-Jewish violence without providing a viable solution to the "Jewish question": "The Jews and their defenders . . . unfold in vivid images the monstrosity of these acts [of anti-Jewish violence]; they remind the Polish people of a whole catechism of religious commandments and a whole code of civil duties. . . . Most people do not care. . . . They harbor open or quiet sympathy and recognition for the anti-Semitic perpetrators."[69]

On the other hand, progressive liberal members of the Polish academic and literary communities unequivocally condemned anti-Jewish violence. Furthermore, the PPS and the Democratic Party, and the social organizations that adhered to their ethos, also engaged in condemnation of violence. They organized special lectures protesting anti-Jewish hostilities, days of solidarity with Jews, and special fund-raising for Jewish victims of violence.[70]

Jewish Provocation

The most salient element of justification of anti-Jewish violence as national self-defense was the concept of "Jewish provocation." Ethno-nationalists used this concept as a direct explanation of hostilities, generally defining it in a very broad sense to suit any situation. They classified the social and political actions of individual Jews in the same terms as those of Jewish organizations— as provocations against the Polish nation. For example, ethno-nationalists cited Jews' alleged or real support for foreign powers, particularly the Soviets, the Ukrainians, and the Germans, as Jewish provocation. They played up Jewish participation in the Communist and Socialist Parties as another Jewish provocation. Parliamentary speeches by Jewish MPs that criticized the actions of National Democracy, the OWP, and the ONR were also viewed as provocation. Ethno-nationalists grouped together the critical reactions of the Polish-Jewish press to anti-Jewish propaganda and the crimes committed by individual Jews against ethnic Poles as Jewish provocations against the Polish nation.

The National Democratic press also interpreted the assassination of the first democratically elected president of the Second Polish Republic, Gabriel Narutowicz (1865–1922), by the National Democrat Eligiusz Niewiadomski on 16 December 1922 at the Warsaw art gallery Zachęta as a Jewish provocation.[71] Narutowicz, a PPS member, had been elected president of Poland on 9 December 1922. He won the election against Maurycy Zamoyski, the candidate of National Democracy, with the support of left-wing, Jewish, and other minority votes. Immediately after the results of the election became known National Democracy organized a wave of antipresidential demonstrations in Warsaw. Its press insisted that Narutowicz represented Jewish and not Polish interests. On 11 December 1922 the *Gazeta Warszawska* stated:

> Who would expect that the first elected president of the Polish Republic would be greeted with silence by the Polish parliament . . . and with waves of protesting demonstrators on the streets. . . . Who would dare to think that the majority, the Poles, would not be responsible for casting the decisive vote on their presidential candidate. . . . Among newspapers published in Polish only two expressed unreserved joy at the outcome of the presidential election: the Zionist *Nasz Kurier* and Rosner's *Kurier Polski*. . . . The Polish nation has to defend itself against the Jewish invasion. The Jews have made a terrible political mistake and have provoked an outburst of anger against them. Poles . . . who allowed the election to be won by Narutowicz have sinned against Poland.[72]

After the political assassination of Narutowicz the National Democratic press insisted that Jews carried the responsibility for it; they had provoked the murder. The twisted logic behind such reasoning was, first, that it was primarily Jews who had voted for Narutowicz and that therefore he was the president of Jews and other nonethnic Poles, not president of the Poles, the true owners of the newly independent Polish state; and second, that as the assassination of heads of state was rare in Polish history—a historical fact—it had to be Jews who were responsible for this assassination. Jews were responsible for provoking a reaction among Poles so out of character with the Polish cultural ethos. Therefore Jews bore responsibility for the crime:

> The murder of the president of the Polish Republic is an event that stands outside political ramifications. This matter has to be seen through the aspect of national sentiments. . . . Outside of the political scene this is a nation with an emotional body and one that has expressed its reactions, even reactions that are politically irresponsible. . . . Our nation has been put under a terrible test, perhaps the most terrible in its entire history. At the moment when finally after years of captivity historical events have given our nation a chance of being an independent sovereign state, this chance has immediately been jeopardized [by the election of Narutowicz] because of the Jewish votes. The Polish nation has been subjugated to a terrible dilemma: to be or not to be, to be sovereign or to give over our sovereignty to the Jews.[73]

Violence and National Martyrdom

In the interwar period core ethno-nationalists identified ethnic Poles who died as a result of active participation in anti-Jewish riots as national heroes and martyrs. The most obvious example is the case of Stanisław Wacławski. Wacławski, a student of the law faculty at the University of Stefan Batory in Wilno, was fatally injured on the second day of the anti-Jewish rioting on the university campus that began on 9 November 1931.[74] His funeral, attended by approximately two thousand students, turned into a national demonstration that had to be dispersed by the police.[75] In the propaganda of All-Polish Youth Wacławski was instantly turned into a national martyr who had died for the cause of the "dejudaization" of Polish universities. News of his death traveled quickly to other academic centers in Lwów, Poznań, and Lublin—where combined anti-Jewish and antigovernment demonstrations took place. Violence also spread to the provincial cities and towns of the Białystok, Kielce, and Łódź districts, where agitated youths smashed windows of Jewish properties and propagated slogans such as "Beat up the Jews and save Poland."[76] In

Date and Place	Events
9 November 1932, University of Warsaw	Members of the OWP from the Faculty of Law throw their Jewish colleagues out of the lecture halls. Twenty Jewish students are injured.
10 November 1932, University of Warsaw	After the Mass dedicated to Wacławski at St. Anne's Church, two thousand students gather in an academic hostel. Attempts to organize street demonstrations are prevented by the police.
14–17 November 1932, University of Warsaw	There is an atmosphere of hostility at the medical and law faculties and fights between Polish and Jewish students. Polish students from the democratic student organizations Myśl Mocarstwowa and Akademicka Młodzież Państwowa sign a petition condemning the anti-Jewish actions of students associated with National Democracy.
12 November 1932, University of Lwów	After the Mass approximately one thousand students form a march to the Dom Technika, where a plaque commemorating Wacławski's death is to be unveiled. The police break up the crowd and confiscate the plaque. Students continue on to other parts of the city, where they smash 120 windows of Jewish properties and beat up Jewish passersby. Police arrest thirty-three students. Anti-Jewish demonstrations last the whole day.
13 November 1932, University of Lwów	Anti-Jewish demonstration takes place throughout the day. Police arrest twenty-three Polish students. The president of the university, Drojankowski, issues a statement condemning the anti-Jewish excesses.

many places police arrested the most violent students, as well as high school pupils who had been drawn into the events by groups of older students. On 14 November the biggest Mass in commemoration of Wacławski's death, attended by seven thousand students, was held in the church of St. Anne, in Warsaw.[77] One year later, on the first anniversary of his death, anti-Jewish violence of varying degrees broke out in the major universities. The table above illustrates examples from the universities of Warsaw and Lwów.[78]

Over the next few years radical ethno-nationalist students continued to refer to Wacławski as a symbol of the national struggle against Jews and as a martyr whose death should be avenged. One ONR leaflet referred to him as a hero and explicitly incited the public to anti-Jewish violence: "On the anniversary of Wacławski's death, Jewish blood must flow. On that day Jewish homes and businesses acquired by wrongs done to Poles, and even by their deaths, must burn."[79]

Jews as a Physical Threat to the Polish Nation

The intensified anti-Jewish propaganda of National Democracy and its off-shoot radical organizations in the 1930s characterized Jews as an economic, political, and cultural threat to the Polish nation and, in a new rhetorical move, also as a physical one. The radical ethno-nationalists interpreted individual murders of Poles by Jews as a sign of the strength and aggressiveness of the Jewish minority. As Emanuel Melzer has observed, the ethno-nationalist propaganda and its audience discounted the real motives behind these killings, such as individual self-defense or individual criminality.[80] To define cases of individual murders of ethnic Poles as a conflict between the Polish and Jewish communities was to touch "raw ethnic sentiment." The notion of "the Jew as the murderer of one of us" engendered heated, spontaneous, and violent reactions against the Jewish community. The dissemination of this notion triggered the most brutal beatings and killings in the interwar period. Following are three examples of such cases from the 1930s.

On 26 November 1932 three Polish students were injured in a fight with Jewish artisans on the streets of Lwów.[81] One of them, Jan Grotkowski, a veterinary student, was mortally wounded. The next day members of the student self-help association and the OWP urged their colleagues to avenge the death of Grotkowski with the slogan "blood for blood" (krew za krew). The reaction to this was instant; several hundred students from the University of Jan Kazimierz took to the streets, mercilessly beating up Jewish passersby and smashing the windows of Jewish shops. Further anti-Jewish rioting continued for another four days, despite police attempts to stop it and despite condemnation by the rector of Lwów University and by the Catholic archbishop of the Lwów diocese. News of Grotkowski's death spread to other universities in the state, and in Warsaw and Cracow Jewish students were beaten up and thrown out of the universities. Other anti-Jewish demonstrations took place at academic centers in Cracow, Lublin, Poznań, Warsaw, and Wilno.

In Przytyk on 9 March 1936 an initial clash between Jews and Poles at the market turned into a full-scale bloody riot after a Jew, Szolem Lesko, killed a Polish peasant, Stanisław Wieśniak.[82] The sight of Wieśniak's corpse being publicly carried by his weeping family to the doctor's house, along with cries of "They've killed one of us!," enraged the crowd, mostly peasants from nearby villages. In its anger the mob launched a large-scale attack on the two Jewish neighborhoods of Podgajek and Zachęta. According to a conclusive statement issued by the deputy public prosecutor, S. Dotkiewicz, the riot proceeded in the following way: "Here groups, twenty to thirty strong, armed mainly with stanchions, ran along the street, forcing their way into houses. Dozens of Jewish apartments had windows and doors wrenched from their frames by metal bars, pegs, stones weighing twelve kilograms or more, and even shafts. . . . Inside the apartments and shops furniture and goods were destroyed; some were looted, although these cases were rare. Some of those wronged maintained that their money from the fair was lost during the sacking. Where the inhabitants were caught, they were beaten up with shouts of: 'Kill them; don't forgive them for what they have done to our brother!' "[83] As a result one Jewish couple, the Minkowskis, were killed, their house completely wrecked. Their children were seriously beaten but were saved by their ethnic Polish neighbor.[84] The violence ceased after police reinforcements were brought to Przytyk from Radom.

In Mińsk Mazowiecki a riot lasting almost four days occurred on 1 June 1936 after Judka Lejb Chaskielewicz shot a Pole, Jan Bujak, out of personal animosity. Only a few hours later a furious crowd smashed windows in all the Jewish shops and private houses. Fearing for their lives three thousand local Jews fled the town. Among the ones who stayed forty-one were injured over the next two days, and some Jewish houses were burned on the last day of the riot.[85]

In the National Democratic propaganda that followed these two deaths became incorporated into a key slogan: "The blood of Bujak and Wieśniak has divided Jews and Poles" (Krew Bujaka i Wieśniaka dzieli Żyda od Polaka).[86] Such slogans aimed to demonstrate that there was no possibility of peaceful coexistence between the two communities and that ethnic hatred and violence were "natural" elements of Polish-Jewish relations.

The postindependence era (1918–39) was the first historical period in which Polish Jews experienced the full force of the most radical form of Polish exclusivist ethno-nationalism in action. In the 1930s, under conditions of thriving exclusivist ethno-nationalism, the Polish government, which was in principle against using violence as a means of solving the so-called Jewish question, had difficulty containing anti-Jewish hostilities. The hostilities resulted in the deterioration of interethnic relations between Poles and Jews on the local, national, and international levels and in the emigration of Jews from Poland to the Yishuv in Palestine and to the West.[87] The myth of Jews as a national threat played an important role in three aspects of anti-Jewish hostilities: their initiation, their evaluation, and their justification.

5. Perceptions of Jews
during the German Occupation of Poland, 1939–45

A New Set of Political and Social Circumstances

For all honest Poles the fate of the Jews going to their death was bound to be
exceedingly painful, since the dying . . . were people whom our people could not
look straight in the face with a clear conscience.

Jerzy Andrzejewski, "Zagadnienia polskiego antysemityzmu"

Introduction

The years between 1918 and 1939 were a crucial period in the dissemination of
the ideology of Polish exclusivist ethno-nationalism. By the end of the Second
Republic both nonelites and a significant section of the Polish political elite and
the Roman Catholic Church perceived Polish Jews as the chief internal enemy
of the Polish nation, harmful to all aspects of its development: political, economic, social, and cultural. Since the ethno-nationalist representation of Jews
was so central to Polish-Jewish relations in interwar Poland and so influential
in the general debate about national life on the eve of WWII, several questions
are compelling: To what extent did the ethno-nationalist vision of Poland
without Jews continue to influence the underground Polish political discourse
in Nazi-occupied Poland? Was it still relevant to plans for the shape of a future
independent Polish nation-state even during the ongoing Nazi genocide of
Polish Jewry? To what extent did it influence attitudes of ordinary members
of society toward Jews, the victims of Nazi genocide? To what extent did the
ethno-nationalist vision contribute to low societal approval of rescue activities?

A wealth of primary sources is available to answer these questions, including
the official documents, reports, and press of the underground Polish state and
the individual testimonies, diaries, and memoirs of both ethnic Poles and
Polish Jews. [1] Analysis of the impact of ethno-nationalist ways of thinking

on Polish society in WWII can provide a better understanding of Polish-Jewish relations during the war and also of the more general problem of the relationship among prejudicial beliefs, prejudicial programs, and prejudicial actions. It can illuminate the nature of the influence of ethno-nationalist perceptions in multiethnic societies under the complex circumstances of war. In the case of Poland the majority ethnic group, the Poles, perceived a minority, the Jews, as the harmful alien; an external social actor, the Nazis, invaded and openly began a program of mass murder and genocide against the Jews, while the Poles, themselves victims of Nazi occupation, also experienced a brutal policy of terror, severe discrimination, and hostility, aimed at the mass murder of Polish political and cultural elites. [2] Wars often strengthen ethnic self-consciousness and ethnic imagery and weaken or destroy the cohesion of multinational societies. [3] Such developments can be particularly intensified in societies in which the "core nation" shows a high level of support for the ethno-nationalization of the state and the exclusion of a minority prior to the outbreak of war. Poland between 1939 and 1945 was such a society.

In the study of Polish-Jewish relations in WWII the representation of the Jew as harmful alien has to be considered one of the main causes for the marginalization of Polish Jews by the ethno-nationalist political camp and by its supporters within the network of the so-called underground Polish state. Polish ethno-nationalists who resisted the Nazi occupation thought of Polish Jews as outside the "universe of Polish national obligations" and did not consider Jewish suffering part of the unfolding tragedy of Poland. [4] The representation of the Jew as harmful alien played a major role in the decision of Poland's underground political parties to exclude Jews from the vision of the future postwar Polish state they endorsed in their political programs. This was true of the National Democrats and the extreme right-wing political parties and also of the Christian Democrats, the leaders of the Peasant Party, and Christian organizations such as the Front for the Rebirth of Poland (Front Odrodzenia Polski, FOP). Negative representations of Jews in the interwar period and in Polish publications during WWII should be viewed as one of the causes of three major developments: the low level of general approval in Polish society for ethnic Poles rescuing Jews from the Nazis; the hostile or indifferent attitude of a significant segment of ethnic Poles toward the fate of their Jewish fellow citizens; and anti-Jewish actions by some Poles, including Polish-initiated anti-Jewish violence during WWII. At the same time the persistent and widespread representation of the Jew as the national enemy in Polish culture cannot be treated as the only and sufficient factor in explaining these phenomena. Explanations of ethnic Poles' attitudes toward their Jewish fellow citizens during this period must take into account the roles of the Nazi and Soviet occupations of Poland, Nazi policies toward Jews and Poles, and the war itself.

One should also bear in mind that even as the negative portrayal of the Jew as the hostile other in Polish society persisted, other representations of Jews were also part of the discourse among members of the Polish political and cultural elite and ordinary members of society during WWII. Advocates of civic nationalism presented Jews as wretched, unfortunate human beings, victims of the terrible atrocities committed by the German occupier/enemy, and intrinsic members of Polish society. Such visions of Jews can be found in the writings of members of the pps, the Democratic Party, and other small left-wing organizations, as well as among members of the liberal cultural elite and ordinary citizens.

One should also recognize that Polish anti-Jewish actions in WWII were not equal or similar to Nazi policies for the genocide of European Jews. At the same time arguments that Polish anti-Jewish perceptions and actions were basically the product of Nazi anti-Semitic propaganda, not rooted in pre-1939 Polish exclusivist ethno-nationalism, are empirically false. Polish underground circles in WWII first presented the argument that Nazi influence was the sole cause of negative Polish actions toward Jews, and later historians in the post-1945 period adopted up this argument. The historical record, however, reveals a different picture: only an insignificant segment of the Polish population was under the direct influence of Nazism. Although there were similarities between some anti-Jewish themes used in the Nazi press and the clandestine core ethno-nationalist Polish press, the main discourse on Polish Jews within the Polish underground state rested in the ideology of Polish exclusivist ethno-nationalism and took on a distinct course of development in WWII.

Of course German propaganda in WWII exploited "domestic" Polish anti-Semitism for its own goals.[5] Soviet propaganda also exploited Polish anti-Semitism and Polish anti-Ukrainian and anti-Belorussian ethno-nationalist policies and practices of the pre-1939 period for two reasons. First, such propaganda sought legitimacy for the Soviet regime among minorities in the eastern territories during the Soviet occupation of 1939–41.[6] Second, in the aftermath of the German invasion of the Soviet state in June 1941, when the Soviet Union became the ally of the free Western powers, the Soviets presented these issues skillfully in negotiations with British and American politicians about the "new postwar order" in Eastern Europe, the Soviets demanding control over western Belarus and western Ukraine. However, Polish anti-Jewish attitudes and behavior in WWII cannot be seen as a Soviet "product" or "construction" either.

Polish anti-Jewish attitudes were also not a product of Jewish "construction" or Jewish "imagination," created by Polish and American Jews in WWII for the purpose of "harming the Polish cause" in the eyes of the Western powers. This claim was common among the right-wing circles led by the National Democracy movement in the Polish underground state in WWII and was also uncritically incorporated into some salient historical interpretations of WWII events in the post-1945 period. One of the more recent explicit examples of the incorporation of the wartime ethno-nationalist perspective is Tomasz Gąsowski's *Pod sztandarami orła białego*, in which the author argues that anti-Semitism in Polish armies in WWII was simply a biased and exaggerated Jewish construction that had no basis in reality.[7] This interpretation ignores historical data, including the voices of Polish PPS politicians such as Józef Beloński (1897–?), a member of the National Council in the Polish government-in-exile who in September 1943 condemned anti-Jewish attitudes and behavior among units of the Polish Army that were led by General Władysław Anders (1892–1970) in the Soviet Union in the second half of 1941. Beloński was also one of the first individuals to challenge the notion of "unique Jewish desertions" from the Polish armed forces, a notion that originated during the war in political circles and later became cited as "historical fact" by historians like Gąsowski. Citing the official number of desertions from the Polish Army provided by the government in the second half of 1943 and juxtaposing the number of Jewish and Polish desertions, Beloński asserted that both ethnic Jews and ethnic Poles deserted the Polish armed forces in similar numbers as the Polish Army passed through Palestine.[8]

Many other Polish historians make claims similar to Gąsowski's attempt to "reverse the cause and result" of anti-Semitism and thus reject the issue of Polish anti-Jewish stereotyping as a crucial aspect of modern Polish ethno-nationalist political and social thought. These historians mention anti-Semitism only in a defensive reaction to what they perceive as unjust anti-Polish accusations and actions. This interpretation is rooted in Polish ethno-nationalist writings going back to the preindependence phase (1880–1918).

Scholarly literature about WWII has neglected the continuing presence and impact of negative tropes about Jews in Polish society for two reasons.[9] First, the subject of Polish-Jewish relations in WWII is a relatively young field of studies. Scholars like Shmuel Krakowski, who have researched this field for some time, recognize the need for further analysis and the methodological challenges the subject poses: "Despite the 50 years which have elapsed since the end of . . . WWII, historians still have a long way to go before they can be seen to have provided a full and objective representation of the intricate problems connected with the relations between the Polish underground and the Jewish population during the most tragic period in its history."[10] Most pioneering historical works on this subject describe anti-Jewish policies and practices and do not analyze the anti-Jewish beliefs and perceptions that shaped such policies and practices. For example, Israel Gutman and Shmuel Krakowski provide the first detailed description of anti-Jewish actions within Polish underground institutions and organizations in Nazi-occupied Poland, while David Engel provides the first detailed historical examination of a similar problem within the Polish government-in-exile.[11]

Second, the lack of empirical analysis of anti-Jewish idioms can be attributed to the dominant approach that developed in the Polish post-1945 historiography of WWII and also in the post-1945 Polish collective memory of WWII. This approach was oriented toward examination neither of the nature of anti-Semitic idioms, policies, and practices nor of their consequences. Instead it was based on the premise that the issue of Polish anti-Semitism was not an important element of Polish social history of the twentieth century but "an exaggerated and biased problem," created by enemies of the Polish cause. This approach was common in sections of the Polish underground political elite in WWII, where it was interwoven with the notion of saving the national Polish honor and good name. In practice this meant suppressing or denying any information about attitudes and actions that would reflect negatively upon ethnic Poles in Nazi-occupied Poland and thus jeopardize the Polish cause in the international arena. The writers and historians who propagated various versions of this approach in the post-1945 period had often themselves been leading, remarkable members of the underground Polish state in WWII. In their writings they produced arguments and interpretations that, in light of the wealth of historical evidence that became available following the end of the Communist regime in Poland, do not stand the test of empirical inquiry.[12] In all, their interpretations do not provide a necessarily complex picture of the history of Poland in WWII and deny the existence of agreed-upon historical truth, implying the existence of "Polish and Jewish truths on the matter." These authors present "apologetics" for Polish anti-Jewish attitudes, practices, and policies and a narrative of denial of any Polish wrongdoing toward Jews.[13] This narrative is characterized by a strong defensive stance on the national level, ranging from minimizing or completely dismissing Polish anti-Jewish attitudes and actions, to the notion that the Polish nation and the Polish underground state acted in a principled way toward Jews during the Holocaust, to charges of "antipolonism" against both Polish and foreign authors who argue differently. Acknowledgment of the destruction of Polish Jewry is intertwined with three types of accusations voiced against Jews: that they lacked gratitude toward those Poles who saved them; that they evidenced anti-Polish behavior and actions during WWII; and that they behaved passively in the face of the Nazi destruction of their own people and even collaborated with the Nazis. The latter two issues are treated in a purely instrumental way, contributing nothing to any kind of empirical analysis of what can be considered the most challenging aspects of Jewish history in the Holocaust. They are simply employed to create an image in which Poles appear in a better light than Jews in the realities of the Nazi occupation.[14]

A glance at Polish post-1945 historiography reveals the impact of ethno-nationalist perspectives. During the Communist era Polish historians wrote history in which Polish Jews were not part of the Polish nation-state, but an alien group that had historically benefited from dwelling in the territory of Poland, although incompatible with the interests and development of Poles. The self-defensive approach of these historians tended to emphasize the notion that the Jewish perspective on the subject of Polish-Jewish relations in WWII was biased and inappropriate, representing Polish anti-Semitism as "unique" and "even more severe" than Nazi anti-Semitism. The development of this approach in the 1980s, 1990s, and early 2000s will be treated in the last chapter.

From the perspective of Polish Jews the issue of Polish anti-Jewish attitudes and actions in WWII has been shocking and emotionally painful. Between 1945 and the 1980s the majority of Jews who expressed an opinion on Polish-Jewish relations during the Nazi occupation reached their conclusions on the basis of their own experiences during the war. This point was made by Israel Gutman, a historian born in pre-1939 Poland who survived the Holocaust in Nazi-occupied Poland.[15]

In Polish-Jewish writing the realization that significant segments of Polish society perceived the Jewish community as outside its fabric and that Poles did not see the Nazi extermination of Polish Jews as part of the Polish national tragedy but were generally indifferent is the most difficult aspect of the experience to understand. This realization has often manifested itself in strongly embittered statements about the Polish lack of solidarity, Polish betrayal of Jews, and ill-concealed Polish joy at seeing Jewish citizens being murdered en masse by the Germans. In *The Holocaust Kingdom* Alexander Donat, a Jewish survivor from Poland, makes a bitter comment on positive reactions among Poles toward the Nazi extermination of Jews: "For years the Poles have been dreaming of getting rid of the Jews and now at last Hitler does it for them. . . . At bottom they are delighted, however horrified by the inhuman cruelty. The Krauts devouring the Kikes: what could be sweeter."[16]

In cases in which survivors experienced blackmail and hostility on the part of Poles, or witnessed or were aware of hostilities, including killings of Jews by Poles, the comments sometimes are much harsher, biased, and historically incorrect. They basically equate Poles with Germans and create the impression that Poles were directly associated with the Nazi extermination of Jews. These are the kind of comments that some in the Western media in the 1960s, 1970s, and 1980s used as a major point of departure for discussions of Poland's relations with its Jews in WWII. For example: "Had it not been for the Poles, for their aid—active and passive—in the 'solution of the Jewish problem,' the Germans would never have been as successful as they were. It was the Poles who called 'Yid' at every Jew who escaped from the train transporting him to the gas chambers, it was they who caught these unfortunate wretches and who rejoiced at every Jewish misfortune. They were vile and contemptible."[17]

This portrayal of the Poles is less nuanced than what one reads in the large body of Jewish diaries, memoirs, testimonies, and literary works on the Holocaust; many individual Jews distinguished between "bad Poles" (źli Polacy) and "good Poles" (dobrzy Polacy) or "good Christians" (dobrzy chrześcijanie). In the former category are Poles who were hostile to Jews in a variety of ways and under different circumstances. In the latter category are individuals who helped in various ways without showing anti-Jewish prejudice, or individuals who were simply sympathetic to their Jewish fellow citizens and their plight. Characteristically it appears that every act of help, empathy, or solidarity and every individual "good Pole" has been remembered and registered in such writings. For example, in her testimony Sonia Orbach states: "As we were sitting in the woods contemplating what to do next, a peasant appeared. . . . He approached us and said: 'I know your family and would like to help you.

If you find a place for yourself in the deep woods I will be happy to bring you food.' . . . He came back without police, and a great friendship started between us. What can I tell you? . . . As they used to say [in Poland], if that man was still alive I would wash his feet and drink the dirty water."[18]

Undoubtedly for many Polish Jews their exclusion from the realm of Polish society during the Nazi occupation of Poland and their experience of Polish indifference toward the Nazi extermination of Jews constituted a morally devastating experience. The need for explanation and understanding of this phenomenon was already present in works written during the Holocaust. In September 1943, in one of his early essays on Polish-Jewish relations, Emanuel Ringelblum (1900–1944), a historian of Polish history in pre-1939 Poland, revealed the extent to which this issue was crucial to the already much diminished remnants of Polish Jewry:

> The Polish people and the Government of the Republic of Poland were not in a position to deflect the Nazi steamroller from its anti-Jewish course. But it is reasonable to ask whether the attitude of the Polish people measured up to the scale of the catastrophe that befell their country's citizens. Was it inevitable that the last impression of the Jews, as they rode in the death trains speeding from different parts of the country to Treblinka or other places of slaughter, should have been the indifference or even joy on the faces of their neighbors? Last summer, when carts packed with captive Jewish men, women and children moved through the streets of the capital, was it really necessary for laughter from wild mobs to resound from the other side of the ghetto walls, was it really necessary for such blank indifference to prevail in the face of the greatest tragedy of all time? A further question is whether some sympathy should not have been expressed during the slaughter of a whole people. . . . We ask further, why was it possible to considerably reduce the evil of denunciations, spying and collaboration with the Germans within one's own community, while nothing was done to check the giant wave of blackmail and denunciation of the handful of Polish Jews that had survived the slaughter of a whole people? These and similar questions are being asked every day by the remaining quarter-of-a-million Jews.[19]

In his essay "The Past Refuses to Vanish" Israeli historian Daniel Blatman discusses the methodological difficulties of inquiry into such questions as those posed by Ringelblum in the Warsaw ghetto but insists that scholars are "duty-bound to investigate Ringelblum's final question: 'why, even as they are being hauled away for extermination, are the Jews still "others" '?"[20] An analysis of the representation of the Jew as the harmful other in wartime Poland can take us to the core of the problem posed by Ringelblum.

The Myth in Political Discourse

In September 1939 the Polish state was invaded by two powers: the Third Reich and the Soviet Union. Germany took control of over 48.4 percent of the territory (188,000 square kilometers), with 62.9 percent of the total population, including 18.7 million ethnic Poles, 2.2 million Polish Jews, 600,000 Germans, and 500,000 Ukrainians. The Soviet Union took control over the eastern Polish territories, amounting to 200,000 square kilometers with a population of 13 million, including approximately 5 million ethnic Poles, 5 million Ukrainians, 2 million Belorussians, and 1 million Jews.[21]

By the first half of October 1939 the German authorities had incorporated the western regions Reichsgau Westprussen, with Danzig (Prusy Zachodnie i Gdańsk), and Reichsgau Wartheland (Kraj Warty) directly into the Reich. In the rest of the occupied territories the Nazi regime established the so-called General Government (Generalna Gubernia, GG). The GG, officially proclaimed on 26 October 1939, was divided into four districts, each named after its major city: Warsaw, Cracow, Radom, and Lublin. In August 1941, in the aftermath of the German invasion of the Soviet Union, the Nazi authorities set up a fifth district, Galicia, with its center in Lwów, where Jewish ghettos were established by the end of the same year. A leading Nazi lawyer, Hans Frank (1900–1946), noted for his fanatical devotion to Hitler, was put in charge of the German administration of the GG. The administration was almost entirely staffed by Germans, though some vestiges of Polish local government were maintained.[22]

In the territories directly incorporated into the Reich in September 1939 the Nazis conducted a policy of ruthless Germanization, personally supervised by the head of the ss, Heinrich Himmler (1900–1945).[23] The Germans saw the majority of Poles in these territories as irreconcilable enemies and subjugated them with brutal killings and expulsion to the GG. The remaining minority of Poles, including women and children above the age of twelve, were forced into compulsory labor. The Germans expelled all Jews who lived in these territories to the GG and brutally killed many, beginning as early as September 1939.

The Nazi authorities regarded the occupation of Poland as the first step on the way to creating the "*Herrenvolk* empire," in which the Germans as a "superior race" were to rule over "racially inferior" groups, the Slavs. According to this project, Polish lands were viewed as *Lebensraum* for the Germans and the

Polish population as a nation of slaves whose physical potential should be used to maintain the economic needs of the Reich. In the GG Germans pressed Poles to work for them and seized 1.2 million individuals for forced labor. They were deported to the Reich, where they were subjected to harsh working and living conditions. In all, the Germans sent 2.5 million Poles to compulsory work in the Reich from all the occupied territories. Many of them did not survive the years of labor, whereas others, who did survive, came back in wretched health. An estimated 200,000 racially desirable Slavic children, mainly Polish, were also sent to the Reich for "Aryanization"; only approximately 40,000 of these children were recovered after the war.[24]

Besides physical exploitation of the ethnic Polish population, the Germans embarked on another project aimed at the destruction of Polish cultural elites and the national culture. The arrest of 183 professors of the Jagiellonian University on 6 September 1939 marked the beginning of this process and was followed by the arrests and killings of thousands of teachers, university professors, military officers, and members of the clergy and aristocracy. The German occupiers closed down Polish secondary schools and universities; education was limited to primary and vocational schools only. All Polish political and cultural institutions were banned, and "high-culture" activities were forbidden. In May 1940 the Nazis began the campaign Aktion (Ausserodentliche Befriedungsaktion, AB), designed to kill the Polish intelligentsia, viewed as "the spiritual and political leaders of the Polish resistance movement."[25] In June of the same year Polish political prisoners were interned in a newly opened concentration camp (Auschwitz I). Germans also placed Russian prisoners of war in this camp, but Poles constituted the majority of prisoners between the summer of 1940 and 1941, and approximately 270,000 of them perished. The Germans met Polish resistance to the German "grand plan" with increasing discrimination and terror. Frequent searches, roundups, and mass executions of civilians became the means of controlling the conquered population.[26]

As harsh as Nazi treatment of ethnic Poles was, the Nazis brought to bear an even greater level of terror and legislative discrimination against Polish Jews from the beginning of the Nazi occupation of Poland. During the first two years of the war, as a result of extremely harsh Nazi policy aimed at destroying Polish culture and Polish political and cultural elites, some ethnic Poles thought that they were suffering in equal measure or even more than Polish Jews. For example, Jerzy Stempowski (1894–1969), the liberal writer and essayist known for his sympathetic attitude toward the fate of Jews during and after the war, expressed such an opinion. In a letter from Lisbon to the Ministry of Information in the Polish government-in-exile Stempowski wrote: "Jews appear to be better off because they are confined in ghettos. The ghettos supply the Germans with a labor force but the police do not enter them."[27] By the end of 1939 the Germans had promulgated laws forcing Polish Jews to wear a yellow star and conscripting all Jewish males between the ages of fourteen and sixty to compulsory labor.[28] During the first half of 1940 the German occupiers denied Jews unlimited movement and forbade them to enter restaurants, parks, and the so-called better streets. Nazi laws forbade Jewish medical doctors to treat non-Jewish patients and denied Jewish lawyers the right to practice. The Jewish community was also exposed to what Helen Fein calls increasing violence for profit and for play, frequently exercised by the ss.[29] German control of food rationing led to growing discrepancy between the rations allocated to Poles and Jews by the second half of 1940.[30]

In 1940 the German occupiers implemented the ghettoization of Polish Jewry, establishing four hundred ghettos within Polish territory. During this process the Germans relocated many Jewish communities from small villages and towns to larger towns and cities. By the end of 1940 the Nazis had sealed off many ghettos from the rest of the Nazi-occupied population, including the Warsaw ghetto, with the largest Jewish population in Europe.[31] Slave labor, hunger, and reoccurring epidemics of typhus were the main features of daily existence behind the ghetto walls during 1941. In 1942 the Nazis launched the Reinhard Action operation, designed to exterminate the entire Jewish population.[32] The ghettos were liquidated under the disguise of "resettlement in the East," their inhabitants transferred to the major operating death camps in Bełżec, Sobibór, Treblinka, and Auschwitz II–Birkenau.[33] The entire process was marked by extreme brutality. In July 1942 the Warsaw ghetto fell victim to the "Great Deportation" plan; during a period lasting less than three months 250,000 Warsaw Jews were sent to the death camp in Treblinka. At the end of 1942 it became clear that the majority of Polish Jews had perished and that only a small number still lived in the remaining ghettos. The Nazis continued to clear these ghettos throughout 1943 and 1944; the Łódź ghetto was the last to be destroyed, in August 1944. To escape Nazi extermination some segments of the Jewish population went into hiding: in the forests, bunkers, and sewers and on the Aryan side. In the case of children a number of Catholic monasteries and shelters for Christian orphans also provided refuge. In all, approximately 2.9 million Polish Jews perished; this figure represents 90 percent of the entire pre-

1939 community. Including Polish Jews, Poland lost approximately 6 million people; of these only 660,000 were killed in military operations in WWII.[34]

Despite the first traumatic experiences of the war and the Nazi and Soviet occupations Polish society was capable of creating a "secret state" that had a highly developed network of political, military, and social institutions.[35] By the end of the war three hundred various clandestine organizations existed in Polish territories.[36] They were divided into two major political camps: the non-Communist camp, composed of the majority of prewar political parties; and the Communist camp, represented by one main party, the Polish Workers' Party (Polska Partia Robotnicza, PPR), supported by the Soviet Union. In the course of the war the Communist camp became the major political rival of the anti-Communist camp. This chapter concentrates on the non-Communist camp, since it was identified by the majority of society as the successor of the sovereign pre-1939 state.

The Polish government-in-exile, headed by General Władysław Sikorski as its first prime minister, wielded ultimate authority over the non-Communist camp. From late 1939 the government was based in France, in Angers. After the Germans defeated the French in June 1940 the government was transferred to London, which remained its main base throughout WWII and beyond.[37] The government-in-exile represented a break with the prewar Sanacja government. Its coalition consisted of four political parties: the Peasant Party (SL), the Labor Party (SP), the National Democrats (Endecja, SN), and the Polish Socialist Party (PPS). Inside Nazi-occupied Poland the Delegate's Bureau (Delegatura), appointed by the government-in-exile, held supreme political authority. It oversaw the majority of underground political parties active in the GG, except for some of the most radical right-wing parties. The Home Army (Armia Krajowa, AK), commanded by the government-in-exile, was the main military resistance force, consisting of different military groups originally organized under the authority of individual political parties. By 1943 membership in the AK had reached 350,000 individuals, making it the largest resistance organization in Nazi-occupied Europe.[38]

The underground Polish state created a set of "Ten Commandments" dictating how an honest and patriotic Pole should behave during the Nazi occupation. The "Decalogue" was published on 1 May 1940 in the newspaper *Polska Żyje* (Poland Is Alive).[39] The "Decalogue" played an important role in public life for at least those groups that were actively involved in underground activities. The seventh commandment forbade denouncing Poles to Germans, and the eighth demanded mutual cooperation and societal solidarity. It seems from the memoirs of both Polish Jews and Christian Poles, however, that most Poles did not count Polish Jews as fellow Poles to whom such solidarity was owed.

How were Polish Jews perceived within the chief institutions of the underground state? To what extent did the ethno-nationalist construction of the Jew as the harmful alien continue to have an impact on political discourse within the underground state?

The Government-in-Exile and the Myth

The position of the Polish government-in-exile was delicate; the Western powers recognized the government as an ally, but it was a dependent entity, not their equal partner. Its position became particularly delicate after the Soviet Union joined the Western powers in an anti-Nazi coalition in the summer of 1941 and became a major player in the war against Hitler.

From the beginning of the government's activities in France in late 1939 it became clear to Polish politicians that their attitude toward Jews and stance toward anti-Semitism were important markers of how the government-in-exile and its institutions would be judged by Western powers.[40] In British, American, and Western Jewish circles the government-in-exile was expected to break with the anti-Semitic heritage of its post-1935 predecessor. However, prominent members of the government-in-exile held ambivalent and prejudicial attitudes toward Jews that stood in opposition to the values of the civic and pluralistic concept of the Polish nation. As in interwar Poland some perceived Jews as a group that demanded special privileges and made "provocative demands on the government." A close look at the 9 January 1940 minutes of the parliament of the government-in-exile shows that Stanisław Stroński (1882–1955), deputy prime minister, understood as Jewish provocations requests presented by representatives of Polish Jewry that discriminatory laws and regulations imposed in pre-1939 Poland, such as "numerus clausus," be abolished.[41] What the deputy prime minister perceived as "the most incredible provocation" on the part of Jews was the request for a certain percentage of Jewish civil servants to be employed in Polish institutions. Minister Stroński labeled this "a provocative demand that is simply unthinkable."[42] Stroński also saw Jewish soldiers' complaints about anti-Semitic attitudes in the Polish Army in France in late 1939 and early 1940 as "a Jewish provocation."[43] As in interwar Poland such an approach aimed at transferring blame upon Jews for causing anti-

Semitism; here the deputy prime minister blamed Jewish opposition to anti-Jewish policies and anti-Jewish attitudes and behavior as the main cause of anti-Semitism.

This approach also constituted the major premise of the response to similar complaints voiced by Jewish soldiers in the Anders Army, which was formed in the territory of the Soviet Union but later evacuated through Persia to the West.[44] The Anders Army was created of former prisoners who had been granted amnesty by the Soviet Union in the aftermath of the Polish-Soviet pact of 30 July 1941.[45] It appears that only PPS politicians in the government-in-exile were capable of evaluating anti-Jewish attitudes and behavior in the Anders Army as a product of false and prejudicial perceptions of Jews rooted in the ideology of the National Democrats. PPS politicians unequivocally condemned manifestations of anti-Jewish behavior in the Polish wartime armed forces and other institutions. In September 1943 the earlier-discussed Józef Beloński, a PPS representative in parliament, demanded that members of right-wing political parties be banned from organizing educational activities in the Anders Army since they were responsible for anti-Semitic occurrences and incitement to hatred. But Beloński's position on anti-Semitism in the Anders Army radically differed from that of General Anders. In a secret memo of 30 November 1941 General Anders called upon his ethnic Polish soldiers to avoid provoking Jews (*nie drażnić Żydów*) so they would not claim that Polish soldiers were anti-Semites. According to Anders, anti-Semitism was not a prejudicial ideology and action that deserved condemnation, but the product of Jewish anti-Polish activities in the eastern territories between 1939 and 1940. He sympathized with his soldiers' negative attitudes toward Jews. However, because of Poland's position vis-à-vis the Western Allies, Anders urged soldiers to restrain their anti-Jewish behavior. He believed that Jews constituted a powerful political lobby in the Anglo-Saxon world that could damage the Polish cause in the international arena. Thus anti-Semitic actions had to be curbed for the time being.[46]

As in the interwar period ethno-nationalist circles viewed Polish and Western Jews as "a powerful united group" that could harm the interests of Poland. This perception totally ignored the ideological and political diversity of Polish and Western Jewish communities and the various, sometimes opposing views among them. The government-in-exile viewed the Jewish, Ukrainian, and Belorussian populations in the eastern territories, occupied by the Soviet Union until summer 1941, as a group disloyal to Poland. This generalization prevailed despite evidence that painted a much more complex picture of the attitudes and actions of Jews under the Soviet regime. For example, on 9 January 1940, during the parliamentary session in Angers, General Sikorski acknowledged that according to received information 70 percent of Jews behaved decently under the Soviet occupation (*zachowują się przyzwoicie*), whereas 30 percent showed sympathy with Communists and "often provoke[d] Poles."[47] However, the negative representation of Jews as the harmful other seemed to play a far more important role in the relations of Polish officials with representatives of Jewish organizations in WWII than did the image of Jews as loyal citizens.

As they had during the interwar period, ethno-nationalists in the government-in-exile tended to perceive Jews as a powerful group with great influence over the Western Allies.[48] They treated Jews with suspicion, as a group that did not want to help the Polish cause or explicitly harmed the national cause. One major aspect of the Polish cause in WWII, in which Jews came to be viewed in a negative manner, was the issue of the eastern Polish borders. Before the signing of the Polish-Soviet pact of 30 July 1941 the Polish government-in-exile had insisted that the Soviets nullify the Ribbentrop-Molotov line of Poland's September 1939 partition and guarantee the interwar Polish-Soviet border, established by the Treaty of Riga in 1921 and confirmed by the Polish-Soviet Nonaggression Treaty of 1932.[49] However, the Soviets rejected Polish demands to western Belarus and western Ukraine, skillfully arguing that these territories should belong to the majority nations living within them. The issue of the eastern Polish borders was a diplomatic disaster for Polish politicians because of Stalin's victory in his negotiations with Western Allies; Churchill was not prepared to jeopardize his country's relations with Stalin over the Polish eastern borders since at the time the Soviet Union was carrying a heavy burden of the war effort against the Nazi regime. Still, in what turned out to be failed negotiations with the Western powers Polish right-wing and conservative politicians sometimes aimed at using the "Jewish card" instrumentally in order to gain support for the Polish cause. For example, in January 1942 Stroński became convinced that the service of 15 percent of Jews in the Anders Army was "an excellent argument" that could be presented to the Western Allies in the dispute over the eastern borders.[50]

Nevertheless, despite internal divisions on the matter the government-in-exile officially endorsed the civic model of nationalism, inclusive toward Jews. The presence on the National Council (Rada Narodowa), the parliament of the government-in-exile, of two Jewish representatives—Ignacy Schwarzbart (1881–1961), the representative of the Zionist organizations, and Szmuel Zygielbojm (1895–1943), the representative of the main Jewish socialist party, the Bund—was one manifestation of the endorsement of pluralism and civic values by Polish institutions in exile.[51]

The maintenance of the civic model of nationalism and suppression of anti-Jewish statements proved to be a struggle inside the government and its various institutions. The suppression of anti-Semitic statements was no doubt particularly difficult for the politicians of National Democracy. A case in point is that of Marian Seyda (1879–1967), who was considered moderate in his views in comparison with his main party rival, Tadeusz Bielecki (1900–1982).[52] As early as 9 January 1940 Seyda, who was a general minister (minister without portfolio) in Sikorski's government, agreed at the meeting of parliament that "the use of anti-Semitism is an undesirable strategy at the present time."[53] Thus Seyda showed what could be called calculated political pragmatism on the matter. On the other hand, during the same year he acted in a manner that contradicted his pragmatic position. For example, he contributed an article to the first issue of an extreme right-wing paper, *Jestem Polakiem* (I Am a Pole), which was edited by Adam Doboszyński, the man responsible for one of the worst anti-Jewish riots in the post-1935 period, and by other former members of the owp and onr. The first issue of *Jestem Polakiem* was published in August 1940, and its explicit radical ethno-nationalist content caused a wave of shock and protest among Polish Jews in England. Critical news about the publication appeared in the British press. On 26 and 28 August 1940, during a discussion in parliament, Seyda defended his contribution to the paper on the grounds that he had written a "patriotic statement." At the same time he also stressed that he "sympathize[d] with the views of the editors of the paper." He accused Jerzy Szapiro (1895–?), a Polish Jew who was a member of the pps and a journalist, of bringing the matter to the attention of the British press.[54]

A similar scandal was caused by Karol Estreicher (1906–84), a former professor of art history at the Jagiellonian University in Cracow who was in charge of the Polish Center for Political and Economic Studies in London. In his review of Antoni Słonimski's volume of poetry *Alarm* (Alarm), published on 17 August 1940 in *Dziennik Polski*, one of the official papers of the government-in-exile, Estreicher wrote that "Słonimski's Jewish origin disqualifies him as a good Pole and as a Polish poet."[55] A similar position on Jewish poets and poets of Jewish origin was voiced in late 1943 in Nazi-occupied Poland in the paper *Sztuka i Naród* (Arts and the Nation), one of the papers of the radical ethno-nationalist group National Confederation (Konfederacja Narodu), by the young poet Tadeusz Gajcy (1922–44), killed in the Warsaw Uprising. In the article, meaningfully entitled "Już nie potrzebujemy" ("We Do Not Need [Them] Anymore"), Gajcy, like Estreicher, argued that poets like Słonimski, Julian Tuwim, and Bolesław Leśmian represented alien values and were "alien souls" who had nothing to do with "the spirituality of the true dwellers of Poland."[56] Such opinions show that even during the war the ethno-nationalist project of the purification of Polish culture, advocated by extremists in pre-1939 Poland, had not lost any of its urgency for some of its advocates. Estreicher's review was condemned in the parliament in late August 1941 by Jan Stańczyk (1886–1953), a member of the PPS and minister of labor and social welfare in Sikorski's government.[57]

Many politicians in the government-in-exile issued official and semiofficial statements characterized by contradictions arising from the clash between the inclusive civic and exclusionary ethnic visions of Poland. One important area of contradiction was the proposed status of Polish Jews in a future sovereign Polish nation-state. On the one hand, the government issued a number of declarations and resolutions in which it committed itself to an inclusive civic model of the nation-state in which Polish Jews would be granted political and civic rights equal to those of ethnic Poles. Prime Minister Sikorski made the first such proclamation as early as 6 October 1939. Sikorski's declaration was followed by two resolutions, of 3 November 1940 and 23 February 1942, that confirmed the government's commitment to the civic and pluralistic model of Poland.[58] The first resolution, known as the "Stańczyk Resolution," declared that "the Jews, as Polish citizens, shall be equal with the Polish community in duties and in rights in liberated Poland. They will be able to develop their culture, religion, and folkways without hindrance. Not only the laws of the state but even more the common sufferings in this most tragic time of affliction will serve to guarantee this [pledge]."[59]

In December 1941, in his address to the Jewish Labor Committee in New York, Stańczyk confirmed the declaration of 3 November 1940 and reassured his audience that Polish Jews living abroad would be able to return to a future independent Poland: "The question is often raised whether the Polish Jews who are not at present in Poland will be permitted to return to a liberated Poland. There must be no doubt whatsoever that every Polish citizen, irrespective of creed, race or nationality, will be free to return to his country. The Polish

Government has clearly stated its position with regard to the political rights of the citizens of the future Poland. The constitutional guarantee of legal equality and equal responsibility excludes any possibility of exceptions. The Polish Jew, like any other Polish citizen, will be able to return to Poland."[60]

At the time the issue of legal return to Poland was an urgent matter that representatives of Polish Jewry addressed in discussions with the government-in-exile. That the majority of all persons dispossessed of Polish citizenship in 1938 and 1939 on the grounds of the legislation of 31 March 1938 were Jews was a memory that was still alive in the Jewish community. Furthermore, the discriminatory legislation of 31 March 1938 was still a law of the Polish state.[61] Herman Lieberman (1870–1941), an assimilated Jew and a member of the pps, succeeded in the abolition of this legislation on 28 November 1941 during his short-term appointment as minister of justice in Sikorski's government. The abolition of this legislation was possible because at the time the National Democrats had temporarily withdrawn their participation from the government; they opposed the signing of the Polish-Soviet agreement of 30 July 1941, and only the more moderate faction of National Democracy, headed by Seyda, returned to the government in early 1942.[62]

In his declaration presented to the Jewish Labor Committee in New York in December 1941, less than one month after the abolition of the legislation of 31 March 1938, Minister Stańczyk once again assured his audience that "the Polish Government . . . even now is doing everything in its power to redress all previous wrongs against any group of citizens. The decree of the pre-war Polish Government depriving of their Polish nationality persons who had resided abroad for many years without maintaining contact with the home country was one such wrong. This vicious decree has been revoked by the present Government."[63]

On the other hand, politicians who officially represented the government made contradictory statements to the effect that the majority of Polish Jews would have to leave Poland after the state had regained its independence. In early 1940 Stanisław Kot (1885–1975), minister of information, and Edward Raczyński (1891–1993), the ambassador of the government-in-exile in London, presented such a proposal in separate conversations with representatives of British Jewry in France. In his memoirs S. Brodetzky, one of the members of the British delegation, captured the nature of such contradictions: "Professor Kot gave a long history of the Jews in Poland, which, he said, had treated Jews well for centuries. But Jews were a foreign body in Poland; they did not even speak Polish. . . . He said that there were too many Jews in Poland, Hungary and Romania. About a third of them could remain, the rest would have to go elsewhere."[64]

During a meeting of the parliament on 11 June 1941 Minister Kot, who enjoyed the reputation of being a conservative but moderate politician, expressed his reservations toward the official declarations of Minister Stańczyk, which the latter continued to present to various Jewish audiences in the summer of 1941.[65] In the spring of 1942, when "the moderate section" of the National Democrats returned to the government, parliament-in-exile passed a National Democratic resolution endorsing the project of the emigration of Polish Jews en masse from the country in the future.[66] Thus the members of the parliament-in-exile went against their officially declared commitment to creating an inclusive civic and pluralistic Polish society.

The government also made contradictory statements regarding the plight of Polish Jews in the territory of the GG to various audiences before and during the Nazi extermination. On the one hand, in statements directed at Western Allies and Jewish representatives, leading members of the government spoke about the solidarity of the Polish people with the Jews and referred to the Nazi extermination of Jews as part of Poland's tragedy. However, such references, or other positive statements about Jews, tended to be limited or omitted in the official statements addressed to Poles in Nazi-occupied Poland. One of the reasons for such an omission lay in the government's concern over how the ethnic Polish population in the GG would receive positive statements about Polish Jews. The extreme ethno-nationalists in the GG accused the government-in-exile during the war, as they had the Sanacja government in the early 1930s, of representing Jewish interests. Such accusations caused concern among politicians, including Prime Minister Sikorski and Minister Kot. During a parliamentary session of 11 July 1940 Kot warned that such propaganda should not be dismissed as unimportant and that the authors of it should be found and prosecuted. This shows that politicians like Kot did not perceive radical nationalistic views as irrelevant and marginal but treated them seriously.[67]

Cases of omission of official statements expressing solidarity with Jews were of great concern to the representatives of Polish Jewry in Tel Aviv and other parts of the free Western world. In fact, they were closely monitored by organizations of Polish Jewry and were also reported in the British press. For example, the *East London Observer* of 9 March 1942 reported: "Considerable comment was caused by the omission from the Polish official press of General

Sikorski's references to the courage of Polish Jews. As reported in our last issue, General Sikorski, at the opening of the Polish National Council on the 24th of February, declared, 'The spirit with which the Jews in Poland bear their sufferings must fill us all with admiration.' This remark of the Polish Prime Minister was omitted in the report, which appeared in the Polish press on that occasion, and also was not cited in air broadcast to Poland."[68]

The government's official press and radio broadcasts to the GG also avoided direct calls upon the Polish population to show solidarity and unity with the Jews during the war. Instead official governmental resolutions tended to issue general statements stating that the solidarity and unity of the Polish population with Jews was a common feature of social life in the GG. This type of response was also of great concern to the Representation of Polish Jewry (Reprezentacja Żydostwa Polskiego), based in Tel Aviv. In fact, Jewish representatives in Tel Aviv were disappointed and frustrated with the lack of direct calls for help and solidarity with Jews in governmental communications with the country and complained about this to the Ministry of Information in the Polish government-in-exile: "We must record with pain that in the regular weekly broadcasts by the Ministry of Information, we find not even one word on the need for a common communal life and mutual help between the Poles and the Jews. . . . We hope that the Government will do everything in order to bring to the consciousness of the population how they must react to the bestial aims of the enemy."[69]

To such complaints the Ministry of Information replied: "An appeal to the public in Poland is unnecessary, as it is precisely from those circles that the information and vigorous protests are sent."[70]

The government's coalition was divided on the issue of the model of the future Polish nation-state; this division played an important role in the internal dynamics of this institution. The National Democracy movement was the chief unquestionable advocate of an ethnically homogenous model for the future Polish state. Throughout WWII the National Democrats continued to regard Polish Jews as the harmful other and constantly demanded their removal from a future independent Poland. In contrast, the positions of the Labor and Peasant Parties on this issue were much harder to pinpoint. Polish historian Andrzej Friszke explains the lack of a clear position on Jews among the politicians of these two parties as a result of their general policy of keeping silent on such matters in the light of the German extermination of the Jewish population.[71] This is no doubt a correct but partial explanation. One should also add to it the concerns of these two parties about how the Western Allies would evaluate them, as well as their prewar approach toward Jews.

In the pre-1939 period both parties had already endorsed the ethno-nationalist position that Poland should be a country without Jews. During the war neither their leaders in exile nor their leaders in the country were willing to condemn or dispose of their prewar position: it had become part of their ideological heritage and part of the political platform supported by their respective electorates. This is why, among members of both the Labor and Peasant Parties in the government, there were contradictory statements about Jews and varied versions of the representation of the Jew as the harmful other. Of course their version of this representation differed in its level of intensity and elaboration from that advocated by the National Democrats; it did not constitute a central aspect of their ideologies.

A close examination of both parties' political programs, official statements, and press reveals the main contradiction: support for the official governmental position on Jews as an inclusive group in a future Poland was intertwined with the exclusivist ethno-nationalist view of Jews as an impediment to the development of the Polish population.

For example, on 26 March 1941, at a session of the parliament, the Peasant Party, which was more influential than the Labor Party in both the prewar and wartime periods, issued the following declaration in support of the previously quoted resolution of 3 November 1940: "The Peasant Party announces its solidarity with this resolution—a resolution politically mature, dictated by sound political reason and principles of democracy, as indicated by the Government of National Unity. The fact that we declare our solidarity with this resolution should not come as a surprise to anybody, as it has been always our attitude, as it is now, that the State's treatment of its citizens cannot be differentiated by reasons of religion, race, or origin. . . . This is a just and democratic principle with regard to rights of equality and to the obligations of all citizens of the State. The Peasant Party is committed to the realization of these principles in a future Poland."[72]

However, just a month earlier, on 20 February 1941, a contradictory statement had been made in an official meeting between Stanisław Mikołajczyk (1901–66), a leader of the émigré Peasant Party, and Ignacy Schwarzbart, the Zionist representative of Polish Jewry in the government. During the meeting Schwarzbart criticized the program for the emigration of Jews as a violation of civic and pluralistic values and requested that Mikołajczyk renounce it:

"This project harms our identity as full-fledged citizens. No citizen can commit himself to being a patriot when he knows that his own state might make him an involuntary emigrant. Polish politicians should be aware that the emigration slogans would not bring sympathy for Poland among Jewry. In the past there was peasant emigration from Poland without specific legislation for such an emigration. There was also voluntary Jewish emigration free of the notion that there were too many Jews in Poland. Emigration results from the economic situation. And no state has the right to create economic or political conditions for a particular group of citizens in order to force them to emigrate."[73]

In response Mikołajczyk, who later in July 1943 was appointed prime minister in the aftermath of Sikorski's death, stated that despite the recent historical changes, the Peasant Party would continue to support the emigration project of Jews because the party had endorsed such a policy in the political program in 1935. He added that the party's leadership in exile could not revoke such a decision.[74] This shows both the strength of the pre-1939 ideological heritage of the peasant movement and its instrumental use of the concept of a civic Poland in the wartime period. The continuity of the pre-1939 Peasant Party's position on Jews was more explicitly expressed in the party's press organs published and circulated in the GG. For example, on 30 April 1942 the paper *Ku zwycięstwu* published an article entitled "Sprawa Żydowska" (The Jewish Matter), in which both the arguments and the language in which they were expressed constituted a repetition of the pre-1939 position. The Nazi extermination of Jews did not seem to have any mitigating effect on such a position: "Concerning the Jewish matter, one thing is sure, that the position of Jews in Poland is deteriorating and that a significant number of them will have to emigrate from Poland. . . . The Polish side should do everything in its power to help support emigration of Jews. . . . The Jewish matter is an international one. The presence of large Jewish masses in Poland is the result of the expulsion of Jews from other countries. Thus Poland has the right to demand that the world participate in a solution to the 'Jewish question.' "[75]

The PPS was the only party in the government that opposed any aspects of the ethno-nationalist vision of a Polish state and insisted on the recognition of Jews as members of a future Polish society. Not only were PPS leaders engaged in condemnation of anti-Jewish attitudes and actions within the underground state and émigré Polish institutions and organizations, but they also succeeded in the abolition of some pre-1939 ethno-nationalist legislation, even though National Democrats often obstructed their efforts.[76]

The ethno-nationalist tendencies in the government-in-exile resulted in policies and practices that were contradictory to the officially declared commitment to a civic model for the future postwar Polish state. Yet overall, because of the proximity of the Western Allies, the government-in-exile's dependence on those allies, and internal fluctuations of power between the PPS and the National Democrats, these tendencies were restrained in comparison with the situation of the underground state in Nazi-occupied Poland.

The Delegate's Bureau, the AK, and the Myth

Perhaps the most apparent evidence of the influence of exclusivist ethno-nationalism on the underground state in Nazi-occupied Poland was the ethnic homogenization of its institutions. In contrast to the Polish government-in-exile, which included two representatives of Polish Jewry in its structure, there were no such representatives in the network of the Delegate's Bureau or the AK in the GG. Membership in these organizations seemed to be reserved almost exclusively for ethnic Poles. The underground organizations included as members only assimilated Jewish individuals whom they saw as ethnic Poles, and they sometimes harassed these individuals when their Jewish origins became public knowledge. A body of records exists, including testimonies of both Jews and Poles, that shows that members of the highly culturally assimilated group experienced prejudice and hostility from Polish ethno-nationalists. One revealing testimony on this subject, which is difficult to analyze, is that given by a Jew, Chil (Hillel) Cejlon, in front of the Historical Commission in Stuttgart, Germany, in the early postwar period. Cejlon, born in 1916 in Sandomierz, served in the underground Polish military organization in wartime Warsaw. In 1943 a school acquaintance of his from Sandomierz who had come to Warsaw recognized him and started to blackmail him. When Cejlon revealed to his commander that he was Jewish and asked for help in getting rid of the blackmailer, he was told to leave both the organization and Warsaw.[77] This is not to say that there were no exceptions to this rule. In the underground units of the AK under the control of those commanders who belonged to the PPS, the Democratic Party, or the left-wing Sanacja parties, it was possible for Polish Jews to serve without being harassed for their background.

Other evidence of the spread of exclusivist ethno-nationalist ways of thinking in sections of the underground state can be found in various official statements of prominent individuals. Some leaders of the AK and the Delegate's Bureau were often themselves critical of the official commitment to the inclusive civic model of a future Polish state upheld by the Polish government-in-exile. They were also inclined to disapprove of any positive attitudes and actions toward Jews on the part of the government-in-exile. Expressions of criticism and disapproval can be found in official reports, dispatches, and memorandums sent to the government-in-exile from the GG. For example, in a well-known report of 25 September 1941 Stefan Rowecki (1895–1944) (pseud. Grot, Kalina), first commander in chief of the AK, stated:

> All the government's actions concerning Jews in Poland make a dreadful impression and incite antigovernmental propaganda. This is the case with the celebration of "Jewish Day," [Ignacy] Schwarzbart's speech, the appointment of Liberman [Herman Lieberman], and the offering of good wishes for the Jewish New Year. Please take it as an established fact that the overwhelming majority of the population is anti-Semitic. Even the Socialists are no exception. There are only tactical differences about what to do. Hardly anybody advocates imitating the Germans. However, even those underground organizations under the influence of the prewar executive groups of the Democratic Club or the PPS accept the emigration project for Polish Jews as a solution to the Jewish problem.[78]

In the summer of 1944, in one of his reports, Jan Stanisław Jankowski, the government's last head of the Delegate's Bureau and a member of the Labor Party, conveyed even harsher and more explicit criticism of the government: "The delegate has asked me to state the following. According to him, the government has exaggerated his 'love toward Jews.' Although he understands that this is to some extent necessary as far as Polish foreign relations are concerned, nevertheless he advises restraining such attitudes. Under the previous premiership of General Sikorski and the present premiership [of Stanisław Mikołajczyk] the government has been overtly philosemitic. It should bear in mind that inside the country Jews are disliked."[79]

Jankowski's criticism of the government for allegedly being "philosemitic" echoed similar criticisms of the government-in-exile published in the press of the National Democrats and of extreme ethno-nationalist political groups that were not subordinated to the Delegate's Bureau, such as the Rampart Group. In the aftermath of the Warsaw Ghetto Uprising of April 1943 the National Democratic and extreme right-wing press was often critical of the government-in-exile because of its alleged "sentimental or melancholic" attitude toward the German destruction of Polish Jews, viewing it as a sign of their failure to represent the Polish national interest.[80]

A close examination of the communications of the Delegate's Bureau and AK with the government-in-exile suggests that the concept of an ethnically homogenous Poland without Jews enjoyed popularity among those individuals from the underground elite who were in charge of writing the reports. Characteristically the arguments and language used by the authors of such communications frequently echoed the pre-1939 arguments and language of National Democracy. What is also striking is their ethno-nationalist interpretation of economic and social problems. As in ethno-nationalist writings of the interwar period, underground ethno-nationalist literature continued to portray Jews as preventing the successful modernization of Poles and their economic advancement. These communications express chilling distance toward Jews as victims of Nazi policies.[81] The Nazi destruction of Jewry does not appear to have had any mitigating effect on this way of thinking. For example:

> In the last few weeks Jewish booksellers have been given permits to open a few bookshops in the Warsaw ghetto. These bookshops have attracted huge interest. Thus the hope of Polish booksellers to save Polish books from Jewish hands has failed due to the Nazi regulations.[82]

> Poles have only partially benefited from the disappearance of Jews from industry and businesses as they are now being infiltrated by the German element.[83]

> The migration of Jews to Poland and their high birthrate have resulted in abnormal numbers of the Jewish population in this country. The huge number of Jews in the cities has prevented Poles from participating in crafts and businesses and is one of the main reasons that our peasant population is overcrowded in villages.[84]

Another explicit example of a similarly distant approach toward Jews as victims of Nazi extermination is General Rowecki's report of 10 November 1942, which contemplates the safety of the ethnic Polish population in the aftermath of the Great Deportation, orchestrated by the Nazis in July of the same year in Warsaw: "Polish society is apprehensive that in the aftermath of the current extermination of the Jews the Germans may proceed to apply similar methods of extermination against Poles. I call for restraint and for counteracting these apprehensions with reassurances. The principal German objective in relation to us could be described as the absorption of our nation. Attempts to exterminate the resistant segments of our nation by methods applied against the Jews cannot, however, be ruled out."[85]

In Rowecki's report the Great Deportation, which took a heavy toll on Warsaw Jewry, is not viewed as part of the unfolding tragedy of Poland and

its people under German occupation. The report views Polish Jews as a kind
of separate entity whose well-being and safety did not belong to the realm of
concerns of the chief of staff of the AK.[86] The language of the report reflects
the emotive distance of its author toward the subject he describes. There is a
glaring lack of reference to the Jews as members of the same society as Polish
citizens; Jews are simply presented as "they," not "us."

Various representatives of Polish Jews in the GG requested official statements
from the Delegate's Bureau that would stress the recognition of Polish Jewry
as an intrinsic part of Polish society. Their argument was that such statements
might be beneficial in creating a so-called positive atmosphere toward Jews and
in reducing anti-Jewish actions, mainly blackmail and denunciation among a
section of the Polish community. In one of the appeals to the underground
in 1941 the intelligentsia of the Warsaw ghetto asked the government "to
publish statements to make the Polish population aware that the Jews are
valuable citizens of the Polish Republic and that crimes against them will be
accountable before the courts of the Republic, and that, in particular, any
form of collaboration with the Nazis will be viewed as high treason against
the state."[87] Such appeals were not met with immediate action: a number of
official statements against blackmailers of Jews began to be published by the
Delegate's Bureau only in April 1943. From September 1943 death sentences
began to be meted out to blackmailers.[88]

Polish political and social activists who were members of the PPS and other
democratic organizations also made similar appeals to the Delegate's Bureau.
The collection of the records of the Council for Aid to the Jews (Żegota), an
organization set up in December 1942 under the auspices of the Delegate's
Bureau, speaks volumes about the genuine attempts and frustrations of those
members of Żegota who requested both the publication and the implementation of such appeals. Julian Grobelny (pseud. Trojan), chairman of Żegota
and a member of the PPS-Freedom-Equality-Independence Party (PPS-WRN),
insisted that rescuing Jews was in the interests of a future independent Poland:
"The most important thing is to provide help to individuals . . . who have no
means to save themselves and whose lives would be indispensable to a future
state. The German extermination of Polish citizens will have grave results
for a future independent state. The state will suffer from the lack of every
human being who could be saved today."[89] The treasurer of Żegota, a member
of the Democratic Union, Ferdynand Arczyński (1914–2000) (pseud. Marek,
Łukowski), also insisted that "Polish Jews were the most threatened element of

Polish society and that their chances of survival depended on the special care they would be provided with."[90]

Other members of Żegota also protested to the head of the Delegate's Bureau and to the prime minister, objecting to negative representations of Jews disseminated in some official publications of the underground state. One such protest, of 30 June 1944, sharply criticized the discrepancies among different positions toward Jews in influential official underground publications and demanded from the prime minister and the Delegate's Bureau immediate actions to put an end to ethno-nationalist propaganda. Because of its importance and the fact that this protest has not before been published, following is a long excerpt:

> In the underground press a work has recently appeared that was published by the Agricultural Department of the Delegate's Bureau, entitled "Nowy Wspólny Dom" [New Common Home]. This work constitutes part of the program of the reconstruction of postwar Poland. On page 13 of this document we find the following paragraph: . . . ["]Alien people, alien capital. Since the time of the First Republic the Jews occupied the most prominent role in commerce. Regardless of bad or good developments in the state the merchants and the middlemen always made a profit. When Poles were dying in battle against the oppressors, Jews, always concerned only with business, regarded the occupying powers as 'ours.' The Jews favored our lands because they had a good life here. The petty leaseholders and craftsmen had built great fortunes, and their achievements became a model that the poor Jewish masses could follow. The entire Jewish population—which recently reached the number of 3.5 million—believed in the dream that, thanks to their resourcefulness, they could financially and socially prosper. They grew up on our land but were aliens to us. They obtained a huge amount of national treasure and occupied an important place in our state economy, but they did not constitute a part of Poland, which finds its strength in the love and sacrifice of its sons. With a few exceptions they were not capable of either love or sacrifice for the country. Historical fate led them to their end, and the majority of them were killed. In the aftermath of the genocide of a large number of Jews in Poland an empty place is left that must be filled in.["] On page 21 we also find the following paragraph: ["]Nevertheless, the war would bring us some positive developments. We have already mentioned the disappearance and future reduction of alien forces. This situation will have an important significance for the rebuilding of our lives.["]
>
> Furthermore, certain publications, such as *Głos Polski* no. 10, cite these particular paragraphs from this document with additional commentaries that

are full of racist poison, which have been accepted by certain segments of our society. This is happening at a time when the Polish government-in-exile stresses in many official pronouncements the democratic character of occupied Poland and its tolerance toward minorities. . . .

The abovementioned citations from "New Common Home" can be read as an official statement. Not only does this document undermine the political stance of our government-in-exile and its representative in occupied Poland, but it also offends the honor of the Polish nation by portraying the most horrible crime of Hitler as the historical fate of the Jewish people and by evaluating it as a positive development for Poland. This document uses language and criteria that are alien to the psyche of the Polish nation. Żegota as a rule abstains from uttering statements of a political nature because it is entirely dedicated to rescue activities. However, in this matter the organization is forced to make a statement because this publication, which after all comes from an official channel, paralyzes to a significant degree its activities, which are undertaken with huge effort and risk. Żegota has expected that the publications of official press organs would disseminate humanitarian slogans among broad segments of society and call for the civic responsibility to rescue dying Jews. Instead such a brochure supports well-known groups in deepening ethnic hatred and giving legitimacy to the spreading evil. Therefore Żegota states that the above-cited paragraphs from the brochure oppose the political stance of the Delegate's Bureau and the prime minister. The organization calls upon the prime minister, first, to issue an official statement on behalf of the Delegate's Bureau and also to draw up principal rules for Polish society concerning responsibility for rescuing Polish citizens of Jewish origin hunted by the German occupier. Second, to explain to Żegota what measures the prime minister is planning to undertake to prevent similar dangerous publications from appearing in the future in the official press of the Delegate's Bureau.[91]

A statement like the one above attests to how isolated and frustrated socialist and democratic members of Żegota were within the structure of the underground state. Their isolation came from their commitment to treating Jews as an intrinsic part of Polish society and to evaluating their rescue activities as part of a project of rescuing Poland's most threatened citizens.

Records of the minutes of Żegota also reveal that silence, disapproval, and procrastination were the main responses on the part of the authorities of the Delegate's Bureau and the AK to demands made by the socialist and democratic activists of Żegota. Many of Żegota's projects aimed at creating a more positive atmosphere toward the dying Jewish community failed as a result. In her study of Żegota Teresa Prekerowa, a Polish historian, implicitly indicates the lack of broad support within the underground for Żegota's actions. Although she does not address the issue of the attitudes of Delegate's Bureau and AK authorities toward Polish Jews, she concludes that Żegota's projects were marginalized in underground organizations:

> The RPZ [Żegota] people were aware that neither the council's activists alone, nor a much bigger group including its collaborators, would be able to achieve any meaningful results without broad social support. Therefore efforts were made to create a climate which was favorable to the actions of the relief groups. Members of the presidium, in the first instance, pressed the underground authorities and the government-in-exile to appeal to Polish society to help the hounded Jews in every possible way. . . . There were attempts to offset the opinions of the clandestine nationalistic periodicals which persuaded their public that the lot of the Jewish minority "is not our affair." In order to supply editorial boards of the clandestine periodicals with edited materials, in the autumn of 1943, the council published three issues of the *Komunikaty Prasowe*, which reported the liquidation of the Jewish camps in the Lublin region and the uprising in the ghetto of Białystok, along with other important events. The underground press failed to react in any significant way to the information published, which perhaps, contributed to the closing down of the title.[92]

In all, the ethno-nationalist perceptions of Jews that prevailed within some significant segments of the political and military underground authorities caused a lack of concern over the plight of the Jewish community. They contributed to the obstruction and delay of those actions taken up within the underground state that aimed at providing help to Jews. The position of treating Polish Jews as an integral part of Polish society in WWII was represented by left-wing sections of the non-Communist underground's elite, mainly socialists and Democrats.

The Prevalence of the Myth in the Clandestine Press of the GG

Looking closely at the spectrum of the prominent clandestine press of various political and social organizations, I differentiate among three main groups in terms of their attitude toward Jews as included in or excluded from Polish society and in terms of their attitude toward Jews as victims of the Nazi extermination.[93]

The first group—those who viewed Jews as part of Polish society—includes the entire press of the left-wing parties—the Democratic Party (Partia Demokratyczna), the PPS-WRN, and the Polish Socialist Party (Polscy Socjaliści)—

along with other small independent liberal and left-wing papers. To this group also belong *Dzieci Warszawy*, one of the main papers of the Delegate's Bureau, and the *Biuletyn Informacyjny*, the main weekly of the AK.[94] The leaders of these latter two papers were individuals like Aleksander Kamiński, the editor of the *Biuletyn Informacyjny*, who were committed to the civic model of Poland.

The writing on Jews published by the left-wing press had five common characteristics. Left-wing writers did not refer to Jews as the threatening other. These writers crafted a program for the inclusion of Jews within a future Polish nation-state. They condemned the Nazi genocide of Jews. They saw the Nazi destruction of Polish Jews as part of Poland's tragedy. Finally, they condemned the anti-Jewish statements of Polish right-wing underground circles and anti-Jewish actions within segments of Polish society.

The left-wing political parties were the only political group within the non-Communist camp that considered rescue operation of Jews as a basic civic duty to fellow citizens. Therefore the press of such groups was critical of the underground institutions, as well as society at large, for a lack of recognition of the genocide of Polish Jews as part of the tragedy of Poland. On 7 February 1944 *Nowe Drogi*, the main paper of the Democratic Party, stated: "Within the Polish population there is a lack of understanding and recognition that the German extermination of Jews constitutes not only a crime against the Jewish community but in fact is a crime against the Polish state, which is losing millions of its citizens."

Next, commenting on blackmailing activities against the remnants of Jews, the same paper called upon underground institutions to take efficient measures to curtail such activities: "The conclusion of our reasoning is simple: the Poles have to disassociate themselves utterly and unequivocally from the German crimes. It is not enough to adopt a passive position and noble gestures of shock and disgust. There is an urgent need for a more active stance in counteracting the social demoralization sown by the enemy [the Germans]. At present the Jewish issue concerns the moral well-being of the nation."[95]

On 8 January 1943 WRN, the press organ of the PPS-WRN, condemned anti-Jewish behavior and attitudes, which continued to be exhibited among segments of the Polish underground elite and society at large in the GG: "Browsing through our political world we see many things that show that our nation is not ready [to embrace democracy]. After all, we are supposed to be a democracy, but the ghost of our own fascism is still present. . . . We are supposed to constitute a federation of nations, but chauvinism and zoological nationalism . . . still threaten the ideal of partnership among nations. Despite the terrible tragedy occurring in front of our eyes, anti-Semitism is still alive in some circles of our society."[96]

The members of the PPS, the Democratic Party, and other small left-wing organizations seemed to be the only representatives of the underground political elite in the GG who constantly insisted on treating Jews as an integral part of society, protested against exclusivist ethno-nationalist programs, and called upon the population to accept their position. Such calls appeared not only in the GG but also in the eastern territories. On 1 May 1940 in Wilno, which from October 1939 until June 1940 had been under Lithuanian control, prior to the Soviet imposition of power, one of the local left-wing Polish papers, *Wolność* (Freedom), announced that "in the new independent Poland there is no place for nationalistic wars. The tremendous suffering of the Jewish population that we have been witnessing every day has to teach us how to live together in a peaceful coexistence with those who have been suffering together with us at the hands of a common enemy. Our present stateless situation has to teach us to have respect for the desires of the national movements of Ukrainians and Belorussians."[97]

In the second group, ideologically the most diverse, one can include the press of the following political parties and social organizations: the Labor Party, the peasant movement, and affiliated smaller peasant groups such as Orka and Racławice; the main Catholic organizations, the Front for the Rebirth of Poland (Front Odrodzenia Polski, FOP), and the Union (Unia), headed by Jerzy Braun; and Sanacja's Camp of Fighting Poland (Obóz Polski Walczącej). Although these groups did not hold a single position on the role of Jews, their literature does share the use of the myth of the Jew as the threatening other to varying degrees of intensity and support the exclusion of Polish Jews from a future Polish state.[98] At the same time their stance on the German extermination of Polish Jewry was one of strong condemnation, accompanied by expressions of sympathy toward the plight of Jews on a human level and by condemnation of Polish denunciators and blackmailers.

The third group consisted of the National Democrats, the core ethno-nationalist party, and its extreme offshoot organizations such as the Rampart Group (ONR-Szaniec), the National Party–Great Poland (SN–Wielka Polska), the Confederation of the Nation (Konfederacja Narodu), Sword and Plough (Miecz i Pług), and the Awakening (Pobudka). Their writings consistently used the myth of the Jew as the enemy of the Polish polity and its people and advocated the project of the exclusion of Polish Jews from a future Polish state. On the Nazi genocide of Polish Jews their stance varied between a rather detached disapproval of the genocidal methods of the Nazis and approval of the outcome of the genocide. This position was accompanied by the view that the extermination of Polish Jews was outside of Polish national considerations. The press of this group was also critical of those groups of Poles who expressed attitudes of sympathy toward the plight of Jews.

The crucial difference between the press of the second and the third groups lay in their position toward the Nazi extermination of Jews. Another difference lay in the degree of the intensity and frequency of the ethno-nationalist representation of the Jew as the harmful other. In the third group, the core of the ethno-nationalist camp, this representation appeared in its most uniform and aggressive version. Here Polish Jews were typically described throughout the war as a "Jewish plague," a "Jewish flood," and "the Judeo-Bolshevik enemy and malevolent entity."

Within the second group Jews as a rule were addressed less frequently, and there were greater and "milder" variations of the expression of the representation of the Jew as the harmful alien. In all, more moderate, diffuse, and implicit references can be found in the central press of the Peasant Party and in some of the official press of the Delegate's Bureau. Here one of the main tendencies was not to refer to Jews directly but to describe the relationship between ethnic Poles and Jews as one of irrevocable political and social conflict and antagonism. In the second group the most explicit and aggressive anti-Jewish expressions can be found in the press of the Camp of Fighting Poland and in publications of the Catholic Unia and the Labor Party, as well as in some publications of the peasant groups Orka and Racławice.[99] Some of these representations of Jews are similar to those found in the press of National Democracy and its offshoot radical organizations. For example, on 15 August 1942 *Naród*, the organ of the Labor Party, insisted: "For hundreds of years an alien malevolent entity has inhabited the northern sections of our city—malevolent and alien from the point of view of our interests, as well as our psyche and our hearts."[100] In January 1943 *Polska*, the publication of the Camp of Fighting Poland, noted: "In Poland the Jews had optimal conditions for development. Yet they have always worked to the detriment of our country. They have always loathed Poland and the Poles. After the present war we would have to treat them differently, no matter how reduced their numbers."[101]

Support for an integral vision of Poland without Jews or other minorities was the only project that the parties and organizations of the second and third groups had in common. The National Democrats interpreted this shared position as the "long-awaited victory" of their party. This exaggerated statement boosted the National Democrats' political influence, on the one hand, but on the other it reflected the particular political atmosphere of the time. On 13 October 1943 one of the papers of the National Democrats, *Młoda Polska*, commented on this "common vision" as follows: "Before WWI the National Camp regarded the 'Jewish question' as the most urgent internal political issue to be resolved. However, on this issue the National Camp was opposed by a wide front, ranging from 'the judaized left wing' to the freemasonry centers of the Sanacja and the liberal 'patriots.' . . . And yet before WWII the same political groups supported the 'economic boycott of Jews.' Today, despite tears shed over the burned Warsaw ghetto, programs of all Polish political organizations have agreed on elimination of the Jewish influence. Victory has been achieved."[102]

At the same time the National Democrats and their extreme offshoot parties were engaged in a propaganda war against political parties that advocated the inclusive civic model of the nation-state. In this war delegitimization of political opponents on the basis of their positive attitudes toward Jews was employed. Political opponents were portrayed as traitors acting in the interests of Jews, not in the interests of Poles. The latter image, of course, was a long-established ethno-nationalist strategy, going back to the pre-1918 period. In WWII the pps, as it had before 1918 and in the postindependence period from 1918 to 1939, was the political party most frequently portrayed as representing Jewish interests because of its unchangeable commitment to the inclusive civic model of a future nation-state and its constant recognition of the plight of Polish Jews as part of the national tragedy.

The National Democrats occasionally described the government-in-exile as an institution disloyal to the Polish national cause, one representing the interests of left-wing parties and Jews. On 28 June 1944 *Narodowa Agencja Prasowa*, the press organ of the National Democrats–Great Poland, stated: "Currently in the Polish government in London the Jew Grosfeld [Ludwik Grosfeld, minister of finance], a member of the pps, was appointed to one of the most important positions, chancellor of the exchequer. . . . Various 'Tennenbaumy' and 'Tuwims' are influential in émigré circles. Some of them support the government-in-exile, while others are basically servants of Moscow. Nothing has changed there. A similar situation has developed in Poland. . . . Today the international elements and the left-wing parties, which define themselves as democratic, want to throw Poland into the hands of international Jewry." [103]

Just as they had labeled the pre-1935 Sanacja government as a tool of Jewish interests, the ethno-nationalists labeled the government-in-exile as an anti-Polish institution. Their wartime strategy was slightly different, as the National Democrats were responding to the specific conditions of the war, and four themes predominated: the government's official commitment to the civic model of a future Polish nation-state, the presence of Jews and persons of Jewish origin in its structure, the representation of the pps in the government, and the official underground state's recognition of the plight of Polish Jews as part of the national tragedy. For example, the National Democrats could seize upon the commemoration ceremonies of the first anniversary of the Warsaw Ghetto Uprising, staged by members of the pps in London in April 1944, as evidence of Jewish influence on the pps and the government-in-exile state.

The Myth and Perceptions of the Holocaust: The zsp and the fop

The representation of the Jew as the harmful alien was also present in some publications of two underground organizations that were actively involved in setting up Żegota, certain sections of the left-wing Union of Polish Syndicalists (Związek Polskich Syndykalistów, zsp), and the Catholic Front for the Rebirth of Poland (Front Odrodzenia Polski, fop). The presence of the myth in the press of the zsp shows how far the exclusivist ethno-nationalist model of thinking about Jews had penetrated various segments of the political elite, whose ideologies were not built on the matrix of integral nationalism, a phenomenon that perhaps was unique in underground organizations in Nazi-occupied Europe.

The zsp participated in preliminary work on setting up Żegota in the autumn of 1942. [104] Whereas the fop was not only involved in establishing the organization but participated in its activities until the summer of 1943, at which point the group withdrew. Needless to say, participation in Żegota's actions meant risking one's life. The zsp was an organization composed of various small left-wing and trade-union groups that stayed in opposition to the government-in-exile. At the end of 1943 the ak classified the zsp as one of four among thirteen political parties and organizations that supported the inclusion of Polish Jews in a postwar Polish state. [105] However, some of the earlier political programs of the zsp expressed a contradictory position. For example, in a program published in July 1940 the zsp proclaimed: "The Jews in Poland constitute a foreign element that wants to strengthen its position on the body of the Polish state. . . . The Jews are a nation without sovereignty, and by maintaining their collectivity they have often had a destructive impact on other societies. . . . The position of Jews within the socioeconomic structure of society makes them a destructive element within the Polish organism. . . . Poland should be politically and economically independent and should do everything possible to make the Jews economically benign." The same program also explicitly advocated the exclusion of Jews from the future state: "Jews should leave Poland of their own accord. . . . Polish nationalizing policies should not regard Jews as a group to undergo assimilation; assimilation is neither viable nor desirable in the case of Jews."[106]

The notion of the Jew as alien and historically harmful to Poles can also be found in the press organ of the zsp, *Iskra*, which at the same time insisted on condemning ethnic Polish blackmailers of Jews as "people without morals." On 28 April 1943, during the ongoing Warsaw Ghetto Uprising, the paper stated that what was happening behind the ghetto walls was a horrific human tragedy, but one that did not directly touch upon the Polish people, since Jews, according to the paper, constituted a social, economic, and cultural problem in Polish society. In fact, they were not a part of it:

> We have never been "philosemites." The "Jewish question" has been the most sensitive aspect of our internal politics. There have been many reasons that could explain why the Polish masses have disliked the Jewish element, which is culturally and psychologically alien to us. The "Jewish question" has to be solved and without doubt will be solved in a future independent Poland according to the principles of Polish national interest. However, today, at this moment, when the remnants of Jews are fighting for their lives, we want to state that the entire Polish public feels deeply for the Jewish tragedy, regardless of our personal sympathies and antipathies.[107]

What is striking about this statement is that the prewar perception of the Jew as the threatening other persisted despite the realization that the size of the Jewish community had been greatly reduced as a result of the German mass-murder policy. A similar attitude toward Jews was present in the press of the Catholic Front for the Rebirth of Poland (FOP), founded by Zofia Kossak-Szczucka and Witold Bieńkowski at the end of 1940. This social organization, based in Warsaw, defined itself as the chief representative of the Roman Catholic political and cultural elite. The FOP aimed at the dissemination of Catholic, national, and anti-Communist values. Between 1942 and 1944 the

FOP published three underground papers: two monthlies, *Prawda* and *Prawda Młodych*; and a bimonthly, *Prawda Dnia*. The main contributors were Kossak-Szczucka and Jan Dobraczyński. Both Kossak-Szczucka and Dobraczyński were actively involved in Żegota, despite their affiliation with the prewar Catholic Action and their support for the vision of Poland advocated by National Democracy. Dobraczyński also played an important role in the wartime propaganda section of the underground National Democracy movement; his party nickname was "Hozjusz."[108] Kossak-Szczucka was one of the leading founders of Żegota and was subsequently involved in various Żegota activities, but without becoming an official member of the organization. [109] Dobraczyński was employed by the Warsaw Municipal Social Department, and thanks to his position he was able to assist in providing both false documentation and shelter for Jewish children.[110] Another prominent member of the FOP, Witold Bieńkowski, the editor of *Prawda Dnia*, was officially engaged in Żegota's activities on behalf of the Delegate's Bureau. Such individuals' actions in Żegota and their views about Jews were strikingly contradictory.

An illustration of Bieńkowski's perceptions of Jews can be found in a proposed program, written in the autumn of 1942, that in fact was rejected by the FOP's council because of its extreme radical stance.[111] In it Bieńkowski proposed total social segregation of Jews from Poles in the name of the Polish national interest. According to him, Jews were a "guest nation" in the Polish territories, characterized by "an aggressive psyche" that could only harm the host nation. He viewed the presence of Jews in Polish territories as a misfortune that could be resolved only by the emigration of Jews to Palestine. Therefore he argued for the emigration of Jews as the only viable solution to the "Jewish question" in postwar Poland.[112]

Characteristically in the FOP press the notion that Jews were the enemy of Poles and would have to be excluded from a future Polish nation-state appeared comfortably next to statements of sympathy for their plight and calls for helping them. In an article entitled "Komu pomagamy" (Whom Do We Help), published in *Prawda* in August 1943, Kossak-Szczucka insisted:

> Today the Jews face extermination. They are the victims of unjust murderous persecutions. I must save them. "Do unto others what you want others to do unto you." This commandment demands that I use all the means I have to save others, the very same means that I would use for my own salvation. To be sure, after the war the situation will be different. The same laws will apply to the Jew and to me. At that point I will tell the Jew: "I saved you,

sheltered you when you were persecuted. To keep you alive I risked my own life and the lives of those who were dear to me. Now nothing threatens you. You have your own friends and in some ways you are better off than I. Now I am depriving you of my home. Go and settle somewhere else. I wish you luck and will be glad to help you. I am not going to hurt you, but in my own home I want to live alone. I have the right."[113]

What Kossak-Szczucka's article suggests is that motivation for rescuing Jews in her case was dictated by the Christian duty of providing help to the needy. What is lacking in her motivation is precisely the civic principle of helping Jews as fellow citizens, members of the same society, a principle advocated by the Democratic Party, the PPS, and other minor socialist groups. The rescued Jew is treated by Kossak-Szczucka as an outsider who has no right to remain in the country of the rescuer when the war is over. A future Poland is expected to be a polity of and for ethnic Poles only. Without doubt this view is nothing less than an exposition of the main principles of Polish exclusivist ethno-nationalism. What is also characteristic of Kossak-Szczucka's argumentation is a striking failure to consider that her ideological convictions might not be appropriate at a time when a common enemy, the Nazis, were conducting extermination of Jews.

The same lack of questioning is manifested in Kossak-Szczucka's well-known and frequently cited pamphlet *Protest*, which was circulated in August 1942 during the ongoing Great Deportation. *Protest* was written as proof of Polish condemnation of and disassociation from the Nazi extermination of Jews:

This silence can be tolerated no longer. . . . He who is silent in the face of a murder—becomes an accomplice of that murder. He, who does not condemn, assists. We therefore raise our voices, we Polish Catholics. Our feelings towards the Jews have not undergone a change. We have not stopped regarding them as the political, economic and ideological enemies of Poland. What is more, we are well aware that they hate us even more than the Germans, that they hold us responsible for their misfortune. Why, on what basis—this remains a secret of the Jewish soul, but it is a fact constantly confirmed. Our awareness of these feelings does not free us from the obligation to condemn the crime. . . . We also protest as Poles. We do not believe that Poland can derive any advantage from the German cruelties. On the contrary, in the stubborn silence of international Jewry, in the efforts of German propaganda attempting to shift the odium of the massacre onto the Lithuanians and . . . the Poles, we sense the planning of an action hostile to us. We know also how poisonous are the seeds of this crime. . . . He who does not understand this, who dares to link the proud, free future of Poland to base joy at the misfortune of his neighbor—he is indeed neither a Catholic nor a Pole.[114]

Although *Protest* contains a moving description of the sufferings of Warsaw Jewry and strong opposition to the Nazi genocidal program, it also explicitly portrays Jews as "the political, economic, and ideological enemies of Poland." They are categorized as obsessive Pole-haters who would unjustly plot against Poland and blame Poles for their plight—a representation of Jews typical of the wartime National Democratic press. Thus *Protest* can also be viewed as evidence that the pre-1939 ethno-nationalist representation of the Jew was left intact during the ongoing Nazi genocide of Jews among prominent segments of the cultural Roman Catholic elite. As in the pre-1939 period ethno-nationalists still portrayed Jews as perpetrators and Poles as victims. They still wrote about Jews as a group who could harm the Poles and Poles as a vulnerable group trying to defend their rights.

Even in 1944, when it became clear that the majority of Jews had perished, the ethno-nationalists continued to portray them as powerful and treacherous. For example, in May 1944 *Prawda Dnia* noted: "We are not afraid of being accused of acting against the national interest. We are fulfilling the basic duty of Catholics; our responsibility is to take care of the most persecuted and suffering, the Jews in our country. Our duty has no connection to our political convictions. We demand from the Jews that they respect the Polish national interest and not play any political games in which they might exploit their suffering."[115]

In some of the publications of the FOP on the destruction of the Warsaw Ghetto the myth of the Jew as the harmful other combined modern anti-Semitism, rooted in exclusivist ethno-nationalism, with premodern Christian anti-Judaism. This fusion was a continuation of a particular genre that was typical in the writings of Catholic Action circles in pre-1939 Poland. *Prawda*, published in April–May 1943, categorized Jews as the enemy of all Christian European nations on whose territories they had dwelled:

> The last time Jews fought with arms in their hands was eighteen hundred years ago. . . . Since this time the Jews have been parasites living off the bodies of European nations. This is why they have been universally loathed and detested. And they have fought with everybody cunningly, never openly, with weapons in hand. They have caused three-quarters of all the wars fought in Europe. . . . They have lost all human dignity. . . . Since last year the Ger-

mans have begun the extermination of Jews en masse in the territory of
Poland. Polish society has been watching this terrible crime with shock and
pity for the Jews, who have not attempted to defend themselves. . . . And
suddenly the Jewish nation has decided to fight. . . . This is a very important
moment. Who knows, perhaps from the ashes of the Warsaw ghetto a new
spiritually reborn Israel will emerge? Perhaps the Jews will cleanse themselves
in this present burning and from being wandering persistent parasites will
transform themselves into a normal nation again. . . . We Catholics understand the importance of present events. We cannot remain passive hearing the
voices of those who were murdered. . . . Our duty is to provide help. And we
do not care if they would reciprocate our help now or in the future. Our help
cannot be limited to material support only. We also have to provide spiritual
help. A prayer for the dying . . . making them aware that before death they
could be redeemed by accepting baptism and the true faith.[116]

Some historians interpret the reaction of the FOP, and Kossak-Szczucka in
particular, as proof that prewar Polish ideological anti-Semitism "softened,"
decreased, or simply disappeared in the face of the ongoing Nazi extermination
of Jews.[117] This interpretation, which is basically committed to saving the good
name of Poland and not to empirical study of the problem, is questionable
in many aspects.[118] What it fails to take into account is that the case of
Kossak-Szczucka as the rescuer of Jews is representative of only a small group
within society, the devout ethno-nationalist Catholic elite who were politically
active in the underground.[119] This position also tends to argue that Kossak-
Szczucka and other similar individuals with a strong prewar record of anti-
Jewish beliefs—such as Jan Mosdorf, a distinguished lawyer and prewar member of one of the radical ONR groups; Leon Nowodworski, National Democrat
and dean of the Council of Lawyers in pre-1939 Poland; and the Reverend
Marceli Godlewski—were unique heroic figures in all of Nazi-occupied Europe.[120] This view totally ignores the fact that cases of rescue activities by
declared anti-Semites can be found in other countries, such as Belgium.[121]

Characteristically this interpretation also ignores the issue of Kossak-
Szczucka's political views and the impact of such views on the wartime reader
and the dynamics of the rescue activities. It does not ask complex questions
such as: How could the FOP press make its readers want to help a people
presented as the enemy of the Polish nation? And if a reader was convinced,
what kind of treatment might a rescued Jew expect from any person holding
such convictions? It also does not respond to Michael Steinlauf's important
question: "The point, rather, is that if even a founder of Żegota was an anti-

Semite, what could one have expected of the average Pole, lacking, let us assume, Kossak's extraordinary ethical sensibility?"[122]

In the light of historical evidence, which is still emerging from Poland, it is certain that Kossak-Szczucka's behavior was not typical or representative of the Catholic population at large. This is not to say that no segments of the nonelite were active in rescue operations, but that significant segments of the general population were basically indifferent to the plight of Jews.[123] Some sections of the population at large expressed varying levels of hostility toward Jews. In some areas, such as the Łomża region in northeastern Poland, hostilities took on the most severe form—that of mass killings.[124] The cases of anti-Jewish violence in thirty-five small towns of the Łomża region—like Jedwabne, Radziłów, and Wizna—show that among the local population the ethical constraints advocated by core ethno-nationalist Catholic elites were absent or did not have any tangible influence on those involved in the killings.[125] They did not prevent the murders of Jewish men, women, and children. Of course what has to be borne in mind about the mass killings and anti-Jewish riots in the Łomża region is that they occurred under special social and political conditions such as the interregnum—the change of regime from Soviet to Nazi—and under the official German policy that killing of Jews was allowed.

Jan Błoński, the first scholar to analyze Kossak-Szczucka's *Protest* in detail, argues that this text "takes us into the thinking and feeling of a significant portion of contemporary Polish society."[126] Although it is methodologically difficult to provide any exact figures regarding how many individuals thought the same way as Kossak-Szczucka did, Błoński's thesis appears correct in the light of other wartime records such as diaries of both Christian/ethnic Poles and Polish Jews and the underground press.[127] The sociological study of American Polish-born scholar Nechama Tec on the rescuers' attitudes toward Jews and their rescue activities also confirms Błoński's thesis.[128]

Of course the issue of rescue activities is a little-researched subject and still awaits further empirical investigation. Still, it is possible to establish with certainty that in WWII the Catholic elite's way of thinking was still heavily influenced by the exclusivist ethno-nationalist perspective and that the vast majority of ethno-nationalist elites also identified with the Catholic ethos. As in the interwar period the close relationship between Roman Catholicism and exclusivist ethno-nationalism persisted in producing a particular fusion of nationalism and Roman Catholicism, which in turn gave rise to a peculiar ethno-national-religious ethos. Under such conditions the Catholic principle of providing help to the most needy had no mitigating influence over the perception of the Jew as the enemy of the nation. On the contrary, the two perspectives—of sympathy and aid for Jews and of perceiving Jews as the chief enemy of Poland—appeared to be compatible with each other. In the case of Kossak-Szczucka even her experience in the concentration camp in Auschwitz, where she was a prisoner from August 1943 until May 1944, did not change her views on Jews. In her first postwar collection of writing, *Z otchłani* (From the Abyss), published in 1946, she gives a vivid portrayal of various national groups of women prisoners of Auschwitz.[129] Strikingly, Jewish women, whom Kossak-Szczucka calls "the daughters of Jerusalem," are depicted as the most corrupt, dishonest, and quarrelsome collectivity: the Jewish women prisoners are attributed the most negative characteristics in comparison with other groups of women in the camp.

The majority of Polish core ethno-nationalist political elites in WWII rejected the Nazi method of exclusion of Jews, genocide. As in the interwar period they chose to advocate the project of the emigration of Jews as the main method of excluding Jews from the postwar Polish state. At the same time National Democracy and its offshoot radical organizations, as illustrated earlier, viewed the outcome of the Nazi extermination of Jews as a positive development in the history of Poland.

The issue of why the Nazi policy of exterminating Jews was rejected by the core exclusivist ethno-nationalist elites is worth exploring. Here two important factors must be taken into account. First, biological racism of the type advocated by the Germans was not a crucial aspect of the mainstream ideology of Polish exclusivist ethno-nationalism. Even the radical groups seemed to focus more often on the "dangerous Jewish soul," "spirituality," and "mind" than on "the dangerous Jewish race." This is not to say that racial concepts did not exist in the Polish version of integral nationalism. After all, a "dangerous Jewish soul" and "mind" also imply the existence of a "dangerous Jewish body and race." Perhaps one of the main differences in terms of content between the German and Polish versions of anti-Semitism lay in the way the concept of race was utilized by Polish core ethno-nationalists in comparison to German racial nationalists. At the same time, as far as the general representation of Jews as a harmful other in the national context is concerned, one can see some similarities between the image of Jews painted by ethno-nationalist Germans and the image of Jews painted by National Democrats and their offshoot organizations. Here one can also argue that, just as in the interwar period, Polish radical ethno-nationalist elites failed to recognize that their conceptualization of Polish Jews as the national enemy resembled the ethno-nationalist German perception of German Jews.[130]

The rejection by radical Polish political elites of the Nazi method of disposing of Jews can also be attributed to the fact that Poland was occupied by Nazi Germany. With the exception of a few early attempts to win over a number of Polish aristocratic politicians with conservative views, such as Stanisław Estreicher, professor of law at Jagiellonian University, and Władysław Studnicki, the Nazi regime did not seem to be interested in establishing collaboration with the Poles, unlike in Nazi satellite states.[131]

Collaboration with the Nazis was met with disapproval and condemnation on the part of the entire underground state, including core ethno-nationalist elites. Already at the beginning of the war the National Democrats condemned those members of its fascist offshoot organizations who were inclined to participate with the Germans in the orchestration of a wave of anti-Jewish violence: "We shall not do what they [the Germans] expect us to do. After the war we shall be able to solve the Jewish question according to Polish mentality and morality. That is why we did not approve of the deeds of those members of the [Falanga and ONR] who tried, at the beginning, to cooperate with the Germans in anti-Semitic activities. We have no intention of baking our bread in this fire."[132]

Perhaps another reason why genocide as a form of solving the "Jewish question" was not acceptable to the National Democrats lay in their understanding of Catholic tradition. Even the most extreme right-wing section of the Polish political elite referred to Nazi extermination of Jewry as "a barbaric anti-Christian action" and one that was "alien to the Polish-Catholic ethos." One extreme version of such a position, advocated in the press of such radical groups as Konfederacja Narodu, stated that the Jews and the Germans, as well the Ukrainians and the Lithuanians, belonged to a civilization with which Polish civilization had nothing in common; Polish civilization was superior in its spirituality to the civilization represented by all these groups: "They represented the other world, which caused the disaster, and therefore it has to perish."[133] Ironically one can argue that such intense and peculiar ethnocentrism and megalomania, mixed with intense and radical anti-Jewish prejudice, also contributed to the radical ethno-nationalist political groups' opposition to collaboration with Hitler. The National Democratic party and its radical offshoot organizations viewed the Nazi extermination of European

Jews as a program that had nothing in common with their project of solving the "Jewish question" by emigration. The National Democratic party made a historically correct distinction in terms of the strategy advocated for disposing of an unwanted minority. However, at the same time Endecja failed to address the issue of approval of the outcome of the Nazi genocide of the Jews that was voiced in public by members of Endecja, its radical offshoot organizations, and segments of the nonelite. Encounter with this approval was one of the most shocking and painful experiences for Polish Jews who were in hiding on the Aryan side and became one of the main aspects of their memory of WWII.

As in the interwar period ethno-nationalist elites were convinced that their position concerning Polish Jews was right and justified: the exclusion of Jews from a future Poland by "voluntary" or forced emigration was not only acceptable but the "proper" way of disposing of an unwanted minority. Thus their position lacked critical reflection on the social and moral implications of advocating the project of the emigration of Jews at a time when the Nazis were committing mass murder of Jews. Here one can see the destructive side of exclusivist ethno-nationalism, even when it does not advocate genocide as a form of exclusion.

In interwar Poland the ethno-nationalist political camp claimed "objective grounds" for the project of Jewish mass emigration from Poland. The "objective grounds" were defined as the large size of the Jewish population and its economic position within Polish society: "We have the right to be anti-Semites. . . . In this state in which every tenth citizen is a Jew there are principal grounds for being an anti-Semite." [134] This reasoning should have lost its validity and disappeared during WWII for two logical reasons: the size of the Jewish community underwent a rapid reduction, and its economic status changed drastically under Nazi legislation. Yet despite knowledge of these two developments Polish ethno-nationalist elites continued to perceive Jews as the chief impediment to the development of the Polish nation. This phenomenon fully reveals the nonrational origins and prejudiced nature of the representation of Jews as the harmful other and its easy adaptability to different social contexts. In fact, it demonstrates the validity of Aleksander Hertz's pre-1939 thesis that the mythologization of the other as the enemy can continue regardless of the real position of the group that is being mythologized. [135] It also exposes the flaws and lack of critical thinking in the post-1945 intellectual and historical approach, which also used the argument of "objective causes" in discussing anti-Semitism. [136]

The Concepts of Judeo-Bolshevism and Judeo-Communism

One of the major narratives of the Jew as the national enemy of Poland that was advocated by various ethno-nationalist political elites in WWII was that Jews supported the antinational forces of Bolshevism and Communism. This representation, which many nonpartisan scholars recognize as one of the main pillars of modern anti-Semitism, functioned as a popular "social truth" in interwar Poland. [137] As documented in chapters 3 and 4, by the end of the Second Republic the press of various political parties and organizations, ranging from extreme ethno-nationalist and fascist groups to Roman Catholic and conservative political and social groups, regularly labeled Jews as agents of Communism and ideological traitors to Poland. In WWII the political debates continued to employ the narrative of Judeo-Bolshevism. [138]

From the beginning of the war the narrative of Judeo-Bolshevism and the Jewish betrayal of Poland influenced various political assessments of wartime events. One such event was the Soviet invasion and occupation of eastern Poland, where the Ukrainians, Belorussians, and Jews constituted the majority of the population. Some scholars, such as Jaff Schatz, argue that the record of the prewar Polish government's policies toward minorities aided the Soviet Army's claim that it had come to liberate them from Polish national and class oppression: "The majority of the population—Ukrainian nationalists, Belorussian Socialists, the Jewish poor, refugees from the German-occupied territories, some ethnic Poles who initially regarded the Soviet Army as an ally, and of course, the Communists—enthusiastically welcomed the Red Army." [139] There is no doubt that the twenty-two-month Soviet occupation reinforced anti-Jewish prejudices of the pre-1939 period and led to disastrous consequences for Polish-Jewish relations.

The Soviet Union reversed what Ben-Cion Pincuk calls "a natural order" of things as perceived by ordinary Poles. [140] From the beginning of the Soviet occupation individual Jews, as well as Ukrainians and Belorussians, were accepted as members of the state administration at both the middle and lower levels, a development unthinkable in terms of the functioning of the pre-1939 Polish state. For Jews the Soviets were also a lesser evil than the Nazis, whose anti-Jewish policies were all too well-known. However, Polish political elites, for whom the Nazis and the Soviets were equal enemies, failed to recognize this. Although Polish officials of the underground state represented a Poland that acted as the continuity of the multinational pre-1939 Polish state, they occupied themselves with the fate of ethnic Poles only. They therefore did not recognize Soviet policies that discriminated against Jews as a religious and cultural community and did not register critical attitudes within the Jewish community toward the Soviet regime.

In underground circles the positive reception of the Soviet Army by segments of the Jewish community, particularly youth and the poor, was interpreted as a collective Jewish betrayal of Poland.[141] In their negative assessments ethno-nationalist politicians of the underground state did not take into account the diversity of Jewish responses to the Soviet invasion and occupation and the subsequently varied treatment of Polish Jews by the Soviet authorities, particularly the ruthless treatment of the Jewish middle class and of Zionist and Bundist political elites. Nevertheless, they were aware of such treatment, which was reported in various secret correspondence: memos and reports sent from the eastern territories to the Polish government-in-exile.[142] Looking at some of their statements one can recognize that the notion of Jews as "Bolshevik traitors of Poland" provided a premise for the prevalent model of thinking about the entire Jewish community that lived under Soviet rule between 17 September 1939 and 22 June 1941 and its relations with the Soviet regime. Even moderate conservative Polish politicians seemed to believe in such an assessment as "objective truth." For example, on 5 December 1942 Minister Stanisław Kot, in his conversations with representatives of Polish Jewry, claimed: "The atmosphere in Russia was caused by the behavior of the Jews under Soviet occupation. Many Poles suffered because of denunciations by Jews. In some places Jews joyfully welcomed the entering Soviet troops, helped disarm Polish officers and police . . . , and then collaborated with the Russian regime and brought about many arrests and deportations."

In reply Dr. Stupp, one of the representatives of the Jewish delegation, presented information contrary to Kot's arguments: "If I may interrupt you, Mr. Minister, you probably know that in many areas of the Homeland Polish people, convinced the Soviet Army had come to help, also welcomed the troops with flowers." Kot, however, rejected Stupps's suggestion that some ethnic Poles had also welcomed the Soviets: "Well, let us leave aside the welcome, but [what about] all the other things that happened later on?"[143]

The steady development of the new Polish Communist Party, the PPR, was another wartime event that contributed in underground circles to the intensification of the representation of Jews as Communists and Bolsheviks.[144] The ethno-nationalists applied the prewar belief that all Jews subscribed to Communism and Bolshevism to the PPR and its underground military forces, the

People's Army (Armia Ludowa, AL) and the People's Guard (Gwardia Ludowa, GL). The latter were set up in the GG at the beginning of 1943, while the PPR was set up on 5 January 1942 with two bases, one in the GG and the other in the Soviet Union. In contrast to the KPP, the prewar predecessor of the PPR, the PPR from the beginning declared its commitment to Poland's independence. Still, the base in the Soviet Union consisted mainly of members of the prewar KPP who had escaped Stalin's purge of 1938. Many of them were Polish Jews. In the GG the structure of the PPR was different; most of the newcomers at the various local branches of the PPR were ethnic Poles.[145]

The link between the PPR and the Soviet Union played an important role in the categorization of the PPR as an antinational party. The memory of the Soviet invasion of 17 September 1939 and the Soviet occupation of the eastern territories, which resulted in various Soviet crimes committed against ethnic Poles (and other Polish citizens) and the Polish state, was still fresh within the non-Communist underground.[146] Such a memory was not easily reconciled with the fact that the Soviet Union had joined the Allied Powers in the war against Nazism in the summer of 1941, after having been invaded by the Germans. Thus inevitably in the non-Communist underground the PPR was viewed not only as a political and ideological opponent but also as a national enemy representing a foreign power, the Soviets, and posing a threat similar to that of the Nazi regime. However, the core ethno-nationalist political elites developed a special perception of the PPR that would also play an important role in the early postwar period. According to this perception, the PPR was "exclusively created by Jews and for Jews and other non-Poles." This perception maintained that "true" Poles would not join such an antinational party and could not be its potential sympathizers either.[147] Although this perception had little basis in the face of developments in the GG, it persisted nevertheless. In the context of the complexities of the Polish experience in WWII the notion of a Judeo-Communist conspiracy provided a biased but convenient explanation for the growing strength of the Communist camp in the last two years of the war, without damaging the image of ethnic Poles who had joined the PPR. Such an explanation would also come to play an important role in assessing Communist rule in post-1945 Poland.

References to Jews as Communists and Bolsheviks can be found in reports of the Delegate's Bureau and the AK that were prepared by various members of these institutions. They indicate that their authors disseminated belief in Judeo-Communism. Here are four varied examples:

> The Polish population of Brześć has welcomed the German invasion [of the Soviet Union] as "redemption" from the Judeo-Bolshevik yoke.[148]

> The partisan units are commanded by Bolshevik officers. The vice-commander is often a Jew. . . . Jewish bandits frequently terrorize the local population.[149]

> The "komuna" is preparing for military actions in October. News is spreading that they are planning to begin the disarming of the Germans. . . . The decision makers are Jews and bandits.[150]

> Jews are completely alien to us and are hostile to Poles in various areas. They are threatening the local population with Bolshevism.[151]

Fugitives from the Holocaust, including women, were also referred to as Communists, Bolshevik agents, and helpers posing a serious threat to the ethnic Polish population. They were simultaneously described as "bandits and common criminals." These labels were to be found not only in the press of extreme ethno-nationalists but also in the orders of the local and chief commanders of the AK.[152] For example, in his order of 31 August 1943 Rowecki's successor, General Tadeusz Bór-Komorowski (1895–1966), stated:

> Well-armed gangs roam endlessly in cities and villages, attacking estates, banks, commercial and industrial companies, houses and apartments and larger peasant farms. The plunder is often accompanied by acts of murder, which are carried out by Soviet partisan units hiding in the forests or ordinary gangs of robbers. The latter recruit from all kinds of criminal subversive elements. Men and women, especially Jewish women, participate in the assaults. This infamous action of demoralized individuals contributes in considerable degree to the complete destruction of many citizens who have already been tormented by the four-year struggle against the enemy. . . . In order to give some help and shelter to the defenseless population I have issued an order—with the understanding of the head of the Delegate's Bureau—to the commanders of regions and districts regarding local security . . . instructing them where necessary, to move with arms against these plundering or subversive bandit elements.[153]

This record clearly shows that in the context of the political struggle against the Communist camp, Jews were simply viewed as an ideological and physical threat to the security of the ethnic Polish population; they were the enemy. This representation can provide clues to the lack of concern over the predicament of Jews among the leadership of the AK. Antony Polonsky points, for example, to Bór-Komorowski's lack of concern for the fugitives. According to Polonsky, "nothing in Bór-Komorowski's order (which was later withdrawn in the wake of protests from within the Home Army) indicates any sympathy for fugitives from the Nazi Genocide; no appeal is made to villagers to provide them with the food and shelter that otherwise they could only seize by force; and no understanding is shown of their predicament."[154]

Bór-Komorowski's prejudiced assessment of cooperation between fugitives from the Holocaust and Communist military forces ignored two important developments. First, only AK units that were under control of the left-wing Sanacja, the Democratic Party, or PPS commanders accepted Jews; otherwise the general policy was to deny membership to individuals who were recognized as Jews or who themselves declared their ethnic origin. Second, the gradual acceptance of various military forces representing extreme political parties under the umbrella of the AK in 1943 and 1944 created a dangerous situation for Jews.[155] In fact, from the point of view of Jewish fugitives the consequences of cooperation between the AK and the military organizations of the extreme offshoot political organizations of the National Democrats, such as the Rampart Group or Sword and Plough, were grave. An encounter with extreme right-wing units could result not only in the rejection of a Jewish individual but also in brutal hostility, which sometimes could end in murder.[156]

Of course the obsession with Judeo-Bolshevism was manifested most aggressively in the press of National Democracy and various radical organizations. Characteristically these journals raised the issue of Judeo-Bolshevism in order to rationalize and justify the Nazi destruction of Warsaw Jewry—the Great Deportation and the destruction of the Warsaw Ghetto in the aftermath of the Ghetto Uprising of April 1943. In this strategy the Jewish plight "at the hands of the Germans" was compared to the alleged plight of Poles "at the hands of the Jews" under the Soviet occupation. The National Democrats presented Jews as the main party responsible for the discrimination against and mass killings and imprisonment of Poles in the Soviet-occupied portion of Poland between 1939 and the summer of 1941. Ethno-nationalist writers used this portrayal of the relationship between Jews and Poles in Soviet-occupied Poland to influence the reader to disassociate him- or herself emotionally from the plight of Warsaw Jewry. This representation of Jews echoed that disseminated through Nazi propaganda in the official Polish-language press. On the eve of the Warsaw Ghetto Uprising the Nazi papers cunningly propagated false news of the "Jewish murder" of Polish officers in Katyń, which was the site where the Soviet regime had killed 4,410 Polish officers during its occupation of eastern Poland.[157]

On 30 April 1943 *Nurt Młodych*, one of the papers of the radical organization Miecz i Pług, claimed: "We are aware that the 'chosen people' have chosen the red banner over the Polish White Eagle. We know how the Jews have behaved toward Poles in the territories occupied by Russia. We know what immense casualties the Polish Nation has suffered as a result of the actions of these Jews. Thus the fate incurred by these Jews now, although appearing terrible from a human point of view, seems justified."[158]

Ethno-nationalist writers viewed Jews as servants of the Russians and also accused them of cooperating with the Germans. In the pre-1939 period Roman Dmowski had been the chief disseminator of the concept of the Jew as a long-term supporter of Germany, the long-standing historical enemy of Poland. In the wartime press Dmowski's concept was simply recycled and adapted to the contemporary political and social context. For example, on 21 September 1942 *Szaniec*, the paper of the Rampart Group, noted:

> The present pogrom of the Jews in Poland orchestrated by the Germans is a well-organized job. . . . The Jewish writer Szalom Ash could not invent a better version of a pogrom of the Poles [than the German pogrom of the Jews]. We can imagine what the Jews would have done to the Poles. In fact, we know what they did to us during the Jewish occupation of [the eastern territories]. . . . The Jews have been the servants of the Germans for many hundred years. And they will always support the Germans and anybody else who is against us. Therefore let us not be sentimental over their tragedy. . . . Of course we advise taking up a philosophical posture of indifference toward the fate of the Jews. We should not voice our satisfaction that the unpleasant job of killing our enemy is carried out by our other enemy. Such a position, we must stress, would not be Christian and Polish. . . . This position could in fact be identified as Jewish and German.[159]

The concept of a connection between the Nazi and Jewish spirit followed the pre-1939 ideas advocated by the Catholic historian Feliks Koneczny. Koneczny, who was dismissed from his post at Stefan Batory University in Wilno in the 1920s, was one of the chief proponents of the theory that Jewish civilization allegedly threatened the entire Christian-Latin world.[160] In his wartime writings he went one step further and claimed that Nazism too "was penetrated by the Jewish spirit." In an article entitled "Hitleryzm zażydzony" (The Judaized Hitlerism) Koneczny argued that Nazism was a product of Jewish civilization.[161] Koneczny's arguments demonstrate the correctness of Aleksander Hertz's thesis about the easy adaptability of the image of the harmful other to different sociopolitical contexts.

In light of recently published and analyzed historical evidence the belief in Judeo-Communism was one of main causes of the massacres of Jews that occurred in Łomża province in northeastern Poland during the summer of 1941.[162] Jan T. Gross convincingly demonstrates that there was no evidence to support the position that Jedwabne Jews, or other Jewish communities of the region, were collaborators en masse with the Soviet regime. On the contrary, the number of collaborators among Jedwabne Jews was insignificant in comparison to the number of Soviet collaborators of ethnic Polish origin.[163] However, many members of the local Polish community in Jedwabne believed in the notion of Judeo-Communism in the summer of 1941. This belief was one of the immediate factors inciting anti-Jewish violence. It manifested itself in the act of anti-Jewish violence itself and in a particular ritual that the per-petrators considered to be punishment for alleged Jewish wrongs committed against Poles: a group of Jewish men was forced to carry a statue of Lenin to the barn where they were about to be killed.[164]

Krzysztof Jasiewicz also argues that the testimonies of ethnic Poles who sur-vived the Soviet occupation do not provide evidence that Jews were a dominant or privileged group within the Soviet state apparatus; in fact, collaboration with the Soviet regime was cross-ethnic, with ethnic Poles also within the group of collaborators. Jasiewicz convincingly argues that despite the fact that Jews did not constitute a majority of Soviet elites, they were the only ethnic group for which Poles blamed the Soviet occupation. This situation can only be explained by the fact that Jews prior to the Soviet occupation were already perceived as Judeo-Bolsheviks and Communists. Thus the anti-Jewish riots of summer 1941 reveal the destructive impact of prejudicial perceptions.[165]

The Concept of the "Covert Jew"

During WWII the ethno-nationalist press began to employ with new vigor the notion of the "covert/masked Jew," who was hardly distinguishable from a Pole. The National Democrats and other ethno-nationalists had used the notion of the "covert/masked Jew" before 1939 to describe the culturally assim-ilated Polish-Jewish intelligentsia, which they believed constituted "the most dangerous group" of Jews because of their alleged ability to destroy "the spiri-tual, cultural, and even biological essence" of the Polish nation. *Myśl Narodowa* regularly published a list of Jews who had adopted Polish-sounding names. According to the paper, Jews who adopted Polish names were "covert Jews" pretending to be Poles. Furthermore, the National Democrats categorized the act of adoption of a Polish name by a Jew as a "crime" committed against the Polish nation.[166]

In WWII the notion of "covert Jews" was employed in describing Jews as not only the cultural but also the political enemies of Poland. Furthermore, the notion would be used against any individual whose identity was suspect. The expansion of its use in the ethno-nationalist press was synchronous with the destruction of the majority of Polish Jewry and with the appearance on the Aryan side of Jews who "performed the act of playing a Pole" in their daily lives in order to survive the Nazi hunt. Who were the masked Jews in the eyes of core ethno-nationalists?

Ethno-nationalist writers considered the "covert Jew" the most threatening element in a postwar Poland, an ideological enemy nursing hatred for everything Polish and conspiring with all other enemies of the state. Various themes were interlocked in this particular version of the myth: the Jew as an ideological enemy, the Jew as a traitor of Poland, and the cunning and powerful Jew always aiming at harming the Polish nation. For example, on 16 May 1943 *Kierownik*, the paper of the National Democratic Military Organization, issued a detailed profile of the covert Jew:

> The Jewish hand is turning against us and blames the Polish nation for all the miseries that have befallen us and for the lack of help from our side. Yes, a majority of the Jewish nation is destroyed, but the remnants have not changed their attitude toward us. They are closer to a Russian or German Communist than they are to us Poles. They are waiting to take control over our economic life. They are plotting against us along with other minorities. In our conflict with Soviet Russia they support the Bolshevik side. They would do anything in order to weaken us and prevent the emergence of a Great Poland. We are fully aware that a few hundred thousand Jews are enough to take control of our economy and to infiltrate the centers of our political and cultural life. These particular Jews are even more dangerous than the Jews en masse. There are many signs that covert Jews in Poland and Jewish émigré circles are now preparing to take control over Poland.[167]

Society and the Myth

The support of a significant segment of the Polish population in the GG for an ethnically homogenous future state was an embarrassing topic for the Polish government-in-exile in London, one that they believed could dishonor the good name of Poland and stain its positive image as a democratic country. The government promoted the image of Poland as a democratic and pluralistic country among the Western Allies and insisted that the vision of a civic and pluralistic Poland was supported by the majority of Polish society in the Nazi-occupied GG. This position required providing supporting evidence. What this meant in practice was that Polish officials suppressed any information from the GG that might reveal to the Western Allies and the representatives of Polish Jews abroad any evidence of support for the ethno-nationalization of the Polish state and the extent of negative or indifferent attitudes of Poles toward Jews. [168] Polish officials adopted a "public relations strategy" in which the positive aspects of the interaction between Jews and Poles were emphasized, including exaggerated information about the assistance provided to Jews by the majority of Poles. This is how the narrative of the solidarity of the majority of the Polish population with dying Jews in WWII was created.

A close look at historical documentation from WWII shows a clear discrepancy between the promoted narrative of the solidarity and unity and the information that was received by the government-in-exile from Nazi-occupied Poland. Underground reports and dispatches sent to the government-in-exile reveal that the government's official commitment to the inclusion of Jews in a future Poland, which brought it credibility in the eyes of the Western Allies, enjoyed low public acceptance in Nazi-occupied Poland among the supporters of the ethno-nationalist vision of Poland. This trend remained unchanged throughout the war. The Nazi destruction of Polish Jews did not appear to have any mitigating influence on support for an ethnic Poland without Jews among members of the nonelite whose views were registered by the underground state.

For example, according to a dispatch sent by Janusz Radziwiłł to Minister Kot, even the electorate of the PPS opposed the inclusion of Jews in a future Polish nation-state. The "Stańczyk Resolution" of 3 November 1940, which Minister Stańczyk promoted among Polish Jews abroad, "made a disastrous impression in Poland, even among workers belonging to the Polish Socialist Party." [169]

An official report from the Department of Internal Affairs of the Delegate's Bureau, covering a period from 15 November 1941 until 1 June 1942, also spoke of popular support for the emigration of Jews from a future Poland. Support for an ethnic Poland without Jews was compatible with expressed emotions of shock and horror at the Nazi murder of Jews and of empathy toward Jews as victims of terrible atrocities committed by the Germans. This report indicated that the Polish population generally welcomed the disappearance of Jews from the social and economic sphere and that the potential reemergence of Jews in postwar Poland could justify hostilities directed against them. It also indicated that the ethno-nationalist economic way of thinking that had been promoted in pre-1939 Poland had gained the upper hand among large segments of Polish nonelites: "German bestiality toward Jews has brought about sympathy for them and condemnation of Nazi methods within the Polish population. And it has also caused a decrease of aggressive [Polish] anti-Semitism. Nevertheless, there is a general expectation that 'the Jewish matter' will be sorted out by voluntary or forced emigration after the war. Present economic changes (laws regarding Jewish business and properties) indicate a future rise of political anti-Semitism."[170]

In the summer of 1943 Roman Knoll, a senior official in the Delegate's Bureau who had supported National Democracy in the interwar period, sent a memorandum to the government-in-exile. In a more elaborate manner than the author of the previous report Knoll argued that the return of Polish Jews to their homes after the war would not be acceptable to the Polish population and could erupt into anti-Jewish violence, which should be understood and justified as a "means of self-defense." He also emphasized that the future disappearance of anti-Semitism in Poland was conditional purely upon the disappearance of the Jews. What is clear here is that Knoll's understanding of anti-Semitism did not differ from the party line of National Democracy as articulated in the late preindependence phase (1880–1918):

> In the Homeland as a whole . . . the feeling is such that the return of the Jews to their jobs and workshops is completely out of the question, even if the number of Jews were greatly reduced. The non-Jewish population has filled the places of the Jews in the towns and cities; in a large part of Poland this is a fundamental change, final in character. The return of masses of Jews would be seen by the population not as restitution but as an invasion against which they would defend themselves, even with physical means. . . . The government is correct in its assurances to world opinion that anti-Semitism will not exist in Poland; but it will not exist only if the Jews who survive do not endeavor to return en masse to Poland's cities and towns."[171]

A 27 March 1944 report of the Delegate's Bureau Department of Information and Press stated that the government's commitment to the inclusion of Jews in a future state had been received with shock and mistrust by the Polish peasantry. According to the author of the report, the peasants expressed doubt that Polish authorities could have made such a pledge. The report indicated that the peasants classified Jews, together with the German and Ukrainian minorities, as "unwanted peoples" in a future state. The fact that Jews and Poles were common victims of Nazi aggression was irrelevant in the context of support for an ethnically homogenous polity. The ethno-nationalist perception that it was the Poles who had suffered in their land because of the presence of minorities in pre-1939 Poland resulted in popular understanding of the project of the exclusion of minorities as just and desirable: "In general the prevalent mood of the peasant population is that a postwar Poland has to be purely ethnically Polish and that the return to the prewar situation, where Jews, Germans, and Ukrainians had more rights and better work opportunities and enjoyed a wealthier life than Poles, is not acceptable. All the government's promises concerning minorities published in the [underground] press have been received with shock and mistrust. In fact, the population is convinced that these promises are simply propagated by German sources."[172]

The conclusion to be drawn from these records is that some significant segments of the ethnic Polish population supported the exclusion of Polish Jews from a future Poland and endorsed the negative representation of Jews as harmful aliens. Even if one takes into account the possibility of exaggeration in some of these records, as Krystyna Kersten argues, one cannot ignore the popularity during WWII of the project of the exclusion of Jews from Poland, which had already been presented in the interwar period as a solution that would lead to the end of the unemployment of peasants and workers and to the creation of the immediate prosperity of Poles.[173] After all, during the last two years of the war and the early post-1945 period even Communists felt compelled to propagate the concept of an ethnically homogenous Poland in their political programs in order to gain public acceptance, a process that will be discussed in the next chapter.

It is also important to keep in mind that the popularity of the National Democrats, the core ethno-nationalist party, was on the increase in WWII. According to Jerzy Terej, the National Democrats succeeded in reaching segments of the Polish population that prior to the war had not voted for National Democracy.[174] This increase in popularity was due to the National Democrats' strong ethno-national, Catholic, and anti-German ethos—values with which many identified under conditions of war and the German occupation. [175] National Democracy's press was also an important tool in disseminating its propaganda. In 1944, of 600 continuous titles within the entire underground press, National Democracy and its offshoot organizations published 120 papers. [176] According to Jerzy Terej, the National Democrats and their offshoot radical organizations possessed good technical equipment in comparison with other clandestine parties, and their press enjoyed wide circulation within all parts of Nazi-occupied Poland. [177] Many of the titles were designed to reach particular segments of society, such as peasants, the working class, and youth.

In February 1940 Jan Karski (1914–2000), a secret courier of the Polish underground state, composed the first comprehensive report on Polish reactions toward the plight of Polish Jewry under the Nazi occupation. Karski's report reveals that exclusivist ethno-nationalism influenced the reaction of certain sections of the Polish population toward the plight of Jews. The report argued that significant segments of the Polish population in the GG perceived Polish Jews as an unwanted entity existing outside of the fabric of Polish society. Furthermore, the Polish population was split in its evaluation of the outcome of German anti-Jewish actions; one segment of the population unequivocally condemned Nazi anti-Jewish actions, and the other expressed ill-concealed joy that the Germans were solving the "Jewish question" for them. The effect of ethno-nationalism on interethnic relations between Poles and Jews under German occupation, as described in Karski's report, was so damaging that Polish officials decided to amend the report. In the amended, "censored" version the information concerning negative attitudes toward Polish Jews was omitted, the Polish population depicted as "united in its revulsion toward German anti-Jewish actions." David Engel convincingly argues that the second censored version was prepared because "Polish officials realized that Karski's original statements regarding the extent and nature of Polish anti-Jewish feeling could potentially, if discovered, discredit the Polish cause in the eyes of Poland's two chief allies, Britain and France." [178] The most "devastating" excerpts from the original report confirm the notion of "the egoism of victimization," in which there can be no real empathy for the suffering experienced by a group considered to be the enemy:

> Usually one gets the sense that it would be advisable were there to prevail in the attitude of the Poles toward them the understanding that in the end both peoples are being unjustly persecuted by the same enemy. Such an understanding does not exist among the broad masses of the Polish populace. Their attitude toward the Jews is overwhelmingly severe, often without pity. A large percentage of them are benefiting from the rights that the new situ-

ation gives them. They frequently exploit those rights and often even abuse them. . . . The solution of the "Jewish Question" by the Germans—I must state this with a full sense of responsibility for what I am saying—is a serious and quite dangerous tool in the hands of the Germans, leading toward the "moral pacification" of broad sections of Polish society. It would certainly be erroneous to suppose that this issue alone will be effective in gaining for them the acceptance of the populace. However, although the nation loathes them mortally, this question is creating something akin to a narrow bridge upon which the Germans and a large portion of Polish society are finding agreement. . . .

Furthermore, the present situation is creating a two-fold schism among the inhabitants of these territories—first, a schism between Jews and Poles in the struggle against the common enemy, and second, a schism among the Poles, with one group despising and resenting the Germans' barbaric methods [conscious of the danger in this], and the other regarding them [and thus the Germans, too!] with curiosity and often fascination, and condemning the first group for its indifference toward such an important question.[179]

Regardless of their level of assimilation into Polish culture, and their political affiliation, a noticeable segment of Jews, at least educated elites, were like Karski profoundly shocked by the realization that they were excluded from Polish society and that their own tragedy was not embraced in the unfolding tragedy of Poland:

The Polish people, suffering perhaps more than any other nation from the yoke of misfortune together with the Jewish people, should have, above all and at every opportunity, demonstrated sympathy, solidarity, and brotherhood with the Jews. Alas, this is but a dream. . . .

We know we must not generalize: there is often a compassionate silence, horror in the eyes, a mute expression of solidarity . . . but what the rabble, youngsters, peasant women, idlers, rascals, scoundrels, and outcast . . . express in words, sets the tone, wounds the heart, hurts the dignity of the Jews who have not been granted the satisfaction of having friends and comrades among the Poles.[180]

The diaries and memoirs of ethnic Poles also address the problem of the reaction of Poles toward the plight of Jews.[181] They can be divided into two groups, the first group endorsing the ethno-nationalist vision of Poland and the representation of the Jews as the harmful other and the second group condemning and distancing itself from the former group. In the latter group members of the Polish intelligentsia often reflected on the lack of concern over the fate of Jews on the part of sections of the Polish population and the ease with which individuals, particularly the poor and uneducated, appropriated "post-Jewish property." In the not widely known short story *Gałązki akacji*, published in Poland in 1947, the theater critic Edmund Wierciński wrote: " 'What happened to the Jewish orphanage?'—I asked the maid Marysia. 'They said that the Germans threw a shell in there. Maybe a group of children was saved, maybe somebody was rescued.' Marysia, however, was mostly perturbed by the fact that according to rumor many of us Poles had been shot down in the ghetto.—'Why did they go there?'—I asked Marysia.—'For the goods the Jews left behind'—she replied."[182]

During the Warsaw Ghetto Uprising of April 1943, the event that marked the final destruction of Warsaw Jewry, the underground political elites and local population were also divided in their attitudes and reactions toward the witnessed event.[183] Of course neither the underground military authorities nor the Warsaw civilian population was in a position to alter the course of the destructive German actions. Most of the clandestine press, in fact, praised the uprising as a courageous Jewish revolt against the Germans and condemned the Nazi destruction of the ghetto. However, the underground authorities and the majority of the political parties, with the exception of the PPS and the Democrats, viewed the event as outside the Polish national tragedy. In the press of National Democracy the uprising was referred to as the German-Jewish War.[184]

The lack of recognition of the plight of Warsaw Jewry as a part of Poland's tragedy was also manifested in the reactions of some sections of the Warsaw population. Most of Warsaw met the events taking place inside the Warsaw ghetto with indifference. This indifference can be attributed to other psychosocial factors than simply the impact of ethno-nationalism, such as powerlessness and fear caused by the severe conditions of the occupation and German legislation that decreed the death penalty for Poles rescuing Jews.[185] Nevertheless, the ethno-nationalist approach should also be considered as a factor influencing some attitudes of the Warsaw population at large.

For example, some individuals admitted that "my conscience is burdened with much heavier guilt. . . . I have in mind the indifference bordering on cruelty to the fate of the Jews which amounted to saying: I could not care less about the people dying in the ghetto. They were 'them' not 'us.' I saw the smoke rising from the burning ghetto, I heard about what was going on inside, but they were 'them.' "[186]

One piece of striking evidence of indifference toward the plight of Warsaw Jewry was the participation of a segment of the population in entertainment activities at Krasiński Square in Warsaw, where the Germans set up a merry-go-round in the spring of 1943 that started to operate during the religious festival of Easter: "When the fighting [inside the ghetto] broke out, the merry-go-round did not stop; children, youngsters and passers-by crowded around it as before."[187]

Diaries and memoirs of both ethnic Poles and Polish Jews speak about "ill-concealed joy" at seeing the remnants of Warsaw Jewry being murdered by some segments of the Warsaw population.[188] In *Polish-Jewish Relations* Emanuel Ringelblum reports that such remarks were also made among individuals engaged in rescuing Jews, causing pain and trauma among those in hiding, including children:

> Though the boy was very much liked, he had to leave this flat, since the land-lord's anti-Semitic relatives did not acquiesce in hiding a Jew, and considered it a sin against the Polish nation. The boy had been through the "the hottest" time for the Jews, the April "action." When the Ghetto where his father lived was burning and the explosions reverberated as walls were dynamited, the boy had to listen to anti-Semitic conversations, with the talkers frankly expressing their great satisfaction at the Nazi solution of the Jewish problem. . . . I know an eight-year-old boy who stayed for eight months on the Aryan side without his parents. The boy was hiding with his father's friends who treated him like their own child. The child spoke in whispers and moved as silently as a cat, so that the neighbors should not become aware of the presence of a Jewish child. . . . He often had to listen to the anti-Semitic talk of young Poles who came to visit the landlord's daughters. . . . On one occasion he was present when the young visitors boasted that Hitler had taught the Poles how to deal with the Jews and that the remnant that survived the Nazi slaughter would be dealt with likewise.[189]

In his memoirs Edward Reicher, a medical doctor from Łódź who survived most of the war in Warsaw on the Aryan side, also recollects expressions of approval for the destruction of the Warsaw ghetto: "At Krasiński Square we were passing the market stalls. Near the merry-go-round people were in a jolly and playful mood. There was loud music and a few couples were dancing. It looked as though the rabble was celebrating the fall of the Warsaw Ghetto. A drunken man embraced me and said; 'What a joy, the Jews are burning.' . . . In those days as a part of the ghetto was turning into ashes, life appeared so jolly on the Aryan side."[190]

One Holocaust survivor living in contemporary Poland recollects similar expressions: "For me this was the most painful experience on the Aryan side. This was simply shocking. Crowds of people were on the way to visit their families and friends during the Easter Festival. And I myself with friends was also walking towards Żoliborz [one of the suburbs of Warsaw]. Among the passing pedestrians I heard 'the Jews are burning and are spoiling our festival.' . . . I felt as if I was on Golgotha. People were dying and yet they were saying that their Festival was being spoiled. Not one person remarked how terrible it was."[191]

Although it is impossible to establish precisely what percentage of the Warsaw population perceived the Nazi destruction of the Warsaw Ghetto as a solution to the "Jewish question," one cannot escape the observation that such remarks were made openly, in public, without embarrassment. This indicates some level of public acceptance of such attitudes. The number of remarks reflecting such attitudes, described in diaries and memoirs, suggests that they could not have been limited to a marginal segment of the population, such as the criminal outcast, but were more widespread.

These attitudes stand in sharp contrast to the attitudes of the Warsaw population toward two thousand peasant children from the Zamość region in southeastern Poland whom the Germans took by force from their parents, putting them into transports to the Reich. According to Tomasz Szarota, the city was moved by news of the children dying of cold and hunger at a Warsaw train station in January 1943.[192] Despite the German announcement that spreading news about the children's transport was punishable by prison, members of all Warsaw social classes made an effort to collect money to save some of the children and visited them with food at the train station. In the eyes of the Warsaw population the plight of these children was recognized as part of the Polish national tragedy. Of course the fate of these children was tragic: approximately eleven hundred of them were sent to the concentration camp in Flossenburg, and only a small group of them survived the war.

Ethno-nationalist Perceptions of Jews and
Low Societal Approval of Rescue Activities

Jan T. Gross and Michael Steinlauf were the first to argue that low societal approval of rescuing Jews cannot be explained solely on the basis of fear of German reprisal: such reasoning is misleading, and the legacy of prewar ethno-nationalist perceptions of Jews must be taken into account as a crucial factor determining the scope and nature of rescue activities.[193]

No doubt rescuing Jews in Poland was a high-risk activity; the German occupier classified providing shelter for Jews as a crime punishable by death. Between 1941 and 1943 central and local German authorities frequently announced the death penalty in the press and in the form of posters circulated on Polish streets.[194] However, in the light of other important historical data the fear of Nazi reprisal cannot be treated as the only cause for low societal approval of rescue activities. During WWII there was a noticeable discrepancy between the relatively low societal approval of rescuing Jews and the high societal approval of a range of other underground activities that were classified by the Nazis as illegal and incurring severe penalties, including the death penalty. Steinlauf points out this discrepancy: "What limited Polish aid to the Jews was not just fear of the death penalty. In occupied Poland, death was mandated for a host of transgressions great and small, and was sometimes merely a result of being on the street at the wrong time. Nor did the fear of death keep hundreds of thousands of Poles from joining the underground."[195]

Survivors of the Holocaust who lived on the Aryan side in the GG were also aware of the discrepancy:

> Hiding Jews was a very dangerous activity and no-one could expect from people such heroism. Nevertheless there was no need for denunciation of one's neighbor because he was hiding a Jew. I myself lived in constant fear that the Germans would kill me but I was even more afraid of Poles who were able to recognize that I was a Jew. Living on the Aryan side in occupied Poland I could have told strangers without any hesitation that my father worked for the underground or that he was engaged in sabotage of German military factories. The likelihood that these strangers would betray me to the Germans was quite low. However, telling a stranger or even an acquaintance that I was a Jew living on the Aryan side with false documents would simply mean committing suicide. An act of denunciation of underground activities was regarded as socially unacceptable, whereas the denunciation of a Jew was acceptable.[196]

Importantly ethnic Poles could more easily recognize a Polish Jew passing for a Pole than could German soldiers unfamiliar with the Polish cultural environment and language. By comparison with ethnic Poles, Germans were also less able to distinguish between phenotypes of people encountered on Polish territory.[197] Therefore one can argue that Jews were dependent on Poles for the successful concealment of their identity and support in their passing as Poles.

Other historical evidence also shows that low societal approval of rescuing Jews continued even after the defeat of Nazi Germany, in the early postwar period, between 1945 and 1947. During the early postwar period the newly set up Jewish Historical Commission in Poland began to publish records of Jewish survival, including the names of Polish rescuers. In many cases rescuers would ask local commissions not to make their names public out of concern over potential negative reactions from their neighbors and acquaintances. This situation points to the societal isolation of Polish rescuers of Jews, even after the war had ended.

Maria Hochberg-Mariańska, a Polish-Jewish woman, survived the war by passing as an ethnic Pole on the Aryan side. Hochberg-Mariańska was involved in Żegota rescue operations of Jews in Cracow and was the first to raise the issue of the disapproval experienced by former rescuers of Jews. In her introduction to a collection of the testimonies of Jewish children, published in Polish in 1946, Hochberg-Mariańska cautiously notes: "In this book, in many testimonies, the names of the people who saved the Jewish children are given; in others, only initials are used. Why is this, if their names are known? I do not know if anyone outside Poland can understand the fact that saving the life of a defenseless child being hunted by a criminal can bring shame and disgrace upon someone, and can expose them to harassment."[198]

The requests for nonpublication of names, and concerns over negative reactions on the part of a rescuer's neighbors, were also registered by Michał Borwicz, director of the Jewish Historical Commission in Cracow in the early postwar period: "The Provincial Jewish Historical Commission in Cracow, of which I was then Director, was collecting among other things, accounts concerning the numerous Poles who had helped Jews during the Nazi occupation, very often at risk of their own lives. Within the context of the experiences of our witnesses, we began to publish these in journals quite early on. Many of those mentioned by names (and portrayed in especially good light) came to us with the accusation that by naming them we were exposing them to unpleasant situations and even revenge."[199]

Evidence of low societal approval for rescue activities can be found in the wartime and early postwar testimonies of both Polish rescuers of Jews and rescued Jews, including the testimonies of children.[200] The consistent picture that emerges from these testimonies is that the actions of Polish rescuers of Jews were frequently met with disapproval or condemnation on the part of their neighbors, acquaintances, and even family members. Rescuers referred to such individuals as "unreliable people" (niepewni ludzie), "unreliable neighbors" (niepewni sąsiedzi), and "unwanted people" (niepotrzebni ludzie) because they were responsible for harassing and pressuring rescuers to cease their rescue activities.[201] The testimonies point out, sometimes explicitly and more often implicitly, that societal disapproval of rescue activities was not limited to the fear of German reprisal but also lay in the legacy of the exclusivist ethnonationalist way of thinking about Jews.

In September 1945 Wanda Chrzanowska, who sheltered two Czech Jewish children for more than two years in Warsaw, stated that at the end of the war she experienced disapproval of her activities on the part of some individuals in the bomb shelter where she and the rescued girls hid from the bombing: "The conditions of hygiene were dreadful in the shelter, but what was worse were the comments of some bad people who were saying, 'the moment the Germans leave the Jews come back.'"[202]

Józefa Krawczyk, the rescuer of a Jewish woman with a child who escaped from the Warsaw ghetto at the time of the outbreak of the Ghetto Uprising, stated in her testimony of 1945 that her actions had to be kept secret even from members of her family, out of fear:

> Events in the ghetto were moving so fast that we did not have much chance to think things over. On Monday 19 April 1943 Sara Lewin arrived at our place with her little boy. Things were really bad because she did not have any clothes or money with her. What could I have done? Throwing her out would have definitely meant her death. Therefore [we decided that] she would stay with us. My son-in-law . . . arranged a false *Kennkarte* for her [the required identity document]. Our first action was to separate ourselves from the rest of the world. Anyone who wanted to visit me was told that I had gone away for a short while. And in fact I had to go away for a while in order not to raise suspicion. Even members of our own family were left in the dark about "our matter," as you never knew if someone intended to cause harm and call the Gestapo.[203]

In 1946 Mrs. A. Konarska, a caretaker in a Warsaw block of flats who with her husband looked after a young Jewish girl, Sabina Indych, spoke about the disapproval she met from her neighbors: "During the German occupation I was constantly afraid of my neighbors, who threatened me with denunciation to the police because I was looking after a Jewish child."[204]

Felicja Bolak, who with her husband was engaged in black-market activities in wartime Warsaw and assisted two Jewish boys, also reflected about similar societal disapproval of her help and its consequences: "With shrewd eyes people saw [the Jewish boys] and betrayed us to the Gendarmes, and then the hell began." [205]

Zygmunt Assman, the rescuer of Lusia Kampf, a Jewish woman with a daughter, also recollected similar societal disapproval: "When my neighbors began to say openly that they would harm us if we continued to keep Jews in our place, we spoke to my brother-in-law and decided to move them somewhere else for a while." [206]

Sabina Kryszak, a Jewish woman whose child was saved by a Polish woman, described the problems of sheltering her son. He was not able to remain in the first shelter, with her family's prewar domestic help Genia, who intended to rescue the boy, because of the hostile attitude of Genia's boyfriend: "My sister . . . took my boy to our ex-servant Genia, who was very friendly with the child. However, he only remained with Genia for one day because of the arrival of Genia's boyfriend. . . . He told her that if she did not get rid of the 'Jewish bastard' he himself would sort him out. On the day of my son's departure Genia behaved very well toward him and provided him with money." [207]

Szlama Kutnowski, born in 1929, stated that his rescuer, Mr. Ciemierych, of the village of Zambska, was often harassed by his neighbors on his account: "I had to work at Ciemierych's place, but he provided me with enough to eat. He was very good to me. At first when he did not know that I was a Jew he used to send me to the Church to take Holy Communion. . . . When he became aware that I was a Jew he remained good to me. . . . People tried to persuade him to get rid of me, but he insisted that his conscience would not allow him to leave me without a roof over my head in the frosty winter." [208]

This testimony and others point to a map of complex relationships between rescuers of the Jews and other members of the local communities and neighborhoods in which rescuers lived in WWII. On the one hand, they reveal that rescuers were in a very vulnerable position in their own communities. On the other hand, they reveal that some rescuers were able to stand up to those who opposed their rescue activities.

The general picture that emerges from WWII is that the representation of the Jew as the harmful alien did not undergo reevaluation during and after the Nazi destruction of 90 percent of Polish Jewry. Instead it persisted in the ethno-nationalist political camp and had an impact on the way a significant segment of the underground political and military elite related to Polish Jews throughout the war. As in the interwar period National Democracy and its offshoot radical organizations used this perception in its most elaborate and intense version. Various themes, such as Judeo-Bolshevism, Judeo-Communism, and the "covert Jew," were also further elaborated and adapted to the sociopolitical conditions of WWII.

With the exception of the PPS, the Democratic Party, and other smaller left-wing groups in the non-Communist underground camp and members of the liberal intelligentsia, a significant segment of the clandestine political parties and organizations used the negative image of the Jew as a main reference point in their discourse on Jews and the future Polish nation-state. Most underground government elites thought the most desirable model for postwar Poland was an ethnically homogenous state without Jews, whom they saw as the chief impediment to the development of the ethnic Polish population. The prevalence of this ethno-nationalist perspective, which contradicted the official stance of the Polish government-in-exile, was conducive to the process of excluding Polish Jews from the structure of the underground state and from the fabric of society in the GG, despite moments of unity between Poles and Jews that took place during the defense of Warsaw in September 1939. The exclusivist ethno-nationalist perspective also had a noticeable impact on the way a significant segment of the underground political and military elite related to Jews as victims of Nazi extermination. As a result these elites perceived Jews as a group of suffering human beings, but as outside the "universe of national obligations" and in many cases as deeply inimical to Polish values, interests, and existence. At the same time the majority of the Polish underground political elite disapproved of the Nazi extermination of Jews and condemned it as a "barbaric and anti-Christian practice." However, this position did not prevent instances of individual and group killings of Jews by extreme right-wing military units and by civilians. The most severe case of civilian anti-Jewish violence was in the Łomża province in northeastern Poland.

On the level of daily interaction between Poles and Jews the image of the Jew as the harmful alien contributed to a range of indifferent attitudes. This image was one of the main factors accounting for low societal approval of rescue activities—creating an atmosphere in which both ethnic Polish rescuers and the rescued Jews lived in fear not only of the German occupiers but also of neighbors and acquaintances. In some cases the image was also conducive to approval of the outcome of the Nazi genocide of Jews (not their methods) and to hostile actions toward fugitives.

The persistence of ethno-nationalism among segments of elites and non-elites in WWII suggests that even the physical elimination of a large proportion of the minority by a common enemy (an external social actor) does not change the prevalent image of the minority held by the majority group. Wartime conditions generally lead to increased focus on the sufferings of one's own group and to detachment from the sufferings of minority groups subjugated to the same or even harsher treatment. Under thriving conditions of exclusivist ethno-nationalism the detachment becomes further intensified, and antiminority actions—violence and denunciation—take place.

Still, at the end of WWII in Poland and abroad Poles who were committed to the inclusive civic model of Poland, as well as remnants of Polish Jewry who wished to return to live in their prewar homes, harbored a dream that post-1945 Poland would treat all its citizens equally regardless of their religion and nationality. Julian Tuwim, who had survived the war in the West, expressed such hope in the poem "Kwiaty Polskie" (Polish Flowers):

> Teach us that under your sunny sky
> There is no more Greek and no more Jew.
> . . . .
> Kindle the clouds into a glare, and
> Strike at our hearts with a bell of gold,
> Open our Poland as with a bolt
> You clear up the overcast heavens.
> Allow us to rid our fathers' home
> Of our cinders, and holy ruins:
> Let our house be poor but also clean,
> Our house raised from the cemetery.
> To the land, when it stirs from the dead,
> And is gilded by freedom's luster,
> Give the rule of wise and righteous men,
> Mighty in wisdom and in goodness. [209]

6. Old Wine in a New Bottle

Polish Perceptions of Jews in the Early Postwar Period, 1945–49

It would seem that with barely one hundred thousand Polish Jews remaining alive from among three million, a nation of more than twenty million, if it does not wish to blatantly contradict common sense, cannot continue to feed itself tales of the Jewish Menace.

Jerzy Andrzejewski, "Zagadnienie polskiego antysemityzmu"

Introduction

The Poland that emerged in 1945 was a ruined country and one that had in many ways changed beyond recognition. World War II cost Polish society great human losses. As mentioned earlier, 90 percent of Polish Jews perished in the Holocaust,[1] and approximately 7 to 10 percent of ethnic Poles were killed in WWII.[2] The Warsaw Uprising of 1 August 1944—the last desperate stage of Operation Tempest, launched by the underground Polish state against the Germans in order to seize power in Warsaw and establish a government before the Soviets entered the city—ended in the worst civilian casualties.[3] The uprising cost the city 180,000 lives, including the lives of Jewish survivors who lived in Warsaw at the time. Material losses were also immensely high: many branches of Polish industry and many cities, such as the capital, Warsaw, were destroyed. Precious items of national cultural heritage were also stolen or destroyed.[4]

The state's prewar western, eastern, and northern borders also changed dramatically as a result of negotiations about Poland's postwar territorial shape conducted by the three big powers: the United States, the United Kingdom, and the Soviet Union. In a series of conferences about the "new world order" that began in Teheran in late November 1943, continued in Yalta in February 1945, and culminated in the conference in Potsdam in July 1945, the new Polish eastern border with the Soviet Union was settled on the Curzon line, and its western border with the newly created Socialist German state was settled along the Oder-Neisse River line (Odra and Nysa Łużycka).[5] Thus Poland lost the eastern territories, with such cities as L'viv (Lwów) and Vilnius (Wilno), and instead gained territories in the west and northwest, with such cities as Breslau (Wrocław), Stettin (Szczecin), and Danzig (Gdańsk).

Prewar Poland had been a multinational state, with one-third of its population composed of ethnic minorities. As an outcome of the war and the ensuing territorial-political changes Poland underwent a swift transformation, becoming an almost ethnically homogenous nation-state. The transformation was realized in a series of forced migrations, transfers, and repatriations that began in 1945 and were largely completed by 1949.[6] More than a year before WWII had ended the Western Allies evaluated the strategy of forced migration as a lasting solution to ethnic conflicts in East-Central Europe. In his parliamentary speech of 15 December 1944 Winston Churchill (1874–1965), the British prime minister, expressed his support for this policy: "For expulsion is the method that, so far as we have been able to see, will be the most satisfactory and lasting. There will be no mixture of populations to cause endless trouble, as had been the case of Alsace-Lorraine. A clean sweep will be made."[7]

The newly established Polish Communist Authority, which was recognized by Moscow, was in charge and conducted the forced transfer of approximately 2.9 million German civilians from Silesia, Pomerania, and eastern Prussia.[8] On 9 September 1944 the official Polish authority signed agreements with Moscow concerning the population exchange between the two countries: the transfer of East Slavic populations, mainly Ukrainians and Lemkos, who inhabited the southeastern territories of the "new Poland" in exchange for the transfer of ethnic Poles and Polish Jews from the Soviet Union into Poland.[9] Although transfer into the Soviet Union was supposed to be voluntary, pressure and force were used in the majority of cases. Between late 1944 and 1947 approximately 500,000 Ukrainians and Lemkos were transferred from Poland into the Soviet Union. Some Belorussians and Lithuanians who inhabited areas of northeastern Poland were also subjugated to the policy of transfer.[10] In the case of the remaining Ukrainian and Lemko population, 140,000 were uprooted from their homes, dispersed, and forcibly resettled in different parts of Poland in the "Action Vistula" (Akcja Wisła), which began on 28 April 1947 and lasted a few months.[11]

Between 1944 and 1946 780,000 individuals, ethnic Poles and Polish Jews, mostly people who had survived four waves of Soviet deportations between

February 1940 and early June 1941 or had been evacuated to the interior, were repatriated from the Soviet Union to Poland.[12] During the main phase of repatriation, which began in early 1946 and lasted until 1947, 137,000 Polish Jews arrived in Poland. At the same time, between 1944 and 1947, approximately 140,000 Polish Jews left Poland, mostly for Palestine.[13] Seventy percent of the Jewish community had survived the war in the Soviet Union, whereas the remaining 30 percent had survived in Poland and in concentration camps in Germany and Austria.[14] In the early postwar period the Jewish community was a "community on the move": many did not wish to remain in Poland, because they considered it a "large cemetery" and because they wanted to be reunited with family members in the West and Palestine.

Between 1944 and 1947 Poland's political system also changed dramatically. In the second half of 1944 the Communists (PPR) began to consolidate power, assisted by and under the control of the Soviet Union. On 21 July 1944 the Polish Committee of National Liberation (Polski Komitet Wyzwolenia Narodowego, PKWN), controlled by the Communists, was established in Moscow. The next day the PKWN issued the Manifesto to the Polish Nation (Manifest do Narodu Polskiego), which constituted the Communist political, social, and economic program for the reconstruction of postwar Poland. On 26 July the PKWN began to build the state administration in the Polish territories by moving its base to Lublin, a city in southeastern Poland just liberated from the Nazi occupation. On 31 December 1944 the PKWN announced that it had become a provisional government in Poland. These were the first major steps in the Communist takeover of political power from the London-based government-in-exile.[15]

At the time the Western Allies voiced their concerns to Stalin about the development of democratic institutions in Poland. In 1945 the PPR was still a weak political body without popular support in the country. In June 1945 the Temporary Government of National Unity (Tymczasowy Rząd Jedności Narodowej, TRJN) was established, nominally a coalition of the PPR, a faction of the PPS that had decided to cooperate with the PPR, the Democratic Party, and the Labor Party. Edward Osóbka-Morawski (1909–97), a PPS member, was nominated as the TRJN's first prime minister, and Władysław Gomułka (1905–82) (pseud. Wiesław), who at this time was serving as first secretary of the PPR, became deputy prime minister.

At first Gomułka, the leader of the PPR, was forced to enter political discussions with Stanisław Mikołajczyk, the leader of the PSL, which at the time represented the constitutional opposition to the left-wing coalition. The PSL enjoyed the support of the Western Allies. It also enjoyed the overwhelming support of the majority of the country's population, who viewed it as "our party" (nasza partia). In spite of his awareness of the lack of popular support for the Communists, however, Gomułka had no intention of sharing power with the PSL. In June 1945, in a conversation in Moscow with Mikołajczyk, Gomułka plainly and brutally announced, "We will never surrender the power we have seized."[16]

This event symbolically marked the beginning of the PPR's attaining its goal of eradicating the legal political opposition. In 1946 the PPR began to treat the PSL in the same way it had already treated the illegal political opposition. By 1947 the PPR had crushed the PSL through intimidation, arrests, terror, and a number of political murders.[17] As a result Mikołajczyk, who in late 1944 resigned from the government-in-exile in order to enter political talks with the PPR, left Poland for England in November 1947. Other main PSL leaders, like Stanisław Bieńczyk, also fled to the West.

By 1947 the PPR had also made clear to the left-wing parties in the coalition, the PPS and the Democratic Party, that it expected their total subordination. In 1948 the PPR merged with the PPS to form one party, the Polish United Workers' Party (Polska Zjednoczona Partia Robotników, PZPR), thus establishing a monopoly of power in the government.[18]

Earlier, in 1944 and 1945, the PPR, with the support of the Soviet Army, had launched a successful military operation against the illegal political and military opposition. The opposition intended to fight the PPR and establish a non-Communist government in Poland. The most active anti-Communist organizations were the National Democrats, the extreme right-wing National Armed Forces (Narodowe Siły Zbrojne, NSZ), and the Freedom and Independence Movement (Wolność i Niepodległość, WiN). The latter, the successor to the AK, like the AK comprised both right-wing and left-wing political organizations. The institutions of the underground Polish state that operated in WWII, such as the Delegate's Bureau and the AK, dissolved in early 1945. Communists arrested sixteen prominent leaders of the underground Polish state in late March 1945 and took them to the infamous Łubianka prison in Moscow.[19] By 1947, after illegal and legal political opposition had been crushed, Communist power was firmly established in the country, and Poland moved under the sphere of influence of the Soviet Union.

The Communist Takeover of Power and
the Opposition's Perceptions of Jews

New historical research reveals that the illegal opposition in Poland—the core ethno-nationalist National Democracy, the radical NSZ, and right-wing segments of WiN—categorized the Communist takeover of power as a takeover with a "Semitic face"—the rule of Judeo-Communism. [20] The majority of local and national illegal publications circulating in the early postwar years, including newspapers, brochures, and leaflets, constantly disseminated the theme of Judeo-Communism. One such publication noted: "Every Pole is fully aware that every Jew works for the NKVD [Narodnyi Komissariat Vnutrennikh Del, the Secret Soviet police], belongs to the PPR, and plays a crucial role in enslaving our nation." [21]

Perhaps a new aspect of the theme of Judeo-Communism in the early postwar period was the claim that "Judeo-Polonia" had actually been realized. In the eyes of the illegal political opposition "Judeo-Polonia," which the Polish ethno-nationalist press had feared so much since the late nineteenth century, had been achieved by the remnants of the Jewish community who had survived the Nazi genocide. They interpreted the participation of ethnic Jews in the Communist government as the destruction of the Poles that had been predicted in the myth of "Judeo-Polonia." [22]

As discussed above, Polish ethno-nationalists in the pre-1939 and wartime periods widely disseminated the notion of Jews as both the creators of Communism and the executors of Soviet policies. They also promulgated this idea about Jews during WWII, increasing their dissemination of this portrayal during the Soviet occupation of eastern Poland, between 17 September 1939 and 22 June 1941. In the early postwar period, in the context of what is widely regarded in Polish historiography as a civil war between the Communist and non-Communist camps, this categorization of Jews intensified once again. Perhaps as a result of the Communist takeover of political power, the representation of Jews as pro-Soviet and anti-Polish reached its peak at this time in terms of its impact on post-1945 political culture and popular memory. Vestiges of this thinking have persisted in right-wing political discourse and historical writing in post-Communist Poland. [23]

Ethno-nationalists were able to intensify the spread of the notion of Judeo-Communism because of the visibility of those Polish Jews who had survived the war and were Communists. Some Communist Jews held visible, prominent positions within the PPR and the state apparatus. [24] Individuals like Hilary

Minc, Jakub Berman, and Roman Zambrowski, who had survived the war in the Soviet Union, were among the elected members of the Politburo and the Central Committee of the PPR. They also held important and visible governmental positions: Minc was minister of industry (1944–49) and head of Polish State Planning, and Berman was undersecretary in the Ministry of Foreign Affairs (1945–52). Zambrowski was deputy chairman of the Polish parliament (1947–52).

Poles reacted to the presence of Jews in their own government the same way they had to the presence of Jews in the Soviet Communist Party and the state apparatus in the eastern territories under the Soviet occupation, between 1939 and 1941. The presence of Polish Jews like Minc, Berman, and Zambrowski in high state and party positions in the early postwar period must have seemed to many ethnic Poles a "reversal of the natural order." [25] The presence of Jews in post-1945 governmental positions constituted a sharp contrast with the "natural order" of the prewar period. In pre-1939 Poland, among six hundred persons who held high diplomatic and governmental positions, no more than two were ethnically Jewish: Szymon Aszkenazy (see chapter 4) and Anatol Muelstein (1889–1957). The latter served in the Polish foreign office and was known as "Piłsudski's Jew." [26] In interwar Poland Jews constituted only 3 percent of the one hundred officials in the state administration, municipal administrations, the judiciary, and other public institutions. [27]

Minc, Berman, Zambrowski, and other Jewish Communists were perceived as double enemies: as Jews and as servants of a foreign enemy power, the Soviet Union. Soviet intelligence was aware of the persistence of these negative perceptions of Communist Jews and collected detailed information on the subject. [28] In anti-Communist propaganda the names of Minc, Berman, and Zambrowski were made plural in order to emphasize the enormity of the Judeo-Communist takeover. The anti-Communist opposition also used such linguistic manipulation in the post-1949 period to explain and rationalize the anti-Jewish hostilities of the early postwar years. In 1970 Andrzej Łobodowski, a well-known émigré writer based in London, argued that "if Poland had regained its independence, everything would have developed differently. . . . But Poland did not regain its independence, and the fact that among the Communist elite there were so many 'Mincs, Bermans, Katz-Suchys, Różanskis and Fejgins' had to weigh badly upon the future." [29]

In the context of the widely held belief in Judeo-Communism the fierce political struggle between the Communist and non-Communist political camps and the use of terror and intimidation by the Communists against their political opponents led to intensification of the theme of the destructiveness of Jews. Slogans circulated around the country in the illegal press warning against Jews: "Fellow Poles! Do you know who is in charge of the trials against us? Jews! Do you know who is murdering us? Jews! Do you know who is ruling over us? Jews—and Bolsheviks!"[30]

In the illegal press Communist ethnic Poles were sometimes portrayed as being totally controlled by Jews. They were depicted as puppets in "the hands of cunning Jews." Their disadvantaged background—poor, uneducated, peasant, and working-class—was given as the explanation for their lack of awareness of the "true" nature of political reality and their misguided attraction to Communism. Thus even the ethnic Poles who were members of the Central Committee of the PPR were sometimes portrayed as puppets in the hands of Jews, with no power over decision making.[31]

Consequently in 1947, in some illegal press publications, Jews were blamed for Polish losses not only on the anti-Communist side but also on the Communist side. According to estimates, approximately six thousand members of the anti-Communist opposition were killed between 1945 and 1946, and another forty-five thousand were arrested. In 1947 another two thousand members of the political opposition were killed, and twenty-five thousand were arrested. The losses on the Communist side were also high: each month during 1945 approximately two hundred Communists were killed, and the killing continued into 1946.[32] This particular interpretation of the civil war portrayed the Poles as victims and the Jews as perpetrators. A good example is provided in an illegal leaflet signed by the Committee against the Jewish Influence that circulated in Bydgoszcz in October 1947: "What a disgrace! A disgrace! A handful of degenerate Jews have taken over the state and are ruling over millions of stupid Slavs. . . . Forty-five thousand Poles from the AK, the NSZ, and WiN have been shot or hanged, and thirty thousand Poles from the PPR and the Secret Police [UB] were killed between 1946 and 1947. This is the result of the bloody regime of the Jewish clique; Jews are our mortal enemy."[33]

The early postwar programs of National Democracy devoted a separate section to discussion of the Jews. As in previous periods, in all programs Jews were identified as the most dangerous enemy of Poland, harming the economic, political, and spiritual life of Polish society. The National Democrats insisted that "Polish civilization needed to be purified of Jews" and therefore called for the total emigration of Jews from the country and the establishment of a Jewish state in Palestine.[34] Until the Jewish state was realized Polish Jews were to have the status of foreigners in Poland. One more moderate version of the National Democratic program, written by Władysław Jaworski on 19 September 1945, claimed that as a result of the Nazi destruction of the Jews in WWII, the Jews had ceased to be the most dangerous element in post-1945 Poland; therefore their small percentage of the population could be permitted to remain in the country.[35] As in WWII National Democratic programs of the early postwar period stressed that Polish anti-Semitism was rooted in objective political, social, and economic conditions and that Polish approaches to solving the Jewish question were based on Christian teaching and thus were totally different from Nazi treatment of the Jews. The latter part of this argument is correct; the former is a manifestation of the rationalization of anti-Jewish prejudice to a degree that allows the categorization of such prejudice as factual truth and as qualitatively different from other anti-Jewish ideologies and images. It also indicates the presence of a strong anti-Jewish position within the Roman Catholic Church.

Mikołajczyk and other leaders of the constitutional opposition, the PSL, generally abstained from making any remarks about Jews, either positive or negative. Just as in WWII they were careful not to raise the subject. One reason behind this silence was their concern about the PSL's image in the eyes of the Western powers. The PSL enjoyed the support of the Western Allies, who as in WWII were concerned about the issue of democracy and anti-Semitism in East Central Europe. The other explanation behind the silence of PSL leaders lay in the fact that Communists attempted to damage the image of the PSL by accusing it of responsibility for anti-Jewish actions. This was a calculated strategy to eliminate a serious political opponent. Within the PSL there were those who genuinely opposed anti-Semitism and those who subscribed to exclusivist ethno-nationalist perceptions of Jews. On many occasions the rank and file of the PSL expressed the theme of Judeo-Communism during public meetings and political rallies and conferences. For example, during a local meeting of the PSL in Cracow on 19 August 1945 Leśniak, a PSL activist from Limanowa, claimed that "the Poland we have is not the Poland we have been waiting for. This is a Jewish Poland. Jews are occupying all high positions in the Public Security Office. They should be arresting Jews, not Poles."[36] In a resolution made in autumn 1945 the youth peasant movement Wici similarly demanded "the elimination of 'International Jewry' from the state apparatus. Happiness, for the Jews, is the destruction of all other nations."[37]

During the PSL Congress of 19–21 January 1946 in Warsaw a correspondent from the *Jewish Chronicle*, a weekly published in London, reported that "charges [that Jews ran the secret police] were repeated at the recent Peasant Congress in Warsaw, where some three thousand delegates met to listen to Mr. Mikołajczyk. He condemned excesses against workers and peasants but did not say anything about Jews. Some peasants told me that the reason the security policy often took 'drastic measures' in areas where outrages occurred was 'because there were a lot of Jews in the police and these Jews were taking revenge on us.'"[38]

Secret memos from meetings of the Central Committee of the PPR also contain references to anti-Semitism within the PSL. For example, on 11 August 1945, during a discussion of the Peasant Self-Help Union (Samopomoc Chłopska) by the Central Committee of the PPR, it was reported that certain PSL activists had protested against the presence of Jews in the peasant organization, expressing anti-Semitic attitudes.[39] On 16 August 1945, during the plenum of the Central Committee of the PPR, Zambrowski reported the endorsement of an anti-Semitic resolution by the local PSL during a political rally in Wola Żelichowska.[40]

How many Jews were members of the infamous political police (Urząd Bezpieczeństwa, UB), known as the Bezpieka? How many Jews were responsible for the worst terror of the early postwar years?

The UB, headed by an ethnic Pole, Stanisław Radkiewicz (1903–87), was a section of the Polish security apparatus that in the early postwar years was totally controlled by the Soviet secret police. Recent pioneering research conducted by the historians Andrzej Paczkowski and Lech Głuchowski gives a general picture of the employment of various ethnic groups in the UB.[41] According to Paczkowski, between 1945 and 1946 287 individuals held leadership positions in the UB. The number of those listed as holding "Jewish nationality" totaled 75. This meant that Jews constituted 26.3 percent of UB leadership, while the remaining 66.9 percent was mostly ethnically Polish. According to other available records prepared in the autumn of 1945 for Bolesław Bierut (1892–1956), an ethnic Pole who was a member of the Central Committee of the PPR and became president of Poland in 1947, the UB included 25,600 employees, with Jews numbering 438 persons (1.7 percent of the total number of employees). At the same time, among the 500 members of the top managerial cadre, Jews held 67 positions, thus constituting 13 percent of all managerial positions.[42] Therefore historians argue that there was an overrepresentation of

Jews in various sections of the UB, particularly at the level of leadership and the top managerial cadre.[43] There is no doubt that this argument is correct.

At the same time categorization of the UB as a Jewish institution, as disseminated in the anti-Communist press of the early postwar years and also in later periods, is biased, rooted in belief in Judeo-Communism. Even if one assumes that the percentage of Jews in the UB increased between 1946 and 1949, this institution cannot be viewed as Jewish since this would mean that all remaining Polish Jews who lived in early postwar Poland were employees of the UB, a notion that is historically false. The size of the Jewish population in Poland at the beginning of 1949 was approximately 110,000 individuals. Between 1949 and 1951 the Jewish population shrank as a result of emigration. Thirty thousand Jews left Poland between 1949 and the end of the following year, and by 1951 the Polish-Jewish community was reduced to 57,000 individuals.[44] At the same time the number of UB employees increased slightly. In late December 1949 the UB had 25,989 employees; in December 1950 the UB had 28,584 employees; in 1951 it had 32,247 and in 1952 34,832.[45]

Were all remaining Jews Communists, members of the PPR, and employees of the UB? The political affiliations of the Jewish community in the early postwar period show that this was not the case. Between 1945 and 1949 there was a short-term rebirth of Jewish religious institutions and political organizations in Poland; as in the interwar period the Jewish community was characterized by a diversity of political affiliations. The Central Committee of Jews in Poland (Centralny Komitet Żydów w Polsce, CKŻP) was established in November 1944, its first chairman the Zionist politician Emil Sommerstein. The committee was an "umbrella" institution that included the Jewish section of the PPR, the socialist Bund, and all Zionist organizations with the exception of the banned revisionists. The latter group was active illegally. This diversity lasted until 1949, when the Stalinist regime banned all Jewish organizations except for those that it could totally subordinate to the Communist agenda.

In the early postwar period active support for Communism as a political movement was not high among the Jewish community.[46] The Jewish section of the PPR, set up in 1945 and dissolved by the Stalinist regime in 1949, included four thousand members at the end of 1946. Only in May 1947 did the Jewish section of the PPR succeed in expanding to seven thousand members, reaching the size of the Zionist political party Ichud. Ichud was the most popular Jewish political movement in early postwar Poland. In 1947 it included between seven and eight thousand members.[47]

Although the subject of the self-identification of Communist Jews is outside the scope of this study, it is worth mentioning that some available material indicates that the Jewish community had different perceptions of Communist Jews who were members of the Jewish section of the PPR than it did of those who belonged to the main part of the PPR. The Jewish community viewed Jews in the Jewish section as "Jewish Jews" and Jews in the main PPR as "non-Jewish Jews" ("Aryan Jews").[48] The study of the categorization of Jewish Communists in the West by the sociologist Percy S. Cohen is useful in aiding understanding of the problem of the self-identification of Communist Jews in post-1945 Poland.[49] Cohen differentiates between two categories of Communist Jews: Jewish Radicals and Radical Jews. The former were those Jewish Communists who were purely committed to the Communist cause and for whom ethnicity was of no importance. In the Polish case many Jewish PPR members who played a leading role in the party displayed these characteristics. The second group, Radical Jews, were those who, while Communists, were also affiliated with other Jewish organizations, maintaining a strong sense of their Jewishness. Jews who belonged to the Jewish section of the PPR displayed these characteristics.

The PPR was not "the Jewish party run by Jews for Jews in order to oppress ethnic Poles." Two factors—the size of the party and of the Jewish community itself—contradict such a view. In late 1945 the PPR included 230,000 members; 61 percent of its rank-and-file members had working-class backgrounds, and 28 percent had peasant backgrounds. In autumn 1946 party membership increased to 400,000, and by 1947 it had reached 800,000.[50] Given the fact that between 1946 and 1947 the highest number of Polish Jews staying in Polish territories can be estimated at 250,000, the perception of the PPR as a Jewish party established in order to oppress ethnic Poles is simply incongruent with reality. The anti-Communist opposition disseminated the theme of the rule of Judeo-Communism, a powerful social construction that offered a simplistic and comforting explanation for the political and social upheavals taking place at the time. Belief in Judeo-Communism prevented Poles from realizing that the Communist regime was not a Jewish invention, but a Soviet-imposed government in which Poles, Jews, and members of Slavic minorities of various socioeconomic backgrounds and orientations actively participated.

Perceptions of Jews within the PPR

During WWII the PPR unequivocally condemned the Nazi genocide of Jews, and the Communist military forces the GL and the AL were positively disposed toward Jewish fugitives from the Holocaust.[51] Yet traces of ambivalence and contradiction with respect to the concept of a future Polish nation and equal rights for all religious and national groups were already apparent in some Communist pronouncements during the war. On the one hand, the official Communist stance expressed in the first political credo of the PPR—the Declaration of November 1943—was that in the name of internationalism, workers' fraternity, and brotherhood, Jews and other minorities would be guaranteed equal civic and political rights with Poles in a future Poland.[52] At the same time some Communist leaders declared support for an ethnically homogenous model of the Polish nation-state.[53]

A perusal of various PPR records between 1944 and 1948 confirms the presence of contradictions in respect to the issue of equal rights and the vision of the Polish nation. The PPR officially restated its recognition of equal rights for all citizens in the PKWN Manifesto of July 22 1944. This document adhered to the Polish constitution of March 1921 and pledged agrarian reforms that the pre-1939 governments had failed to introduce. Jews were the only minority explicitly mentioned in the PKWN Manifesto, in the context of the plight of Polish Jewry in the Holocaust. The destruction of Polish Jews in WWII was linked to the issue of granting them equal civic and political rights. On the issue of citizenship the PKWN Manifesto declared that it favored "the restoration of all democratic liberties, the equality of all citizens, regardless of race, creed, or nationality," and the notion that "Jews who were subjected to inhuman tortures by the Nazi occupier are guaranteed full rehabilitation and legal and actual equal rights."[54]

On the other hand, in various addresses to the Polish population prominent PPR leaders, including Gomułka and Bierut, spoke about the PPR's commitment to the creation of a homogeneous (ethno-national) Polish state.[55] Communist propaganda of the years 1944–47 frequently employed both national and Roman Catholic symbols. This phenomenon provides clues about the nature of early post-1945 Polish Communism and the ways in which the PPR attempted to legitimize its power.[56]

PPR propaganda frequently stressed the fact that Poland had regained both sovereignty and the western territories, the so-called Recovered Lands (Ziemie Odzyskane), which were a part of "Piast Poland," the medieval Polish kingdom that for most of its history had been ethnically homogenous. Paradoxically Communist propaganda portrayed "Piast Poland" as the most desirable model of the Polish nation-state, and the PPR delivered this model to the Polish nation. PPR leaders uttered such statements during public events, including national ceremonies and political rallies. In 1944 the Communists also staged ceremonies commemorating national historical events, celebrating the past of the pre-1939 "bourgeois Poland"; Poland's regaining of independence in 1918; and even the "Miracle on the Vistula," the victory of Poland in the Polish-Soviet War of 1920. In 1947, for example, Communists staged the funeral of General Lucjan Żeligowski, who under Józef Piłsudski conquered Wilno and the Wilno region in 1920, as an important national ceremony, making a short documentary film about the event to show in cinemas.[57] The Communist emphasis on the homogenous ethno-national character of the Polish state led certain historians to the conclusion that the Communist regime had paradoxically achieved the chief goal of prewar nationalists (exclusivist ethno-nationalists, members of National Democracy).[58]

Some members of the PPR, both Poles and Jews, criticized the narrative of the homogenous ethno-national character of the Polish state as contradictory to the PPR's principle of equal rights for all national and ethnic minorities. For example, as early as 1945 some members of the Jewish section of the PPR raised concerns over the emphasis on creating "a homogenized nation-state of one people" (ethnic Poles) and the negative effect of this concept on equal rights. They argued that there was a noticeable link between advocating an ethnically homogenized nation-state and the ongoing displacement of minorities and increased anti-Jewish hostilities.[59] For example, at a session of the Jewish faction of the PPR in the autumn of 1945 Marek Bitter (1902–65) argued that "national consolidation is on the increase and follows the line of ousting national minorities from the life of the state."[60]

Stanisław Ossowski, a leading postwar Polish sociologist, was perhaps one of the first members of the Polish intellectual elite to share these concerns. In his article on the Kielce pogrom, "Na tle wydarzeń kieleckich" (The Background to the Events at Kielce), published by the left-wing weekly *Kuźnica* in September 1946, he criticized the manipulation of nationalist resentment by Communist propaganda. He argued that this was an important factor in the increasing intolerance and hatred toward Jewish and other minorities among the ethnic Polish population.[61]

The increasing intolerance of minorities, manifested in open hostilities toward Jews and also Slavic groups, was one of the chief features of early postwar social life. Despite its various political and ideological declarations, the PPR not only failed to alleviate interethnic tensions but in fact contributed to sustaining ethnic tensions. Communist propaganda also used the narrative of the homogenous ethno-national character of the Polish state in rhetoric related to the policy of the expulsion of the German civilian population. In such propaganda expulsion of the Germans was portrayed as "squaring Polish suffering" (wyrównanie krzywd), not surprising given the fact that Poland had just emerged from five years of Nazi occupation that cost Polish society heavy losses. The expulsion was also justified on the grounds of the homogeneity of the state.[62] In a speech at the plenum of the PPR Central Committee on 20–21 May 1944 Gomułka justified the expulsion of the Germans by appealing to the desirability of national homogeneity: "[In] the Western territories . . . a guard must be put on the frontier, the Germans must be expelled, and those who stay must get the kind of treatment that will not encourage them to stay. The change in the Soviet Union's German policy should not concern us. We should simply clear out the Germans and build a national state."[63]

In the case of the Slavic minorities, particularly Polish Ukrainians, the "Action Vistula," dispersing the remaining 140,000 Ukrainians and Lemkos, was explained by references to the suffering of Poles in Wołyń in 1943 and to the war against the Ukrainian nationalists in the Ukrainian Insurgent Army (Ukrayinska Povstanska Armia, UPA), who were active in the early postwar period in southern Poland.[64] The assassination of Polish general Karol Świerczewski by the UPA on 28 March 1947 provided a pretext for the "Action Vistula," in which 3,600 Ukrainian men, women, and children were detained by Polish armed forces in the former Nazi concentration camp in Jaworzno, where some died.[65] Official Communist propaganda portrayed all Ukrainians and Lemkos as anti-Polish, anti-Communist, and supporting Ukrainian nationalism. This constituted the ideological principle for deporting all Ukrainians and Lemkos from their homes. Thus the drive for ethnic homogenization and the exclusion of minorities from early postwar Poland for the first time included Slavic minorities, whom ethno-nationalists had advocated integrating into Polish society through forced cultural assimilation in the pre-1939 period.

Although the PPR proclaimed that it was fully committed to fighting anti-Semitism as a party, historical records suggest that lower-ranking members of local PPR committees and state institutions on occasion displayed anti-Jewish attitudes.[66] Contrary to the principles of the Party, the rank and file did not necessarily treat Jews as equal citizens with the same rights as ethnic Poles, instead allowing anti-Jewish prejudices to guide their actions. This situation was noticeable in various parts of the country, particularly in the province of

Kielce in central Poland, where the wave of early postwar anti-Jewish hostilities was the most widespread and the strongest.[67] On 23 February 1945 the Voivode of Kielce province felt compelled to issue the following letter to members of municipal councils, warning them that discrimination against Jewish clients in offices and institutions would not be tolerated: "The Minister of Public Administration has been informed that citizens of Jewish nationality living in the [Kielce] province are not properly treated by our institutions and offices. Therefore an instruction has been issued that all citizens have to be treated correctly. Officials who breach this instructions will face penalties."[68]

At its meeting on 14 May 1945 the Jewish Committee of Kielce province discussed the issue of the safety of the Jewish community and the way they were treated by the representatives of the new local government. The conclusions were grim: "[In] Ostrowiec [Ostrowiec Świetokrzyski] the size of the Jewish community is 193 members. The state of safety is very poor. There are cases of assaults and robberies. Recently some local officials stated that German legislation still applied to the Jews. There are cases of common hooliganism: Jews are beaten up, and policemen who are present at such assaults do not react but instead openly say: 'Beat him up, I do not see anything.' Jews are arrested for corruption, while the murderers of four persons go free; just before the Red Army entered this province a certain Polish family murdered a Jewish family. They were arrested but later released. In Ostrowiec region leaflets are circulated calling for 'death to any remaining Jews.' "[69]

According to the historian Danuta Blus-Węgrowska, many local PPR committees failed to take any preventative measures against anti-Jewish violence, which spread in 1945 in Poland.[70] In some cases PPR committees ignored Jewish petitions for help to put an end to anti-Jewish hostilities. In other cases local Communist authorities discontinued investigations into the murders of individual Jews, despite sufficient evidence to press charges. In others representatives of the state apparatus, the army, and the militia not only allowed anti-Jewish hostilities to take place but themselves participated in such events. This was the case in the well-documented pogroms that took place in Cracow on 11 August 1945 and in Kielce on 4 July 1946. This situation caused concern in the high ranks of the Central Committee of the PPR, particularly among Jewish members of the Central Committee like Zambrowski, who raised the problem of anti-Semitism among the lower ranks of the state apparatus and the militia and among the working class. For example, at the plenum of the Central Committee of the PPR on 3 July 1945 Zambrowski argued that anti-

Semitism was a living phenomenon and that no effective strategy of combating it had been implemented.[71] More than three weeks after the Kielce pogrom Ostap Dłuski (1892–1964), another Jewish member of the Central Committee of the PPR, called for setting up an institution that would allow Jews to be reunited with their families living abroad. In the same speech he expressed the disappointment of the Jewish community at the lack of democracy in the country, driven by pogroms, and its dismay that Comrade Gomułka had not addressed the situation of Jews in his five-hour speech to the Party.[72] Soviet archival material also confirms the concerns of other leading Jewish Communists, like Michał Mirski (1905–94), who played an important role in the Jewish faction of the PPR.[73]

At the same time some ethnic Poles who were members of the Central Committee of the PPR displayed anti-Jewish attitudes. This breached the Communist principles of internationalism, brotherhood, and friendship.[74] These attitudes can be summarized in a simple statement: "There are too many Jews among us, and we do not want them." These attitudes were openly expressed at various meetings of the Central Committee of the PPR. For example, at the plenum of the PPR's Central Committee on 20–21 May 1945 Ignacy Loga-Sowiński (1914–71), a member of the PPR Central Committee and at this time first secretary of the PPR Provisional Committee in Łódź, expressed views that closely resembled those of the core ethno-nationalist movement National Democracy. Loga-Sowiński claimed that anti-Semitism within the PPR could only disappear with the disappearance of Jews: "The Party School is producing a kind of anti-Semitism. Most of the lecturers are Jews. When Milaj [a prominent PPR member] came for a lecture, he received an ovation because he is an Aryan."[75]

During the same plenum Gomułka complained about the physical features of the new members of local branches of the PPR in Cracow. He indicated that he viewed the enrollment of these Jews into the PPR as a damaging development for the Party: "The director of the Personnel Department in Cracow, which is the responsibility of Jasny [Włodzimierz Zawadzki], took in two thousand people, all obviously Jews by their appearance and by their poor Polish accent. This was a cheap trick, but it is difficult to say to what extent it was sectarianism and to what extent sabotage."[76] Gomułka's concerns about the Jewish physical features and poor Polish accents of the newcomers were colored by negative stereotypes of Jews. At the root of these concerns was the drive for what might be interpreted as a form of the polonization/ethno-nationalization of the

Communist Party. The Polish-Jewish writer Julian Stryjkowski (1905–96), who at the time was a Communist, and the key Communist Jew of the time, Hersz Smolar (1905–93), both claimed that Gomułka's wife, Zofia Gomułkowa, was obsessed with the Jewish physical features and poor accent of Communist Jews and therefore had selected Jewish Communists for particular tasks at the PPR.[77] She was herself by ethnicity Jewish, with a long-standing record of belonging to the KPP in prewar Poland. Her eager attempts at "polonizing" Communist cadres by "polonizing" Jewish names of PPR members was a subject of jokes among Jewish Communists, since they saw her own facial features as clearly Jewish/Semitic.

Gomułka's conversation of 9 December 1948 with the head of the Soviet state, Joseph Stalin (1879–1953), is perhaps the most important example of an expression of anti-Jewish attitudes by a key ethnic Polish leader of the PPR.[78] This conversation occurred not long before the PPR and the PPS merged into the Polish United Workers' Party (PZPR).[79] Stalin, who wanted Gomułka to join the Politburo of the PZPR, initiated the conversation. Gomułka confirmed it in a letter of 14 December 1948 addressed to Stalin. At the time of the conversation Gomułka and some other PPR leaders were already accused of representing "the nationalistic line in the Party." The conflict over the ethos of the Party and Gomułka's vision of the Party was visible at the plenum of the Central Committee of the PPR in June of the same year and reemerged again at the 31 August–3 September plenum. At the latter plenum Bierut, one of Stalin's most trusted subordinates, condemned Gomułka's vision of Polish Communism.[80]

Addressing the issue of the membership of the PPR and the state apparatus with Stalin, Gomułka indicated that there was a need for "the regulation of the Communist cadre along national [ethno-national] lines." By this he meant a reduction in the number of Jews within the PPR and an increase in the number of ethnic Poles, particularly within the top echelons of the PPR. Gomułka also provided a negative evaluation of Jewish members of the PPR, accusing them of "national nihilism," a quality that, according to him, was alien to the Polish working class. This statement suggests that, according to Gomułka, only Jews displayed a lack of concern for the Polish nation and national cause:

> Basing my views on some observations, I can state with certainty that a segment of Jewish Comrades does not have a strong attachment to the Polish nation and therefore cannot have a strong attachment to the working class. In fact, their position can be defined as national nihilism. I have plenty of evidence that their presence in the Party leadership and employment in

the state apparatus cause bitterness and discontent [among ethnic Polish comrades]. Furthermore, a particular atmosphere . . . in which no one is allowed to criticize this issue openly has been created since the eighth plenum of the Party. Nevertheless, discontent is expressed covertly. . . . In my opinion it is important to put an end to the increase in the number of Jewish Comrades both in the Party and in the state apparatus. In fact, the number of Jewish Comrades should be decreased, particularly at the top level.[81]

Gomułka's position on membership within the PPR and the state apparatus resembled prewar ethno-nationalist arguments about polonization of the cities and the employment policy for ethnic Poles (peasants) at the expense of the Jewish population. In his letter to Stalin Gomułka also implied that the positions of Polish Jews in the PPR leadership offended the Polish working class. The fact that Gomułka felt no constraints in making these statements to Stalin indicates that he might have been aware of Stalin's own growing obsession with the Jews at this time.[82] The fact that Gomułka, leader of a Communist party, had no difficulty in uttering anti-Jewish comments also reveals the extent to which leading ethnic Polish Communists in the PPR had been shaped by ethno-nationalist moral sentiments rather than by the doctrine of internationalism and brotherhood. In this respect Gomułka followed the voice of a significant segment of Polish society. As various wartime communications between the Delegate's Office and the government-in-exile reveal, the Polish population had voiced a wish that post-1945 Poland become a country for ethnic Poles only. In political decisions some leading members of the PPR, like Gomułka, appeared to succumb to this voice of ethnic nationalism.[83] This phenomenon also reveals the salient contradictions on the Jewish matter within the PPR. The negative image of Jews as national nihilists, as outsiders whose character was so different from that of Polish Communists, was to play an important role in anti-Jewish propaganda within the PZPR, particularly in the late 1960s.

Until 1948 Gomułka had a chance to become the Polish version of Tito (1892–1980), the independent leader of Communist Yugoslavia, who gathered all nationalities into "one Yugoslavian nation." However, in his desire to follow "the national way to socialism" (narodowa droga do socjalizmu) Gomułka failed to become the Polish Tito. Various documents indicate Gomułka's compelling desire that the Polish population would see the PPR he led as a Polish Communist party, not as a foreign Soviet entity.[84] In his attitudes toward Jews Gomułka did not oppose the anti-Jewish stereotypes prevailing in Polish society at the time; his own political decisions were colored by these stereotypes.

How can one otherwise explain Gomułka's opposition to the repatriation of Polish Jews from the Soviet Union to Poland in 1946, which other party members knew about as early as 1945?[85] No doubt Gomułka's awareness of his portrayal as the leader of the Jews and a servant of the Soviets—expressed in anti-Communist slogans like "Let's get rid of the PPR," "Gomułka is a Jew," and "No Catholic joins the PPR"—also played a role in his attitudes toward Jews.[86]

The PPR presented two different images of itself. First, it declared adherence to the principle of equality for all citizens of Communist Poland; at the same time it emphasized the ethno-national homogenization of the Communist Polish nation-state. The first image was directed at the Western Allies, who were concerned about the development of democracy and anti-Semitism in post-1945 Poland. The second image was directed at the ethnic Polish population. The leaders of the PPR wished to exercise political power over Polish society and to be seen as representatives of a legitimate power. In the PPR's efforts at seeking legitimacy in the eyes of the Polish population some leading members of the Central Committee of the PPR, including Gomułka, "courted" Poles with the core ethno-nationalist notion "Poland for [ethnic] Poles"—a strategy arguably brought about by the Party's awareness of widespread support for the ethnic nationalization of Poland. Thus the process of the ethno-nationalization of Communism, with anti-Jewish and antiminority elements, crystallized in some ethnic Polish segments within the PPR and the state apparatus in the early postwar period.[87] This process was "frozen" in the dark years of Stalinism, between 1949 and 1953, when hard-line internationalists and committed subordinates of the Soviet state, including both ethnic Poles and Jews, took control over the PZPR. But the issue of the ethno-nationalization of the PZPR began to reemerge again in 1956.

Rationalization and Justification of Anti-Jewish Violence

The social experience of individual Polish Jews returning home in the early postwar period was characterized by lack of safety, fear of assault and robbery, and fear for their lives. Various local branches of the newly established Central Committees of Jews in Poland (CKZP) raised the subject of such fears at their meetings. For example, the minutes of the meeting of the Jewish Committee of Kielce Province of 14 May 1945 provide insight regarding the extent to which this was a major social problem for local Jewish communities:

> Town of Szydłowiec—the size of the Jewish community 100 individuals, personal safety very poor.

Zwoleń—the size of the Jewish community 47 individuals. They all wish
to leave the town.

Radom—the size of the community 402 individuals. They are depressed
and live in fear. Attitude of local Polish population hostile and raises concerns.[88]

Accounts of hostility—ranging from verbal harassment, including supposedly "friendly" advice to "leave the village or something bad is going to happen
to you", to robbery, beatings, and even murder—were frequently recorded in
individual statements, diaries, and official records of the CKZP and the PPR.
In some instances various local Jewish communities resettling in small villages
and towns received threats ordering them to leave under threat of punishment:
"Jewish hordes, if you do not leave the city by 15 May, we will take appropriate
action!"[89] The Jewish community of Jedlińsk, in Radom province, received
a similar warning: "To the Jewish Community of Jedlińsk, 9 July 1945. It
has been observed that many of you work in intelligence in the service of a
government brutally imposed on us and that therefore you are acting against
the well-being of Polish society. As a representative of the Polish people, I order
all Jews to get out of Radom and Radom province by 15 August 1945. I warn
you that if you do not leave by this date or if you attempt to ask the local
government for help, you will be punished."[90]

In the summer of 1945 the CKZP became alarmed by the frequency of anti-
Jewish attacks in central and eastern parts of Poland, where one hundred people
were murdered in only two months. Six months later, with the repatriation of
Jews from the Soviet Union that began on 8 February 1946, an anti-Jewish
atmosphere spread all over the country.[91] Even in the western "Recovered
Territories," where both ethnic Poles and Polish Jews were newcomers, anti-
Jewish hostilities had become noticeable by the spring of 1946.[92] In his article
"Na tle wydarzeń kieleckich" Ossowski noted that separate food lines of ethnic
Poles and Polish Jews formed in this region and that the two communities kept
to themselves.[93]

Until the discovery of the Jedwabne massacre of 1941 scholars considered the
anti-Jewish violence of the early postwar period the most severe in the history
of anti-Jewish hostilities in Poland. Some studies have evaluated the anti-
Jewish violence in early postwar Poland as the most severe of this period for
the entire region of East-Central Europe.[94] By the end of 1947 there had been
a number of casualties among Jews, including two hundred persons killed in
the so-called train actions (*akcje pociągowe*). Units of the illegal military group

NSZ orchestrated these anti-Jewish "train actions." [95] The number of people killed in individual attacks was much higher than at any time between the two world wars, except for the early post-1918 period of civil war. For example, seven people, including a fourteen-year-old boy, were killed near Czorsztyn on 30 April 1946; out of a group of twenty men, women, and children on a road near Krościenko on 2 May 1946 twelve were shot and six seriously injured. [96] The Kielce pogrom of 4 July 1946 was the worst case of anti-Jewish violence during this period, ordinary civilians, together with soldiers and militiamen, murdering forty-two Jews and injuring more than one hundred individuals. [97]

Polish historiography tends to focus on one individual pogrom, not to discuss the entire postwar wave of anti-Jewish violence. [98] The Kielce pogrom stands out as the key individual case of anti-Jewish violence, widely discussed in both scholarly and popular works in Poland. In discussion of the Kielce pogrom Polish historians have focused on two aspects: the description of the event and investigation into the "forces" responsible for masterminding the pogrom. In respect to the latter the main historical interpretation, represented by distinguished scholars like Krystyna Kersten, asserts that Soviet security forces or some special secret units of the Communist regime in Poland orchestrated the pogrom. [99] A small group of historians, represented by Józef Adelson, argue that the pogrom was a spontaneous grass-roots event. [100] The historian Andrzej Paczkowski was the first scholar in Poland to point to clues of the relative lack of interest in investigating the role of the local population in the Kielce pogrom. [101] According to him, for some historians to accept the idea of a spontaneous pogrom would mean to accept the embarrassing fact that a substantial section of Polish society was intensely anti-Semitic. [102]

In recent years a new, empirically false interpretation of anti-Jewish violence has appeared in the work of Marek J. Chodakiewicz. According to Chodakiewicz, one cannot apply the concept of a pogrom to the anti-Jewish violence of the early postwar period because at this time Poles and Jews were engaged in a "zero-sum game war": Poles killed Jews, and Jews killed Poles. [103] In the popular book *Szkice z dziejów i stosunków polsko-żydowskich 1918–1949* Józef Orlicki, a former member of the UB in Szczecin, presents an even more intellectually disturbing interpretation of anti-Jewish violence. According to Orlicki, the Zionists themselves orchestrated the Kielce pogrom in order to force the Jewish community to emigrate from Poland to Palestine. Orlicki also claims that Poles, not Jews, were the main victims of the Kielce pogrom. [104]

The intensity of the brutality of postwar violence resembled to some degree the brutality of the anti-Jewish hostilities that took place during the wartime period in the northeastern area of Łomża. Łomża saw the most extreme case of wartime anti-Jewish violence, rooted in the specific conditions created by Germany's policy of exterminating Jews and the Nazi permission to kill Jews. The postwar wave of violence also included brutal killings extended to children and women, including pregnant women.[105] This violence can be attributed to the following factors: the impact of WWII, familiarity with the Nazi extermination of Jews, the Communist takeover; and the ongoing civil war in the years 1944–47.[106]

Yet in contrast to the wartime anti-Jewish violence in Łomża, the early postwar anti-Jewish violence in Poland constituted more of a classic case of ethnic cleansing.[107] Its intent, despite its severe brutality, was not to kill all Jews but to force them to leave Poland. Because of its intent this violence can be seen as similar to the anti-Jewish violence of the interwar period. The practice of ethnic cleansing in early postwar Poland was extremely effective.[108] For example, in August of 1946 alone, one month after the Kielce pogrom, approximately thirty-three thousand Jews left Poland.[109]

In the early postwar period ethnic cleansing was also used to solve the problems of other minorities. The Communist armed forces exercised the policy of ethnic cleansing against the Ukrainians and the Lemkos. The local NSZ armed forces exercised ethnic cleansing against Belorussians living in small villages of the Bielsko Podlaska region in January 1946.[110]

As in the interwar and wartime periods the representation of the Jew as the threatening other provided grounds for the rationalization and justification of anti-Jewish violence. Anti-Communist leaflets circulated in early postwar Poland recycled the same anti-Jewish lexicon that had been used in the interwar period. Jews were once again constantly referred to as a "menace," a "plague," and a "curse." Expressions of hatred and hostility were extremely explicit when they arose out of the image of Jews as executors of the new Communist regime. An example of this extreme hatred is the text of a leaflet circulated in Frydland, in the western territories, in May 1948: "Attention! A Jewish plague has swamped our town; every townsman agrees . . . that Jewish faces and their deceitful eyes look at us as if to say: We will show you Poles! However, we are not afraid, and we are going to beat the Jews back on each and every street until this Jewish plague is gone."[111]

The Kielce pogrom shows that such phrases proliferated in times of anti-Jewish violence, and ordinary citizens were not afraid to repeat them to representatives of the Communist regime during public meetings that were held in factories to allow the working class to condemn the Kielce pogrom. In a report from the meeting at the Dęblin railway factory on 11 July 1947 Stefan Tomaszewski, head of the Warsaw Department of Communication, stated: "The meeting lasted two hours and was very stormy. Comrade Chodkiewicz and I both made our statements. During the speeches people shouted back 'Get rid of the Jews! It's a disgrace that they have come to defend Jews!' These shouts received a big round of applause from the workers. . . . We had control over the meeting, but I knew that the prepared resolution would not be accepted because of the hostile atmosphere, so I didn't bother to read it out. After the meeting the workers spoke among themselves. I heard them saying: 'They are servants of the Jews, fuck them all!' "[112]

The way Jews were perceived in the early postwar period can also be interpreted in terms of "moral panic," as the Jewish community was perceived as a threat to the rest of society.[113] As in the interwar period all five key elements of "moral panic" can be detected in the early postwar period: expressions of concern over the behavior of the Jewish minority, with Jews allegedly responsible for the Communist takeover of Poland and Communist crimes against the opposition and against Polish society at large; wildly exaggerated claims of the Jewish threat, with Jews portrayed as the "ultimate destroyers" of Poland and its people; wide consensus among the illegal political opposition, a segment of the constitutional opposition, the Catholic Church, and society at large on the threat posed by Jews; an increased level of hostility toward members of the Jewish minority and outbursts of violence; and a sense of the self-righteousness of this position.

The image of the Jew as a physical threat to the Polish nation served as the trigger for spontaneous violent reactions against members of the Jewish community. This image of the Jew acquired a particular dimension in the early postwar period that it did not seem to have in the interwar period. In the early postwar period the accusation of ritual murder became the immediate cause of anti-Jewish demonstrations and violence.[114]

How can one explain the willingness of segments of early postwar Polish society to believe in an old medieval myth? The myth of ritual murder grew on psychologically well-prepared soil, Polish society having been exposed to cruelty beyond understanding over five years of Nazi occupation. The experience of war generated a profound sense of insecurity among many Poles, which was only reinforced by the terror, arrests, and murders perpetrated by the new Communist regime in the early postwar period. Historians stress that during the early postwar period the population felt a deep fear not only for their material goods but also for health and life itself. This fear was sometimes manifested in the most incredible rumors.[115] Officers of the UB collected these rumors and published them in bulletins for strict internal use among members of the Central Committee of the PPR. For example, in July 1947 they registered the following two rumors:

> Members of the Union of the Youth Fighting Movement ZWM have abandoned a course in "industrial instruction" in Częstochowa. They tell stories about forced blood donations, infertility, shortages of food, and Russian and Jewish female lecturers running the course (23 July 1947, Kielce, Starachowice).[116]

> We suspect that the Jews have stolen the atomic bomb from the United States and are transporting it in a coffin to the Soviet Union (31 July 1947, Białystok).[117]

Given the openness of society to superstition and to the myth of the Jew as the new ruler of the Polish nation-state, it becomes even clearer how the psychological fear of losing one's life could find its ultimate nonrational expression in the accusation of ritual murder.[118] These allegations reinforced the belief in a Jewish enemy who murdered Christian Poles and plotted both world domination and Polish servitude. In this sense many Poles saw Jews as a powerful nation with the ability to destroy future generations of Poles.

The Roman Catholic Church, the only institution that enjoyed real authority among various sections of the population, did virtually nothing to counter these allegations. Only a tiny group within the clergy opposed accusations of ritual murder. For example, on 9 July 1946 Bishop Teodor Kubina of Częstochowa issued an appeal to the population of his diocese, adamantly rejecting the idea of ritual murder: "No Christian, either in Kielce, Częstochowa, or anywhere else in Poland, has been harmed by Jews for religious or ritual purposes. . . . We therefore appeal to all citizens of Częstochowa not to be influenced by criminal rumors and to counteract any excesses against the Jewish population."[119]

Senior clergy themselves believed in ritual murder.[120] Records from the British embassy in Warsaw illustrate this situation well. One and a half months after the Kielce pogrom Victor Cavendish-Bentinck, the British ambassador to Poland, recorded a discussion he had held with Juliusz Bieniek (1895–1978), the auxiliary bishop of Upper Silesia:

> Dear Rubin,
>
> My telegram no. 1332 of today's date [28 August 1946][:]
>
> Bishop Bienik [Bieniek], Auxiliary Bishop of Upper Silesia, astonished me yesterday by stating that there was some proof that the child [Henryk Błaszczyk] whose alleged maltreatment by Jews had provoked the Kielce pogrom had in fact been maltreated and that the Jews had taken blood from his arm. If a bishop is prepared to believe this, it is not surprising that uneducated Poles do so too.
>
> I am sending a copy of this letter to the Holy See.[121]

There is also historical evidence that some Catholic churches preserved religious artifacts commemorating the alleged victims of ritual murder. For example, in the church of the Jesuits in Łęczyca a little coffin with a skeleton of a child allegedly killed by the Jews in 1639 was exhibited in 1945 and 1946 with an accompanying manuscript describing the event and a painting depicting a group of religious Jews actually committing the murder. In November 1946, during the relocation of the Jesuits from the church, the artifact and the painting disappeared.[122]

The theme of ritual murder recurred repeatedly during the many attempts to create panic and anti-Jewish pogroms before and after the Kielce pogrom. The bulletins of the Ministry of Public Security, which carefully registered rumors and so-called whispered propaganda, provide examples of the presence of the theme of ritual murder in the daily life of some segments of society:

> Rumors have spread in the Brzesk district that two Jews in Silesia have allegedly killed a Christian child in a ritual murder (31 March 1947, Cracow).[123]

> Once again a nine-year-old girl has disappeared. It may be that the Jews from Rzeszów have eaten her and have now run away from the town in fear (7 July 1947, Rzeszów).[124]

> Jews have murdered Christian children in Łódź. The police have already discovered some corpses during a one-day search (20 September 1947, Kielce).[125]

On 11 August 1945 rumors spread in Cracow that the bloody corpses of Polish children were lying in the Kupa synagogue at Miodowa Street. Instantly a crowd broke into the synagogue and started to beat up members of the Jewish congregation, who were praying at the Saturday-morning Sabbath service.

The synagogue was demolished, and violence spread to other parts of the city. Among the many injured were four fatalities, including two women; in addition two Jewish institutions were plundered. [126]

A similar situation occurred in Kielce during the notorious pogrom of 4 July 1946. Mojżesz Cukier, an eyewitness who lived at 7 Planty Street, remembered it thus: "At about nine o'clock on 4 July crowds started to surround the building. I heard voices from the crowd: 'You Jews have killed fourteen of our children! Mothers and fathers unite and kill all the Jews!' "[127] The rumor that a nine-year-old boy, Henryk Błaszczyk, had escaped from Jewish captivity and that other Polish children had been killed led to the murders of forty-two Jews, including ten women. The records of the CKZP reported that thirty more Jews were murdered in several trains on that day. [128]

Referring to the public mood in Kalisz in the aftermath of the Kielce pogrom, an official report prepared by one of the special committees from Warsaw also indicated widespread belief in the accusation of ritual murder: "The rumor grew. People were talking about four, eight, and twenty-four boys being killed. One woman whom we could not identify stated that she had seen fourteen boys' heads and that their flesh had been taken by the Ukrainians or Soviets, and their blood drunk by the Jews." [129] Recent research reveals that even in 1949, in cities like Częstochowa and Cracow, there were attempts at inciting anti-Jewish hostilities by spreading rumors that Polish children had already been killed or were being targeted by Jews. [130]

As in the interwar period some individuals actively involved in anti-Jewish hostilities were categorized by a section of society as national heroes and martyrs. This was the case with nine men who were hastily sentenced to death on 11 July 1946 at the first trial for the Kielce pogrom. [131] The men were charged with battery and murder and with incitement to ethnic hatred. [132] They were of peasant or working-class background and little education. Among them were two low-ranking policemen. Their executions took place on 12 July 1946 in the presence of an official from the supreme military attorney's office, a military priest, and two members of the UB. Neither the families of the nine sentenced nor the press were informed of the executions. Polish historians of the Kielce pogrom observe that this trial was conducted in a hasty and biased fashion with important material on the participation of the militia and the army suppressed. They also correctly observe that the trial had a political nature. At the same time they seem reluctant to analyze the reactions of ordinary members of society to the trials and to those who were sentenced to death.

Anonymous correspondence addressed to members of the government and special PPR reports prepared for strict internal circulation among members of the Central Committee of the Party reveal that segments of the population opposed the 11 July decision of the courts and the executions that followed. Those who participated in the pogrom and were sentenced to death in the first trial were identified in these communications as patriots fighting for the "dejudaization of the Polish nation-state."

This position was not limited to the lower, uneducated classes, but extended even to members of the clergy.[133] An anonymous priest's letter sent in July 1946 to Prime Minister Edward Osóbka-Morawski explicitly describes the people involved in the pogrom as patriots committed to the national cause and warns the government about the potentially hostile mood of the nation should the executions take place. Here the execution appears to be seen as a crime against the entire Polish nation: "On behalf of the entire nation I warn you that the sentencing to death of these great Polish patriots [the nine people sentenced to death] who acted only in self-defense and despair after six years of fighting for their lives . . . will be the beginning of your ruin and will cause harm to the whole nation. Instead of getting rid of the Jews from Poland now when there is a good chance, you are instead murdering your own brothers. In any case you should protect this eight-year-old hero [Henryk Błaszczyk]; otherwise the Jews will try to poison him as an inconvenient witness."[134]

In big cities members of the working class launched protest actions that in some cases turned into sit-down strikes against the sentences. In Radom railway workers went on strike. Strikes also occurred in all the textile factories in Łódź. A special Communist report on the situation in Łódź at the time stated:

> The social situation in Łódź is serious. The strikes have moved swiftly from one factory to another, and the women are very aggressive. . . . Women have been calling for revenge if the death sentences are to be carried out. . . . Their anti-Semitic arguments are as follows: "A pregnant Jewess gets sixty thousand zlotys and I get nothing! The Jews are running Poland!" The Jews of Łódź insist that there is an atmosphere of pogrom in the city. In trams people spread rumors that Jews killed a child in Bałuty [the poorest suburb of Łódź]. The Provincial Party Committee organized a meeting. . . . It was decided to mobilize the whole Party to take counteraction against this reactionary movement [the official Communist interpretation was that reactionary forces were responsible for the Kielce pogrom] that is spreading anarchy in the factories.[135]

The tendency of shifting responsibility for anti-Jewish violence to Jews was not only limited to perpetrators and supporters of physical violence: it was also found among social institutions that in principle condemned the use of physical violence. The most salient example of this phenomenon was the position of the Roman Catholic Church.

The stance of the Roman Catholic Church on anti-Jewish violence in the early postwar period was similar to the Church's position on violence during the interwar period; on the one hand, the Church condemned physical violence, but on the other it blamed Jews themselves for anti-Jewish incidents and reinforcement of the myth of the Jew as the threatening other. The only significant difference lay in the use of different themes of this representation of the Jew. In the interwar period the Church accused Jews of a variety of "crimes" against the Polish nation: of spreading atheism and Communism; of permissiveness; and of destroying the culture, economy, and morals of the Polish population. In the early postwar years the Church focused on Judeo-Communism and on Jewish responsibility for imposing the Communist regime on the Polish nation.

After the Kielce pogrom, in July 1946, the Jewish delegation of the Lublin district met Bishop Stefan Wyszyński of the Lublin diocese.[136] Two members of the delegation, M. Szyldkraut and S. Słuszny, prepared a report from this meeting in which they discussed Wyszyński's negative attitude toward Jews:

> The delegation presented its analysis of the political situation in the country that is contributing to anti-Jewish excesses. Bishop Wyszyński disagreed with this analysis; he stated that the reasons behind anti-Jewish excesses were far more complex and were based on the population's anger against Jews, who take a very active role in the present political system. The Germans murdered the Jewish nation because the Jews were the propagators of Communism. . . . The bishop stressed that the Nazi [concentration] camps had their roots in the Soviet [labor] camps, which were the first schools of barbarism for the Germans.
>
> According to the bishop, the contribution of the Jewish community to Polish life was minimal. . . . The bishop condemned all kinds of murders from the point of Christian ethics; regarding the Kielce incident, he had nothing to add or particularly condemn, as the Church [the bishop claimed] had always condemned evil. . . . [He stated that] in Poland not only were Jews murdered but also Poles. Many Poles were in [Communist] jails and camps.[137]

Cardinal August Hlond issued a similar statement to foreign journalists on

11 July 1946. Hlond's position caused great controversy among the foreign media, which were shocked by the primate's claim that anti-Jewish violence was a reaction of the frustrated Polish population against the rule of the Communist Jews. Hlond argued: "The course of the highly regrettable events in Kielce shows that they did not occur for racial reasons, but, rather, they developed on a totally different, painful and tragic basis. . . . Numerous Jews in Poland are alive today because of the help of Poles and Polish priests. The fact that this condition is deteriorating is to a great degree due to Jews who occupy the leading positions in Poland's government and endeavor to introduce a governmental structure that a majority of the people do not desire."[138]

Hlond's position on the causes of anti-Jewish violence proved to be totally biased in the light of empirical research conducted in the 1990s by the historian David Engel. According to Engel's analysis, there were significant differences in gender and age among casualties of members of the Jewish community and those of the non-Jewish Communist political camp: twice as many Jewish youths under the age of seventeen were killed than were Polish youths of the same age group, and 20 percent of the overall casualties were Jewish women, as opposed to 7 percent of ethnic Polish women.[139] This discrepancy indicates that Jews were not killed because of their Communist affiliation but because of their ethnicity.

The most detailed, albeit not verified, example of the Church's interpretation of the Kielce pogrom as national self-defense was found in the Kielce Cathedral on 12 January 1952.[140] A document signed there by the Reverend R. Zelek calls the Kielce pogrom a "guilt-free event." This document, like Hlond's statement, expresses the righteousness of national self-defense and denies any racial basis for anti-Jewish attacks:

> Both the workers and the intelligentsia in general say that we are under a Jewish-Bolshevik occupation and that the Communist Jews are acting on behalf of the Russians. . . . Our impression of the incident [the Kielce pogrom] is that the Jews have become a symbol of the present political oppression and of the hated government. The crowd was often heard to shout, "Get rid of the Jewish government!" during the incident.
>
> The actions of the Kielce population during the incident of 4 July were an unusual reaction of an oppressed nation against the new regime dominated by Jews. . . . The entire incident was not directed against Jews as a different religious or ethnic group, but against Jews who rule over the country. This is the opinion of the whole of society after the Kielce incident.[141]

The myth of the Jew as the threatening other was also used as a means of minimizing the unethical and criminal nature of anti-Jewish violence. Members of the state apparatus and the Central Committee of the PPR condemned anti-Jewish violence but at the same time categorized it as an antistate activity, orchestrated and perpetrated by the anti-Communist camp, the so-called reactionary forces. The Communists also portrayed these reactionary forces as enemies of the working class and the Polish people. According to the Communists, the reactionary forces were attempting to slander the good name of Poland. Thus in the official Communist condemnation of anti-Jewish violence the stress was placed on fighting the opposition, not on Jewish victims. Characteristically the topic of Jewish victims was carefully phrased and mentioned in a very limited way. Communist propaganda tended to omit reflections on the spread of anti-Jewish hostilities among society at large, and the idea of questioning and challenging anti-Semitism within society was not raised. In public pronouncements Communists avoided discussion of the topic of anti-Jewish attitudes and hostilities within the rank and file of the Party and the state apparatus. For example, the Appeal of 4 July 1946 to the community of Kielce contains all the elements of the official Communist approach to anti-Jewish violence: "Irresponsible elements of society caused the incidents of 4 July in our town [Kielce] and tarnished Poland's reputation. Our nation has always been well-known for its tolerance. Irresponsible individuals have exploited the crowd, which gathered as a result of false and biased news spread by hired servants of the aristocracy. . . . In the name of innocent blood shed on the stones of the streets of our town, we appeal for calm and urge citizens to resist these elements, which incite hatred and deliberately attempt to sabotage the rebuilding of Poland."[142]

Jerzy Andrzejewski (1909–83), one of the leading Polish writers of the twentieth century, who in the postwar period began to write for left-wing papers, condemned this official Communist strategy of dealing with anti-Semitism. In his article "Zagadnienie polskiego antysemityzmu," published in the summer of 1946, Andrzejewski argued that there had been continuity of pre-1939 negative patterns of thinking about Jews in Polish society in the post-1945 period. He criticized the Communist government's stance on anti-Semitism as worthless and leading to confusion among the public. In fact, he argued that the Communist interpretation of the Kielce pogrom could only obstruct the emergence of necessary and urgent questions about the nature and roots of anti-Jewish prejudice within Polish society. For him blaming reactionary forces for anti-Jewish violence was part of the political struggle of Communists with non-Communists and had little to do with a meaningful analysis of anti-Jewish attitudes and behavior.[143]

The tendency to play down anti-Jewish violence was also noticeable within the local Party and state institutions, including those of law and order. Cases in which investigations into various anti-Jewish hostilities were discontinued and lenient sentences issued in courts were common in the early postwar period.[144] In the third trial for the Kielce pogrom, which took place in December 1947, two men responsible for not stopping the pogrom, Major W. Sobczyński, chief of Kielce public security, and Colonel W. Kuźnicki, chief of the provincial police, received very lenient sentences. Both individuals were, in fact, acquitted of any responsibility for the pogrom, despite evidence of negligence on their part.[145]

In a recent legal and historical analysis of the first trial of the perpetrators of the Jedwabne massacre of 10 July 1941, which occurred on 16 May 1949 before the district court in Łomźa, Andrzej Rzepliński, a distinguished lawyer, discussed misconduct on the part of the judges and investigators. The first trial of the perpetrators of the Jedwabne massacre was like the first trial for the Kielce pogrom, conducted in a hasty and biased fashion. Furthermore, in the case of Jedwabne the accused were only charged with bringing the Jews to the market square and keeping guard over them, not with murdering them. They were accused of collaborating with the Nazis, but it was only the Germans who were seen as responsible for the massacre. Rzepliński argues that the main judge in this trial, who passed lenient sentences, was a local person of peasant background who himself might have been influenced by anti-Jewish attitudes, widespread in the region.[146] One can infer from this case that other courts that conducted trials against perpetrators of early postwar anti-Jewish violence behaved similarly.

The main newspaper of the constitutional opposition party, the PSL's *Gazeta Ludowa*, published many reports and statements about the Kielce pogrom, but Mikołajczyk's pronouncement on the event was vague and avoided any direct references to Jews as victims.[147] There were two reasons for this. First, the PSL was in an increasingly fragile position vis-à-vis the PPR, which treated the PSL as an enemy by 1947. In addition many PSL members seem to have believed that Jews were the chief executors of the new Communist regime.

The illegal opposition argued that Poles and not Jews were the "true" victims of the Kielce pogrom. Articles in the illegal press after the Kielce pogrom plainly categorized Jews as enemies of Poles and anti-Jewish violence as an element of political conflict rather than an unethical and criminal activity. The NSZ forces, which perpetrated various acts of anti-Jewish hostilities in the name of national self-defense, presented the most extreme version of this position.

Statements made by various groups of the illegal opposition accused the Communist government of master-minding the Kielce pogrom in order to turn international attention away from the results of the rigged referendum of 30 June 1946. This referendum was a pivotal political event of the early postwar period. In it Polish society was supposed to decide on three key issues: agrarian reforms, the Polish-German border on the Oder-Neisse line, and a single-chamber parliament. Polish opposition insisted on voting "No" three times, whereas Communists organized a propaganda campaign under the slogan of voting "Three Yes." In a move to cling to power the Communists falsified the official results of the referendum, which were published more than a week after the Kielce pogrom.[148] In this tense political atmosphere the illegal opposition categorized the Kielce pogrom as a ruse to defame the good name of Poland and turn international opinion away from the referendum of 30 June and its falsified results. This interpretation was rooted in their political battle with the Communists. Therefore, unsurprisingly, the opposition press did not reflect on the fate of the Kielce victims: Jewish men and women, including the elderly, and children. For example, an article entitled "Kielce" published by the chief paper of WiN, *Honor i Ojczyzna*, in August 1946 claimed:

> The anti-Jewish pogrom [at Kielce] was neither the first such event nor an isolated incident. We should not deceive ourselves. It was neither the first nor the last incident in a chain of murders committed by the UB. The Kielce pogrom is a classic example of provocation. . . . The following are the facts, which shed some light on the methods of the NKVD and the UB and on the secret tactics of Bolsheviks in Poland. The Kielce incident should be considered as part of a broader issue: Communism—Jews—reactionary movements. Among the small numbers of Jews in Poland the majority of them, four out of five, work for Public Security. . . . Thus the Warsaw government has created perfect conditions for the spread of anti-Semitism and racism. This in turn led the West to develop a hostile attitude toward Polish nationalism and gave Moscow the excuse it has been waiting for—to provoke the Polish population and to repress us.[149]

Leaflets and anonymous correspondence addressed to local Jewish communities in the aftermath of the Kielce pogrom presented a similar point of view.

For example, the chairman of the Jewish community in Włoszczów received an anonymous letter stating: "As I know you personally from our village I would have feelings of remorse if I were not to warn you. Something bad might happen to your people. No one is going to forgive you for Kielce [the pogrom]. Revenge is on its way because you have treated Poles badly. Nothing can help your people, not even the UB. A terrible revenge against you is coming from the entire country. I advise you to leave Poland for 'the Promised Land'; otherwise there will be bloodshed in the spring."[150]

On the other hand, a segment of Polish cultural elites unambiguously condemned anti-Jewish violence. Left-wing journals such as *Kuźnica* and *Odrodzenie* were the main papers in which serious attempts at questioning anti-Jewish prejudices and hostilities within Polish society were made in the early postwar period.[151] Stanisław Ossowski, the sociologist, and writers like Jerzy Andrzejewski, Kazimierz Wyka (1910–75), and Stefan Otwinowski (1910–76) were adamant in their condemnation of anti-Jewish attitudes and behavior in society in the early postwar period. In the article "Our Role in It" the scholar Witold Kula (1916–88) depicted the "darkest" image of Polish society, including the Polish intelligentsia, as a community characterized by strong anti-Jewish prejudices. Kula described the scope of encounters with anti-Jewish attitudes in daily life: "The current situation in Poland is unbearable for the Jews. I recently traveled by train between Łódź and Wrocław. Nearby sat a Jewish family. Honestly, I am not exaggerating when I say that fifteen minutes did not go by in which I did not hear some derogatory remark, joke, comment, warning mocking parody, or imitation of a Jewish accent directed at them."[152]

Because of the tone of Kula's condemnation of early postwar anti-Semitism and his grim analysis of the spread of anti-Semitic attitudes among various social classes of Polish society, the editors of *Kuźnica* rejected his article for publication. The article appeared for the first time in Polish only in 2004, in the book *Uparta sprawa*, written by Marcin Kula, Witold Kula's son.[153]

Tygodnik Powszechny, the chief paper of the progressive Catholic intelligentsia, which became one of the main forums of the Open Church in the post-1945 period, also published articles condemning anti-Jewish violence.[154] *Prawo Człowieka*, the monthly journal of the All-Polish Antiracist League (Polska Liga do Walki z Rasizmem), the first issue of which appeared on 15 September 1946, published articles calling for a self-critical examination and questioning of anti-Jewish prejudices and actions that persisted in early postwar Poland.[155] The Communist regime permitted only a small number of these articles to be published in *Prawo Człowieka*. In 1948 the All-Polish Antiracist League, established in the spring of 1946, was ordered to "drop" discussion of anti-Jewish hostilities and prejudices in Poland. Instead, in the growing atmosphere of the Cold War, the monthly was ordered to concentrate on racism in the capitalist world and discuss issues of prejudice against Blacks in the United States.

In all, backward-looking ethno-nationalism, intolerant of multiethnic and multicultural diversity, was a powerful force in early postwar Poland. It was represented not only by the illegal right-wing anti-Communist elites but also by segments of the new Communist elites who were already susceptible to it. Thus, despite the official Communist principle of equal civic and political rights for Jews and other minorities, the ethno-nationalist perspective played an important role in the discussion and treatment of Jews and other minorities.

The myth of the Jew as the threatening other, in varying degrees of intensity, persisted within significant segments of Polish society, reinforced by the stormy political situation of the early postwar period: the Communist takeover of power, which was controlled by the Soviets and carried out by Communist Poles, Jews, and members of Slavic minorities. This representation of the Jew played an important role in outbreaks of anti-Jewish violence between 1945 and 1947 and in the rationalization and justification of this violence. The continuity of this representation of the Jew in early postwar Poland reveals the persistence and adaptability of such an image in different historical, political, and social contexts.

7. "Judeo-Communists, Judeo-Stalinists, Judeo-anti-Communists, and National Nihilists"

The Communist Regime and the Myth, 1950s–80s

Anti-Semitism persists within us as a vestige of old prejudices and not as a phenomenon typical of socialist countries. Comrade Werblan interestingly noted that the moment we came to face to face with the construction of socialism, each Marxist Party found itself faced with the responsibility for its own nation. On these grounds our internationalism has gone through defined evaluation. Now we too are trying to unite two phenomena: the responsibility for one's nation and our internationalist obligations. These matters are not as simple as they had appeared in theory.

Comrade Włodzimierz Sokorski, 1965

The students must know if [Adam] Michnik and his group are defenders of student rights or rather defenders of Zionism.

Walka Młodych, 24 March 1968

One popular misconception about the post-1945 Communist regimes in Poland and other Eastern European countries is the belief that these regimes suppressed all expressions of ethnicity and nationalism and all national traditions, symbols, and sentiments. In the last two decades this belief has been successfully contested. Various studies on the links between Communism and nationalism have concluded that the ethno-nationalization of Communism took place in all Communist states to varying degrees and in various forms. While in theory Communist regimes preached the Marxist ideology of internationalism, working-class brotherhood, and friendship, in practice they used ethnicity, national traditions, sentiments, and myths of the "dominant nation" to legitimize their rule. Thus ethno-nationalism came to constitute an essential aspect of the Communist system and at the same time created contradictions and tensions within Communist doctrine.[1] The power of ethno-nationalism in Communist countries should not be underestimated merely because Communist regimes collapsed. As Andre Gerrits, a key scholar of the subject, points out: "Nationalism, in its particular Communist form, was a constituent part of the post-war experience. All Communist regimes attempted to legitimize their rule by placing it in the framework of national history and tradition. The fact, that these endeavors largely failed, does not in itself diminish the relevance of nationalism."[2]

In Poland the crystallization of the ethno-nationalization of Communism with anti-Jewish elements began in the early postwar period (1945–49), when these elements emerged within a segment of the PPR leadership, the rank and file of the PPR, and the state apparatus, although they were not officially endorsed as political propaganda by any factions within the PPR. This situation began to change in the 1950s and reached its apogee in the late 1960s when anti-Jewish policy, expressed in the slogan "Party free of Jews, Poland free of Jews," was endorsed by the Communist regime. Given the scope and impact of anti-Jewish propaganda in the years 1967–69, the following questions are compelling: What were the similarities and differences between the ethno-nationalist Communist version of the myth of the Jew as the harmful other and the original version of the myth disseminated by non-/anti-Communist ethno-nationalist political elites? In what ways was the ethno-nationalist Communist version manifested? And what social functions did it play in political culture under the Communist regime?

Next to the years 1944–47 and October 1956 the political events of 1967–69 constitute one of the most dramatic moments in Communist Poland. Along with the purge of the majority of Jews from the PZPR, cultural and scientific institutions, and the state apparatus, this period was also marked by a deep ideological and political crisis within the PZPR and student demonstrations against state censorship and the lack of democratic reforms in the country that had been promised by the Communist regime during the "political thaw" in 1956. Many organizers of the 1968 student demonstrations in time would become leading members of anti-Communist dissident movements: the KOR and the first Solidarity.

In the last two decades the events of 1968 have been the subject of various academic conferences, scholarly research, and public debate. In late 1980, in the aftermath of the emergence of the first Solidarity movement, members of the academic community and students began calling for rehabilitation of the victims of 1968 policies. In the spring of 1981, at the University of Warsaw, an exhibition dedicated to the events of 1968, including their anti-Jewish aspect, was opened, and a scholarly conference lasting a few days was held.[3] The thirtieth anniversary of 1968 also proved to be an important political and social event in post-Communist Poland. In early March 1998 Aleksander Kwaśniewski (1954–), president of the Third Polish Republic, apologized on behalf of the state to all individuals who had been forced to leave the country in what is known as the anti-Zionist purge of 1968–69, announcing that they had the right to reclaim their Polish citizenship.[4] At the same time the Polish government passed new legislation that granted this right to all individuals who had been so affected.[5]

In the post-1989 period certain important archival collections of secret PZPR and state documents about the events of 1967–69 have also appeared in print.[6] The historian Dariusz Stola published a detailed historical account of the anti-Jewish policies of March 1968 based on archival research.[7] The historian Jerzy Eisler also published a useful monograph on March 1968, although the archival research in his book is limited.[8] Michał Głowiński, a historian of Polish literature, conducted a valuable analysis of the language of official anti-Jewish propaganda in the Communist press of 1968, revealing its repetitive and schematic character.[9] Other authors who were among the first to write about the anti-Jewish aspect of 1968 are Josef Banas, Paul Lendvai, Celia Stopnicka Heller, and Łukasz Hirszowicz. The latter was himself a victim of the anti-Zionist purge of 1968.[10] All aspects of the events of March 1968 continue to raise popular and scholarly interest.[11]

The Prelude to 1968

The years 1954–56 saw the end of the Stalinist era in Poland. Nikita Khrushchev (1894–1971), who became the new Soviet Party and state leader in May 1955, announced the end of Stalinism in February 1956 at the Twentieth Congress of the Communist Party of the Soviet Union. At the congress Khrushchev gave a "green light" to the concept of "separate national roads to socialism."[12] In his secret speech delivered to the members of the Soviet Communist Party Khrushchev listed and condemned all the horrors that had accompanied Stalin's rule. This revelation seriously undermined the authority of local Stalinists in Poland.

The end of Stalinization began in Poland with the dismissal from the government and the Politburo of the most discredited and notorious Stalinists, such as Jakub Berman and Stanisław Radkiewicz. Major changes took place within the infamous security apparatus, its separate status abolished. In April 1956 Edward Ochab (1906–89), the new prime minister and a former Stalinist turned into moderate reformer, announced mass amnesty for prisoners of the Stalinist era, and some twenty-eight thousand were released.[13] These developments were followed by the events of October 1956, which constituted the apogee of the "political thaw" (odwilż) that began in 1954 with the emergence of critical voices from the intelligentsia asking for democratization of the system. The "thaw" of 1956 lasted until late 1957 and resulted in some visible political, social, and economic changes, such as the abolition of the collectivization of farms, the establishment of a new relationship between the state and the Roman Catholic Church, the introduction of Catholic religion in schools, and the lifting of censorship on publishing.[14]

In late October 1956, at the plenum of the Central Committee, Władysław Gomułka was reelected to the position of first secretary of the PZPR, with the population's approval. Other close associates of Gomułka also joined the Central Committee, such as Ignacy Loga-Sowiński, Marian Spychalski (1906–80), and Zenon Kliszko(1908–89).[15] Gomułka was at this time a national hero; Poles saw in him the only Communist leader able to conduct in-depth reforms of the political and economic system and thus implement "the Polish national road to socialism."[16] Factors that contributed to his popularity in 1956 were his ethnic Polish and working-class background, his record of having been removed from the Party in November 1949 for the so-called nationalist deviation, his stress on the Polish Communist Party's independence from Moscow, and his record of having spent time in a Stalinist prison with his wife between 1951 and 1954.

Gomułka returned to power with the help and cooperation of the faction of reformers in the PZPR that had emerged at the third plenum of the Central Committee in January 1955. However, the policies and practices that Gomułka implemented starting in late 1957 would prove that he was not the true potential reformer of the Communist system that he initially seemed.

Accompanying the "political thaw" between 1954 and October 1956 was an overt public outburst of anti-Jewish attitudes and sentiments, manifested simultaneously in the conservative segments of the PZPR leadership, the rank and file of the PZPR and the state apparatus, and some segments of society at large.[17]

Such sentiments were particularly visible in April, May, and October of 1956 in Łódź and Dolny Śląsk (Lower Silesia), areas where there was still a relatively high concentration of Jews. These sentiments and attitudes were sometimes manifested in both verbal and physical anti-Jewish hostilities among not only adults but schoolchildren. As in the early postwar period (1945–47) in some schools children refused to have contact with Jewish children.[18] This situation indicates that at this time anti-Jewish sentiments were being transmitted in families from the older to the younger generation and were also encouraged or supported by some teachers. For example, one article of 6 June 1956 published in *Trybuna Ludu*, the main paper of the PZPR, discussed the case of a teacher in one of the Warsaw primary schools who seated a Jewish girl separately from the rest of the class because she was Jewish.[19]

As with the ethno-nationalists of the interwar period, some factions of the PZPR came to view personal animosities and conflicts between individual ethnic Poles and Polish Jews collectively. In every case these factions of the PZPR saw conflicts between individuals as antagonism between Poles and Jews in which Poles were the victims and Jews were the perpetrators. For example, a PZPR. newspaper reported that in Łódź the mother of a child who had been fighting with his Jewish classmate publicly protested her perception that "Jewish children beat up Polish kids and no one takes any action."[20]

Hostile reactions toward Jews were also noticeable in contacts between members of the Jewish community and the rank and file of the PZPR and the state apparatus, especially at the local level. This was manifested in policies of employment and promotion: in some factories ethnic Poles began to be given preferential treatment over Jews. The Warsaw Yiddish newspaper *Folkshtimme* advised individual Jews to get in touch with members of the Polish parliament and bring to their attention all instances of anti-Jewish discrimination. The paper also reported that a number of governing and communal institutions preferred not to notice that certain groups among them attempted to put pressure on Jews to leave the country. Such pressure was also applied to Jews who returned to Poland from the Soviet Union in the last wave of repatriation in the spring of 1956.[21]

Anti-Jewish sentiments and actions reached a high level by the end of 1956 and were even noted in the Western press. In January 1957 a journalist for the *New York Times* reported that a few weeks earlier the Union of Students at Wrocław University had demanded the expulsion of all Jewish students from the university.[22] The reporter found similarities between the anti-Jewish sentiments some segments of society at large were expressing and the anti-Jewish sentiments expressed by segments of the Party and the state apparatus.[23] Both groups seemed to share the convictions that "Jews have ruled over Poland," were "responsible for the Stalinist terror," and constituted an impediment to the development of ethnic Poles. Both groups also seemed to make similar demands for the removal of Jews from the Party, the state apparatus, and even the country. This indicates the strength of the anti-Jewish sentiments that persisted in various sections of society in the 1950s.

On the other hand, various Polish intellectuals, such as then–Marxist philosopher Leszek Kołakowski (1927–) and the émigré writer Konstanty A. Jeleński (1922–87), condemned anti-Semitic attitudes and actions.[24] Jerzy Turowicz (1912–99), the editor in chief of the progressive Catholic journal *Tygodnik Powszechny*, published an editorial in which he argued that anti-Semitism could not be reconciled with Catholicism and that Jews had an equal right with Poles to live in the country.[25] In 1960, in another Catholic progressive monthly, *Więź*, whose first issue appeared in 1958, Tadeusz Mazowiecki published the article "Antysemityzm ludzi łagodnych i dobrych" (Anti-Semitism of Good and Kind People). In his article Mazowiecki put a finger on the presence of anti-Jewish attitudes among "ordinary decent people." He discerningly observed that anti-Semitism would not disappear without the deconstruction of these anti-Jewish attitudes. He argued that "the law and the state may ban anti-Semitic propaganda, but they alone cannot finally liquidate it. Anti-Semitism will not disappear until a reevaluation of attitudes and concepts already present in society takes place. That is why I say that the main problem lies in the attitude of 'good, kind people.' "[26] In a commentary on this article written in 1998 Mazowiecki admitted that at the time he did not foresee that the Communist government would endorse anti-Semitism in the late 1960s.[27]

The first sign that such an official endorsement might take place appeared in the year 1956, which witnessed the crystallization of an overt anti-Jewish stance among the elite of the PZPR. The first faction of the PZPR that endorsed an anti-Jewish position as part of its program and as a strategy to delegitimize internal opponents was the so-called Natolin group. The Natolin group appeared on the political scene around late March 1956, simultaneous with the emergence of its main opponent, a new reformist faction called the Puławska group. Both groups were named after the neighborhoods in Warsaw where they held their meetings.[28]

The Natolin group consisted of strongly pro-Soviet and ethnic Polish Communists "who wanted to replace the old Stalinist leadership but were opposed to any reforms of doctrine and political methods which could exceed the political reforms of the Soviet Party." [29] Its members were known for their dogmatism, their support for authoritarian rule, and their anti-intelligentsia stance.

In contrast, the Puławska group was internally much more diverse, including both ethnic Polish and Jewish Communists. This group advocated a more independent stance in relation to the Soviet Union and enjoyed the support of the PZPR's intelligentsia. It was regarded as the reform-oriented faction of the PZPR, since many of its members "out of ideological disillusionment or for opportunistic reasons" favored liberalization and the democratization of the political system. [30] Some members of the Puławska group became the main revisionists of institutionalized Marxism in the early 1960s.

The Puławska and Natolin groups competed for political power within the PZPR and state apparatus between 1956 and 1960. October 1956 brought about a short-term defeat for the Natolin group and a short-term victory for the Puławska group, but Gomułka's departure from the course of reform in late 1957 changed this balance of power. By early 1958 Gomułka started to support and "court" the Natolin group. Adam Bromberg, the former chief editor of the *Wielka Encyclopedia*, dismissed from his post in 1968, described Gomułka's drift toward the Natolin group as his "imprisonment" by the conservative Natolin group. [31] Nevertheless, in the political realities of the early 1960s both factions lost their prominence.

The rivalry and animosity between the Puławska and Natolin factions were reflected in the groups' names for each other. The Puławska group called members of the Natolin group "Boors" (Chamy), a pejorative term meaning slow-witted peasants, and the Natolin group called the members of the Puławska group "Yids" (Żydy), a pejorative form of "Jews" (Żydzi). [32] This is a good example of their imitation of the long-lived ethno-nationalist strategy of labeling political opponents as Jews.

Although within both groups there were Communists with a clear record of a "Stalinist past," members of the Natolin group emphasized that only Jews as a group should be held responsible for the errors of Stalinization in Poland. Therefore they called for the removal of Jewish members of the PZPR from important positions in the Party and the state apparatus. [33]

An illustration of this approach may be found in Zenon Nowak's speech of 18 July 1956 at the seventh plenum of the Central Committee of the PZPR. Nowak (1905–70), who was at this time deputy prime minister and a member of the Politburo, was the leader of the Natolin group. In his cleverly structured speech he introduced the theme of Judeo-Stalinization into the vocabulary of the PZPR by placing sole blame on "the Jewish apparatchiks" for the Party's past failures, errors, and repressions.[34] He argued: "I would like to ask if the arrests of [Roman] Romkowski, [Anatol] Feigin, and [Józef] Różański for the abuses of the UB brought a positive outcome. In my opinion it was a good thing that we arrested them, but the bad thing is that they are all of Jewish origin. And I would like to ask if it is a good or a bad thing [for the Party] when people say the Jews arrested the Poles."[35]

Characteristically Nowak's speech held neither Stalinist Soviet apparatchiks who were based in Poland between 1945 and 1956 nor Stalinist ethnic Poles responsible for the crimes of the Stalinist era. Furthermore, Nowak accused Jews and "other alien powers" of being responsible for more recent events, namely the workers' demonstrations in Poznań on 28 June, during which approximately seventy people were killed by soldiers on the orders of the Communist regime.[36] Nowak also called for the "ethno-national regulation of the Party and state apparatus cadres," arguing that the presence of Jews within the PZPR and the state apparatus had a bad effect on the popularity of the Party among the population. At the same time he insisted that anti-Semitism did not drive his position. This claim is a typical rationalization of anti-Jewish prejudice as based on objective factors and was common among members of pre-1939 National Democracy and among ethno-nationalist anti-Communist groups in the post-1945 period.

The Natolin group's project for the "purification" of the PZPR from Jews was not realized in 1956. In April 1957 the Central Committee of the Party issued a letter to all PZPR committees condemning anti-Semitism.[37] This letter also urged Jewish Communists to persuade members of the Jewish community not to leave the country. The outburst of anti-Jewish sentiments and attitudes in parts of the population and in the rank and file of the PZPR was undoubtedly one of the main factors that contributed to the emigration of Polish Jews during the late 1950s. It is estimated that between 1956 and 1958 approximately forty thousand Jews left Poland, including twenty thousand who had returned to Poland from the Soviet Union in early 1956.[38] By the early 1960s the remaining Jewish community in Poland numbered approximately thirty thousand members, an insignificant percentage of the population.

The first six years of the 1960s, described by the Polish poet Tadeusz Różewicz (1921–) as the time of a "small stabilization" (mała stabilizacja), were characterized by growing stagnation of political, economic, and cultural reforms and by social opportunism and petty compromise. The PZPR regime headed by Gomułka launched a major campaign against any interpretations of Marxist doctrine different from the official institutionalized version.[39] That is how the PZPR came to view revisionism of Marxist thought as one of the main enemies of the Party. At the same time, by the middle of the 1960s membership in the PZPR had increased to approximately 1.5 million. In 1967 158,507 new members joined the rank and file of the PZPR, and in 1968 another 213,098 individuals joined.[40] This was the result of the Party's new recruitment policy, which offered fresh opportunities for social advancement. In turn the fact that the PZPR included almost 2 million people in 1968 shows that by this time the PZPR had achieved a high level of legitimacy in society.

Although there was a decrease in the number of overt anti-Jewish statements within the PZPR in the early 1960s, anti-Jewish sentiments and attitudes did not disappear from political culture. Such utterances by important members of the Central Committee of the PZPR occurred but as a rule were immediately covered up. According to Paul Lendvai, this was the case with Zenon Kliszko's lecture at a meeting of historians in Cracow in 1966. In this lecture, which was not published in full, Kliszko, one of the closest associates of Gomułka and then one of the main theoreticians of the Party, supposedly "hinted at the 'diabolic role'" of Jewish intellectuals.[41] Kliszko's anti-Jewish position was also reported by Mieczysław F. Rakowski, who as the editor in chief of the weekly *Polityka* had free access to the members of the Central Committee of the PZPR. In his diary Rakowski recollected some anti-Jewish comments uttered by Kliszko and other close associates of Gomułka, such as Loga-Sowiński.[42]

On the whole, it is possible to differentiate among three main developments concerning Jews within the PZPR during the first half of the 1960s. First, Party leadership denied the presence of anti-Jewish sentiments and attitudes within the PZPR. This denial was an important feature of ethno-nationalist Communism, although it certainly contained anti-Jewish themes, found not only in the Polish People's Republic but also in other countries of the Soviet Bloc, such as the Soviet Union.[43] In Poland the origin of this phenomenon can be traced to the pronouncements of Gomułka and Loga-Sowiński in the early postwar period (see chapter 6) and of the Natolin group in the 1950s.

In the early 1960s the elites of the PZPR started to make the charge of "bogus anti-Semitism" against any members of the PZPR who raised the issue of the presence of anti-Jewish sentiments and attitudes within the Party. A good illustration of the exploitation of this charge, used against critics of anti-Jewish attitudes, is the responses of the PZPR's Central Committee to Adam Schaff's book *Marksizm a jednostka ludzka*, published in 1965. Schaff, a Polish Jew, was at this time still a member of the Central Committee of the PZPR and director of the Institute of Philosophy and Sociology of the Polish Academy of Sciences. He enjoyed a reputation as one of the chief theoreticians of Marxism in Poland. In *Marksizm a jednostka ludzka* Schaff argued that anti-Semitism was a serious social problem in Communist states, including Poland, and that Communist governments had not properly tackled it. He also argued that nationalism constituted a danger to Communism and that in fact a huge gap between Communist theory and practice was visible in the PZPR. [44] Schaff's arguments were met with general condemnation and raised a heated discussion within the Party. The discussion was published in *Nowe Drogi*, the main theoretical press organ of the Central Committee of the PZPR. Except for some members of the Communist elite such as Jerzy Wiatr, the majority evaluated Schaff's book as revisionist and thus dangerous. Some of the negative evaluations contained clear anti-Jewish overtones. For example, Andrzej Werblan (1924–), then head of the Central Committee's Department of Science, interpreted Schaff's arguments as a manifestation of "the Talmudist approach to the theory of the classics of Marxism." [45] Another member of the Central Committee, Wincenty Kraśko, argued that Schaff's position on anti-Semitism in the PZPR was unfair, biased, and unacceptable to the Party: "Comrade Schaff sharply flays the alleged absence of the struggle with anti-Semitism in our Communist countries. . . . Undoubtedly anti-Semitism is a very painful and revolting phenomenon, but equally painful and revolting is the charge of anti-Semitism, a charge that is both unjust and groundless." [46]

The second development that began to crystallize in the first half of the 1960s was the preparation and collection of data on the remaining Jews who occupied important positions in public life, including converts to Catholicism, their spouses Jewish and non-Jewish, their children, and even their in-laws. Index cards on Jewish members of the PZPR's Central Committee and the government were prepared by a section of the Ministry of Internal Affairs that dealt with Jewish matters. A similar system of index cards with the names of Jewish officers remaining in the Polish Army was prepared by military counterintelligence for the Ministry of Defense. [47] The process of collecting the index cards was completed by the second half of the 1960s and was used in the anti-Jewish purge of 1968.

Simultaneously, in the first half of the 1960s the PZPR and government institutions were forcing gradual demotion and early retirement on Jewish members of the Central Committee of the PZPR, Jewish personnel employed by the Ministry of Interior Affairs, and Jewish military servicemen in the Polish Army.[48] The new policy of the ethno-nationalization, or "full polonization," of the PZPR and the state apparatus was conducted in a discreet and unpublicized manner. Sometimes this policy also affected ethnic Poles married to Jews or ethnic Poles accused of revisionism. Soviet leaders supported this policy; Nikita Khrushchev, in a conversation with Gomułka as early as 1956, complained about too many "Semitic faces" in the PZPR.[49]

The Rise of the "Partisans"

Many members of the Ministry of Interior Affairs, responsible for the preparation of index cards with Jewish names and orchestrating the removal of Jewish personnel, belonged to the informal "Partisan" group (Partyzanci), which emerged in the early 1960s as the most dynamic faction within the PZPR. At the Fourth Party Congress in June 1964 the Partisans already constituted a significant force.

This group included former members of wartime Communist military forces based in Nazi-occupied Poland. They were placed in secondary political positions, or dismissed from any positions, in the PPR and PZPR and the state apparatus between 1949 and 1956. They gradually returned to power in the post-1956 period, and within a short span of time, by the mid-1960s, they had succeeded in taking control of all influential positions within the Ministry of Internal Affairs, the security apparatus, and the police. The Partisans, like the Natolin group of the 1950s, were characterized by a strongly authoritarian, anti-intellectual, anti-Jewish stance. Unlike the Natolin group the Partisans did not advocate complete subservience to the Soviet Union. In fact, the Partisans portrayed themselves as an anti-Soviet and nationally oriented political group. The Partisans stressed their patriotism, the strong national aspect of their ideology, and their local roots in order to gain public support and legitimacy.[50]

The driving force behind the Partisan faction, its founding father and un-questionable leader, was Mieczysław Moczar (1913–86).[51] Moczar, a Ukrainian by origin, was the head of the local UB forces in Łódź between 1945 and 1948. In 1948 he was dismissed from his position on the same charges as were being raised at this time against Gomułka, namely of holding a "right-wing nationalistic position." In 1956 he was reinstated to the position of deputy minister of interior affairs, and in 1964 he was nominated minister of interior affairs. The same year he was also elected president of the Union of Fighters for Freedom and Democracy (Związek Bojowników o Wolność i Demokrację, ZBOWiD), an organization that, according to Moczar, acted as "the guardian of patriotism, love, and service to one's homeland."[52]

ZBOWiD, which emerged as a small, irrelevant Communist organization, quickly transformed itself into a formidable political base that aimed at uniting all those who had fought for the victory of Poland in WWII, irrespective of their political convictions and affiliations. Although many former soldiers of the AK did not accept ZBOWiD, small groups of servicemen joined the organization.[53] Given the fact that Moczar was, after all, heavily involved in the actions of the infamous security apparatus between 1945 and 1948, and had supposedly remarked in 1948 that "a good member of the AK is a dead one," the growth of ZBOWiD's organization in the early 1960s constituted a remarkable success.[54] In the first two years of the 1960s ZBOWiD reached approximately a quarter of a million members. This situation allowed Moczar to strengthen his position vis-à-vis Gomułka and to implement his version of the campaign against Jewish members of the PZPR and the state apparatus.[55] The network of ZBOWiD's organization, as convincingly argued by the historian Michael C. Steinlauf, "gave Moczar and his associates popular legitimization to appropriate the entire heritage of anti-Nazi resistance. . . . ZBOWiD, which hinted that it represented, better than the Party, the interests of all Poles, became Moczar's ideological base, the driving force of the anti-Jewish campaign of 1968."[56]

Another organization supportive of the Partisans' anti-Jewish campaign of 1968 was the government-sponsored Catholic organization PAX (Stowarzyszenie PAX), chaired by Bolesław Piasecki (1915–79), a well-known extreme right-wing political figure of the interwar and wartime periods. In pre-1939 Poland Piasecki was first a member of National Democracy and OWP and later became a leader of one of the fascist groups, ONR-Falanga. During WWII Piasecki headed another extreme ethno-nationalist political group, the National Confederation, which published strongly anti-Semitic articles in its various underground papers. In 1943 its military group subordinated itself to the command of the AK. At the end of the war, in unclear circumstances, Piasecki, who was captured by the Soviets, was released from prison and became a Soviet agent.[57] In the early post-1945 period Piasecki was allowed to establish PAX, which promoted a certain mixed Communist-Catholic perspective to counterbalance the anti-Communist Roman Catholic position. In fact, the organization's main role was to neutralize the influence of the Roman Catholic Church and the progressive Catholic intelligentsia, concentrated around two Cracow-based papers: the weekly *Tygodnik Powszechny* and the monthly *Znak*.[58] PAX enjoyed a well-developed press network. Its first paper, *Dziś i jutro*, was established in 1945, with Piasecki as its editor in chief. Other PAX papers included the daily *Słowo Powszechne* and *Wrocławski Tygodnik Katolicki* and the weekly *Kierunki*. Between 1967 and 1969 all these papers played an important role in disseminating the myth of the Jew as the harmful other in Poland. *Słowo Powszechne* was the first paper to participate in the anti-Jewish campaign.[59] By 1968 Piasecki, as chairman of PAX, had already served four years as an MP in the Polish parliament and therefore was an influential political figure.

Other supporters of Mieczysław Moczar included former members of National Democracy and its offshoot radical organizations, such as Czesław Pilichowski. Moczar maintained close links with such individuals and promoted them to high positions in governmental and state institutions. For example, Pilichowski was appointed head of the High Commission to Investigate Nazi Crimes in Poland (Komisja do Badania Zbrodni Hitlerowskich w Polsce) in 1968 and maintained this position until 1984. Under Partisan control the High Commission assumed the role of "guardian of [ethno]-national history and [ethno]-national traditions."[60] The year 1968 would show that individuals like Pilichowski excelled in the dissemination of the ethno-nationalist Communist version of the myth of the Jew as the enemy of Poland and the Poles. In all, the fact that these individuals belonged to the Communist political elite both before and after 1968 reveals how porous the border was between some factions of Communist leadership and the prewar core ethno-nationalist parties and how easily this border was crossed in the so-called climate of national unity promoted by Moczar. Moczar also succeeded in winning the support of three important Communist journals: *Kultura*, *Stolica*, and *Żołnierz Wolności*.

The Myth and the Issue of "Zionism" in Communist Propaganda in the Late 1960s

One of the problems in the analysis of the ethno-nationalist Communist version of the myth of the Jew as the enemy of Poland in the late 1960s comes from the fact that during this period the term *Jew* was, as a rule, replaced by the term *Zionist*. The popular slogans of the late 1960s were "Purge the Party of Zionists" (Oczyścić Partię z Syjonistów), "Zionists, go to Zion" (Syjoniści do Syjonu), and "Zionists represent Israel, not Poland" (Syjoniści reprezentują Izrael nie Polaków).[61]

PZPR publications' use of the term *Zionist* instead of *Jew* can be explained by the reluctance of PZPR leadership to openly express anti-Jewish positions, knowing that this would breach the Communist ethos and contradict the Party's official stance opposing anti-Semitism. Thus during the anti-Jewish campaign of 1968 the condemnation of anti-Semitism was maintained throughout the entire period of the officially sponsored anti-Jewish purge.[62] This phenomenon, called "anti-Semitism without anti-Semites," was rooted in a highly rationalized anti-Jewish perspective that blamed anti-Semitism on Jewish cultural qualities and the size of the Jewish population. In this case Communists saw the number of Jewish Communists in the PZPR as the objective cause of their own anti-Jewish actions. The phenomenon of "anti-Semitism without anti-Semites" would reemerge in post-Communist Poland.

In the late 1960s the term *Zionism* also carried two other meanings in PZPR propaganda. Zionism was understood as an instrument of imperialism, a tool used by the enemy of Communism to destroy all Communist countries. Zionism was also defined as the "source" of the successful Israeli campaign in the war of 1967 against the Arab world, which at this time was the official ally of all the countries of the Soviet bloc.[63] The use of the latter two meanings of *Zionism* in Polish Communist propaganda corresponded with the use of the term in official Soviet propaganda of the late 1960s, whereas the myth of the Zionist/Jew as the enemy of the Polish state, its people, and the "Polish spiritual essence" had domestic roots in pre-1939 exclusivist ethno-nationalist traditions, integrated into the Polish ethno-nationalist version of Communism.[64]

Characteristically all three meanings of Zionism were intertwined to varying degrees in PZPR propaganda in the late 1960s. Of course Zionism as a movement and ideology was nonexistent among the remaining Polish Jewry in Poland in the late 1960s. Between 1949 and 1950 the Stalinist regime banned all Zionist parties and social organizations. Furthermore, any remaining Jews who supported Zionism had almost certainly left Poland in the various postwar waves of emigration between 1945 and 1957. Therefore the PZPR's "hunt" for Zionists was conducted in a reality in which no Zionists were present in Poland.

The criteria for singling out a person and labeling him or her a "Zionist" were not openly stated in official Party propaganda. However, it is possible to differentiate between two types of criteria that were applied at this time.

The first was the biological or racial/ethnic origin of a person. This criterion was advocated by the Partisan group, which treated all remaining Polish Jews, including individuals of partly Jewish origin, as biological polluters of the Polish state. This explains why Partisans were labeled "fascists" by those who condemned their anti-Jewish actions in the late 1960s; the similarities between their categorization of Jews and the categorization of Jews in the pre-1939 core ethno-nationalist political camp were obvious. [65]

The second criterion was the subjective notion of belonging to and loving Poland, introduced by Gomułka in his 19 March 1968 speech to three thousand PZPR activists in Warsaw. [66] In this speech, which was aired on radio and television, Gomułka divided Polish Jews into three categories. The first group was composed of individuals defined as attached by "reason or emotion to Israel"; Gomułka's speech implicitly advised such individuals to leave Poland for good. The second included "cosmopolitans and national nihilists" who considered themselves neither Polish nor Jewish and therefore should not occupy any important positions in the Party or state apparatus. This definition implied that these individuals constituted "a lesser worst type" of citizens who could not be trusted. The third group, according to Gomułka, was constituted of Polish patriots, who, in contrast to the two previous groups, regarded Poland as their sole homeland.

Gomułka's motivation to distinguish among different types of Jews and thus ameliorate the anti-Jewish ideas espoused by the Partisan division may have stemmed from his marriage to a highly assimilated Polish Jew. His contemporaries speculated that this had a mitigating influence on Gomułka's approach toward the concept of purifying Poland from all remaining Jews and viewing them all as enemies of socialist Poland without any differentiation. Gomułka was also on some level an old-fashioned Communist believer who did not simply treat Communism instrumentally, as many of Partisans did, and this might also have had a mitigating influence on the scope of his use of right-wing ethno-nationalist and anti-Semitic traditions. In the popular anti-Communist student songs of the late 1960s, which also constituted a voice of protest against the anti-Jewish campaign, Gomułka's categorization of Jews and the Jewish origin of his wife came to symbolize the absurdity of the Communist regime's anti-Jewish policies. For example, the song "Open Letter to Comrade First Secretary of the Central Committee of PZPR" began with the words: "Although under our heaven Mosiek and Srulek are no more, sometime, somewhere a Zionist 'reappears' and this disturbs you, Herr Gomułka." [67]

What criterion for marking who was a Jew/Zionist was the most popular and accepted within the PZPR, the state apparatus, and society at large? The records of various reactions to Gomułka's speech of 19 March 1968 indicate that the biological or racial/ethnic criterion advocated by the Partisans was more accepted than was Gomułka's categorization of Jews. The Partisans' advocacy of purging all remaining Jews from the Party, the state apparatus, and the country also seemed to be a popular and accepted project at this time.[68]

The leadership of the PZPR criticized Gomułka's speech of 19 March 1968 for not being assertive enough in terms of cleansing the country of Zionists, or "dealing with the Zionists." For example, according to a secret report prepared for internal circulation among the leadership of the PZPR by the Ministry of Internal Affairs on 21 March 1968, members of the academic staff of institutes of higher education in Poznań argued that Gomułka had not solved the Zionist issue properly, despite the population's full support for such a project.[69] The same report also stated that in primary schools in Olsztyn in northern Poland teachers argued that Gomułka's speech "could only bring peace" to the Jews, not to the Poles.[70]

A report of April 1968 sent to Gomułka by Franciszek Całka, a Jew who was at this time still head of one of the main Warsaw factories, Predom, indicates that the rank and file of the local branch of the PZPR in the Warsaw suburb of Żoliborz were keen on dismissing any Jews who worked for the factory, regardless of their qualifications and contributions. During a local Party meeting that took place on 10 April 1968, at which Całka had to be present, Mr. Kacperczyk, chairman of the local Żoliborz branch of the PZPR committee, demanded that the Jewish employees of Predom be dismissed. He also stated that "Poland should be ruled by Poles and Jews are not Poles."[71] This indicates that the policy of employment was interpreted in a collectivist ethno-nationalist way by some ethnic Polish members of the PZPR. In turn this way of thinking about employment and the right to a position was an echo of the ethno-nationalist way of thinking about the labor market and the economy that was persistent in the interwar period.

Police conducting interviews with students arrested in the campus demonstrations of March 1968 also expressed anti-Jewish sentiments of a clearly racial character. They verbally abused individuals of Jewish origin and used racist language toward ethnic Poles who had Jewish partners. For example, in one of her two letters to "Comrade" Gomułka the student Beata Dąbrowska, whose boyfriend Andrzej Duracz had a Jewish mother, complained about the way the police abused her during the interviews because she had a sexual relationship with a Jew: "They laughed at my attraction to 'black and curly-haired guys.' "[72]

As in the early postwar period and 1956 some Polish children seemed to be under the influence of the anti-Jewish propaganda advocated by the Partisan group in the late 1960s. For example, in a letter of 8 May 1968 written to the weekly *Polityka* Józef Lidwoń voiced concerns about children's anti-Semitic harassment by their peers. Lidwoń was the father of a ten-year-old girl whose schoolmates in the small town of Gliwice in western Poland thought she was Jewish. The father asked the editors of *Polityka* to condemn this phenomenon as immoral: "For some time my daughter has been coming back home from school crying because children do not want to play with her because they think that she is a Jewess. In fact, she is not Jewish, but it is below human dignity to explain such a thing to everybody. . . . I can imagine the situation of other children who are exposed to such verbal abuse in their environment. A saying such as: 'My mother forbade me to play with a Jewess' does not originate in the heads of children."[73]

Comrade Zenon Kliszko, in his speech of 8 July 1968 at the Twelfth Conference of the Central Committee of the PZPR, admitted that Poles both within and outside the PZPR understood the term *Zionist* as the equivalent of *Jew*.[74] Kliszko's speech referred to "Zionism as a dangerous ideology of the recent past," while at the same time suggesting that this danger was no longer relevant. Thus the speech was possibly a sign of retreat from the use of the term *Zionism* in the political culture of the Communist regime. Gomułka and his close inner circle of "comrades" may have been attempting to put an end to the most intense anti-Jewish campaign led by the Partisans. Kliszko argued:

> The antisocialist actions in March of this year [1968] were the work of an alliance of various reactionary forces. The common denominator of these forces was revisionism. Zionism, as one of the reactionary tendencies, also joined this struggle. This is a tendency that in recent times has been particularly vicious in its hostility toward our Party. . . . At present, when this problem [Zionism] has been solved we should remove it from the Party's agenda. . . . In some Party organizations, especially in various bureaus and departments, an atmosphere of struggle against Zionism is still artificially maintained. This atmosphere sometimes becomes tense, preventing a calm analysis of the real sources of the current difficulties and problems. Moreover, it prevents recognition of the true opponent of our Party . . . and of the real enemies of socialism and of our nation. A Jew is identified as a Zionist, and thus a justified suspicion of a concrete individual case turns into a generalized

suspicion of all persons of Jewish origin. Severe measures are particularly applied in cases of minor offenses committed by persons of Jewish origin, offenses that are ignored when committed by non-Jews.[75]

Although Gomułka was responsible for the abatement of the anti-Jewish campaign in the second half of 1968, there is no doubt that he himself initiated it in his speech of 19 July 1967, at the Sixth Congress of Polish Trade Unions. On this occasion, for the first time the first secretary made reference to Zionists as an internal enemy. Referring to Israel's victory over the Arabs in the Six-Day War of June 1967, Gomułka condemned all individuals in Poland who supported "the Israeli aggressor and politics of imperialism," labeling such people "a Fifth Column."[76] He argued: "We cannot remain indifferent toward people who in the face of a threat to world peace, that is, also to the security of Poland and the peaceful work of our nation, support the aggressor, wreckers of peace and imperialists. . . . We do not wish a 'Fifth Column' to be created in our country."[77]

The expression "Fifth Column," which was also used in the underground Polish lexicon in WWII to describe collaborators with Nazi Germany, suggested that an internal enemy whose intention was to harm the country and its people had reappeared in Poland in the late 1960s. This expression closely resembled the popular pre-1939 anti-Jewish core ethno-nationalist slogan "the Jews as the Fourth Partition," which portrayed Jews on a par with the three partitioning powers of Poland in the late eighteenth century, the Prussian, Russian, and Austrian Empires. The reference to the "Fifth Column" was removed from any publications of Gomułka's speech of 19 July 1967. Nevertheless, because the speech was aired on radio and television the expression "Fifth Column" became a "hit" of 1968 anti-Jewish propaganda. It was a popular slogan of the time, used in such expressions as "Down with the 'New Fifth Column'" (Zniszczyć nową piątą kolumnę), a saying that was displayed by workers at various demonstrations and meetings organized by local branches of the PZPR all over the country.

Gomułka's speech of 19 June 1967 gave a "green light" to Moczar and his Partisan group to embark on their expanded version of the anti-Jewish campaign. It paved the way for the emergence of the myth of the Zionist/Jew as the enemy of the Polish People's Republic in official Party propaganda.[78] The myth was disseminated in the state-controlled mass media, on both national and local levels.[79] At this time the majority of the mass media were controlled to a great extent by Moczar's Partisan faction. Therefore the anti-Jewish campaign in the press was widespread and intense. Among the leading papers that propagated the myth were *Trybuna Ludu*, the PZPR's central ideological paper; *Sztandar Młodych*, the official Communist youth paper; *Życie Warszawy*, the most popular Warsaw daily; the weekly *Prawo i Życie*; all journals of PAX; and *Żołnierz Wolności*. The anti-Jewish propaganda was especially intense in local Communist papers such as *Trybuna Robotnicza*, published in Łódź, the second-largest city in Poland. The weekly *Polityka*, run by Mieczysław Rakowski, was the only prominent paper that refused to publish anti-Jewish propaganda.

The Ethno-Nationalist Communist Version of the Myth

The ethno-nationalist Communist version of the myth of the Jew as the harmful other was versatile and multifaceted, like the anti-Communist ethno-nationalist image of the Jew in pre-1945 Poland. However, the Communist representation of the Jew as the enemy of Poland and its people was limited in theme and expression in comparison to its non-Communist predecessor. In this respect the Communist government was constrained both by its official opposition to anti-Semitism and by the limitations on expression of the socialist lexicon.[80]

Nonetheless, as in previous attempts to exploit Jewish stereotypes, the Polish government in the late 1960s linked the Zionist/Jewish enemy of Poland with other external enemies of the country. Socialist Poland of the 1960s had three main external enemies: "the imperialist United States," seen as the most powerful ideological enemy of socialism and Communism; Israel; and West Germany. International relations with the West German state were particularly strained in the 1960s because West Germany, until the change in its political government in 1969, did not recognize the post-1945 Polish western border on the Oder-Nisse River.[81] This situation was of great concern to Gomułka, who was also alert to new developments in international relations between West Germany and the Soviet Union in the 1960s.[82]

Local Communist newspapers incorporated the issue of insecurity over western Polish borders and the notion of West Germany as the enemy of Poland into the theme of the destructive nature of the Zionist enemy who conspired with other enemies of Poland in order to destroy the country. The Communist media accused all Polish Jews who were members of the minute remaining network of Jewish social organizations, such as the Social and Cultural Society of Jews and the youth club Babel, of representing foreign interests:

Israeli, American, and West German. They also accused Jews of slandering the good name of Poland and spreading "lies" about the presence of anti-Semitism in Poland.

In the Communist version of the myth, as in the non-Communist version, Jews were ungrateful guests living in the midst of the host (ethnic) Polish nation. This reveals that the pre-1945 ethno-nationalist interpretation of the concept of nationhood remained potent and persistent in the Communist Poland of the 1960s. An article published in the local paper *Trybuna Mazowiecka* on 25 March 1968 is a typical example of the ethno-nationalist Communist version of the myth, in which the theme of Jewish destructiveness is linked with external enemies of socialist Poland and Jews are portrayed as ungrateful guests of the Poles: "The Zionists seem to forget that the Poles are in their own home and that they are not. They would like to impose upon the people of socialist Poland the policies of Israel, the German Federal Republic, and imperialism. And as they are failing to so do and will continue to fail, they have begun to clamor about the anti-Semitic traditions in Poland. While they impute to us all kinds of barbarism and crimes, they 'smile' at the 'German henchmen of their relatives' in West Germany. . . . We would like to know with whom we are living under the same roof. We wonder what is going to be the attitude of society toward such slanderous and hostile attacks against Poland."[83]

As in the pre-1945 period contemporary social and political developments were incorporated into the main themes of the representation of the Jew as the enemy. One such development was an ideological crisis of Communist doctrine, accompanied by the emergence of revisionist Marxist theories opposing the official version. Among the leading Marxist revisionist intellectuals of the 1960s were some Polish Jews, such as Adam Schaff, Zygmunt Bauman (1929–), and Jerzy Morawski (1918–), and non-Jews such as the philosopher Leszek Kołakowski. Many of them belonged to the so-called humanistic school of Marxism. Official PZPR propaganda did not tolerate open ideological discussion and criticism and accused all Jewish intellectuals of "being Zionists," non-Jewish intellectuals of "being Zionist sympathizers," and their intellectual work and stance on Communist doctrine of being anti-Polish.[84]

Another important political and social development of the 1960s that was incorporated into the representation of the Jew as the enemy were student demonstrations against censorship and the suppression of individual freedoms.[85] These demonstrations, which took place between 8 and 23 March 1968, were a reaction against a ban on the production of Adam Mickiewicz's famous national drama *Dziady*. The well-known theater director Kazimierz Dejmek (1924–2002) was permitted to stage the play in late 1967 in the National Theater in Warsaw. However, soon after, on 31 January 1968, the Communist regime imposed a ban on the play because of its anti-Soviet, anti-Russian, and religious content and because of Dejmek's staging of the final scene, in which a character emerges in chains—a powerful allusion to the lack of freedom of expression in Communist Poland. In Warsaw students of the Warsaw Theater School organized the first demonstration against the ban of the play after its last performance. As a result they were arrested. Adam Michnik and Henryk Szlajfer, two Polish-Jewish students of Warsaw University, were arrested for speaking to a French journalist from *Le Monde* about these student arrests. Michnik and Szlajfer were also suspended from Warsaw University. Their suspension led to further student demonstrations.[86]

Police brutally suppressed the student demonstration that took place on 8 March in Warsaw. News of this suppression spread around the country and led to a new wave of student demonstrations in other major universities in the country. The official PZPR propaganda described these demonstrations as the outcome of the destructive influence of Jews on the ethnic Polish youth and intelligentsia. The portrayal of student demonstrations as a "Jewish conspiracy" was carefully arranged without direct reference to Zionists or Jews. Instead well-known Polish-Jewish students such as Adam Michnik, Józef Dojczgewant, Aleksander Smolar, Wiktor Górecki, and Irena Lasota were cited as the "ringleaders" of the demonstrations. The names of two other Jewish students— Antoni Zambrowski, the son of Roman Zambrowski, the only remaining Jew on the Central Committee of the PZPR in 1968; and Ewa Zarzycka, the daughter of Janusz Zarzycki—were also added to the list of the organizers of the student demonstrations, although they were not present in the country at the time.[87] The ethno-nationalist Communist propaganda of March 1968 referred to all of them as "Commandos," as "banana youths," as "infant-revisionists" who worshipped "the revisionist sky in which glitter stars of the first magnitude such as Prof. Adam Schaff, Prof. Włodzimierz Brus, [Leszek] Kołakowski, [Zygmunt] Bauman, [Bronisław] Baczko, and [Jerzy] Morawski."[88] State-sponsored media typically described the student protesters as representing foreign/Zionist interests and "hostile, aggressive, anti-Polish, and anti-socialist elements."[89] For example, on 14 March 1968 Edward Gierek (1913–2001), then first secretary of the PZPR in Silesia and future first secretary of the PZPR, made a speech in which he used such expressions. Although Gierek was not a member

of the Partisan group, but a leader of his faction within the PZPR—the so-
called Technocrats, or supporters of "Consumer Communism"—his speech,
addressed to one hundred thousand individuals in Katowice, resembled in
content typical comments issued by the Partisan faction.[90] Gierek said:

> It is a fact that "Michniks, Szlajfers, Grudzińskis, Werfels" . . . and the like
> have found themselves through the logic of demonstrations outside the bound-
> ary of the majority of Polish students. But we would be shortsighted if we
> ascribed these excesses only to this "hair-raising group" among students whose
> names I have mentioned. . . . One should ask the following questions: Whom
> do they want to serve by leading our youth astray? Who has an interest, for
> example, in inciting students against the Soviet Union? Who has an interest in
> slowing down the pace of work in the Polish People's Republic? The answers
> to all these questions are not difficult to find. . . . This is done in the interests
> of old political speculators who act without any scruples. This is a case of
> people who wish to slide on stage by devious means. They do not respect
> the cause and goals of socialism. Who is their master? What kind of people
> are they, these Zambrowskis, Staszewskis, Słonimskis, and their cohorts, and
> men like Kisielewski, Jasienica, and others? They have irrefutably proved that
> they have served foreign interests.[91]

What is characteristic in Gierek's speech of 14 March 1968 is his use of the
plural form for the names of those individuals whom he blamed for student
unrest and for serving foreign interests. All of the listed individuals, with the
exception of the writer Stefan Kisielewski (1911–91), were known to be Jewish or
of Jewish origin. Thus, without referring to them as Jewish or Zionist, Gierek
skillfully portrayed the student demonstrations as "a Jewish conspiracy."

The use of Jewish names in plural form was not a new strategy invented
in the 1960s by the ethno-nationalist Communists, but a tested strategy of
the interwar and early post-1945 periods. In the latter period anti-Communist
political elites applied this strategy in order to emphasize the scale of Jewish
participation in the forced implementation of the Communist regime in the
state. In the late 1960s Polish ethno-nationalist Communist elites seemed to
adopt this strategy in order to show that Jews were responsible for all social
and political problems in the Polish People's Republic and for all past errors
of socialism in Poland. Here one can see the persistent and versatile nature
of the strategy, aiming at "scapegoating" Jews for all the national and social
misfortunes of the Poles.

The official statement about student demonstrations issued by ZBOWiD on 12 March 1968 also blamed the Zionist enemy for orchestrating the student demonstrations. The characteristic element of ZBOWiD's statement was its frequently repeated accusation of "the enemy for perfidiously misleading our youth" and causing "the painful incidents." This was an attempt to shift responsibility for the brutal suppression of demonstrations onto Jewish students and away from the police:

> The continuous development of our country and our achievements has led to the intensification of the ideological-political campaign conducted by the imperialist and "revanchist" centers in the United States and West Germany. . . . In this slanderous campaign against Poland and Socialism a particularly active role is being played by international Zionism and its agents. The enemy employs propaganda and lies. . . . Recent incidents in Warsaw [student demonstrations] supply plenty of evidence of this. We know the instigators of these painful incidents. . . . They are, principally, the very same people who for a long time have been known as national nihilists. Today they . . . operate under the slogans of freedom and patriotism. . . . We are convinced that they should be punished, irrespective of whatever position they occupy, and that they should meet with general condemnation, not only for inspiring painful incidents but first and foremost for perfidiously misleading our youths.[92]

The theme of Judeo-Communism underwent a major transformation in the ethno-nationalist Communist version of the myth of the Jew as the enemy of Poland and its people. In fact, it was reversed into the theme of Judeo-anti-Communism, a phenomenon first noted in the midst of the anti-Jewish campaign by the writer Antoni Słonimski at the executive meeting of the Warsaw Section of the Union of Polish Writers on 29 February 1968.[93]

Ethno-nationalist writings on the theme of Judeo-anti-Communism depicted the anti-Communist Jew as the ideological enemy of the Polish socialist system and of socialism and Communism, responsible for all past ideological and political errors of the PPR (1944–49) and the PZPR (1948–1990). In particular these writing made Jews responsible for the terror and crimes committed by the Communist government during the Stalinist era (1949–54). The theme of the Jewish anti-Communist as the polluter of the PPR and the PZPR was invariably intertwined with the basic ethno-nationalist theme of the Jew as the polluter of the Polish state. The important message conveyed in these two intertwined themes was that if it were not for "Jewish comrades," Polish Communism could have developed in agreement with Polish national traditions since 1944 and would thus have become a popular people's ideology. If it were not for the "Jewish Communists" in the Polish Communist movement, the Polish People's Republic would have become a prosperous country, not incurring any economic, social, and political difficulties.

This explanation of all problems that had troubled Communist Poland since its rise in 1945 resembled the National Democracy movement's explanation of all Polish social, economic, and political problems during the interwar period. The use of such arguments by the Communist regime in the 1960s was the Party's attempt to present itself as the people's party and achieve greater popularity within the ethnically homogenous society. These arguments drew on the stock of popular ethno-national sentiments that were shared by the majority of the ethnic Polish rank and file of the PZPR and its leadership.

A good illustration of the portrayal of Zionist/Jewish "comrades" as an anti-Communist and antinational element within the PPR and the PZPR is a speech made by Mieczysław Moczar on 12 April 1968. In this rare personal public statement issued to a journalist of the Polish Press Agency (PAP) Moczar argued that the Jewish Communists who came to Poland in 1944 from the Soviet Union did not have respect for national Polish values or for ethnic Polish Communists in the PPR. They unlawfully captured power in the PPR and the government in 1944. Moczar further asserted that Jewish Communists were those responsible for the horrors of Stalinism between 1949 and 1956:

> The arrival in our country, together with the heroic soldiers of the Kościuszko Division [the first Polish military group to be set up in the Soviet Union under Communist patronage], of certain politicians masquerading in officers' uniforms, the Zambrowskis, the Radkiewiczs, the Bermans, who later were of the opinion that it was they and only they who had the right to leadership, to a monopoly on deciding what was right for the Polish nation. . . . From the moment of their arrival the evil began, and it continued until 1956. Although their mouths were full of phrases of unity, they did not like that our Party disseminated beautiful policies on a broad-based front, a front in which there would be room for every Polish patriot who wanted to raise up his fatherland, make it more prosperous, wiser, and more beautiful. . . . For that reason men such as Radkiewicz, Romkowski, Różański, Światło, and Feigin persecuted spokesmen of the broad-based patriotic national front, calling it a swamp. To these men Polish patriots were nothing but a swamp.[94]

Andrzej Werblan, head of the Department of Science and Learning in the Central Committee of the PZPR in the late 1960s, himself a former Stalinist who acted as political secretary to President Bolesław Bierut in the early 1950s, used arguments similar to Moczar's in his presentation of the history of the Communist Party in post-1944 Poland. In his long article "Przyczynek do genezy konfliktu" (A Contribution to the Genesis of the Conflict), published in June 1968 in *Miesięcznik Literacki*, Werblan went so far as to claim that the qualities and ethno-cultural makeup of Jews rendered them incapable of being good Polish Communists.[95] Werblan argued:

> A group of activists with sectarian cosmopolitan tendencies sought to domi-
> nate the Party through a specific cadre's policy. . . . One of the peculiar char-
> acteristics of this policy was to give people of Jewish origin particular respon-
> sibilities in certain organs of the power apparatus, in propaganda, and in the
> Foreign and Internal Affair Ministries. . . . The majority of them [people of
> Jewish origin] no longer had anything in common with the leftist movement
> of the prewar period, and they frequently came from among the well-to-do
> city-dwelling strata of the Jewish bourgeoisie, who during WWII had sought
> asylum from "Hitlerism" in the Soviet Union. . . . The participation of these
> people in the ranks of the First Polish Army in the fight against "Hitlerism"
> was their duty as Polish citizens. But this should not have given people like
> Brus, Baczko, Bauman, and many others the right to make such swift political
> careers. . . . Objective circumstances meant that these activists [Communists
> who spent WWII in the Soviet Union] did not undergo the ideological re-
> newal that took place in the underground Communist movement in German-
> occupied Poland, where new Party cadres emerged and became politically
> educated, where the Party's bonds with the broad masses became established,
> where the Party of the working class became the Party of the people.[96]

Werblan's perspective on the membership of the Polish Communist Party represented an ethno-nationalist orientation, excluding Jewish Communists. According to Werblan, the ethnic Polish composition of the PPR in post-1944 Poland would have guaranteed the proper development of Communism, with no deformations or mistakes. Jews, however, had polluted the Party with their ideas, which Werblan did not consider grounded in a working-class or Polish national ethos, but in a bourgeois ethos. He saw both their Jewishness and their social background as a problem; both made Jewish comrades "outcasts" in the PZPR.

Werblan's accusation against Jewish Communists of holding sole respon-
sibility for the "errors" of the Party during the Stalinist period continued the approach that emerged in the Natolin group in the PZPR of the 1950s. Some segments of the PZPR in the post-1968 period took the same position, blaming only Jews for the errors of the Stalinist system. For example, on 8 March 1981,

during the anniversary of March 1968, the Grunwald Patriotic Union, an organization with a strong ethno-nationalist Communist provenance, organized a rally in front of the building in Warsaw that had formerly housed the infamous Ministry of Public Security. Speakers at the rally voiced accusations against Jews as the sole criminals of the era of Stalinism. People attending this rally carried placards with sayings such as "Hands off Poland, you successors of the Zionist clique of Berman and Zambrowski."[97]

Some segments of the anti-Communist right-wing political elite advocated a similar stance toward the crimes of Stalinism both before and after the anti-Jewish campaign of 1968.[98] In fact, the extreme right-wing press still publishes writing forwarding the notion of the Jew as the sole agent of Stalinist crimes committed against the Polish nation between 1949 and 1956, often using these claims as justification for the anti-Jewish violence of the early post-1945 period.[99] The extreme right-wing anti-Communist press also describes the anti-Zionist purge of 1968 as an event from which Jews benefited because they were allowed to leave Communist Poland for the West, whereas for ethnic Poles in the late 1960s it was extremely difficult if not impossible to travel to the West.[100]

In the late 1960s Jews were portrayed as polluters not only of the PPR and the PZPR but also of Polish culture. As discussed in chapter 3, core ethno-nationalist elites in the interwar period exploited the image of the Jew as the polluter of Polish culture without any success in eliminating assimilated Polish Jews and their literary and artistic contributions from the arena of high Polish culture. In 1968 the theme of the Jew, or an individual of Jewish origin, as the carrier of values spiritually alien to Polish cultural traditions returned to public life. Once again ethno-nationalist Communists portrayed the contributions of Jewish authors to Polish literature, history, and visual arts as cosmopolitan and lacking in national values. Once again they portrayed the contributions of Jews to Polish culture as having a negative and demoralizing influence on Polish youth. As in the Catholic press of the interwar period the ethno-nationalist Communist press accused works of Jewish artists and writers of polluting the public morale and spreading eroticism.

The ethno-nationalist Communist press of the late 1960s provides a substantial body of examples of a further failed attempt to remove the contributions of Polish-Jewish writers, journalists, and artists from the Polish cultural canon.[101] The image of Jews as polluters of Polish culture can be found, for example, in the resolution of 16 March 1968 issued by the Congress of the

Association of Polish Journalists. The resolution stated that "forces ideologically alien to the Polish culture, which represent nihilism and cosmopolitanism, are capable of sowing unrest and poisoning the minds and hearts of our youths."[102] Perhaps the most intellectually and morally disturbing example of the exploitation of this image was the August 1969 publication in the leading literary monthly *Poezja* of the wartime article "We Do Not Need [Them] Any Longer," by the poet Tadeusz Gajcy.[103] This article, discussed in chapter 5, presents poets such as Julian Tuwim and Bolesław Leśmian as polluters of Polish literary language and the Polish canon of poetry. In December 1969 the poet Julian Przyboś condemned the reissuing of Gajcy's article without commentary as a "shocking and painful event."[104]

The rediscovery and imitation by the 1960s ethno-nationalist Communist press of the pre-1945 theme of the Jew as a cultural and spiritual polluter shows how the same theme could persist in political and social groups that were otherwise ideologically opposed. What social functions did the myth of the Zionist/Jew as the harmful alien play in the political culture of the 1960s?

As in the pre-1945 period it is possible to speak about the myth's polyfunctionality in the 1960s. Ethno-nationalist Communist elites used the representation of the Jew as the enemy of the Polish People's Republic and its people in four ways. First, they exploited it as the rationale and justification for the purification of the PZPR's leadership of any remaining Jewish Communists who still held important positions within the Party. Jewish Communists representing different political orientations, such as revisionism or liberalism, were stripped of their functions and in some cases expelled from the PZPR. The purification of the PZPR's leadership also included non-Jewish Communists who were either accused of Zionist and revisionist sympathies on the grounds of their ideological orientation or were involved in protests against the dismissal of their Jewish colleagues and therefore were also seen as Zionist sympathizers.[105] Individuals from both groups were dismissed from their positions within the PZPR, the state apparatus, and the army.

The ethno-nationalist Communist elites also used the myth as a rationale and justification for firing Jewish employees from scientific and cultural institutions, publishing houses, and national radio and television stations. The majority of individuals who lost their jobs in these institutions were members of the Polish-Jewish middle class and intelligentsia. These people were replaced by ethnic Poles, who were either faithful followers of the PZPR's propaganda, opportunists, or both.[106]

Third, ethno-nationalist Communist elites used the myth as a rationale for the purification of the Polish state from the remaining Polish Jews. Jewish Communists, members of the middle class and intelligentsia from large cities like Warsaw, Cracow, and Łódź, as well as members of Jewish communities from small towns like Wałbrzych and Dzierżoniów in western Poland, were forced to relinquish their Polish citizenship and leave the country. The state issued these Jews one-way travel documents out of the country. Many of these emigrants were highly acculturated or assimilated Polish Jews. Therefore in many cases they represented a social group of individuals whom Paul Lendvai calls "Jews by force" and "not by choice."[107] In the case of the most assimilated Jews of the young generation many were not aware of their Jewish roots or identity until the events of March 1968 took place.[108] The emigration started in the summer of 1967 and lasted until the end of 1970.[109] It included approximately twenty thousand people, out of a community of thirty thousand.

Finally, ethno-nationalist Communist elites used the themes of Judeo-Stalinism and Judeo-anti-Communism as a means of cleansing the PZPR of its "dark past" by attributing all errors of the PPR and the PZPR and all inadequacies of the Communist system to Jewish Communists. This strategy was also designed to improve the Party's image and increase its popularity in society at large. The theme of the Jew as "the anti-Communist," and therefore as the ideological enemy of the Polish People's Republic, was the only original aspect of the ethno-nationalist Communist version of the representation of the Jew as the harmful other. Apart from this aspect, and the socialist lexicon in which the myth was expressed, the themes of the ethno-nationalist Communist version of the myth did not differ much from the major themes advocated by non-/anti-Communist right-wing political elites.

Historians of March 1968 are divided on the issue of public response to the anti-Jewish campaign and purge orchestrated by the Communist regime. For example, Jerzy Eisler argues that society at large watched the events from a distance without being engaged in the anti-Jewish campaign.[110] Marcin Zaremba was the first historian to assert that a significant segment of the population received the anti-Jewish campaign in a positive way and that by the late 1960s a majority of Poles perceived the PZPR as the "People's Party in the sphere of maintaining national values." Zaremba's proposition seems more convincing because it is based on archival research into secret reports of the Ministry of Interior Affairs and local PZPR committees about society's mood in 1968.[111] Data concerning PZPR membership for the month of March 1968, at the peak of the anti-Jewish campaign, supports Zaremba's argument that the PZPR succeeded in gaining broader social legitimacy at this time. During that month 670 new members joined the local Warsaw PZPR organization, a substantial increase over the 179 newcomers who joined the party in January 1968.[112] However, it is difficult to establish beyond a doubt whether this dynamic increase of newcomers to the PZPR in March 1968 was motivated only by the anti-Jewish campaign or whether other social and economic factors were also involved.

On the other hand, sections of the intelligentsia did not approve of the anti-Jewish campaign and purge of 1968.[113] Some groups of academic youth, liberals, and members of the Catholic progressive intelligentsia, concentrated around the journals *Znak*, *Tygodnik Powszechny*, and *Więź*, opposed the events of March 1968, including the anti-Jewish aspect of these events.[114] In addition members of the Communist political elite concentrated around the weekly *Polityka*, edited by Mieczysław Rakowski, also refused to participate in the anti-Jewish campaign.

In December 1970, in the midst of mass strikes and demonstrations that broke out among shipyard workers in the three northern cities of Gdańsk, Gdynia, and Szczecin, Edward Gierek replaced Gomułka as first secretary of the PZPR.[115] Gierek was a very different Communist politician from Gomułka. He lacked Gomułka's ideological zealousness and seemed to focus primarily on raising living standards, providing consumer goods and better housing, and revising the disastrous economic policies of the 1960s.[116] His slogan, first uttered in November 1972 at the plenum of the Central Committee of the PZPR, reflected his goals: "We will build a second Poland" (Zbudujemy drugą Polskę).[117] Thus he projected an image as the champion of modernization and the builder of a better and more prosperous socialist Poland.

Although during the decade of Gierek's leadership of the PZPR official anti-Jewish propaganda decreased in comparison to the 1960s, anti-Jewish sentiments and the representation of the Jew as the harmful alien did not vanish from political culture. Gierek, who had himself participated in the anti-Jewish campaign of 1968, neither dissociated his Communist government from the events of 1968 nor condemned their anti-Jewish aspect.

In the second half of the 1970s, when his promises of economic prosperity ran into major obstacles and new political opposition arose, Gierek's regime did not hesitate to employ anti-Jewish themes in official propaganda.[118] These themes were first employed during the events of 1975 and 1976, when a debate about Poland's new constitution was followed by a rise in food prices and work-ers' riots in Radom. They were used against the Committee for the Defense of the Workers (KOR), which was set up in September 1976 and included a number of prominent members of the intellectual opposition.[119]

Regardless of the ethnic origin of the members of the KOR, Communist papers such as *Życie Warszawy, Sztandar Młodych, Żołnierz Wolności,* and *Słowo Powszechne* portrayed this dissident organization and its founders and par-ticipants as serving foreign and anti-Polish interests. To discredit the KOR in the eyes of the population the Communist press portrayed its members as having Stalinist pasts, foreign-sounding names, and some "revisionist-Zionist" connections and of being fundamentally alien to Polish workers and to society as a whole.[120] Thus in a time of crisis Gierek's regime resorted to employing the old strategy of delegitimizing political opponents by labeling them as Jewish and therefore as representing anti-Polish values and interests.

In a desperate attempt to hold onto power the next Communist regime in the 1980s also employed the myth of the Jew as the harmful alien as a propaganda weapon against the first Solidarity movement (Solidarność), which emerged in August 1980 in the midst of a dramatic confrontation between the Communist government and the workers of the Lenin Shipyard in Gdańsk.[121] The government portrayed the leaders of the Solidarity movement, particularly those who were members of the KOR, as constituting "anti-Polish forces that want to take over power in order to use it against the Polish nation." The official press advised Poles not to trust the Solidarity movement because indi-viduals of Jewish origin "whose interests and goals were incompatible with the Polish national interests ran the movement."[122] Indeed, the press portrayed leading members of Solidarity with non-Jewish backgrounds, such as Jacek Kuroń (1934–2004), as connected with Jews and with foreign and dangerous powers.[123]

Sometimes the government labeled Solidarity as a Jewish-run movement by using sinister tactics, such as fabricating alleged Solidarity leaflets that spoke about the Jewish majority in the Solidarity leadership who wished to capture power in order to rule over Poles. For example, *Dziennik Bałtycki,* on 10 March 1982, published such a fabricated leaflet, stating: "We, the undersigned loyal citizens of Jewish descent, protest the campaign of slander conducted by the regime press. . . . The allegation that we constitute a decisive majority in Solidarity is untrue. We are a majority only in its leading bodies, and it is thanks to this that the movement has already lasted for over a year. We believe that after the elections our group will continue to shape the image of the new Poland."[124]

Perhaps one of the most sinister and morally disturbing examples of such fabrication is the alleged interview with Bronisław Geremek conducted by Hanna Krall, a well-known Polish-Jewish writer. *Żołnierz Wolności* published excerpts from this interview, which portrayed Geremek as an individual who hated Poles and wished to take control over the government in order for Jews to rule over Poles again: "We hate the Poles because they are now better off than we are. . . . So you will understand that this entire social movement [Solidarity] that we are now creating and invigorating by various ways and means aims at changes in the structure of the Polish state and economy that will make the Jews always better off than the Poles."[125]

However, the strategy of delegitimizing political opponents by labeling them Jewish proved to be entirely unsuccessful in the 1980s because both the economic and the political goals of the Communist regime became increasingly discredited in the eyes of the population. The first Solidarity movement of 1980–81, led by the charismatic electrician Lech Wałęsa (1943–), was an alliance between workers and the intellectual opposition of the KOR organization. This alliance appeared to be a tangible alternative to the Communist regime.[126] In the fight against the discredited Communist regime the Solidarity movement united people of widely differing political orientations, such as members of the KOR organization, adherents of the political orientation of the Roman Catholic Church, some followers of more radical and ethno-nationalist groups, and many disillusioned Communists. Solidarity was also one of the fastest-growing political and social movements in the Soviet bloc; the historian Timothy Garton Ash calls it "a civil crusade for national regeneration."[127] Solidarity claimed a membership of ten million people within a few weeks of its founding.

Between the summer of 1980 and 13 December 1981 Solidarity acted more as a national movement than as simply a trade union, making both social and political demands.[128] In its program of October 1981 Solidarity called for the establishment of a self-governing republic and defined itself as a movement committed to "building a new just Poland for everyone." In the same program Solidarity defined itself as "a force invoking common human values" and uniting people "adhering to various ideologies, with various political and religious convictions, irrespective of their nationality," "united in protest against injustice, the abuses of power, and against the monopolized right to determine and to express the aspirations of the entire nation."[129]

The ethos of the Solidarity movement could not be destroyed even after the imposition of martial law, introduced on 13 December 1981 in order to bring the threat to Communist rule under control.[130] In the summer of 1986 General Wojciech Jaruzelski (1923–), first secretary of the PZPR and the prime minister responsible for the imposition of martial law, granted full amnesty to those leaders of Solidarity arrested in the aftermath of 13 December 1981. New strikes in the country and a growing national crisis forced the Communist government to surrender and agree to open direct talks with Solidarity. The political discussion between the Communist government and the Solidarity movement, conducted around a "round table" (okrągły stół), began in February 1989 and ended on 5 April of the same year.[131] The outcome of the round table was agreement on the pluralization of the political system in Poland. The Solidarity movement was legalized, and the end of Communism was approaching fast. On 29 December 1989 Poland formally ceased to be called the Polish People's Republic. The new crucial phase in the battle between backward-looking ethno-nationalism, exclusive toward Jews and intolerant of cultural diversity, and civic and pluralistic nationalism, inclusive of Jews and other minorities, was about to begin in post-Communist Poland.

8. Conclusion

The Beginning of the End of the Image, 1989–2000s

The Institute of National Memory has been attacked because it has investigated crimes committed by Poles and not against Poles. I should like to underline what Professor [Leon] Kieres has repeatedly emphasized, speaking about Jedwabne, and remind you that "those who died there were also citizens of Poland—of a different faith, with different customs and traditions. The Jews of Jedwabne were Poles. . . ." This is simple and obvious, yet at the same time how difficult it is for us to comprehend it.

Father Adam Boniecki, on the debate about Jedwabne

Two opposing developments accompanied the political and economic transformation of Poland between 1989 and the early 1990s. On the one hand, the first post-Communist government, headed by Prime Minister Tadeusz Mazowiecki, announced its commitment to building a civil society in which cultural and religious diversity would be respected and cherished. This commitment was translated into a number of new laws and regulations that subsequent post-Communist governments gradually introduced and implemented in the 1990s and the early 2000s. These new laws protect members of minorities against discrimination and guarantee communal rights to maintain linguistic, religious, and cultural differences.[1] On the other hand, an outburst of intense antiminority sentiment, particularly anti-Jewish beliefs and attitudes, emerged in public discourse at the same time as the crucial events of political transformation.

Between 1989 and 1990 various newly established and restored right-wing political parties and a significant section of the institutionalized Roman Catholic Church began to disseminate references to Jews as aliens and as a menace to the Polish nation. Slogans stating that Poland "has fallen into Jewish hands" and that "the Jews have already ruled over or want to rule over Poland again" reappeared in political discourse.[2]

The Solidarity movement was also affected by this trend. In the aftermath of the split of Solidarity into two factions in May 1990 members of the right-wing section, Solidarity Center Alliance, raised accusations against members of the left-wing Solidarity faction, the Citizens' Movement for Democratic Action, charging them with "not being true Poles" (prawdziwi Polacy). At the same time some hard-line ethno-nationalist Communist groups, such as Grunwald, continued to claim that the political camp under the banner of Solidarity represented antinational interests, that is to say Jewish interests.

Various themes of the Jew as the harmful other appeared in the press and public discourse. New historical and contemporary events were incorporated into these narratives; new disseminators of the myth blamed Jews for the decline of Poland in the past, particularly during the Communist period. These disseminators also blamed Jews as a group for hindering the political and economic transformation of 1989–90. Another narrative claimed that Jews might prevent the future development of a great Polish nation. As in the past the disseminators of the myth again referred to the Jew as the pernicious enemy of Poland and its people, as the exponent of international finance, and as the carrier of cosmopolitan and spiritually debased Western values.

Anti-Jewish sentiments reached their peak during the first free presidential election of the late 1990s. In the presidential race right-wing anti-Communist political circles labeled Mazowiecki, the leading member of the progressive Catholic intelligentsia and the chief opponent of Lech Wałęsa, a Jew. One high-ranking Roman Catholic clergyman undertook a thorough investigation into Mazowiecki's family genealogical tree, going back to the early modern period. He accused Mazowiecki of having Jewish ancestry and thus of being a "hidden Jew."[3]

Attempts to delegitimize Mazowiecki as a political leader by claiming his alleged Jewishness were not limited only to right-wing members of the clergy. During a press conference on 29 July 1990 Mazowiecki's political rival Wałęsa suddenly demanded that "persons of Jewish origin should not conceal [their] origin."[4] Furthermore, on a few occasions Wałęsa also described himself as "a full-blooded Pole with documents going back to his great-grandfathers to prove it."[5]

Wałęsa's pronouncements were shocking to members of the left-wing Solidarity movement, particularly to Wałęsa's former advisers. During the ten years of Solidarity's struggle against the Communist regime Wałęsa had displayed no anti-Jewish sentiments. This indicates that in 1990 Wałęsa resorted to the strategy of delegitimizing his political opponents by labeling them Jewish. He seems to have been doing this for purely instrumental reasons, in order to increase his share of the electorate and bring himself political victory. Therefore Wałęsa's strategy appears to have been a carefully calculated action to bring himself in line with the stock of cultural sentiments in the population. Thus it illustrates the persistence in the post-1989 period of the post-1880 ethno-nationalist political tradition of discrediting political opponents by calling them Jewish. This function of the myth of the Jew as the threatening other is perhaps most persistent and long-lived not only in post-1989 political culture but also in popular culture.

In the latter case the strategy of discrediting opponents by labeling them Jewish has clearly influenced the culture of the national sport: football. One of the most verbally and visually pronounced manifestations of this strategy, reoccurring on football pitches in the 1980s, the 1990s, and the early 2000s, is the casual labeling of rival football teams as Jewish. For example, fans of the Łódź-based ŁKS team often label their well-known and accomplished rival Łódź football team Widzew as Jewish. This post-1880 ethno-nationalist tradition has succeeded in transforming the word *Jew* into a term of political and social abuse. In the summer of 2003, during the annual Woodstock rock festival, the association Nigdy więcej (Never Again), which was set up in the summer of 1996 in order to combat anti-Semitic, racist, and xenophobic traditions, organized a tournament under the banner "Let's Kick Racism out of the Football Pitches." [6] At this event the leaders of Nigdy więcej called upon the Polish Football Association to take effective steps in eradicating racism from Polish sport.

Various surveys conducted during the 1990 presidential election also indicated that anti-Jewish sentiments enjoyed significant public acceptance. For example, according to one survey, 50 percent of Lech Wałęsa's electorate and 25 percent of Tadeusz Mazowiecki's were convinced that "Jews had too much power in Poland." [7] Some schoolchildren living in the capital, who likely had no interaction with members of the Jewish community in their lives, shared the opinion that "the Jews wanted to govern Poland and wished to have power over the Poles." Their negative attitudes toward Jews were rooted in ethno-nationalist themes of the representation of the Jew as the threatening other. According to one poll conducted in three Warsaw high schools, 25 percent of those interviewed expressed such views. This indicates that the children had absorbed these views through their families and also perhaps through their schools and the mass media.[8]

The sudden, intense, and widespread outburst of an "anti-Jewish mood" in the newly free, sovereign, post-Communist Poland shocked many members of the Polish liberal, left-wing, and progressive Catholic intelligentsia, as well as members of the minute Jewish community in Poland. An inquiry into the nature of Polish anti-Semitism and the concept of Polish national identity followed this first reaction of astonishment and shock. In the sea of conflicting views about anti-Semitism and its scope in Polish society, claiming it as either a salient or an irrelevant social issue, some scholars began to point to the historical connection between contemporary anti-Jewish sentiments and the pre-1939 historical period.[9] It has emerged that, as in the pre-1939 period, in the early 1990s attitudes toward Jews came to represent a "litmus test of Polish democracy": the choice was between ethnic nationalism, exclusive of Jews and intolerant of multireligious and cultural diversity, and civic nationalism, inclusive of Jews and accepting of multireligious and cultural diversity.

Questions about the definition of Polishness and attitudes toward Jews and other minorities, which intensified in the intellectual discourse of the 1990s, originated in left-wing Solidarity circles in the early 1980s. From its inception the left wing of the Solidarity movement, represented by politicians and statesmen such as Jacek Kuroń, had been committed to reckoning with the "dark past" of Polish treatment of religious and cultural minorities. The underground Solidarity press was in fact the first forum in which adherents of this approach presented their position. They all shared the conviction that this dark past needed to be aired in the name of social and moral necessity.[10] Some intellectuals also observed that the subject of anti-Semitism and xenophobia toward national and cultural minorities is one of the most challenging issues in public discourse. In their work, published as a samizdat publication in 1980 under the meaningful title *O czym myśleć nie lubimy czyli o niektórych dylematach zasady narodowej* (The Issues We Do Not Like to Think About, Namely Certain Problems of National Principle), the late Stefan Amsterdamski and Tadeusz Kowalik were perhaps the first intellectuals to point out this situation.[11] They defined anti-Semitism and xenophobic attitudes toward "others" as an important social problem that Poles "do not like to think about."[12] In 1990 some public intellectuals, such as the historian Jerzy Jedlicki, returned to this topic and acknowledged a series of failures on the part of the Polish intelligentsia in the past to oppose and eradicate anti-Semitic traditions in Polish society.[13]

Various samizdat publications of the left-wing Solidarity movement in the 1980s and sociological studies conducted in the 1980s and early 1990s pointed to particular patterns in national self-identification and attitudes toward Jews and other "others." Many left-wing Solidarity intellectuals considered these patterns dominant and characteristic of a significant cross-section of post-1945 Polish society. Some intellectuals observed that the majority of Poles tended to define Polishness not according to the civic and legal concept of citizenship, but according to the ethno-national model of Polishness. Many Poles identified a person's Polishness as based on having genealogical ethnic Polish roots, being a member of the Roman Catholic Church, following Polish moral and cultural traditions defined in the ethno-national sense, and having the Polish language as a mother tongue.[14]

Sociological studies of the 1980s and 1990s also revealed that society generally evaluated its ethno-cultural homogeneity as a positive feature.[15] Thus Polish society as a collectivity was characterized by what is described in sociological terms as "low internal tolerance" toward religious and cultural minorities. The dissemination of various slogans such as "Poland for the Poles" (Polska dla Polaków) and "Poland Yes, Jews No," (Polska tak, Żydzi nie) are good illustrations of this phenomenon.[16] In the early 1990s the conflation of ethno-nationalism with homogeneity in Polish society was a serious obstacle to improvement of the position of national and ethnic minorities in Poland. According to the *Report on the Situation of Persons Belonging to National and Ethnic Minorities in Poland*, published in 1994, nationalist behavior and attitudes were the chief markers of "intolerance of 'others.'" These markers were also listed as a key factor in the excessively lenient treatment, by Polish courts and police, of individuals guilty of various antiminority actions, such as verbal abuse of members of minority groups, drawing antiminority graffiti, and disseminating antiminority publications.[17]

One of the most recent examples of such leniency by Polish legal institutions was the decision of the Warsaw prosecutor's office not to prosecute Marcin Dybowski, the owner of the right-wing nationalistic publishing house Antyk. This publishing house, which is based in the crypt of All Saints' Church in Warsaw, sells various anti-Jewish works written in contemporary Poland and reprints of anti-Semitic books published in the interwar period.[18] In early 2003 the leaders of the Jewish community in Poland filed suit against Antyk. In

June 2003 the Warsaw prosecutor's office decided that there were no grounds for prosecution. The prosecutor argued that although negative opinions were expressed in the books, the content of the reprints "arose in a specific situation in which inter alia the demographic structure and the prognosis for its further development were unfavorable for persons of the Polish nationality."[19] Thus the prosecutor concluded that the content of such books "was not anti-Semitic but patriotic." This indicates not only that some employees of institutions of justice have difficulty identifying anti-Semitic material but that their own way of thinking is rooted in a highly rationalized ethno-nationalist representation of the Jew as the harmful other.

Although the eruption of antiminority sentiments in the first half of the 1990s was not limited only to Jews but also included strong outbursts of anti-Ukrainian sentiments in Przemyśl and Supraśl in southeastern Poland and anti-Roma sentiments in central Poland, anti-Jewish sentiments were the most intense and the most clearly interlinked with the issue of national identity.[20] Once again the ethno-nationalist publications of a relatively large number of small right-wing political parties represented Jews as the most dangerous enemy of Poles. In the extreme version ethno-nationalists defined Jews as the embodiment of other groups that had historically constituted a threat to Poland, such as the Germans or even the Ukrainians. This sentiment was expressed in the slogan "All Germans are Jews" (Wszyscy Niemcy to Żydzi) or in the label "Jew-Ukrainian" (Żydo-Ukrainiec).[21] This indicates that the anti-Jewish sentiments expressed in the early 1990s were not new and original but belonged to the anti-Jewish heritage of the past. Their persistence in the early 1990s can be explained in sociological terms as "the social inheritance of position."[22]

In the 1980s and 1990s intellectuals and scholars of religion observed that the dominant version of Roman Catholicism in post-1945 Poland manifested itself in a peculiar form, becoming a national religion in which ethno-national values appeared to be of greater importance and relevance than universal Christian values.[23] Tadeusz Mazowiecki was perhaps the first progressive Catholic intellectual who voiced criticism of this model of Polish Roman Catholicism. In 1985, four years before the political transformation of Poland, Mazowiecki posed a salient question about the future development of Roman Catholicism in the country and its relationship to nationhood. He put a finger on what was to become the core problem within the institutionalized Roman Catholic Church in the post-1989 period: "The second problem is the question of whether this rendezvous of Polishness and Christianity will be shaped into a kind of Polish-Catholic triumphalism and narrowness, or whether it will be a meeting of open Polishness with open Catholicism."[24]

In the post-1989 period two distinct movements emerged in the Polish Catholic Church: the "Closed Church" movement, a conservative or even reactionary trend characterized by "Polish-Catholic triumphalism and narrowness," and the modernizing "Open Church."[25] These two movements differ widely on a number of issues, including the modernization of the Church, its position within the state, and its relations with other Christian and non-Christian religions. The members of the Open Church, whose spiritual father was the late Pope John Paul II (Karol Wojtyła), have frequently condemned the core ethno-nationalist orientation of the Closed Church as a deformation of Christian principles and have accused it of failing to reject the anti-Jewish traditions condemned by Vatican II. Open Church clergy and intellectuals have displayed their commitment to eradicating anti-Semitism within the Church and have endorsed the principle of dialogue with Jews and Judaism.

In contrast, the formation of the Closed Church is rooted in the pre-1939 model of Polish Roman Catholicism and thus represents a backward-looking, traditional, conservative, and "folkish" type of religiosity.[26] In its perception of Polish society the Closed Church tends to differentiate between two groups: "true Poles" and the rest of society, including progressive Catholics, liberals, social democrats, Protestants, Jews, and masons. In the 1990s the ethos of this formation began to be disseminated in a wide range of right-wing ethno-nationalist Catholic publications, such as *Niedziela*, *Ład*, *Słowo-Dziennik Katolicki*, and *Nasz Dziennik*. The latter daily is the most important and long-lasting representative of such publications: it enjoys a nationwide circulation of between 250,000 and 300,000 copies. The Closed Church also propagates its ideas through other forms of mass media, such as two radio stations, Radio Niepokalanów and Radio Maryja. The latter, established in Toruń in 1994 by Father Tadeusz Rydzyk, is not an ordinary radio station, but a social organization with an extensive network of cultural and educational institutions.[27] In 2003 Father Rydzyk established another outlet for the Closed Church: the nationwide television station Trwam (I Endure).[28]

Since the early 1990s one of the key representatives of the Closed Church has been the bishop of Gorzów, Józef Michalik (1941–), who was appointed chairman of the episcopate in March 2004.[29] Another influential bishop representing the Closed Church is Sławój Leszek Głódź, currently bishop of Warsaw-

Praga. In February 2005 Bishop Głódź became an ardent defender of Father Rydzyk in Lech Wałęsa's dispute with Radio Maryja.[30] On 23 February 2005, in a letter published in *Gazeta Wyborcza*, Wałęsa criticized Rydzyk for spreading extreme right-wing political allegations claiming that many former Solidarity members, including Wałęsa himself, had collaborated with the Communist regime, and called upon the Church to take Rydzyk to task.[31] At the meeting of the episcopate in early March 2005 the extent of the influence of Głódź's support was revealed. In spite of Lech Wałęsa's calls for the episcopate to deny recognition to Radio Maryja, and Archbishop Józef Życiński's earlier public condemnations of Father Rydzyk as a propagator of anti-Semitic and anti-Christian values, the bishops' conference once again failed to take a firm position on Father Rydzyk.[32] Rydzyk's latest initiative, announced in February 2005, is the establishment of a political party, Maryja, that would aim at uniting the right-wing political spectrum and promoting the values of the Closed Church.[33] Another figure similar to Father Rydzyk is Father Henryk Jankowski, the legendary priest of the Solidarity movement of the 1980s, known for a series of anti-Semitic actions and pronouncements throughout the 1990s and early 2002.[34] In late 2004, in the midst of scandal over his professional conduct, the archbishop of Gdańsk, Tadeusz Gocłowski (1931–), dismissed Father Jankowski from his position as the vicar of St. Brigida Church in Gdańsk.[35]

In the early 1990s the Closed Church also gained supporters among members of the Catholic Information Agency and the Catholic University of Lublin. Reverend Czesław Bartnik and Professor Ryszard Bender have since become the most important representatives of this position at the university. The support of the Closed Church in the post-1990 period by members of the university faculty is intellectually disturbing, because in the 1980s the Catholic University of Lublin was known for its liberal and progressive traditions. Most recently there are some indications that within the university supporters of the Open Church have also reemerged.[36]

The long-term prevalence of the Closed Church, with its strong historical connection to Polish exclusivist ethno-nationalism, has led to difficulty among significant segments of Polish society in perceiving a person of any denomination other than Roman Catholic as a Pole.[37] Studies conducted in the 1980s revealed the extent of the impact of this phenomenon. In post-1989 Poland non–Roman Catholics represent a miniscule community of religious minorities, constituting approximately 4 percent of the Polish population. For example, in a study of the Protestant religious minority conducted in the early 1980s Ewa Nowicka and Magdalena Majewska concluded that Warsaw Lutherans saw themselves as second-class citizens and felt social disapproval in the national context.[38]

In the early 1990s members of the Closed Church uttered many overt and covert references to Jews as the harmful other in Poland. At the same time they denied holding anti-Semitic views. This indicates that, as with ethno-nationalist Communist groups in the 1960s, the clergy representing the Closed Church highly rationalized its anti-Jewish prejudices. As a result their attitude toward Jews falls under the category of the phenomenon of "anti-Semitism without anti-Semites."[39] This situation is not only typical of Poland but represents a more universal phenomenon.[40] A good example of it in Poland's Closed Church is the speech Primate Józef Glemp (1929–) made at the press conference of the Roman Catholic delegation in Paris in April 1990. During this conference Glemp echoed ethno-nationalist arguments going back to the first half of the twentieth century, saying, "Anti-Semitism in Poland is a myth created by the enemies of Poland."[41]

By the second half of the 1990s most of the high-ranking clergy of the Closed Church had stopped making overt anti-Jewish pronouncements. Only the most ideologically extreme individual clergymen, such as Reverend Jankowski and Father Rydzyk, continued to issue overt anti-Jewish statements. At the same time the major Closed Church media organs, such as Radio Maryja, continue to broadcast anti-Jewish, anti-secular, and anti-Western material. According to Father Stanisław Obirek, a representative of the Open Church, the teachings and actions of the late Pope John Paul II were conducive to a reduction in overt anti-Jewish statements among the hierarchy of the Roman Catholic clergy in the 1990s.[42] In the aftermath of the death of John Paul II on 2 April 2005 lay members of the Open Church, such as Stefan Wilkanowicz of the monthly *Znak*, expressed worries about the strength of his legacy in the Church in Poland.[43]

In the second half of the 1990s right-wing parties and organizations also curtailed expressions of intense overt anti-Semitic sentiments. By the second half of the 1990s a large number of active right-wing political parties constituted a highly divided political scene, and many of them were confined to the outside of the mainstream political arena.[44] In the mainstream political spectrum the Solidarity Electoral Alliance (AWS), headed by Marian Krzaklewski, in 1997 formed the government in coalition with the liberal Union of Freedom. Within the AWS, an umbrella-like movement consisting of various right-wing parties and organizations, there were groups and individuals who advocated the representation of the Jew as the harmful other. Nevertheless, the frequency of overt anti-Jewish pronouncements in the AWS decreased by the late 1990s.[45] This can be attributed to pressure from Western democracies, which assisted in the economic transformation of Poland in the 1990s and would not tolerate anti-Semitism.

The 1990s also saw the emergence of a totally original phenomenon with regard to attitudes toward Jews in one right-wing political party, the Conservative Party (Partia Konserwatywna), headed by Aleksander Hall (1953–).[46] Although the heritage of this party is directly rooted in the ethno-nationalist traditions of Roman Dmowski, it has not employed any anti-Jewish images since its inception in 1992. This indicates that a political party with a ethno-nationalist heritage is capable of disposing of the anti-Semitic legacy of its ideological predecessor.[47]

The presidential election of 1995, in which President Lech Wałęsa competed against former Communist Party member Aleksander Kwaśniewski, seemed to be the last important political event in post-Communist Poland in which various right-wing politicians and members of the Closed Church expressed overt anti-Jewish attitudes to a significant degree.[48] For example, in his criticism of Kwaśniewski Father Rydzyk went so far as to claim that Kwaśniewski's mother, who died during the presidential campaign, should be denied the right to burial in a Roman Catholic cemetery because Kwaśniewski's family had hidden their Jewish origins.[49] Kwaśniewski, whose political slogan was "Let us choose our future," won the presidential election of 1995. This indicates that the representation of the Jew as Poland's threatening other has lost its political relevance and that other social and economic factors play a more important role in the choice of political leader than do anti-Jewish sentiments.

The second half of the 1990s and the early 2000s was a period during which the civic and pluralistic model of Poland, inclusive of Jews and other minorities, established itself more firmly in the political and cultural life of the country. A new sense of an inclusive civic and pluralistic Poland was manifested in various initiatives put forward by members of the cultural elite and representatives of the younger generation of Poles. In 1997 the Polish Roman Catholic Church added an annual "Day of Judaism" to the Church calendar. Students at the University of Warsaw set up "Jewish Day" in 2002. In addition students established new organizations and initiatives such as Hatikva-Nadzieja and Kolorowa Tolerancja (see chapter 1).[50]

In 1995 a Polish-Israeli commission was set up to remove negative stereotypes of Jews from Polish history textbooks and biased stereotypes of Poles from
Israeli textbooks. [51] This was an important event in the history of the Polish
educational system because the scholars who investigated historical knowledge
about Jews in Polish textbooks used in primary and high school education in
the 1980s and early 1990s had concluded that "the description of the annihila-
tion of the Jews on Polish territory is rather confusing, and the subject of the
relations between the Polish and the Jewish populations is riddled with omis-
sions, half truths, and overt inaccuracies, to say the least." [52] This initiative was
followed by another important educational and cultural event. In May 1999
in Warsaw two hundred intellectuals and students established an association
named Open Republic (Otwarta Rzeczpospolita), dedicated to fighting anti-
Semitism, racism, and xenophobia in Polish society. [53]

By the late 1990s public intellectuals such as the distinguished literary critic
Maria Janion and the sociologist Hanna Świda-Ziemba, and members of the
Open Church such as the late Father Stanisław Musiał, had published works
highly critical of the representation of the Jew as the harmful other. These
works, which seemed to gain greater resonance in cultural circles in the 1990s,
constitute an important contribution to challenging the myth of the Jew as
the enemy of Poland and re-creating a multifaceted image of Poland and
the Poles. [54] Yet Jan T. Gross's *Neighbors*, published in Poland in May 2000,
marked the beginning of a profound debate over the deconstruction of the
representation of the Jew as the harmful other. The book's publication led to a
fierce battle over the memory of the "dark aspects" of Polish relations with the
Jewish minority in WWII and the model of Polishness in post-Communist
Poland.

Neighbors is perhaps the most powerful fulfillment of the call voiced in the
summer of 2000 by Hanna Świda-Ziemba. In her article "Rozbrajać własne
mity," which appeared in the June issue of the monthly *Znak*, Świda-Ziemba
urged Polish intellectuals to "deconstruct at once the distorted popular representation of the history of Polish-Jewish relations and not to leave this task to
future generations." [55]

Neighbors is an unconventional history book that calls for and at the same
time introduces itself as a revolution in "historical awareness." This revolution
is structured according to the logic of inclusion into the official historical
memory of events that were manifestations of discrimination and exclusion
of minorities by the dominant national community.

Neighbors is a slender book that covers a remarkably broad range of topics. As earlier mentioned, its central topic is the discussion of the 10 July 1941 collective mass murder of the Jewish community by its ethnic Polish neighbors in the small town of Jedwabne, in the Łomża region in northeastern Poland. The Jedwabne massacre represents—to use, as Gross does, the metaphor coined by the British-Polish writer Joseph Conrad (1857–1924)—"the heart of darkness" in Polish-Jewish relations in World War II.[56] Until the publication of *Neighbors* the Jedwabne massacre existed as an event that belonged to "unthinkable history." It was a "nonevent" in Poland, and forgetting had occluded it. Gross contextualized the murder of Jedwabne Jews within the social history of Poland in World War II and linked it with other subjects, which can be divided into two groups. The first includes historical issues such as Polish society and its attitudes toward Jews in eastern Poland under the Soviet occupation (1939–41); the response of Polish society to the German invasion of the Soviet Union in June 1941; the role of Polish society in the Holocaust; and society's participation (collaboration) in the Communist takeover in 1944. The second group includes topics related to the areas of the methodology and historiography of Holocaust studies and twentieth-century Polish history; the role of Holocaust survivors' testimonies in understanding the genocide; the memory of the "dark past" and collective self-image of Polish society; the responsibilities of a historian; and truth and its relativization in history writing. In *Neighbors* Gross raised many original, salient questions and historical hypotheses that past Polish historians had avoided.[57]

Neighbors triggered a profound public debate about anti-Semitism and Polish-Jewish relations in WWII.[58] This debate was also echoed abroad in various countries, connoting various meanings and raising questions essential for particular national communities. In a sense this debate was the culmination of two earlier debates about Polish-Jewish relations in WWII, which took place in Poland in 1987 and 1994. The article "Biedni Polacy patrzą na ghetto" (The Poor Poles Look at the Ghetto), written by well-known literary critic Jan Błoński, triggered the first of these debates.[59] The second debate was initiated by Michał Cichy's short article "Polacy-Żydzi: Czarne Karty Powstania Warszawskiego" (Poles and Jews: Black Pages in the Annals of the Warsaw Uprising), published in *Gazeta Wyborcza* on 29–30 January 1994.[60]

One observer described Błoński's article, published in *Tygodnik Powszechny* on 11 January 1987, as "sparking off the most profound debate on the implications of the Holocaust in Poland since WWII."[61] In his article Błoński raised the issue of the moral responsibility of Poles for the Holocaust and also plainly stated that prewar Polish anti-Semitism had an impact on Polish attitudes toward Jews in WWII. Similar reflections on the behavior of Poles toward Jews in WWII also appeared in the personal memoirs of Jacek Kuroń, which were first published two years after Błoński's article.[62] In his memoirs Kuroń, born in Lwów in 1934, noted: "The wartime sources of hatred toward the Jews compounded existing anti-Semitic feelings. There was a folk anti-Semitism based on a feeling of separateness, and there was anti-Semitism whipped up by Endecja, supported by a considerable section of the clergy and National Radical Camp propaganda."[63]

Most of the two hundred individuals who took part in the debate over Błoński's article rejected his position. They accused Błoński of taking an anti-Polish stance and even of betraying the Polish state and the Polish nation. Some voices even called for his prosecution under articles 178 and 270 of the Polish criminal code, for "slandering the Polish nation." Błoński's voice was a lonely one.[64] A similar situation developed in the debate over Michał Cichy's article, which discussed anti-Jewish attitudes and actions on the part of some right-wing military organizations in the sixty-three-day Warsaw Uprising of 1 September 1944. He briefly described well-known cases of individual and group murders of Jews by the National Armed Forces (NZS) and some right-wing units of the Home Army. Although three distinguished Polish historians, Andrzej Paczkowski, Andrzej Friszke, and Teresa Prekerowa, supported Cichy's discussion of the ambiguous and negative side of the Polish treatment of Jews in the Warsaw Uprising, a majority of discussants dismissed his article as untrue.

The outcome of the debate over Gross's *Neighbors* differed significantly from the outcome of the debates over Błoński's and Cichy's articles. Gross's call for putting an end to the self-image of Poland as a community of victims and heroes only, and thus rewriting the Polish collective past and the history of Polish-Jewish relations in a more balanced and truthful manner, was not without support. Many intellectuals, particularly nonhistorians such as anthropologists Dariusz Czaja and Joanna Tokarska-Bakir, psychologist Krystyna Skarżyńska, sociologist Jacek Kurczewski, and the well-known journalist Konstanty Gebert (Dawid Warszawski), supported Gross's stance on the participation of ethnic Poles in the Jedwabne massacre and on the need for a more truthful image of Polish society.[65] Various representatives of the Open Church—such as Archbishop Henryk Muszyński; Archbishop Józef Życiński;

Bishop Tadeusz Pieronek, the rector of the Papal Theological Academy in Cracow; and Reverend Michał Czajkowski—also actively supported Gross's position. [66] Some leading members of the mainstream political elite, including President Kwaśniewski, Jacek Kuroń, and Henryk Wujec and Waldemar Kuczyński of the Union of Freedom, also supported Gross's main arguments. [67] Leon Kieres, then chairman of the Institute of National Memory, who was responsible for overseeing the forensic and historical investigation into the mass murder of Jedwabne Jews on 10 July 1941, stressed that the murdered Jews of Jedwabne were Polish compatriots and "not others." [68] Well-known national dailies such as *Gazeta Wyborcza, Rzeczpospolita,* and the weekly *Wprost,* as well as the three progressive Catholic journals—the weekly *Tygodnik Powszechny* and the monthlies *Więź* and *Znak*—published articles supporting and endorsing Gross's position.

On the other hand, individuals and groups that strongly opposed Gross's theses used the representation of the Jew as the harmful other in the debate over Jedwabne to prove that they were allegedly wrong. His opponents' arguments took up various ethno-nationalist themes of Jewish destructiveness; Jewish collaboration with Poland's other enemy, the Soviet Union; and the tropes of Judeo-Bolshevism and Judeo-Communism. These arguments circulated in right-wing ethno-nationalist, conservative, and Catholic publications such as the daily *Nasz Dziennik,* associated with Radio Maryja, and the weeklies *Angora, Myśl Polska, Niedziela, Najwyższy Czas, Tygodnik Głos, Tygodnik Solidarność,* and *Życie.* [69] Representatives of right-wing nationalist political parties such the League of Polish Families (Liga Polskich Rodzin, LPR), a recently established Christian-Nationalist party that won 7.87 percent of the seats in the parliamentary election of September 2001, representatives of the Closed Church, and right-wing nationalist historians used the various themes of the Jew as the harmful other in order to rationalize and minimalize the criminal nature of the Jedwabne massacre. [70]

Many of those who tried to downplay Jedwabne's ethnic Poles' culpability in the mass murders rehearsed the theme of Judeo-Communism, which claims that a majority of Jews, if not the entire collectivity, actively supported Poland's chief enemy of the twentieth century—the Soviet regime. According to those who based their argumentation on this theme, not only did Jews collaborate with the Soviets against the Poles during the Soviet occupation of the Polish eastern territories between 1939 and 1941, but they did so again in the early postwar period during the imposition of the Communist regime. The meaning of this proposition is that the Jews were twice guilty of crimes against the Polish nation, understood in an ethnic sense, and that it was the Poles who were the "real victims" vis-à-vis Jews. In the case of the Jedwabne massacre this proposition was mainly used as a strategy for rationalizing the involvement of any Poles in the massacre and thus neutralizing its criminal nature.

For example, the late Tomasz Strzembosz, a respected historian of the Polish underground during World War II, used such arguments consistently in his contribution to the debate over *Neighbors*. In his first article, with the significant title "Przemilczana kolaboracja" (Covered-up Collaboration), Strzembosz criticized Gross for presenting an untruthful version of events and provided his own evaluation of the historical background to the massacre.[71] Characteristically his article was not concerned directly with the Jedwabne massacre and its Jewish victims—to whom Strzembosz dedicated a single sentence—but served one purpose only: to show ethnic Poles in a good light and Polish Jews in a bad light. Strzembosz not only applied different categories of judgment toward the two communities but also oversimplified the German occupation of Poland in relation to the history of the Soviet occupation of eastern Poland in order to neutralize the criminal nature of the Jedwabne massacre; he considered the Soviet occupation somehow worse than the German occupation of Poland. Strzembosz's main argument was that prior to the German occupation of the eastern territories in June 1941 Polish Jews willingly served as the chief agents of Soviet anti-Polish politics. He categorized them as "traitors to the Polish state" and "collaborators with the mortal enemy of Poles," who welcomed the invasion of the Soviet Army and were later responsible for the suffering of thousands of ethnic Poles who were taken to Siberia in 1940. Strzembosz also claimed that in contrast to the Jews the ethnic Polish population acted honorably throughout the Soviet occupation. He argued: "Apart from a small group of Communists in towns and even smaller ones in the countryside, the Polish population responded to the USSR's aggression and the imposed Soviet system in those territories the same way it had reacted to the German aggression. . . . In contrast, the Jewish population, especially youths and poor town-dwellers, staged a mass welcome to the invading army and took part in introducing the new order."[72]

In his next article, "Inny obraz sąsiadów" (A Different Picture of the Neighbors), Strzembosz also insisted that Germans, not ethnic Poles, were responsible for the Jedwabne massacre.[73] He claimed that individual Jewish testimonies used by Gross were unreliable sources, while at the same time insisting that

Polish testimonies of a similar nature were reliable historical sources. Finally, he dismissed *Neighbors* altogether as a "weak" and "fake" work that could not be taken seriously as historical writing. Four other historians, including Marek Jan Chodakiewicz, Bogdan Musiał, Leszek Żebrowski, and Piotr Gontarczyk, endorsed and propagated similar positions.[74] The extreme right-wing nationalist press cited these historians as the chief authorities on both Gross's book and the Jedwabne massacre.[75]

The right-wing nationalist press also used the theme of "Poles as servants in the hands of the Jews" to discredit the forensic findings regarding the Jedwabne massacre, which were commissioned and announced by the Institute of National Memory (IPN). These findings confirmed Gross's main thesis about the participation of the local population of Jedwabne in the murder of their Jewish neighbors. In the right-wing nationalist press Leon Kieres was described as a Polish traitor—the "Polish Quisling."[76] The most severe attack on Kieres occurred on 27 February 2002 at a session of the Polish parliament.[77] At this session Kieres delivered a report on the activities of the Institute of National Memory conducted between the summer of 2000 and the summer of 2001, the peak period of debate about the Jedwabne massacre. A group of MPs representing the League of Polish Families launched a personal attack against Kieres. He was called a "servant of the Jews" and was blamed, together with President Aleksander Kwaśniewski, for "stoning the Polish nation."[78]

In all, the debate about the Jedwabne massacre raised issues that Poles had resisted facing for a long while: questions about anti-Jewish prejudices and the scope of past anti-Jewish actions and attitudes and about what kind of a national community Poland desires to be in the future. The debate was a reflection of the process of the democratization of political and social life in Poland and as such could not have taken place before the country regained full sovereignty in 1989.[79] It reflected the reemergence of pluralistic culture in Poland, representing two competing concepts of Poland: one a civic and pluralistic model—inclusive of the memory of "others" and acknowledging wrongdoings—and the second based on an ethnic model—excluding the memory of "others" and nurturing the narrative of unique (ethnic) Polish sufferings. In the debate among the participants representing the mainstream political and cultural elite and also among segments of youth the civic and pluralistic vision of Poland took the upper hand over the ethno-nationalist vision.[80]

In the aftermath of the 9 July 2002 announcement of the final IPN report on the massacre of Jedwabne Jews *Gazeta Wyborcza* published an opinion poll about perceptions of Jews in Polish society.[81] The opinion poll, conducted earlier that year, which questioned 1,009 individuals representing a cross-section of the population, indicated that some themes of the representation of the Jew as the threatening other, such as that of Jewish rule in Poland, still resonated in some sections of society. According to this poll, members of the urban and educated population were as susceptible to anti-Jewish perceptions as were members of the rural and less educated population. The opinion poll also revealed that politicians of right-wing ethno-nationalist groups such as the Solidarity Electoral Alliance (AWS), Law and Justice (Prawo i Sprawiedliwość, PiS), and the League of Polish Families and Self-Defense (Samoobrona) tended to display the strongest anti-Jewish prejudices, whereas politicians of liberal parties such as the Union of Freedom and the Civic Platform (Platforma Obywatelska) did not display such prejudices.

This opinion poll also indicated that anti-Jewish themes function on the basis of a "reflex" rooted in the old post-1880 ethno-nationalist image of the Jew; 19 percent of respondents showed signs of active anti-Jewish stereotyping, whereas 24 percent showed signs of holding passive anti-Jewish images. Respondents in the latter group, when asked about Jews, simply recycled a negative image of Jews that echoed the ethno-nationalist perspective.

Thus this opinion poll confirms that social constructions such as the myth of the Jew as the harmful other are persistent and long-lived phenomena, rooted in a prejudiced and nonrational way of evaluating the world characteristic of the exclusivist ethno-nationalist perspective. The poll also suggests how important it is to challenge and deconstruct the representation of the Jew as Poland's threatening other, which in the past constituted one of the main causes behind damaged intercommunal relations between ethnic Poles and Polish Jews and led to the exclusion of the Jewish community from the fabric of society. Furthermore, far from providing benefits to ethnic Poles, this representation of Jews has retarded the development of Polish society along the lines of a modern inclusive civic nationalism that advocates Western liberal democracy and pluralistic values.

History teaches us that making long-range firm predictions about the future of any nation and its development of a culture of civic nationalism and pluralism is potentially riddled with errors. This also holds true for predictions about the future of the two models of Polishness, the ethnic and the civic. Yet current indicators show that the balance between the ethnic model of Poland, which advocates the representation of the Jew as the harmful other, and the civic model of Poland, inclusive of Jews as Poles in a civic sense (past and present), has gradually shifted in favor of the latter.

In recent years increasing sections of mainstream political elites, cultural elites, and ordinary citizens, particularly of the younger generation, seem to have endorsed the model of Polishness that embraces every culture and faith of all those who have lived in Poland and still do. These social groups are capable of developing a more balanced collective self-image of Polish society. They are also capable of integrating into collective memory the (ethnic) Polish "dark past" regarding relations to Jews and other minorities. The latter is particularly important, because Jews and other religious and ethnic groups constitute a tiny percentage of contemporary Polish society, which means that the process of learning respect for minorities' cultures and the deconstruction of old anti-Jewish prejudices must encompass the history of the pre-1939 multinational and multireligious Poland. Jan Błonski, Hanna Świda-Ziemba, Maria Janion, the late Stanisław Musiał, the late Jacek Kuroń, Reverend Michał Czajkowski, Leon Kieres, and above all Jan T. Gross and his supporters in the debate about Jedwabne should be given credit for taking a leading role in reinforcing and strengthening the civic and pluralistic model of Poland. Poland's entry into the European Union in May 2004 may also strengthen this development because of the greater exposure of younger generations of ethnic Poles to information and education from the Western world.

At the same time one should not ignore the persistence of the backward-looking ethno-nationalist vision of Polishness, intolerant of multiethnic and multicultural diversity and still making overt and covert pronouncements advocating the representation of the Jew as the harmful other. This is not a phenomenon that belongs to the past; it is still a living vision of Poland. This model of Poland is still to a significant degree present among members of right-wing nationalist groups, both those outside the mainstream of political elites and those who constitute a legitimate part of the current mainstream political elite. One cannot rule out the possibility that parties such as the LPR—some of whose individual members have strong links to the extreme and openly anti-Semitic movement All-Polish Youth, whose ideological origins go back to interwar Poland—will become important political actors in the future.[82] The increasing fragmentation of the political scene on the left and the right and the search for transformations at the center between 2004 and the early 2005 suggest a certain level of unpredictability in contemporary Polish politics. [83] The representatives of the Closed Church also cannot be ignored as irrelevant in contemporary Polish Roman Catholicism. The backward-looking ethno-nationalist vision of Poland has a hold on some sections of the population, particularly those that still struggle with the social and economic changes brought about by the political and economic transformation of 1989.

The question of "what Polishness Poles need" is essential for Polish society in the post-Communist era. It is not a closed historical question, but a salient contemporary issue open to contestation. The deconstruction of the representation of the Jew as the harmful other constitutes one of the main features of the forward-looking, secure, civic, and pluralist vision of Poland. In the post-1989 period this vision of Poland has reached a level of confidence and influence that it has never had before. Its current development is a good indicator that national identities undergo change involving reselection, recombination, and recodification of previously existing values, symbols, and memories, as well as the addition of new cultural elements. It remains to be seen whether this vision of Poland will achieve long-term prevalence over the backward-looking vision of Poland, exclusive of Jews and intolerant of religious and cultural diversity.

Notes

1. Introduction

1. Narodowa Demokracja, which constitutes the core ethno-nationalist Polish movement, has changed its name a few times since its emergence in the 1880s. The organization's first name, Stronnictwo Narodowo-Demokratyczne (National Democracy), was in use during the late preindependence period (1897–1918). In the interwar period (1918–39) the movement appeared first under the name Związek Ludowo-Narodowy (National-Popular Union). In 1928 it renamed itself Stronnictwo Narodowe (National Party). The movement was also commonly called Endecja during the interwar period. In this work, for the sake of simplicity I mostly use "National Democracy" and "Endecja" to refer to the National Democrats in both the late preindependence and postindependence periods.

2. Tadeusz Mazowiecki was the first liberal Catholic politician and writer who used the term "Open Catholicism," in "Questions to Ourselves," published in English in *Dialectics and Humanism*, no. 2 (1990): 13. This essay was originally published in Polish in *Przegląd Powszechny*, no. 6 (1985). For a discussion of the subject of the "Open" and "Closed" Church, and further literature on it, see chap. 8; see also Joanna Michlic-Coren, "The 'Open Church,' the 'Closed Church,' and the Discourse on Jews in Poland, 1989–2000," *Communist and Post-Communist Studies*, no. 37 (2004): 461–76.

3. Kolorowa Tolerancja is a social initiative of high school youth that began in Łódź in 1999. One of its main actions is to clean up anti-Semitic and racist graffiti in Łódź and other cities. Regarding Hatikva-Nadzieja, *hatikva* is a Hebrew word for hope, while *nadzieja* is a Polish word for hope. The organization Hatikva-Nadzieja was established in 2000 as an educational circle at the University of Wrocław. I would

like to thank Joanna Czernek, a member of Hatikva, for discussing with me the aims of the organization.

4. According to the latest census, carried out in 2002, there are nine national minorities, four ethnic minorities, and one linguistic minority living in contemporary Poland. The German, Belorussian, and Ukrainian communities are the largest national minorities, whereas the Jewish, Armenian, and Czech groups are the smallest. See, e.g., Zbigniew Lentowicz, "Mniejszości narodowe," *Rzeczpospolita*, 23 June 2003,the special section *Nasza Europa*, 2.

5. Tadeusz Mazowiecki, speech in Polish parliament, Aug. 1989, cited in Michał Czajkowski, "Chrześcijanin na czasy trudne," *Tygodnik Powszechny*, 28 Aug. 2003, *http:// tygodnik.onet.pl/1629.1131005_dzial.html*.

6. For a discussion and examples of this new language in reference to Jews, see Antony Polonsky and Joanna B. Michlic, eds., *The Neighbors Respond: The Controversy over the Jedwabne Massacre in Poland* (Princeton and Oxford, 2004), 40–42, 130–32, 155–65. See also Joanna Michlic, "Coming to Terms with the 'Dark Past': The Polish Debate about the Jedwabne Massacre," *Acta: Analysis of Current Trends in Anti-Semitism*, no. 21 (Jerusalem) (2002): 29–32.

7. Chap. 8 contains a discussion of the views of these intellectuals. For examples of their views, see Polonsky and Michlic, *The Neighbors Respond*, 75–86, 103–13, 173–80, 344–70.

8. Robert N. Bellah, Richard Madsen, William M. Sullivan, Ann Swidler, and Steven M. Tipton, *Habits of Heart: Individualism and Commitment in American Life* (New York, 1985), 153.

9. There is a vast literature on European nationalism. On the development of late nineteenth-century nationalism, see, e.g., Anthony D. Smith, *Theories of Nationalism* (Oxford, 1982), chap. 5; Eric J. Hobsbawn, *Nations and Nationalism since 1780* (Cambridge, 1994), 101–62; and Elie Kedourie, *Nationalism* (Oxford and Cambridge MA, 1993), 100–102.

10. In the literature on the development of modern European nationalism two models of nation building are generally recognized. The first is civic nationalism, which, e.g., provided the matrix for the development of the modern French nation, and the second is ethnic nationalism, which, e.g., provided the matrix for the development of the modern German nation. Of course I recognize that in practice real-world nationalisms usually combine ethnic and civic claims. However, one type of nationalism is usually more crucial in the process of conceiving of modern nations. For the application of this paradigm and the historical development of the modern French and German nations, see the important study by Liah Greenfeld, *Nationalism: Five Roads to Modernity* (London and Cambridge MA, 1992), 89–184, 275–386.

11. Stefan Świeżawski (1907–2004), one of the key representatives of the liberal Catholic intelligentsia, has voiced such an opinion. See Stefan Świeżawski, *Lampa wiary. Rozważania na przełomie wieków* (Cracow, 2000), 145–46. Also see the following arti-

cles about Jacek Kuroń (1934–2004), a politician dedicated to the civic and pluralistic vision of Poland: Adam Michnik, "Wolność sprawiedliwość, miłosierdzie. Rzecz o Jacku," and Paweł Smoleński, "Przyda się w niebie taki pomocnik—wspomnienie o Jacku Kuroniu," both in *Gazeta Wyborcza*, 18 June 2004.

12. See, e.g., a collection of articles by historians and social scientists on the role of the "other" in forming national identity in Habsburg Central Europe: Nancy M. Wingfield, ed., *Creating the Other: Ethnic Conflict and Nationalism in Hapsburg Central Europe* (New York and Oxford, 2003). Also see Anna Triandafyllidou, "Nationalism and the Threatening Other: The Case of Greece," ASEN *Bulletin*, no. 13 (Summer 1997): 15–25.

13. Triandafyllidou, "Nationalism," 20–23.

14. See, e.g., two works by the historian Tadeusz Łepkowski: *Uparte trwanie polskości* (Warsaw, 1989), 67–68; and "Historyczne Kryteria Polskości," in Antonina Kłoskowska, ed., *Oblicza Polskości* (Warsaw, 1990), 88–99. Also see Zdzisław Mach and Andrzej K. Paluch, eds., *Sytuacja mniejszościowa i tożsamość* (Cracow, 1992), 11–18; the sociological study by Ewa Nowicka, "Narodowe samookreślenie Polaków," in Ewa Nowicka, ed., *Swoi i obcy* (Warsaw, 1990), 55–100; and Stefan Treugut, "Posłowie do Swojskości i Cudzoziemszczyzny," in Maria Prussak, ed., *Geniusz Wydziedziczony. Studia Romantyczne i Napoleońskie* (Warsaw, 1990), 428.

15. See Jan S. Bystroń, *Megalomania narodowa. Źródła, teorie, skutki*, 2d ed. (Cracow, 1924,); Aleksander Hertz, "Swoi przeciwko obcym," *Wiedza i Życie*, no. 6 (1934): 458–69. Hertz's article was republished in Jan Garewicz, ed., *Aleksander Hertz. Socjologia nieprzedawniona. Wybór publicystyki* (Warsaw, 1992), 145–64.

16. For a discussion of interwar works on attitudes toward the "other" by Jan Stanisław Bystroń and other authors such as Józef Obrębski and Florian Znaniecki, see Ewa Nowicka, "Wprowadzenie. Inny Jako Obcy," in Ewa Nowicka, ed., *Religia a obcość* (Cracow, 1991), 19–20.

17. A good example of this approach is the acclaimed book by Brian Porter, *When Nationalism Began to Hate: Imagining Modern Politics in Nineteenth-Century Poland* (New York and Oxford, 2000). Porter completely ignores the influence of the moral and cultural sentiments present in post-1864 Polish society on the National Democracy movement and fails to assess the reception of National Democratic traditions in the Roman Catholic Church and among nonelites. The latter problem was first pointed out by Richard J. Butterwick in his review of Porter's book in the *Journal of Modern History* 73, no. 3 (2001): 710–12.

18. Good examples of this approach in a version that neutralizes the importance of anti-Semitism in the National Democracy movement are two biographies of Roman Dmowski: Roman Wapiński, *Roman Dmowski* (Lublin, 1988); and Krzysztof Kawalec, *Roman Dmowski* (Warsaw, 1996).

19. Alina Cała, "The Question of the Assimilation of Jews in the Polish Kingdom (1864–1897): An Interpretive Essay," *Polin* 1 (1986): 130–50. Also see the work of Belgian

scholar Alix Ladngrebe, *"Wenn es Polen nich gäbe, dann müsste es erfunden werden":*
Die Entricklung des polnischen National be Wussteins im Europäischen kontext von 1830
bis in die 1880er Tahre (Wiesbaden, 2003).

20. Michael Steinlauf, *Bondage to the Dead: Poland and the Memory of the Holocaust* (New
York, 1997), 14. The importance of anti-Jewish ideas in the formation of Polish ethnic
nationalism generally tends to be omitted as an analytical problem in historical studies
on Polish anti-Semitism. For an overview of the historical literature on anti-Semitism
in Poland, see Antony Polonsky, "Approaches to Anti-Semitism," in Michael Brown,
ed., *Approaches to Antisemitism: Context and Curriculum* (New York, 1994), 290–308.

21. See Ireneusz Krzemiński, introduction, in Ireneusz Krzemiński, ed., *Czy Polacy są*
antysemitami? Wyniki badania sondażowego (Warsaw, 1996), 19–20.

22. Marcin Kula, "Problem postkomunistyczny czy historycznie ukształtowany polski
problem?" *Biuletyn Żydowskiego Instytutu Historycznego (BZIH)*, no. 4 (1991): 27.

23. Richard Pipes, *VIXI: Memoirs of a Non-Belonger* (New Haven and London, 2003), 20.

24. See, e.g., Zvi Gitelman, "Collective Memory and Contemporary Polish-Jewish Relations," in Joshua D. Zimmerman, ed. *Contested Memories: Poles and Jews during the*
Holocaust and Its Aftermath (New Brunswick and London, 2003).

25. The figure of five thousand constitutes the number of Jews affiliated with Jewish organizations in the 1990s. The highest figure, including individuals of mixed marriages, is
estimated at between fifteen and twenty thousand. See Alina Cała and Helena Datner-
Śpiewak, *Dzieje Żydów w Polsce 1944–1968. Teksty źródłowe* (Warsaw, 1997), 176.

26. See Andre W. M. Gerrits, "Paradox of Freedom: The 'Jewish Question' in Post-
Communist East Central Europe," in Ian M. Cuthbertson and Jane Leibowitz, eds.,
Minorities: The New Europe's Old Issues (Prague, 1993), 88–109.

27. Marcin Kula, "Problem," 45–49.

28. Jolanta Ambrosiewicz-Jacobs and Anna Maria Orla-Bukowska, "After the Fall: Attitudes towards Jews in post-1989 Poland," *Nationalities Papers*, no. 2 (1998): 267.

29. See, e.g., Israel Gutman, "Historiography on Polish-Jewish Relations," in Chimen
Abramsky, Maciej Jachimczyk, and Antony Polonsky, eds., *The Jews in Poland* (Oxford, 1986), 179; Marcin Kula, "Problem," 22–23; Konstanty A. Jeleński, "Od Endeków Do Stalinistów," *Kultura*, no. 9 (1956): 14–15 (*Kultura* is an émigré journal based
in Paris); Artur Sandauer, *Pisma Wybrane* (Warsaw, 1985), 3: 445–62; and Zygmunt
Bauman, "The Literary Afterlife of Polish Jewry," *Polin* 7 (1992): 273–99.

30. See Iwona Irwin-Zarecka, *Neutralizing Memory: The Jew in Contemporary Poland*
(New Brunswick and Oxford, 1989), 165.

31. Michał Jagiełło, *Próba rozmowy. Rodowód* (Warsaw, 2001), 1: 223.

32. Frank Golczewski, "Anti-Semitic Literature in Poland before the First World War,"
Polin 4 (1989): 88.

33. Jan Tomasz Gross was the first scholar to carefully analyze anti-Semitic idioms such
as Judeo-Communism in Polish society in WWII. See, e.g., the following works by
Jan Tomasz Gross: *Upiorna Dekada* (Cracow, 1998), 61–92; *Neighbors* (New York and

London, 2002), 21–42, 110–12; and "The Jewish Community in the Soviet-Annexed Territories on the Eve of the Holocaust," in Lucjan Dobroszycki and Jeffrey Gurock, eds., *The Holocaust in the Soviet Union* (Armonk NY, 1993), 155–71. See also the analysis of Judeo-Communism by Krzysztof Jasiewicz, *Pierwsi po Diable. Elity sowieckie w okupowanej Polsce 1939–1941* (Warsaw, 2002).

34. See chap. 3 in Omer Bartov, *Mirrors of Destruction* (Oxford, 2000), 91–142.

35. For a typology of the project purifying a nation-state, see Anthony D. Smith, "Ethnic Nationalism and the Plight of Minorities," *Journal of Refugee Studies* 7, nos. 2–3 (1994): 187–89.

36. In the tradition of political thought that originated in late eighteenth-century Enlightenment discourse, assimilation is viewed as a means of the inclusion of a minority in the nation. Currently this position is questionable, since it is recognized that assimilation generally leads to the disappearance of the culture and physical presence of a minority. In contemporary literature on ethnic minorities it is agreed that the most acceptable forms of inclusion of minorities within a nation are through policies of pluralism and integration, both aiming at the unity of various groups within a society, while allowing minorities to maintain their characteristics. See Ivan Gyurcsik, "New Legal Ramifications of the Question of National Minorities," in Cuthbertson and Leibowitz, *Minorities*, 1–49.

37. See Steinlauf, *Bondage*, 66–69.

38. See Michlic, "Coming to Terms," 15–17.

39. Irwin-Zarecka, *Neutralizing*, 172.

40. Jerzy Tomaszewski, "The History of Jews in Poland 1944–1968," *The Best of Midrasz*, special issue of *Midrasz* (1998): 47.

41. In chap. 8 I discuss the major representatives of this approach in the post-1989 period.

42. Jan Tomasz Gross, *Sąsiedzi: Historia zagłady żydowskiego miasteczka* (Sejny, 2000).

43. See Joanna Michlic-Coren, "The Troubling Past: The Polish Collective Memory of the Holocaust," *East European Jewish Affairs* 29, nos. 1–2 (1999): 77–78.

44. Michlic-Coren, "The Troubling Past," 77.

45. See, e.g., David Engel, *In the Shadow of Auschwitz: The Polish Government-in-Exile and the Jews, 1939–1942* (Chapel Hill, 1987); David Engel, *Facing the Holocaust: The Polish Government-in-Exile and the Jews, 1943–1945* (Chapel Hill, 1993); Israel Gutman and Shmuel Krakowski, *Unequal Victims: Poles and Jews during World War Two* (New York, 1986); and Yehuda Bauer, introduction, in Gutman and Krakowski, *Unequal Victims*, 1–3.

46. See http://www.polonia.net/Zydzi-w-Polsce.htm, accessed Dec. 2004.

47. For a short discussion of the reactions of Jewish organizations to the news about the Jedwabne massacre and the commemorative events in Jedwabne on 10 July 2001, see Polonsky and Michlic, *The Neighbors Respond*, 403–7.

48. See http://www.hidingandseeking.com.

49. See, e.g., Piotr Wróbel, "Double Memory: Poles and Jews after the Holocaust," *East*

European Politics and Societies, no. 3 (1997): 569–73; and Robert Cherry, "Contentious History: Polish-Jewish Relations during the Holocaust," partially published in Polish as "Sporna Historia," *Midrasz*, no. 4 (2003): 38–42. I would like to thank Professor Cherry for giving me the English version of his article.

50. See Gitelman, "Collective Memory," 271–72.

51. On the subject of communitarian rights in liberal thought, see Will Kymlicka, *Liberalism Community and Culture* (Oxford, 1989); and Will Kymlicka, ed., *The Rights of Minority Cultures* (Oxford, 1995).

52. On the perception of the Jew as the threatening other in twelfth-century Europe, see Roger I. Moore, *The Formation of a Persecuting Society* (Oxford, 1994), 34–45. On similar perceptions of Jews in English popular culture of the early modern period, see Frank Felsenstein, *Anti-Semitic Stereotypes: A Paradigm of Otherness in English Popular Culture* (London, 1995). On the perception of Jews as the threatening other and polluter in twentieth-century Europe, see Saul Friedländer, "Europe's Inner Demons: The 'Other' as Threat in Early Twentieth-Century European Culture," in Robert. S. Wistrich, ed., *Demonizing the Other: Anti-Semitism, Racism, and Xenophobia* (Jerusalem, 1999), 210–22; other articles in Wistrich, *Demonizing the Other*; and Bartov, *Mirrors*, 91–142.

53. Smith, "Ethnic Nationalism and the Plight of Minorities," 190–92.

54. The scope of this research does not allow for comparisons with other minorities perceived as the "threatening other" in various societies.

55. On myths and their social functions, see, e.g., William G. Doty, *Mythography: The Study of Myths and Rituals* (University AL, 1986), 11–25. On national mythologies, see Anthony D. Smith, *The Ethnic Origins of Nations* (Oxford, 1986), 86–100; and George Schöpflin, "The Functions of Myth and a Taxonomy of Myths," in Geoffrey Hosking and George Schöpflin, eds., *Myths and Nationhood* (London, 1997), 19–35, 18–19, 23.

56. Schöpflin, "The Functions," 22.

57. Doty, *Mythography*, 12–13.

58. Doty, *Mythography*, 14–20.

59. Leonard W. Doob, *Patriotism and Nationalism: Their Psychological Foundations* (New Haven and London, 1964); Aleksander Hertz, *The Jews in Polish Culture* (Evanston IL, 1988) (first published in Polish in 1964); Hertz, "Swoi," 145–64; and James Aho, *The Thing of Darkness: A Sociology of the Enemy* (London, 1994).

60. See Walter P. Zenner, *Minorities in the Middle: A Cross-Cultural Analysis* (New York, 1991), 48–49.

61. Hertz, "Swoi," 158–59.

62. Aho, *The Thing*, 3–15.

63. See William G. Sumner, *Folkways* (Boston, 1906).

64. See, e.g., the psychosocial study of ethno-nationalism in the former Yugoslavia by Dusan Kecmanovic, *The Mass Psychology of Ethno-nationalism* (New York and London, 1996), 36.

65. On the subject of war and creating a sense of national cohesiveness, see Anthony D. Smith, "Warfare in the Formation, Self-Images and Cohesion of Ethnic Communities," *Ethnic and Racial Studies* 4, no. 4 (1981): 375–97.

66. Doob, *Patriotism*, 249–53.

67. Hertz, *The Jews*, 53.

68. Hertz, *The Jews*, 144.

69. For a position questioning the existence of civic nationalism, see articles by such scholars as Bernard Yack in Ronald Beiner, ed., *Theorizing Nationalism* (New York, 1999), 103–18.

70. The concept of the "multivocalness" of all national communities is expressed in Porter's *When Nationalism*.

71. See Smith, "Ethnic Nationalism," 187–89.

72. Smith, "Ethnic Nationalism," 188.

73. The prevailing tendency in historical studies of the Polish nation, its nationalism and minorities, is to apply the narrower definition of nationalism. For a recent debate on the use of the continental and Anglo-Saxon definitions of nationalism in Polish scholarly discourse, see the special issue of *Znak*, no. 3 (1997): 4–94.

74. Rogers Brubaker, "Nationalizing States in the Old 'New Europe'—and the New," *Ethnic and Racial Studies* 19, no. 2 (1996): 411–37. See also Rogers Brubaker, *Nationalism Reframed: Nationhood and the National Question in the New Europe* (Cambridge, 1996), 79–106.

75. Brubaker, "Nationalizing," 414.

76. Brubaker, "Nationalizing," 414.

77. Brubaker, "Nationalizing," 416.

2. The Representation of the Jew

1. There is a huge body of literature discussing modern anti-Semitism and integral nationalism in France, Germany, Hungary, and Romania. On the general developments of exclusivist ethnic nationalism and anti-Semitism in Europe, see, e.g., the classic pioneering studies Shmuel Almog, *Nationalism and Anti-Semitism in Modern Europe 1815–1945* (Oxford, 1990), 66–72; and Jacob Katz, *From Prejudice to Destruction: Anti-Semitism, 1700–1933* (Cambridge MA, 1994), 260–300.

2. Polish anti-Jewish literature of the late nineteenth century and interwar period (1918–39) refers to foreign anti-Semitic works by authors such as Houston S. Chamberlain and Charles Maurras. Polish writers called *Protocols of the Elders of Zion* a work of "authors of prophetic vision, who had foreseen in great detail the Jewish conquest of the world." See, e.g., Stanisław Trzeciak, *Program światowej polityki żydowskiej. Konspiracja i dekonspiracja* (Warsaw, 1936); and *Pamiętnik I Konferencji Żydoznawczej odbytej w grudniu 1921 roku w Warszawie*, ed. Mieczysław Czerwiński (Warsaw, 1923), 15–25. The influence of various European anti-Semitic authors on Polish modern anti-Semitic writing is a still-unexplored subject requiring a separate scholarly study. On the reception of *Protocols of the Elders of Zion* in Poland, see Janusz Tazbir, "Conspiracy

Theories and the Reception of the *Protocols of the Elders of Zion* in Poland," *Polin* 11 (1998): 171–82.

3. The scope of this book does not allow for a comparative analysis of the negative perceptions of Jews in different European countries at the time of the rise of integral nationalism. Such an analysis would be extremely useful in identifying common and unique features of anti-Jewish images as well as in discussing their differences.

4. See Ezra Mendelsohn, *The Jews of East Central Europe between the World Wars* (Bloomington, 1983), 1–17. On the emergence of modern political movements among East European Jewry, see the seminal book by Jonathan Frankel, *Prophecy and Politics: Socialism, Nationalism and the Russian Jews, 1862–1917* (Cambridge, 1981). On the relationship between the young Jewish socialist movement and the young Polish Socialist Party (PPS), see Joshua D. Zimmerman, *Poles, Jews and the Politics of Nationality* (Madison, 2004). For a concise summary of the social and political changes in East European Jewry, see David Vital, *A People Apart: The Jews in Europe 1789–1939* (Oxford, 1999), 353.

5. Krystyna Kersten, "The 'Jewish Communism' Stereotype (The Polish Case)," in Andre Gerrits and Nanci Adler, eds., *The Vampires Unstaked: National Images, Stereotypes and Myths in East Central Europe* (Amsterdam and Oxford, 1995), 146.

6. See, e.g., J. Taylor, *The Economic Development of Poland 1919–1950* (Ithaca, 1952), 101–5. On the development of this approach in Polish historiography in the interwar period, see Israel Oppenheim, "Polish Jewry in the Nineteenth Century as Reflected in Twentieth Century Polish Historiography," in John Micgiel, Robert Scott, and H. B. Segel, eds., *Poles and Jews: Myth and Reality in the Historical Context* (New York, 1986), 168–202. Some of the articles presented in this volume were republished in different versions in the Polish-Jewish studies journal *Polin*, which first appeared in 1986.

7. For one of the most elaborated versions of the third approach, in which the author, along with the above-mentioned causes, also includes religious anti-Semitism and the individual choices of political leaders, see the important article by Stephen D. Corrsin, "Polish Political Strategies and the 'Jewish Question' during the Elections in Warsaw to the Russian State Dumas, 1906–1912," in Micgiel, Scott, and Segel, *Poles and Jews*, 140–67.

8. Theodore R. Weeks, "Poles, Jews and Russians, 1863–1914: The Death of the Ideal of Assimilation in the Kingdom of Poland," *Polin* 12 (1999): 256. This is an example of the third approach, characterized by fine scholarship and a nonprejudiced perception of Jews.

9. See Andrzej Jaszczuk, *Spór Pozytywistów z Konserwatystami o przyszłość Polski 1870–1903* (Warsaw, 1986), 207–8. On the early position of PPS toward Jews, see Zimmerman, *Poles, Jews*, 126–90; and Alina Kowalczykowa, *Piłsudski i Tradycja* (Chotomow, 1991), 46–50.

10. On Warsaw positivism in general, see Stanisław Blejwas, *Realism in Polish Politics*

(New Haven, 1984);and Jaszczuk, *Spór.* On the evolution of the attitudes of Warsaw Positivists toward Jews, see Stanisław Blejwas, "Polish Positivism and the Jews," in Micgiel, Scott, and Segel, *Poles and Jews,* 112–39. This article also appeared in a slightly different version in *Jewish Social Studies* 1, no. 46 (1984): 21–56. Also see Tadeusz Stegner, *Liberałowie Królestwa Polskiego* (Gdansk, 1990), 113–30; and Tadeusz Stegner, "Liberałowie Królestwa Polskiego wobec kwestii żydowskiej na początku XX wieku," *Przegląd Historyczny* 80, no. 1 (1989): 69–88.

11. In the modern era two opposite theories about Jewish origins in Poland emerged. The first, much criticized theory claims an Eastern origin for Polish Jewry, whereas the second, less questionable theory claims a Western European origin. On this subject, see Bernard Weinryb, "The Beginnings of East European Jewry in Legend and Historiography," in Meir Ben-Horin, Bernard D. Weinryb, and Solomon Zeitlin, eds., *Studies and Essays in Honor of Abraham A. Neuman* (Leiden, 1962), 445–502.

12. The earliest evidence for permanent Jewish settlements in Poland, mainly in Silesia, dates back to the twelfth century. See, e.g., Bernard D. Weinryb, *The Jews of Poland: A Social and Economic History of the Jewish Community in Poland from 1100 to 1800* (Philadelphia, 1973), 10–20. For the most recent literature on the origin of Jews in Poland, see Gershon David Hundert, *Jews in Poland-Lithuania in the Eighteenth Century: A Genealogy of Modernity* (Berkeley and Los Angeles, 2004), 1–31.

13. For a discussion of Casimir the Great's achievements, see Adam Zamoyski, *The Polish Way: A Thousand-Year History of the Poles and Their Culture* (New York, 2001), 36–40. In this book the author makes a conscious effort to discuss all ethnic and religious-cultural groups that lived in premodern Poland.

14. On the first increase in newcomers in thirteenth-century Poland, see Benedykt Zientara, "Melioratio Terrae: The Thirteenth-Century Breakthrough in Polish History," in J. K. Fedorowicz, *A Republic of Nobles: Studies in Polish History to 1864* (Cambridge, 1982), 28–47.

15. On the various charters of rights granted to Jews in medieval Poland and the reaction of Polish statesmen, political thinkers, historians, and Catholic clergy, see the important article by Shmuel A. Cygielman, "The Basic Privileges of the Jews of Great Poland as Reflected in Polish Historiography," *Polin* 1 (1986): 117–33. For the most comprehensive history of Jewish privileges in Poland, see Jacob Goldberg, *Jewish Privileges in the Polish Commonwealth: Charters of Rights Granted to Jewish Communities* (Jerusalem, 1985).

16. Jan Długosz lived during the Reformation and was critical of the Reformation movement. In his main work, *Annales,* considered the most important Polish historical chronicle of the medieval period, he expresses hostility toward Jews and other groups, such as Lithuanians, whom he considered half heathen, and Czechs, whom he viewed as heretics. On his attitudes toward Jews and Casimir's decision to grant them privileges, see Hundert, *Jews in Poland-Lithuania,* 8; and Czesław Miłosz, *The History of Polish Literature* (Berkeley, Los Angeles, and London, 1983), 18–19.

17. See, e.g., Antoni Zawadzki, *Polska przedrozbiorowa a Żydzi* (Warsaw, 1939), 20–25; and Antoni Marylski, *Dzieje sprawy żydowskiej w Polsce* (Warsaw, 1912), 72–80.

18. See Hundert, *Jews in Poland-Lithuania*, 6.

19. On Polish society under the Jagiellonian dynasty, see, e.g., Henryk Samsonowicz, "Polish Politics and Society under the Jagiellonian Monarchy," in Fedorowicz, *A Republic*, 49–69.

20. On the role of Jews in the colonization of the Ukraine, see, e.g., Shmuel Ettinger, "Helkam shel ha-Yehudim be-kolonizatsyah shel Ukr'enah 1569–1648," *Zion* 21 (1956): 119–24. Ettinger estimates that across the Ukraine, in 1569, Jews lived in 24 settlements with a total population of 4,000. By the 1648 uprising Jews lived in 115 settlements and numbered approximately 51,525.

21. Miłosz, *The History*, 60.

22. For a detailed discussion of the issue of Poland as a "paradisus Judaeorum," see Gershon Hundert, "Second Goldman Lecture," *Journal of Jewish Studies* 48, no. 2 (1997): 335–48.

23. For Jewish evaluations of their existence in sixteenth-century Poland, see Edward Fram, *Ideals Face Reality: Jewish Law and Life in Poland 1550–1655* (Cincinnati, 1997); and Hundert, *Jews in Poland-Lithuania*, 6–7.

24. The upper house of the Council of Jews of Four Lands ceased to exist in the second decade of the eighteenth century, and the council as such was dissolved in 1764. On the internal structure of premodern Polish Jewry, see Fram, *Ideals*, 38–47; and Hundert, *Jews in Poland-Lithuania*, 79–118. Hundert provides an updated bibliography of the latest works on the subject by Jacob Goldberg, Andrzej Link-Lenczowski, and Moshe Rosman (13).

25. See introduction and chap. 1 in Hundert, *Jews in Poland-Lithuania*, 1–31.

26. Zamoyski, *The Polish*, 91.

27. See Irena Gieysztorowa, "Research into Demographic History of Poland: A Provisional Summing-up," *Acta Poloniae Historica*, no. 18 (1968): 11. Weinryb cites similar figure in *The Jews* (107).

28. Fram, *Ideals*, 17. On the fate of Protestantism during the Counter-Reformation, see Janusz Tazbir, "The Fate of Polish Protestantism in the Seventeenth Century," in Fedorowicz, *A Republic*, 198–217.

29. Hundert, *Jews in Poland-Lithuania*, 21–24, 233–37.

30. Hundert, *Jews in Poland-Lithuania*, 236.

31. Fram discusses the variety of social interactions, including close, friendly contacts with the Christian population in the sixteenth century. See Fram, *Ideals*, 29–32.

32. Kedourie, *Nationalism*, 113.

33. On the definition of *naród* in seventeenth- and eighteenth-century Poland, see Janusz Maciejewski, "Pojęcie narodu w myśli republikanów lat 1767–1775," in Janusz Goćkowski and Andrzej Walicki, eds. *Idee i koncepcje w polskiej myśli politycznej czasów porozbiorowych* (Warsaw, 1977), 21–41.

34. See Jerzy Łukowski, *Liberty's Folly: The Polish-Lithuanian Commonwealth in the Eighteenth Century, 1697–1795* (New York, 1991), 27. According to some other estimates, the nobility in Poland constituted 9 percent of the population: see Edmund Lewandowski, *Character narodowy Polaków i innych* (London and Warsaw, 1995), 105.

35. See M. J. Rosman, "Jewish Perceptions of Insecurity and Powerlessness in 16th–18th Century Poland," *Polin* 1 (1986): 19.

36. On the regulations prohibiting the engagement of the nobility in trade and commerce, see Taylor, *The Economic*, 101–2.

37. On the economic ties between the nobility and the Jewish community, see Moshe Rosman, *The Lord's Jews: Magnate-Jewish Relations in the Polish-Lithuanian Commonwealth during the Eighteenth Century* (Cambridge MA 1990); and Hillel Levine, *Economic Origins of Anti-Semitism: Poland and Its Jews in the Early Modern Period* (New Haven and London, 1991), 10–11.

38. *Hajduk Miklosz Odmienia Art u Żyda*, cited in Urszula Augustyniak, *Koncepcje narodu i społeczeństwa w literaturze plebejskiej od końca XVI do konca XVII wieku* (Warsaw, 1989), 62.

39. See Salo Wittmayer Baron, *A Social and Religious History of Jews* (New York, 1976), 16: 138–39.

40. See Janusz Tazbir, *Szlaki kultury polskiej* (Warsaw, 1986), 160.

41. See Augustyniak, *Koncepcje*, 57; and Jacob Goldberg, "Poles and Jews in the 17th and 18th Centuries: Rejection or Acceptance," *Jahrbucher fur Geschichte Ost Europas* 22, no. 2 (1974): 250–51. For observations about perceptions of Jews and also Lutherans (Germans) by burghers in the seventeenth and eighteenth centuries, see William W. Hagen, *Germans, Poles, and Jews: The Nationality Conflict in the Prussian East, 1772–1914* (Chicago and London, 1980), 20–30.

42. Jan Jurkowski, *Poselstwo z dzikich pól*, cited in Augustyniak, *Koncepcje*, 58.

43. On the issue of the conversion of Jews in premodern Poland, see Magda Teter, "Jewish Conversions to Catholicism in the Polish-Lithuanian Commonwealth of the Seventeenth and Eighteenth Centuries," *Jewish History*, no. 17 (2003): 264. Teter is also author of the book *Jews and Heretics in Catholic Poland: A Beleaguered Church in the Post-Reformation Era* (Cambridge NY, 2006). I am grateful to Magda Teter for sharing with me the outline of her book.

44. See Augustyniak, *Koncepcje*, 62.

45. Teter, "Jewish," 264.

46. On the changes in attitude toward internal others and the development of xenophobia among the Roman Catholic population in the seventeenth century, see Tazbir, *Szlaki*, 133–219.

47. Hundert notes this development in *Jews in Poland-Lithuania*, 57–58.

48. The last time the Polish Army faced Roman Catholics in a military battle was in 1588 at the Battle of Byczyna; see Tazbir, *Szlaki*, 160. On the history of seventeenth-century wars and their effects on *szlachta*, see Zamoyski, *The Polish*, 144–74.

49. Teter, "Jewish," 265.

50. See, e.g., Teodor Jeske-Choiński, *Poznaj Żyda* (Warsaw, 1912), 190–92; and Józef Caderski, *Co nasi ojcowie sądzili o żydach* (Kielce, 1923), 1–10.

51. See Stanisław Tworkowski, *Polska bez Żydow* (Warsaw, 1939), 30. For an extensive description of this viewpoint, see Michał Morawski, *Stanowisko kościoła wobec niebezpieczeństwa żydowskiego w dawnej Polsce* (Wloclawek, 1938), 10–23.

52. On the Roman Catholic Church's economic entanglements with the Jewish community in the form of credits and loans and managerial arrangements, see Hundert, *Jews in Poland-Lithuania*, 77–78; and Judith Kalik, "Patterns of Contact between the Catholic Church and the Jews in the Polish Lithuanian Commonwealth: The Jewish Debts," in Adam Teller, ed., *Studies in the History of the Jews in Old Poland in Honor of Jacob Goldberg* (Jerusalem, 1993), 102–22. In her article Kalik discusses the contradiction between the Church's ideology and its practice toward Jews. One could argue that the relationship between the Church and the Jewish community in the seventeenth and eighteenth centuries shows that close economic ties do not alleviate anti-Jewish attitudes but comfortably coexist with them.

53. In the last two decades Artur Eisenbach, Gershon Hundert, Krystyna Zieńkowska, and Jacob Goldberg have explored this aspect in a variety of ways. See Artur Eisenbach, *The Emancipation of the Jews in Poland 1780–1870* (Oxford, 1991), 67–73; Hundert, *Jews in Poland-Lithuania*, 57–78, 211–32; Krystyna Zienkowska, "Stereotyp Żyda w publicystyce polskiej w drugiej połowie XVIII wieku," in Jerzy Michalski, ed., *Lud żydowski w narodzie polskim* (Warsaw, 1994), 81–98; Jacob Goldberg, "The Changes in the Attitude of Polish Society toward the Jews in the 18th Century," *Polin* 1 (1986): 35–48.

54. On the position and rights of different sections of Polish society and various political developments in the eighteenth century, see Łukowski, *Liberty's Folly*.

55. For a discussion of the interference of foreign powers in Polish politics of the early eighteenth century, see Zamoyski, *The Polish*, 206–21.

56. For a good summary of this problem, see Zienkowska, "Stereotyp," 81–98.

57. See Gershon D. Hundert, "Some Basic Characteristics of the Jewish Experience in Poland," *Polin* 1 (1986): 31.

58. On the impact of Jesuit education of the nobility in the first half of the eighteenth century, see, e.g., Anatol Leszczyński, *Sejm Żydów Korony 1623–1764* (Warsaw, 1994), 31–33. On the Jesuit educational system, see Henryk Samsonowicz, Janusz Tazbir, Tadeusz Łepkowski, and Tomasz Nałęcz, *Polska, losy państwa i narodu* (Warsaw, 1992), 217–19.

59. See Baron, *A Social*, 16: 138.

60. Popes Benedict XIV and Clement XIII condemned the ritual-murder trials; see Zenon Guldon and Jacek Wijaczka, "The Accusation of Ritual Murder in Poland, 1500–1800," *Polin* 10 (1997): 99–140. Guldon and Wijaczek give a detailed history of the accusation of blood libel in premodern Poland.

61. This figure does not include the less frequent accusation of host desecration. See Guldon and Wijaczka, "The Accusation," 99–140.

62. In post-Communist Poland in 2000 a debate began over what should be done with the painting in the cathedral of Sandomierz. For a detailed discussion of the debate and examples of the persistence of the belief in ritual murder in contemporary Poland, see Anna Landau-Czajka, "The Last Controversy over Ritual Murder? The Debate over the Paintings in Sandomierz Cathedral," *Polin* 16 (2003): 483–90.

63. Gershon Hundert describes Stefan Żuchowski as "the leading antisemite in the history of the Polish Commonwealth." See Hundert, *Jews in Poland-Lithuania*, 74.

64. Gaudent Pikulski, *Złość żydowska przeciwko Bogu i bliźniemu, prawdzie i sumieniu na objaśnienie przeklętych talmudystów na dowód ich zaślepienia i religii daleko od Prawa boskiego przez Mojżesza danego* (L'viv, 1758). For a detailed analysis of Roman Catholic clergy's anti-Jewish writings, and for a bibliography on the subject, see Hundert, *Jews in Poland-Lithuania*, 67–77; and Guldon and Wijaczka, "The Accusation," 99–140.

65. Zienkowska, "Stereotyp," 92.

66. Janusz Tazbir, *Świat Panów Pasków* (Lodz, 1986), 225.

67. On the economy of *szlachta*, see Łukowski, *Liberty's Folly*, 26–35.

68. Hundert points out that in some areas, like the Ukraine, the Jewish innkeeper became such a characteristic figure that the terms *arendarz* (leaseholder) and *Jew* became synonymous. See Hundert, *Jews in Poland-Lithuania*, 14–15.

69. Stanisław Staszic, "Przestrogi dla Polski," in Stanisław Suchodolski, ed., *Pisma filozoficzne i społeczne* (Warsaw, 1954), 299–300.

70. According to Artur Eisenbach, approximately seventy thousand Jews (fifteen thousand Jewish families) ceased to be *arendarze* of taverns in the countryside between 1815 and 1830. See Artur Eisenbach, *Wielka Emigracja wobec kwestii żydowskiej 1832–1849* (Warsaw, 1976), 60.

71. Eisenbach, *Wielka*, 60. An interesting example of the persistence of this myth of the Jewish innkeeper is the late nineteenth-century publication of an author who supported the forceful assimilation of Jews into Polish culture. See Władysław Smoleński, *Stan i sprawa Żydow polskich w XVIII wieku* (Warsaw, 1876), 12–18.

72. Staszic, *Przestrogi*, 298–99.

73. Mary Douglas, *Purity and Danger* (London, 1966), esp. 140–58.

74. For the data and a summary of the most important literature on Jewish demography in premodern Poland, see Hundert, *Jews in Poland-Lithuania*, 21–31.

75. John Thomas James, *Journal of a Tour in Germany, Sweden, Russia, Poland, in 1813–1814* (London, 1819), cited in Hundert, *Jews in Poland-Lithuania*, 19.

76. On the Jewish debate during the Four-Year Parliament and for the major literature on the subject, see Hundert, *Jews in Poland-Lithuania*, 216–31.

77. On the stance of leading figures of the Polish Enlightenment toward Jews, see Eisen-

bach, *Emancipation*, 77–82; and Zdzisław Libera, *Rozważania o wieku tolerancji ro-
zumu i gustu: Szkice o XVIII stuleciu* (Warsaw, 1994), 75–94.

78. Zalkind Hurwitz also played an important role in the discussion of the political
emancipation of Jews in France. On the discussion of the Haskalah movement in
Poland, see Eisenbach, *Emancipation*, 87–91.

79. On the phases of emancipation, see Jacob Katz, *Emancipation and Assimilation: Studies
in Modern Jewish History* (Franborough, 1972), 22. On the political theory of Jewish
emancipation, see Amos Funkenstein, *Perceptions of Jewish History* (Berkeley and
Oxford, 1993), 221–22.

80. Hundert, *Jews in Poland-Lithuania*, 230.

81. Eisenbach, *Emancipation*, 82–87.

82. On the definitions and problems of acculturation and assimilation, see Jonathan
Frankel and Steven Zipperstein, eds., *Assimilation and Community: The Jews in Nineteenth-Century Europe* (Cambridge, 1992); and Marsha Rozenblit, *The Jews of Vienna,
1867–1914: Assimilation and Identity* (Albany, 1983).

83. On the issue of responses of the late premodern Polish-Jewish community to the
Polish discourse on Jewish emancipation and cultural assimilation, see Eisenbach,
Emancipation, 125–45.

84. On Staszic's proposal and the general problems of the inclusionary model based on the
concept of strong assimilation, see Eisenbach, *Emancipation*, 91–101. Eisenbach defines Staszic's proposal as "compulsory polonization and complete denationalization"
(97).

85. According to Andrzej Walicki, "the gradual replacement of the political definition
of the nation [premodern Poland] by the ethno-linguistic conception was certainly
one of the most important shifts in the Polish thought of the late Enlightenment."
This process was fostered by the growing radicalism of certain writers, like Franciszek
Jezierski, who wanted to put stress on language and culture, or "commonality," but
its main cause was certainly the impact of the partitions. See Andrzej Walicki, *The
Enlightenment and the Birth of Modern Nationhood: Polish Political Thought from Noble
Republicanism to Tadeusz Kosciuszko* (Notre Dame, 1989), 89. On the emergence of
ethno-cultural concepts of the Polish nation in the writing of Stanisław Staszic and
Franciszek S. Jezierski, see also Maciejewski, "Pojęcie," 39–41.

86. Wiesław Władyka, ed., *Inni wśród swoich* (Warsaw, 1994), 75, 107.

87. Mirosława Zakrzewska-Dubasowa, *Ormianie w dawnej Polsce* (Lublin, 1982), 311.

88. The emergence of this distinction was first suggested in Zienkowska, "Stereotyp," 97.
See also Hundert, *Jews in Poland-Lithuania*, 77.

89. First Baron Acton, *Essays on Freedom and Power* (London, 1956), 147.

90. For a discussion of the Polish ideal of a nation during the romantic period, see
Stanisław Eile, *Literature and Nationalism in Partitioned Poland, 1795–1918* (London,
2000), 1–20; and Andrzej Walicki, "The Three Traditions in Polish Patriotism," in

Stanisław Gomułka and Antony Polonsky, eds., *Polish Paradoxes* (London and New York, 1991), 22–30.

91. For the political history of insurrectionary developments in the first half of the nineteenth century, see Zamoyski, *The Polish*, 259–300.

92. On the history of the January Uprising, see Stanisław Kieniewicz, *Powstanie styczniowe* (Warsaw, 1972).

93. Eile, *Literature*, 12.

94. For the literary representation of Jankiel, see Adam Mickiewicz, *Pan Tadeusz* (New York, 1992), 165–66. On the discussion among Polish émigré circles of Mickiewicz's representation of Israel as the Older Brother, including critical reactions, see Maria Janion, *Do Europy tak, ale razem z naszymi umarłymi* (Warsaw, 2000), 53–71, 73–90. On the contradictions and complexities of Mickiewicz's messianism, see also Eile, *Literature*, 46–54.

95. Cyprian Kamil Norwid, "Żydowie polscy," trans. Harold B. Segel, in Harold B. Segel, *Stranger in Our Midst: Images of the Jew in Polish Literature* (Ithaca and London, 1996), 89.

96. According to Eisenbach, the appeal of 23 Feb. 1846 was an act of great historical importance, the first document in the Polish territories that in a revolutionary way abolished the estate barriers separating the Jewish population from the other inhabitants of the country. See Eisenbach, *Emancipation*, 326.

97. On the revolutionary movements in Galicia and Prussia in the 1840s, and on the various reactions of the Polish and German populations toward the Jews in these areas and Jewish and German relations in the province of Poznań, see Hagen, *Germans*, 85–116; and Sophia Kemlein, "The Jewish Community in the Grand Duchy of Poznań under Prussian Rule, 1815–1848," *Polin* 14 (2001): 49–67. On developments within the Jewish community in the province of Posen, see Sophia Kemlein, *Die Posener Juden 1815–1848. Entwicklungsprozesse einer polnischen Judenheit unter preussischer Herrschaft* (Hamburg, 1997).

98. For a discussion of Polish-Jewish relations and the Brotherhood in the January Uprising of 1863–64, see Magdalena Opalski and Israel Bartal, *Poles and Jews: A Failed Brotherhood* (Hanover and London, 1992), 19–21.

99. See Porter, *When Nationalism*, 37–38.

100. Andrzej Walicki raises the issue of the German model of survival as a community of history and language inspiring Polish romantic elites in "The Three," 28.

101. See Irena Grudzińska-Gross, *Alexis De Tocqueville. Listy* (Cracow, 1999), 33–34.

102. Walicki, "The Three," 23–24; and Eile, *Literature*, 9–20.

103. On the importance of the gentry and its ethos in shaping the ethos of modern Polish elites, see Walicki, "The Three," 27–28.

104. On the importance of Catholicism, conservatism, and traditionalism in Polish national traditions of the nineteenth century, see Walicki, "The Three," 29–31; and Łepkowski, *Uparte*, 30–31. On negative perceptions of the capitalist West by Polish

elites of the first half of the nineteenth century, see Jerzy Jedlicki, "A Stereotype of the West in Post-Partition Poland," *Social Research* 59, no. 2 (1992): 345–64.

105. The Jewish families of Samuel Kronenberg, Antoni E. Fraenkel, Izaak Rosen, and Michal Ettinger-Rawski, among others, were the major entrepreneurs. The Warsaw Jewish bourgeoisie was also involved in creating the modern food and textile industries. On the subject of the contribution of the Warsaw Jewish bourgeoisie to the economic modernization of the country in the first half of the nineteenth century, see Eisenbach, *Emancipation*, 207–13.

106. Eisenbach, *Emancipation*, 212.

107. See Alina Kowalczykowa, "Kraszewski w Warszawie," *Rocznik Warszawski* (1992): 206. On the evolution of Kraszewski's perception of Jews, see Opalski and Bartal, *Poles*, 64–65.

108. For a description of the event known as the "Jewish war," see Eisenbach, *Emancipation*, 398–400.

109. Jędrzej Giertych, *Polski Obóz Narodowy* (Warsaw, 1990), 30.

110. See Eisenbach, *Wielka*, 44–80.

111. Eisenbach was the first to write about such transmission of images from one generation of nobility to another. See Eisenbach, *Wielka*, 50.

112. On Jewish participation in insurrectionary Polish movements and various reactions toward them, see Eisenbach, *Emancipation*, 248–55. See also Hanna Węgrzynek, "Ludność żydowska wobec powstania listopadowego," and Krzysztof Makowski, "Ludność żydowska wobec wydarzeń Wiosny Ludów na ziemiach polskich," both in Jerzy Tomaszewski, ed., *Żydzi w obronie Rzeczypospolitej: Materiały Konferencji w Warszawie 17–18 października 1993* (Warsaw, 1996), 31–42, 43–64.

113. For a detailed discussion of this problem, see Eisenbach, *Wielka*, 50–60. The attitudes of Wielka Emigracja toward Jews and other groups is a subject that needs further research.

114. They were advocates of the unconditional integration of Jews into society. In concert with a group of acculturated Jews they propagated the concept of the Pole of the Mosaic Persuasion (Polak Mojżeszowego Wyznania)—the Polish equivalent of the concept of the Frenchman or Englishman of Mosaic Persuasion. See Eisenbach, *Emancipation*, 142–46, 183–84; and Janusz Detka, "Żydowska Kwestia," in Józef Bachórz and Alina Kowalczykowa, eds., *Słownik Literatury Polskiej XIX Wieku* (Warsaw and Wroclaw, 1991), 1051.

115. In the last two decades there has been a renewal of academic interest in the Frankists. For a basic description of the history of the Frankist movement, see Weinryb, *The Jews*, 237–40.

116. Excerpts from the pamphlet *O Żydach i judaiźmie* are cited in Mateusz Mieses, *Z rodu żydowskiego* (1938; Warsaw, 1991), 18. On Zygmunt Krasiński's negative perspective on Jewish converts, see Opalski and Bartal, *Poles*, 19. On Zygmunt's father, Wincenty

Krasiński-Korwin, and Zygmunt's private tutor L. A. Chiarini, who held similar views on Jewish converts to Christianity, see Janion, *Do Europy*, 66–71.

117. Julian U. Niemcewicz, entry, 19 Jan. 1834, in *Pamiętniki*, 2: 222, cited in Eisenbach, *Wielka*, 324. Jan Czyński, political activist and journalist, was one of the most attacked among the group of Polish democrats with the same background. He was a member of the Paris Historical and French Literary Associations. On Czyński and attitudes toward him among Wielka Emigracja, see Eisenbach, *Wielka*, 325–28; and Adam Gałkowski, "Jan Czyński and the Question of Equality of Rights for All Religious Faiths in Poland," *Polin* 7 (1992): 31–56.

118. *Moszkopolis* is made of two words: *Moszko/Moshko*, a diminutive of the name Moses; and *polis*, which means "city" in Greek. For an important essay about Niemcewicz's pamphlet, see Janion, *Do Europy*, 121–24.

119. Roman Brandstaetter, "Moszkopolis," *Miesięcznik żydowski* (1932): cited in Janion, *Do Europy*, 123.

120. These figures are drawn from Piotr Wróbel, *Zarys dziejów Żydów na ziemiach polskich w latach 1880–1918* (Warsaw, 1991), 10–11.

121. This figure is cited in Maria Nietyszka, *Ludność Warszawy na przełomie XIX i XX wieku* (Warsaw, 1971), 122.

122. This figure is cited in Samsonowicz et al., *Polska*, 379.

123. For a discussion of some of the alarming forecasts, see Eisenbach, *Emancipation*, 259–62.

124. On the failure of integration of the Polish territories, see Eisenbach, *Emancipation*. For a discussion of this problem and its consequences for Polish-Jewish relations in the twentieth century, see Antony Polonsky, "The Failure of Jewish Assimilation in Polish Lands and Its Consequences, The Third Goldman Lecture," Oxford Center for Hebrew and Jewish Studies, 2000.

125. On Wielopolski's Emancipatory Act, see Eisenbach, *Emancipation*, 440–60.

126. Illustrations of such reactions are provided in Eisenbach, *Emancipation*, 520–21; and in Golczewski, "Anti-Semitic," 93–95.

127. For the history of the Warsaw Positivist movement, see Blejwas, *Realism*. The late Blejwas is one of the leading historians of the Warsaw Positivist movement. On the Positivists' debate with the conservative press, see Jaszczuk, *Spór*, 144–202.

128. On Warsaw Positivist attitudes toward Jews and their evolution, see Alina Cała, *Asymilacja Żydów w Królestwie Polskim (1864–1897)* (Warsaw, 1989), 216–76; and Blejwas, "Polish," 112–39.

129. On the pogrom of 25–27 Dec. 1881, see Cała, *Asymilacja*, 268–78. The pogrom was part of the wave of anti-Jewish violence that swept the Russian Empire after the assassination of Tsar Aleksander II. On the general history and causes of pogroms in late Imperial Russia, see John D. Klier and Shlomo Lambroza, *Pogroms: Anti-Jewish Violence in Modern Russian History* (Cambridge, 1992).

130. Bolesław Prus, *Lalka* (Warsaw, 1972), 1: 202. The novel *Lalka* was first published as a serial in the paper *Kurier Codzienny* between 1887 and 1889.

131. Klemens Junosza-Szaniawski, *Nasi żydzi w miasteczkach i na wsiach* (Warsaw, 1889), 124, cited in Cała, *Asymilacja*, 213.

132. Bolesław Prus, *Kroniki* (Warsaw, 1965), 16: 419.

133. For a discussion of the Positivists' critical stance toward the vicious anti-Jewish position, represented by the weekly *Rola* in the 1890s, see Jaszczuk, *Spór*, 229–36.

134. Świętochowski supported the anti-Jewish campaign of Endecja that started in the aftermath of the Duma elections of 1912. In 1913, in agreement with Endecja's concept of antagonism between Poles and Jews, Świętochowski prophesized the "war" between the Polish and Jewish nations. This event is discussed in Michael C. Steinlauf, "The Polish-Jewish Daily Press," *Polin* 2 (1987): 219–45. On the same subject, see also Stegner, "Liberałowie," 69–88; Theodore R. Weeks, "Polish 'Progressive Anti-Semitism,' 1905–1914," *East European Jewish Affairs* 25, no. 2 (1995): 49–68; and Frank Golczewski, *Polnisch-Jüdische Beziehungen 1881–1922* (Wiesbaden, 1981), 92–96.

135. See Polonsky, "The Failure," 12–13.

136. Blejwas, "Polish," 127–28.

137. Poseł Prawdy Aleksander Świętochowski, "Liberum veto," *Prawda*, 1882, cited in Blejwas, "Polish," 128.

138. On the evolution of the Positivists' attitudes toward integration of Jews through assimilation, see Cała, *Asymilacja*, 216–67.

139. See Polonsky, "The Failure," 12.

140. On German liberals' attitudes toward Jews in the late nineteenth century, see Uriel Tal, *Christians and Jews in Germany: Religion, Politics and Ideology in the Second Reich, 1870–1914* (Ithaca and London, 1975). On historical and contemporary problems inherent to liberalism in its treatment of the cultural rights of groups, see Kymlicka, *The Rights*.

141. Benjamin Nathans, *Beyond the Pale: The Jewish Encounter with Late Imperial Russia* (Berkeley, Los Angeles, and London, 2004), 7.

142. Adam Boryna, *Antysemityzm a kwestia żydowska*, cited in Adolf Nowaczyński, *Mocarstwo Anonimowe (ankieta w sprawie żydowskiej)* (Warsaw, 1921), 237.

143. This opinion was expressed by Stanisław Koźmian, a representative of a conservative political group based in Cracow, in his review of Theodor Herzl's *Der Judenstaat* (1896), cited in Nowaczyński, *Mocarstwo*, 232.

144. For examples of this vocabulary in literary writings, see Krzysztof Stępnik, "Powieść antysemicka w ostatnich latach Kongresówki," *Krytyka*, no. 39 (1992): 88–90.

145. Smoleński, *Stan*, 95.

146. On the categorization of free-thinking Western liberalism, socialism, and Communism as anti-Polish doctrines, see Łepkowski, *Myśli*, 36–37; and Michał Śliwa, *Polska myśl polityczna w I połowie XX wieku* (Wroclaw, 1993), 239–54.

147. See Jaszczuk, *Spór*, 202–57. For a detailed description of the crystallization of such

groups in literary circles see Mieczysław Inglot, "The Image of the Jew in Polish Narrative Prose of the Romantic Period," *Polin* 2 (1987): 199–218.

148. See Jaszczuk, *Spór*, 207–8; and Cała, *Asymilacja*, 276–78.

149. On the importance of Catholicism in shaping Polish nationalism and national identity, see Z. Anthony Kruszewski, "Nationalism and Politics: Poland," in George Klein and Milan J. Reban, eds., *The Politics Of Ethnicity in Eastern Europe* (New York, 1981), 151.

150. Jaszczuk was the first scholar to argue that there was no difference in the image of the Jew presented in *Rola* and *Niwa* and in *Niwa Polska*. See Jaszczuk, *Spór*, 223.

151. For a detailed description of Jeleński's anti-Jewish opinions and activities, see Jaszczuk, *Spór*, 212–20; and Cała, *Asymilacja*, 278–84.

152. Jan Jeleński, *Wrogom własnej ojczyzny* (Warsaw, 1906), 6–10.

153. For a concise biography of Teodor Jeske-Choiński, see Władysław Niemirycz and Wacław Olszak, eds., *Polski Słownik Biograficzny* (Wroclaw, 1978), 10: 194–95.

154. Jeske-Choiński, *Poznaj*, 238–39.

155. See Niemojewski's defense of the Lithuanian priest Justyn Pranajtis, included in the booklet *Skład i Pochód Armji Piątego Zaboru* (Warsaw, 1911), 3–8. On Niemojewski, see Niemirycz and Olszak, *Polski*, 10: 3–10.

156. Andrzej Niemojewski, *Etyka Talmudu* (Warsaw, 1917), 127.

157. On Father Marian Morawski, see Jaszczuk, *Spór*, 221–23; and Jagiełło, *Próba*, 1: 36–40. On the Jesuit *Przegląd Powszechny*, see Jagiełło, *Próba*, 1: 29–70; and Michał Jagiełło, *Trwałość i zmiana. Szkice o "Przeglądzie Powszechnym" 1884–1918* (Warsaw, 1993).

158. Father Marian Morawski, "Asemityzm," *Przegląd Powszechny* 49 (Feb. 1896): 161–89. The article was reprinted in *Niwa Polska* in 1898.

159. See Jaszczuk, *Spór*, 221.

160. Iwan Franko himself was not free of anti-Jewish prejudices in the context of his own society. On the subject of Franko's attitudes toward Jews in the Russian Empire see Yaroslav Hrytsak, "Between Semitism and Anti-Semitism: Iwan Franko and the 'Jewish Question' " (work in progress, 2005). I would like to thank Professor Hrytsak for sharing this paper with me.

161. Iwan Franko, "Jezuityzm w kwestii żydowskiej," *Tydzień*, no. 12 (1898): 89, 90–91, cited in large excerpts in Jagiełło, *Próba*, 1: 38–39.

162. Jaszczuk, *Spór*, 223.

163. Jagiełło, *Próba*, 40. For an apologetic approach to Father Marian Morawski that emphasizes his opposition to anti-Jewish violence and undermines if not dismisses his anti-Semitic idiom, see Brian Porter, "Making a Space for Anti-Semitism," *Polin* 16 (2003): 425–27.

164. For a questionable position claiming the "multivocalness" of the Roman Catholic press on the "Jewish question" in the late nineteenth and early twentieth centuries, see Brian Porter, "Marking the Boundaries of the Faith: Catholic Modernism and the Radical Right in the Early Twentieth Century," in Elwira M. Grossman, ed., *Studies*

in Language, Literature and Cultural Mythology in Poland (Lewiston, Queenston, and Lamperet, 2002), 261–86.

165. See Wróbel, *Zarys*, 22–23.

166. On the founders and development of PPS's movement and ideology, see Śliwa, *Polska*, 22–37.

167. For an extensive discussion of the treatment of Jews in the ideology and programs of PPS during the preindependence period, see Zimmerman, *Poles, Jews*, 165–90, 255–74. See also Michał Śliwa, "The Jewish Problem in Polish Socialist Thought," *Polin* 9 (1996): 26; and Kowalczykowa, *Piłsudski*, 46–50. See also Timothy Snyder, "Kazimierz Kelles-Krauz, 1872–1905: A Polish Socialist for Jewish Nationality," *Polin* 12 (1999): 257–70.

168. In Piłsudski's early political writing of 1893 a critical voice directed at the Jews in the kingdom of Poland can be found. However, a year later criticism of the Jewish masses for being politically passive and of Jewish elites for not opposing Russification is replaced by a positive evaluation of Jews and their commitment to the Polish national cause. This was first pointed out and discussed by Alina Kowalczykowa. See Kowalczykowa, *Piłsudski*, 47–48.

169. See Zimmerman, *Poles, Jews*, 255–72.

170. On the general history of the early Endecja movement and its leader Roman Dmowski, see Alvin Marcus Fountain II, *Roman Dmowski: Party, Tactics, Ideology, 1895–1907* (New York, 1980); and Porter, *When Nationalism*, 157–233. Barbara Toruńczyk published an anthology of texts from Endecja's major press organ, *Przegląd Wszechpolski: Antologia myśli politycznej "Przeglądu Wszechpolskiego (1895–1905)* (London, 1983). This anthology also includes an important introduction of Endecja's political thought. National Democracy's attitudes toward Jews in the formative period of the movement are still relatively unexplored. A separate descriptive work dedicated to this issue is Israel Oppenheim, "The 'National Democrats'–Endecja Attitude to the Jewish Question at the Outset (1895–1905)," *Studia Podlaskie* 2 (1989): 105–20.

171. See Walicki, "The Three," 34–35; Andrzej Walicki, "Intellectual Elites and the Vicissitudes of 'Imagined Nation' in Poland," *East European Politics and Society*, no. 2 (1992): 227–53; and Andrzej Walicki, "Naród i terytorium. Obszar narodowy w myśli politycznej Dmowskiego," *Dziś*, no. 7 (2002): 22–41.

172. In 1890 eleven socialist members of Zet left the organization as a sign of protest against the admittance of Dmowski to the Warsaw branch. See Toruńczyk, *Narodowa*, 297.

173. Endecja's press and its circulation and readership are discussed in Bogumil Grott, *Nacjonalizm Chrześcijański* (Cracow, 1991), 11–20. Grott belongs to the ethno-nationalist historical school.

174. Barbara Toruńczyk cites this data in *Narodowa*, 13.

175. On the early development of National Democracy, see Grott, *Nacjonalizm*, 11–16.

176. Wilhelm Feldman, *Rzecz o Narodowej Demokracji* (Cracow, 1902), 4.

177. See Toruńczyk, *Narodowa*, 21–23.

178. Toruńczyk, *Narodowa*, 22.
179. For a discussion of the relationship between the Roman Catholic Church and National Democracy, see Grott, *Nacjonalizm*, 90–130; Toruńczyk, *Narodowa*, 59–63; and Oppenheim, "The 'National Democrats.'" Oppenheim was the first author to insist on a close relationship between the elite of Endecja and the Roman Catholic Church in the pre-1918 period, but he does not acknowledge the contradictions of such a relationship, given the secular stance of the Endeks.
180. American scholar Norman Naimark was the first to discuss the anti-Semitic aspects of the conservative, Catholic, democratic, patriotic, peasantist groups of the politically active 1880s Polish intelligentsia, associated with the journal *Głos*. Naimark identifies this political group as representing populist nationalism of the "new patriotism" and discerningly evaluates it as a bridge between the democratic traditions, socialism, positivism, and socialist patriotism of the 1880s and the National Democrats of the 1890s. See Norman Naimark, *The History of the "Proletariat": The Emergence of Marxism in the Kingdom of Poland, 1870–1887* (New York, 1979), 191–95.
181. On anti-Jewish thought among National Democrats, see the brief discussion in Andrzej Friszke, "Pytania o polski nacjonalizm," *Więź*, no. 11 (1993): 74–85. See also Toruńczyk , *Narodowa*, 24–25; and Porter, *When Nationalism*, 227–32.
182. Walicki briefly discusses the use of the Jew as the "other" in raising national cohesiveness and national awareness. See "Naród," 31. It is perhaps also striking that none of Walicki's past major works on Polish nationalism addresses the issue of Polish anti-Semitism in detail. Walicki has begun to address the problem of anti-Semitism only in his recent articles, such as "Naród."
183. On various levels of national awareness within Polish society, see Łepkowski, *Uparte*, 24–28.
184. On the lack of development of national consciousness among the peasantry in the early twentieth century, see Jan Jerschina, "The Catholic Church, the Communist State, and the Polish people," in Gomułka and Polonsky, *Polish*, 93–95. On the peasants' association of Polishness with the gentry and serfdom, see Roman Wapiński, *Polska i małe ojczyzny Polaków* (Wroclaw and Warsaw, 1994), 145–47.
185. See Roman Dmowski, *Upadek myśli konserwatywnej w Polsce* (1914; Częstochowa, 1938).
186. On the categorization of secularism, Western liberalism, socialism, and Communism as anti-Polish doctrines, see Łepkowski, *Myśli*, 36–37; and Michał Śliwa, *Polska myśl polityczna w I połowie XX wieku* (Wroclaw, 1993), 239–54.
187. This type of representation of the Jew was disseminated in the main press organ of the National Democrats in the preindependence period, *Przegląd Wszechpolski*. See, e.g., the excerpt from "Listy warszawskie," by Ignotus (pseud.), in *Przegląd Wszechpolski* (1903): 459–69, cited in Toruńczyk, *Narodowa*, 157–58.
188. See Grott, *Nacjonalizm*, 67–69; and Norman Davies, "Polish National Mythologies," in Hosking and Schöpflin, *Myths*, 151.

189. On the attitudes of the peasant movement toward Jews in Galicia, see Kai Struve, "Gentry, Jews, and Peasants: Jews and Others in the Formation of the Modern Polish Nation in Rural Galicia during the Second Half of the Nineteenth Century," in Wingfield, *Creating the Other*, 235–94.

190. Struve, "Gentry," 244–49.

191. On the treatment of Jews by SL, see Struve, "Gentry," 261–71; and Golczewski, *Polnisch-Jüdische*, 64–70. Walicki argues that Bolesław Wysłouch was the first theoretician who introduced the concept of an ethnic/racial Polish nation in "Szkice programowe," published in *Przegląd Społeczny* in 1886. See Walicki, "Naród," 23.

192. This is an excerpt from the article "Skutki nędzy i ciemnoty," published in the main press organ of SL, *Przyjaciel Ludu*, on 1 July 1898 (283), cited in Struve, "Gentry," 264–65.

193. See Edward D. Wynot, "The Polish Peasant Party and the Jews, 1918–1939," in Israel Gutman, Ezra Mendelsohn, Jehuda Reinharz, and Chone Shmeruk, *The Jews of Poland between Two World Wars* (Hanover and London, 1989), 39–41.

194. On the importance of the long historical conflict with Germany in shaping modern Polish nationalism, see Kruszewski, "Nationalism," 147–49. On the policy of Kulturkampf, see Piotr S. Wandycz, *The Lands of Partitioned Poland 1795–1918* (Seattle and London, 1984), 233–35.

195. Roman Dmowski, *Myśli Nowoczesnego Polaka*, 2d ed. (L'viv, 1904) 88–90. For an analysis of Dmowski's attitudes toward Germans, see Antony Polonsky, "Roman Dmowski and Italian Fascism," in R. J. Bullen, H. Pogge von Strandmann, and Antony Polonsky, eds., *Ideas into Politics: Aspects of European History 1880–1950* (London and Sydney, 1984), 132.

196. For a description of Polish ethno-nationalists' attitudes and policies toward the ethnic German minority, see Włodzimierz Mich, *Obcy w polskim domu* (Lublin, 1994), 114–20.

197. See Roman Dmowski, "Podstawy polityki polskiej," in Toruńczyk, *Narodowa*, 73.

198. On the self-perception of some Russians as representatives of a lower civilization vis-à-vis Poles, see Theodore R. Weeks, "Defining Us and Them: Poles and Russians in the Western Provinces, 1863–1914," *Slavic Review* 53, no. 1 (1994): 26–40.

199. For a general discussion of Zionist and Bundist aspirations for equal rights and minority rights for Jews, see Frankel, *Prophecy*; and Vital, *A People*, 610–16.

200. See, e.g., Dmowski, *Upadek*, 69–70, 120–21; and another excerpt from "Listy warszawskie," by Ignotus (pseud.), in *Przegląd Wszechpolski* (1903): 459–69, cited in Toruńczyk, *Narodowa*, 158.

201. Theodore R. Weeks, "Polish," 49–68

202. See Toruńczyk, *Narodowa*, 22; and Walicki, "Naród," 32.

203. On the importance of the concept of national conflict between Poles and Jews in Polish anti-Semitism, see Steinlauf, *Bondage*, 14. On Endeks' anti-Semitism between 1905 and 1914, see Theodore R. Weeks, "Fanning the Flames: Jews in the Warsaw Press,"

East European Jewish Affairs 28, no. 2 (1998–99): 63–81; and Golczewski, *Polnisch-Jüdische*, 101–20.

204. On Endecja's anti-Jewish stance during and after the fourth Duma election in Warsaw in 1912, see Stephen D. Corrisin, "The Jews, the Left, and the State Duma Election in Warsaw in 1912: Selected Sources," *Polin* 9 (1996): 45–54.

205. Report from the Ministry of Internal Affairs, Warsaw Oberpolitseimeister, no. 11379, 29 Oct.–11 Nov. 1912, cited in Corrisin, "The Jews," 54.

206. This was a popular presentation of the economic boycott in Endecja's press at the national and local levels. On the use of these slogans in violent attacks on Jewish shopkeepers in Kielce, see, e.g., Stanisław Wiech, "Polacy a Żydzi w Kielcach w latach 1911–1916," in *Społeczeństwo województwa kieleckiecjo wobec niepodległości 1918 roku* (Kielce, 1991), 140–41.

207. Ludwik Oberlaender, "Ewolucja poglądów Narodowej Demokracji w sprawie żydowskiej," *Miesięcznik żydowski*, no. 1 (1931): 5–6.

208. Polonsky, "Roman Dmowski," 130.

209. On Edouard Drumont, see, e.g., Pierre Birenbaum, "Gregoire, Dreyfus, Drancy and the Rue Copernic: Jews at the Heart of French History," in Pierra Nora, ed., *Realms of Memory* (New York, 1996), 1: 381–87.

210. Andrzej Walicki gives two examples of this type of approach in history writing: Wapiński, *Roman Dmowski*, 107–8; and Kawalec, *Roman Dmowski*, 69–70. See Walicki, "Naród," 30. Interestingly Kawalec's position on Roman Dmowski shows the author's strong identification with the vision of the nation advocated by National Democracy; his work represents an uncritical approach toward Endecja. Wapiński's work, which presents more sophisticated arguments than Kawalec's, also shows inconsistencies on the matter of the treatment of National Democracy and its leaders. Although the author is well-informed about the ideological anti-Semitism of the Endeks, he is inclined to view anti-Semitism as a result of the actions of the Jewish community, specifically the rise of Zionism. Similar inconsistencies on Polish anti-Semitism are present in Wapiński's other studies. See, e.g., Wapiński, *Polska*, 152–92.

211. See Walicki, "Naród," 30 n. 31.

212. Fountain, *Roman Dmowski*, 11. Dmowski was one of the founders of the clandestine Straźnica youth club. Although Fountain acknowledges Dmowski's anti-Jewish prejudicial views at an early age, he does not ask questions about their social origin and impact in shaping Dmowski's views at a later stage. On the contrary, he insists that Dmowski's mature position on Jews had "objective grounds." Fountain's position is inconsistent.

213. Dmowski, *Myśli*, 40.

214. Dmowski, *Myśli*, 214–15.

215. *Gazeta Warszawska*, 19 Apr. 1935, cited in Harry M. Rabinowicz, *The Legacy of Polish Jewry* (New York and London, 1965), 184.

216. Roman Dmowski, *Kwestia żydowska. Separatyzm Żydow i jego źródła* (Warsaw, 1909), 29.
217. Dmowski, *Upadek*, 118–21.
218. Dmowski, *Upadek*, 118–19.
219. Roman Dmowski, "Speech of 1 October 1912," cited in Nowaczyński, *Mocarstwo*, 238.

3. The Myth of the Jew as Threatening Other

1. These figures represent the results of the second census conducted in Poland in 1931, cited in Juliusz Bardach, Bogusław Leśnodorski, and Michał Pietrzak, eds., *Historia ustroju i prawa polskiego* (Warsaw, 1994), 468–67. For demographic data on the population of interwar Poland, see also Mendelsohn, *The Jews*, 23–25.
2. On the reconstruction of the Polish state, see Antony Polonsky, *Politics in Independent Poland: The Crisis of Constitutional Government* (Oxford, 1972), chap. 1; and R. F. Leslie, A. Polonsky, J. M. Ciechanowski, and Z. Pełczyński, *The History of Poland since 1863* (Cambridge, 1980), 112–38.
3. For the text of articles 110 and 111 of Poland's constitution of 1921, see, e.g., Stephan Horak, *Poland and Her National Minorities 1919–1939* (New York, 1961), 196.
4. There is a vast literature on the subject. For a more recent and fascinating historical analysis of the conflict between Piłsudski and Dmowski, and the problem of territorial settlements in the early postwar period, see Timothy Snyder, *The Reconstruction of Nations: Poland, Ukraine, Lithuania, Belarus, 1569–1999* (New Haven and London, 2003), 52–72.
5. The term *Sanacja* means "healing" or "restoration" and comes from the Latin *sanatio*. It refers to Piłsudski's aim to restore "health" to the political, social, and moral life of Poland after his coup d'état of May 1926.
6. For the composition of the parliament in 1930, see Leslie et al., *The History*, 175–76.
7. See Szymon Rudnicki, *Obóz Narodowo-Radykalny. Geneza i działalność* (Warsaw, 1985), 58–59.
8. On the merging of Piłsudski's ethos with that of Endecja by the ozn camp, see Grott, *Nacjonalizm*, 61–63; and Jacek Majchrowski, *Silni Zwarci Gotowi. Myśl polityczna Obozu Zjednoczenia Narodowego* (Warsaw, 1985), 34–53. Majchrowski, a well-respected Polish historian, also adopts the thesis of "objective conditions" for the development of Polish anti-Semitism in interwar Poland. Also see Israel Gutman, "Polish Anti-Semitism between the Wars: An Overview," in Gutman et al., *The Jews*, 103–6.
9. On the ozn movement, see Majchrowski, *Silni*; and Edward D. Wynot, *Polish Politics in Transition: The Camp of National Unity and the Struggle for Power, 1935–1939* (Athens GA, 1974).
10. On the subject of three generations of Polish political elites in the interwar period, see Roman Wapiński, *Pokolenia Drugiej Rzeczypospolitej* (Wroclaw, 1991).
11. On the history of onr, see, e.g., an important study by Rudnicki, *Obóz*; and an important article by Jan Józef Lipski, "Antysemityzm onr Falangy," in Jan Józef Lipski, *Tunika Nessosa* (Warsaw, 1992), 85–138.

12. For the history and historiography of the treatment of Jews in interwar Poland, see Mendelsohn, *The Jews*, 32–40; Ezra Mendelsohn, "German and Jewish Minorities in the European Successor States between the World Wars—Some Comparative Remarks," in Ezra Mendelsohn and Chone Shmeruk, eds., *Studies in Polish Jewry* (Jerusalem, 1987), 51–64; and William Hagen, "Before the 'Final Solution': Toward a Comparative Analysis of Political Anti-Semitism in Interwar Germany and Poland," *Journal of Modern History* 68, no. 2 (1996): 368–81.

13. See Salo Wittmayer Baron, *Ethnic Minority Rights: Some Older and Newer Trends* (Oxford, 1985), 19.

14. On the history and historiography of the Minorities Treaties, see Baron, *Ethnic*, 1–45; and Gershon Bacon, "Polish Jews and the Minorities Treaties Obligations, 1925: The View from Geneva (Documents from the League of Nations Archives)," *Gal-Ed* 18 (2002): 145–76.

15. See Polonsky, *Roman Dmowski*, 135.

16. On the division among the American and Eastern European Jewish representatives organized in the Comité des Délègations Juives, see Baron, *Ethnic*. On the approach of British Jewish representatives, see Eugene C. Black, "Lucien Wolf and the Making of Poland: Paris, 1919," *Polin* 2 (1987): 1–36; and Mark Levene, *War, Jews and the New Europe: The Diplomacy of Lucien Wolf, 1914–1919* (Oxford, 1992).

17. See Black, "Lucien Wolf," 15.

18. Baron, *Ethnic*, 10–11.

19. For such views, see, e.g., Tworkowski, *Polska*, 36; and Józef Kruszyński, *Żydzi i kwestia żydowska* (Wloclawek, 1920), 100–101.

20. The interwar ethno-nationalist interpretation of the Minorities Treaties has been uncritically integrated into post-1945 historical writings. For its post-1989 manifestations in history books, see, e.g., Antoni Czubiński, *Walka Józefa Piłsudskiego o nowy kształt polityczny Europy środkowo-wschodniej w latach 1918–1921* (Torun, 2002), 70–75; and Marek Wierzbicki, *Polacy i Żydzi w zaborze sowieckim. Stosunki polsko-żydowskie na ziemiach północno-wschodnich II RP pod okupacją sowiecką (1939–1941)* (Warsaw, 2001), 30.

21. For statistics on the elections to the parliament in Nov. 1922, see Leslie et al., *The History*, 153.

22. On similarities of political perspectives on Jews among otherwise ideologically diverse political parties, see, e.g., Mich, *Obcy*, 25–27. For a detailed analysis of anti-Jewish positions within the conservative movement, see Włodzimierz Mich, *Problem mniejszości narodowych w myśli politycznej polskiego ruchu konserwatywnego (1918–1939)* (Lublin, 1992), 59–154. See also Anna Laudau-Czajka, *W jednym stali domu . . . Koncepcje rozwiązania kwestii żydowskiej w publicystyce polskiej* (Warsaw, 1998), 240–59; Jerzy Holzer, "Polish Political Parties and Anti-Semitism," *Polin* 8 (1994): 194–205; and Jerzy Jedlicki, "How to Grapple with the Perplexing Legacy," in Polonsky and Michlic, *The Neighbors Respond*, 237–46.

23. Hagen, "Before," 374.

24. See Grott, *Nacjonalizm*, 61–63.

25. The scholar Anthony Kruszewski states: "Poles could not understand, except for a few politicians on the Socialist Left, the re-awakening of national aspirations of the Lithuanians, Ukrainians and Belorussians." See Kruszewski, "Nationalism," 158.

26. The most detailed study of the policies and practices of the Obóz Niepodległościowy and Sanacja toward minorities before and after 1935 is Waldemar Paruch, *Od konsolidacji państwowej do konsolidacji narodowej. Mniejszości narodowe w myśli politycznej obozu piłsudczykowskiego (1926–1939)* (Lublin, 1997).

27. See Snyder, *The Reconstruction*, 65–67, 148–50.

28. See Majchrowski, *Silni*, 167–69.

29. Majchrowski, *Silni*, 152.

30. Such a view is expressed in the article signed by "B.," "Prawdziwi Polacy," published in *Prawda* in 1906. A long excerpt from this article is included in Toruńczyk, *Narodowa*, 252–55.

31. Joel Cang, "The Opposition Parties in Poland and Their Attitude towards the Jews and the Jewish Problem," *Jewish Social Studies* 1 (1939): 245.

32. For a pre-1918 representation of such a position, see, e.g., Roman Dmowski, *Problems of Central and Eastern Europe* (London, 1917).

33. See, e.g., three articles by the historian Peter D. Stachura in a book he edited, *Poland between the Wars, 1918–1939* (London, 1998). Stachura's views represent an uncritical endorsement of the ideology of National Democracy.

34. See Olaf Bergman, *Narodowa Demokracja wobec problematyki żydowskiej w latach 1918–1929* (Poznan, 1998). See critical reviews of Bergman's book by Szymon Rudnicki, in *Polin* 14 (2001): 399–402; and by Israel Oppenheim, in *Gal-Ed* 18 (2000).

35. Ezra Mendelsohn, "Interwar Poland: Good or Bad for the Jews?" in Abramsky, Jachimczyk, and Polonsky, *The Jews*, 135–36. Polish social historian Jan Kofman makes a similar critical evaluation of such an approach in *Nacjonalizm gospodarczy—szansa czy bariera rozwoju* (Warsaw, 1992), 80–81.

36. Mendelsohn, *The Jews*, 37.

37. Bacon, "Polish," 149–50.

38. For statements of loyalty to the Polish state expressed by a variety of Jewish political parties in the interwar Polish-Jewish press, see, e.g., the collection *Ten Years of Poland's Independence in the Polish-Jewish Press* (Warsaw, 1931).

39. On the history of Agudat Yisrael in interwar Poland, see Gershon C. Bacon, *The Politics of Tradition: Agudat Yisrael in Poland, 1916–1939* (Jerusalem, 1996).

40. On the SD and its activities combating anti-Semitism, see Aharon Weiss, "The Activities of the Democratic Societies and Democratic Party in Defending Jewish Rights in Poland on the Eve of Hitler's Invasion," *Polin* 7 (1992): 260–67. For the general history of the SD, see Antoni Czubiński, *Stronnictwo Demokratyczne (1937–1989). Zarys dziejów* (Poznan, 1998), 17–111.

41. On the opposition of the PPS and the Democratic Party to anti-Semitism, see Emanuel Melzer, "Anti-Semitism in the Last Years of the Second Polish Republic," in Gutman et al., *The Jews*, 133–34; and Abraham Brumberg, "The Bund and the Polish Socialist Party in the Late 1930s," in Gutman et al., *The Jews*, 86–88.

42. The problem of the liberal intelligentsia's opposition to the ideology of anti-Semitism and anti-Semitic actions awaits further research. Rabinowicz makes some first basic observations in his popular book *The Legacy* (104–6).

43. See *Polacy o Żydach. Zbiór artykułów z przedruku* (Warsaw, 1937). Among other contributors were Adam Próchnik, Leon Kruczkowski, professors; Stefan Czarnowski, Witold Rubczyński, Zygmunt Szymanowski, and Józef Ujejski; and Wanda Wasilewska.

44. See "Głos ks. Biskupa gr. katol. Grzegorza Chomyszyna," in *Polacy*, 91–92.

45. In Yiddish a "shabbes goy" is a Gentile who is asked by Orthodox Jews to light a fire, put out candles, or perform a chore on the Sabbath. See Leo Rosten, *The Joys of Yiddish* (London, 1988), 331.

46. Apolinary Hartglas, "Żółta łata (Sprawa ograniczeń prawnych)," part 1, in Yitzhak Gruenbaum, ed., *Materiały w sprawie żydowskiej w Polsce* (Warsaw, 1922), 5: 8.

47. Moshe Sneh (Kleinbaum), "Hoser omez ba-zad ha-yehudi," cited in Vital, *A People*, 799.

48. For a discussion of parliamentary speeches about Jews, see Isaac Lewin, *The Jewish Community in Poland* (New York, 1985), 216–40.

49. Wincenty Witos, speech, 17 Oct. 1923, cited in Lewin, *The Jewish*, 225.

50. Władysław Sikorski, speech, 19 Jan. 1923, cited in Lewin, *The Jewish*, 221.

51. On the history of the NPR, see Antoni Czubiński, *Ewolucja systemu politycznego w Polsce w latach 1914–1998*, vol. 1, *Odbudowa niepodległościowego państwa i jego rozwój do 1945 r* (Poznan, 2000), 245–55.

52. See the NPR program in the following collection of political programs: Ewa Orlof and Andrzej Pasternak, eds., *Programy partii i stronnictw politycznych w Polsce w latach 1918–1939* (Rzeszow, 1993), 143.

53. See the PSKL program in Orlof and Pasternak, *Programy*, 180.

54. The last two decades have seen growing research on this small political group. See, e.g., Antony Wacyk, *Mit polski Zadruga* (Wroclaw, 1991).

55. See Władysław Studnicki, *Sprawa polsko-żydowska* (Warsaw, 1936), 5. For a contemporary critical review of Studnicki's work, see *Sprawy Narodowościowe*, no. 3 (1936): 319–20.

56. On Bogusław Miedziński's speech at the Budget Commission session on 10 Feb. 1934, see "Żydzi w Sejmie," *Sprawy Narodowościowe*, no. 1 (1934): 89–90.

57. On the PPS position on the Jewish minority in the interwar period, see Śliwa, "The Jewish," 14–31; and Antony Polonsky, "The Bund in Polish Political Life, 1935–1939," in Ezra Mendelsohn, ed., *Essential Papers on Jews and the Left* (New York and London, 1997), 166–97.

58. The issue of *shekhita* has given rise to a vast literature. For the history and historiography of *shekhita*, see Emanuel Melzer, *No Way Out: The Politics of Polish Jewry 1935–1939* (Cincinnati, 1997). This book first appeared in Hebrew as *Maavak medina be-malkodet: Yehudey Polin, 1935–39* (Tel Aviv, 1982).

59. On the problem of the violation of equal rights for Jews in interwar Poland, see Bernard D. Weinryb, *Jewish Emancipation under Attack* (New York, 1942), 32–34, 63–64; and Jerzy Tomaszewski, "The Civil Rights of Jews in Poland," *Polin* 8 (1994): 115–28.

60. Jerzy Tomaszewski, "Beck-Drymmer-Zarychta (w dyplomatycznej kuchni lat trzydziestych)," forthcoming in a festschrift dedicated to Andrzej Garlicki. I would like to thank Professor Tomaszewski for giving me this article.

61. See Brubaker, "Nationalizing," 421–25.

62. Mendelsohn, "German and Jewish," 51–64.

63. See Melzer, "Anti-Semitism," 126–40.

64. On the Roman Catholic Church's position on Jews in the Catholic press, see Jagiełło, *Próba*, 1: 77–164; Ronald Modras, *The Catholic Church and Anti-Semitism: Poland, 1933–1939* (Chur, 1994), 79–87; Ronald Modras, "The Catholic Press in Interwar Poland and the 'Jewish Question': Metaphor and the Developing Rhetoric of Exclusion," *East European Jewish Affairs* 24, no. 1 (1994): 49–69; Anna Laudau-Czajka, "The Image of the Jew in the Catholic Press during the Second Republic," *Polin* 8 (1994): 146–75; Franciszek Adamski, "The Jewish Question in Polish Religious Periodicals in the Second Republic: The Case of the *Przegląd katolicki*," *Polin* 8 (1994): 129–46. On the attitudes of the Roman Catholic Church in Cracow toward Jews, see Victoria Pollmann, *Untermieter im Christlichen Haus: Die kirche und die "judische Frage" in Polen anhand der Bistumspresse der Metropolie Krakau 1926–1939* (Wiesbaden, 2001).

65. Jagiełło, *Próba*, 1: 140–50; and Dariusz Libionka, "Kwestia żydowska -myślenie za pomocą clichés. 'Odrodzenie' 1935–1939. Przyczynek do historii antysemityzmu w Polsce," *Dzieje Najnowsze*, no. 3 (1995): 31–46.

66. "Deklaracja ideowa Stowarzyszenia Młodzieży Akademickiej Odrodzenie," *Prąd*, nos. 4–5 (1923). A large excerpt is cited in Jagiełło, *Próba*, 1: 144–45.

67. Stefan Świeżawski, "Plantacja Ducha Świętego," *Apokryf*, no. 12, special section of *Tygodnik Powszechny*, Dec. 1997, 18.

68. On the importance of the Catholic Church in the Polish society of interwar Poland, see, e.g., Kruszewski, "Nationalism," 150–52.

69. See Gutman, "Polish," 152.

70. This data is cited in Andrzej Paczkowski, *Prasa polska 1918–1939* (Warsaw, 1980), 222–23.

71. On the history, popularity, and circulation of *Mały Dziennik*, see Paczkowski, *Prasa*, 222–23; and Witold Mysłek, *Kościół katolicki w Polsce w latach 1918–1939* (Warsaw, 1966), 201–5.

72. "How the Jew Was Stealing Money from the Treasury and at the Same Time Poisoning

the Goys," *Mały Dziennik*, 26 June 1936; "Terrible Conditions in the Jewish Factory," *Mały Dziennik*, 28 June 1935; and "Jewish Educators Poison Our Children with the Venom of Hatred and Atheism," *Mały Dziennik*, 25 June 1935.

73. "A myśmy . . . ślepi," *Przegląd Powszechny*, 7 Dec. 1922, cited in Laudau-Czajka, "The Image," 169. Similar rhyming poems were published in the radical ethno-nationalist monthly for university students *Alma Mater*. See, e.g., *Alma Mater*, no. 10 (1938): 7.

74. Ryszard Michalski, *Obraz żyda i narodu Żydowskiego na łamach polskiej prasy pomorskiej w latach 1920–1939* (Torun, 1997), 26–30.

75. On the links between Endecja and the Roman Catholic Church, see Grott, *Nacjonalizm*, 89–93; and Mysłek, *Kościół*, 199–205.

76. Mysłek, *Kościół*, 201.

77. Dariusz Libionka, "Duchowieństwo diecezji łomżynskiej wobec antysemityzmu i zagłady Żydów," in Pawel Machcewicz and Krzysztof Persak, eds., *Wokół Jedwabnego* (Warsaw, 2002), 1: 105–28.

78. See, e.g., Franciszek Błotnicki, "Kościół- Naród i Państwo," *Pro Christo*, no. 3 (Mar. 1937): 42. This article was reprinted from another Catholic paper, *Gazeta Kościelna*, 17 Jan. 1937.

79. "Katolicyzm, rasizm i sprawa żydowska," *Myśl Narodowa*, no. 51 (1935): 1–2.

80. On the perception of Jews as the chief threatening other to the German nation and state during the interwar period, see Omer Bartov, "Defining Enemies, Making Victims: Germans, Jews, and the Holocaust," *American Historical Review* 13, no. 3 (1998): 771–816; and Bartov, *Mirrors*, 91–142. For a comparison of Polish and German political anti-Semitism prior to 1939, see Hagen, "Before," 351–81. On the little-researched subject of German evaluation of Endecja's attitudes toward Jews, see Paweł Stachowiak, "Rozwoj ruchów nacjonalistycznych w Polsce w opiniach publicystyki niemieckiej lat trzydziestych," in Czesław Mojsiewicz and Krzysztof Glass, eds., *Przezwyciężenie wrogości i nacjonalizmu w Europie* (Torun-Poznan, 1993), 45–52.

81. "Trzy synagogi zapłonęły w Berlinie na wieść o śmierci vom Ratha. Obłąkani żydzi nie zaspokoili się krwią trzeciorzędnego urzędnika," *Mały Dziennik*, 11–12 Nov. 1938, 2. On the little-researched subject of the perception of German atrocities in Endecja's press, see Karol Grunberg, "The Atrocities against the Jews in the Third Reich as seen by the National-Democratic Press," *Polin* 5 (1990): 103–13.

82. See Colonel Adam Koc, "Ideowo-polityczna deklaracja płk. A. Koca," *Przegląd Katolicki*, 28 Feb. 1937, 130–32.

83. Leslie et al., *The History*, 145.

84. For the history of the economic structure of Polish Jewry, see Rafael Mahler, *Yehude polin ben shte milhamot ha-olam* (Tel Aviv, 1968). For a concise overview of the subject, see Mendelsohn, *The Jews*, 26–28; and Steinlauf, *Bondage*, 16–17.

85. See, e.g., *Alma Mater*, nos. 6–7 (1938): 14; and *Mały Dziennik*, 2 June 1935, 3.

86. A forthcoming bibliography, *The "Jewish Question" in Interwar Poland, 1918–1939*, prepared by two scholars, Hanna Volovici and Eugenia Prokop-Janiec, provides a

good picture of the various anti-Jewish idioms employed in books and booklets of the interwar period. I would like to thank both scholars for showing me their work and discussing particular publications.

87. "Głos Prymasa Polski," *Rycerz Niepokalanej*, May 1936, cited in Landau-Czajka, "The Image," 170.

88. The theme of Judeo-Communism deserves its own monograph. On the problem of studying Judeo-Communism, see Andre Gerrits, "Anti-Semitism and Anti-Communism: The Myth of 'Judeo-Communism' in Eastern Europe," *East European Jewish Affairs* 25, no. 1 (1995): 49–72.

89. On Communist revolts and the fear of Communism in the Weimar Republic, see Richard J. Evans, *The Coming of the Third Reich* (London, 2005), 156–75.

90. For incisive remarks on the popularity of identifying Jews with Communism in the aftermath of the Russian Revolution, see Richard Pipes, "Jews and the Russian Revolution: A Note," *Polin* 9 (1996): 55–57.

91. For an analysis of this phenomenon, see Irena Kamińska-Szmaj, *Judzi, zohydza, ze czci odziera. Język propagandy politycznej w prasie 1919–1923* (Wroclaw, 1994), 143–49.

92. Stanisław Rybarkiewicz, *O Żydach wiadomości pożyteczne* (Warsaw, 1920), 1–15.

93. See Andrzej Korboński, "The Revival of the Political Right in Post-Communist Poland: Historical Roots," in Joseph Held, ed., *Democracy and Right-Wing Politics in Eastern Europe in the 1990s* (New York, 1993), 16.

94. On the subject of attempts at Communist rebellion and Communist attitudes to the Polish-Soviet War of 1920, see Antoni Czubiński, *Komunistyczna Partia Polski (1918–1938). Zarys historii* (Warsaw, 1985), 42–71.

95. Stanisław Trzeciak, "W obliczu grozy," *Pro Christo*, no. 3 (Mar. 1937): 1.

96. Waldemar Olszewski, *U źródeł antysemityzmu* (Wilno, 1937), 1–12.

97. Karol Stojanowski, *Chłop a państwo narodowe* (Poznan, 1937), 21.

98. See Rudnicki, *Obóz*, 300–303.

99. Koc, "Ideowo-polityczna deklaracja," 131.

100. On the popular interwar interpretation of KPP as a party representing foreign ideology, see Krystyna Trembicka, *Między apologią a negacją. Studium myśli politycznej Komunistycznej Partii Polski w latach 1918–1932* (Lublin, 1995), 11.

101. On the internal divisions within the leadership of the KPP on the issues of Polish national traditions and identity, and independence, see Trembicka, *Między apologią*, 135–63; and Bogdan Kolebacz, *Komunistyczna Partia Polski 1923–1929. Problemy ideologiczne* (Warsaw, 1984), 11–97.

102. On the history of the KPP, see Czubiński, *Komunistyczna Partia*; and Gabriele Simoncini, *The Communist Party of Poland 1918–1929: A Study in Political Ideology* (Lampeter, 1993).

103. In the new scholarship on Polish thought about Bolshevism in interwar Poland the scope of Judeo-Communism seems to be ignored or only partially acknowledged and discussed. For example, in the first anthology of Polish thought on Communism in

English the theme of Judeo-Communism is not mentioned at all, despite the fact that the author notes some texts, including one by Roman Dmowski, in which Judeo-Communism is advocated as a historical and social fact. See Bogdan Szlachta, *Polish Perspectives on Communism* (Lanham MD, 2004). In his two-volume study Marek Kornat discusses the presence of Judeo-Communism in the ideology of the radical right-wing ONR camp and in the writings of some Catholic thinkers such as Feliks Koneczny. However, Kornat displays some difficulty in dealing with the theme of Judeo-Communism as pronounced in the writings of Roman Dmowski. See Marek Kornat, *Bolszewizm totalitaryzm rewolucja Rosja. Początki sowietologii i studiów nad systemami totalitarnymi w Polsce (1918–1939)* (Cracow, 2004), 2: 216–21.

104. This slogan comes from a lecture by Stanisław Trzeciak, cited in *Mały Dziennik*, 22 Mar. 1936, 5.

105. On the membership of Jews in the KPP and their role in the party, see Jaff Schatz, *The Generation: The Rise and Fall of the Jewish Communists of Poland* (Berkeley, Los Angeles, and Oxford, 1991), 75–102. See also Moshe Mishkinsky, "The Communist Party of Poland and the Jews," in Gutman et al., *The Jews*, 56–74. The latter also contains an important discussion of the Communist perspective on anti-Semitism.

106. See Czubiński, *Komunistyczna Partia*, 130–31.

107. The data regarding support of Jewish voters for the Communist movement in 1928 is cited in Schatz, *The Generation*, 98.

108. Jeffrey S. Kopstein and Jason Wittenberg, "Who Voted Communist? Reconsidering the Social Bases of Radicalism in Interwar Poland," *Slavic Review* 62, no. 1 (2003): 106.

109. Czubiński, *Komunistyczna Partia*, 214–15.

110. Roman Dmowski, "Przewrót," in Roman Wapiński, ed., *Roman Dmowski. Wybór pism* (Warsaw, 1990), 323.

111. Roman Dmowski, *Dziedzictwo*, 2d ed. (Poznan, 1935).

112. Czerwiński, *Pamiętnik*, 28 (voice of Wacław Sobieski).

113. Leslie et al., *The History*, 142.

114. For a discussion of the major social and economic problems of Poland in the interwar period, see Leslie et al., *The History*, 139–46.

115. Kazimiera Muszałówna, "Antysemityzm—wróg Polski," in *Polacy*, 112.

116. On Jewish MPs in the Polish parliament, see Szymon Rudnicki, *Żydzi w parlamencie polskim* (Warsaw, 2004).

117. "Report of the Parliamentary Session," no. 71, 17 Feb. 1938, 156, *Sprawozdania Stenograficzne*, Sejm Rzeczypospolitej Polskiej, Kadencja IV, Sesja zwyczajna 1937–38 (voice of MP Emil Sommerstein). *Sprawozdania Stenograficzne* of Sejm Rzeczypospolitej Polskiej of the interwar period are held in the collection of the Archiwum Akt Nowych (Archives of New Documents) and the Archiwum Sejmu (Archives of the Parliament). I would like to thank Dr. Poldek Lustig and Helga Lustig for giving me the collection of *Sprawozdania Stenograficzne*, 1935–39, which were part of their private collection.

118. Jaszczuk, *Spór*, 232.
119. Roman Dmowski, "Historia szlachetnego socjalisty—przyczynek do psychologii politycznej społeczeństwa polskiego," *Przegląd Wszechpolski* (1903), 758–72, cited in Toruńczyk, *Narodowa*, 174.
120. Mieczysław Skrudlik, *Sprawa Skrudlika* (Poznan, 1923), 10–14.
121. On this subject, see Jerzy Tomaszewski, "Dokumenty o zaburzeniach antysemickich na Uniwersytecie Warszawskim na jesieni 1931 roku," *BZIH*, no. 2 (1997): 77; and Rudnicki, *Obóz*, 112–13.
122. PPS *wrogiem ludu pracującego i sługa żydowskiego kapitału* (Lodz, 1938), 1–30 (publication of Stronnictwo Narodowe).
123. Rudnicki discusses such a strategy in *Obóz*, 113.
124. Małgorzata Domagalska describes the episode of the public labeling of Wojciech Wasiutyński as a Jew in " 'Najpilniejsza sprawa,' Publicyści 'Prosto z mostu' wobec kwestii żydowskiej," *BZIH*, nos 3–4 (2002): 483–500. See also Paweł Wroński, "Pan Wojciech," *Gazeta Wyborcza*, 13–14 Jan. 2001, 18–19. Wasiutyński himself never alluded to this episode in his prolific post-1945 writings.
125. Councilor Kowalski, speech, Łódź Municipal Council, 27 Mar. 1935, Łódź State Archives, Municipal Council 1935, Protocol 10, 34 (87).
126. Jewish converts, a large number of whom lived in medieval Spain, remained clearly identified as "new Christians." They formed a separate community between Christians and Jews, indicating that their conversion did not automatically incorporate them fully into Spanish Christian society. There is a large body of literature dedicated to the treatment of Jews and Conversos in medieval Spain. On medieval Spanish attitudes toward "new Christians," see, e.g., the classic study Almog, *Nationalism*, 3–4; Edward Peters, "Jewish History and Gentile Memory: The Expulsion of 1492," *Jewish History*, no. 9 (1995): 9–34; and Jonathan Elukin, "From Jew to Christian: Conversion and Immutability in Medieval Europe," in James Muldoon, ed., *Varieties of Religious Conversion in the Middle Ages* (Gainesville, 1997), 171–89.
127. Landau-Czajka describes cases of denying converted Jews membership within the Polish nation in "Image," 152–54.
128. On cases of the negative approach of well-known conservative intellectuals toward converted Jews, see Melzer, "Anti-Semitism," 135–36; and Laudau-Czajka, *W jednym*, 251–52. The subject of converted Jews in interwar Polish society still needs a separate scholarly analysis.
129. Zofia Kossak-Szczucka, "Nie istnieją sytuacje bez wyjścia," *Kultura* (1936), cited in Landau-Czajka, "Image," 165–66.
130. Rudnicki describes this event in *Obóz*, 307.
131. See the column "Przegląd prasowy" about the debate in Ateneum Kapłańskie on the "Jewish question," in *Przegląd Katolicki*, 23 June 1935, 433.
132. "Przegląd prasowy," *Przegląd Katolicki*, 23 June 1935, 433.
133. Linguistic and cultural assimilation among Polish Jews, particularly among the

younger generation, was on the increase during the postindependence phase (1918–39). In the 1921 census a quarter of those who declared their religion as Jewish declared their nationality as Polish. See Mendelsohn, *The Jews*, 23, 29. According to the same author, "polonization of the Jewish community certainly increased in the 1930s, and Polish became the main language of even Zionist publications, all this despite the dramatic rise of anti-Semitism." See Mendelsohn, "German and Jewish," 60.

134. On the importance of language in ethno-nationalist projects of the self-purification of nations, see Kedourie, *Nationalism*, 108–9; and Smith, "Ethnic Nationalism," 190–91.

135. *Kurier Warszawski*, 21 Feb. 1921, 2.

136. See, e.g., Stanisław Pieńkowski, "Poezja kryptożydowska," *Myśl Narodowa*, no. 41 (1926): 234–36; Jan Rembieliński, "Na Widowni," *Myśl Narodowa*, no. 45 (1931): 178–79, and no. 47 (1931): 209–10; and Zygmunt Wasilewski, "Na Widowni," *Myśl Narodowa*, no. 10 (1935): 170–71. On the anti-Semitism of Zygmunt Wasilewski, see Eugenia Prokop-Janiec, *Literatura i nacjonalizm. Twórczość krytyczna Zygmunta Wasilewskiego* (Cracow, 2004). On anti-Semitism among various cultural leaders of National Democracy, see Małgorzata Domagalska, *Antysemityzm dla inteligencji?* (Warsaw, 2004).

137. On the subject of National Democratic treatment of acculturated Polish Jews, see Eugenia Prokop-Janiec, *Polish-Jewish Literature in the Interwar Period* (Syracuse, 2003), 69–82 (originally published in Polish in 1992); and Domagalska, " 'Najpilniejsza,' " 483–500. See also essays on Julian Tuwim and Antoni Słonimski written by the controversial Marxist literary critic Artur Sandauer, in *Pisma*, 3: 463–74; Bauman, "Literary Afterlife," 273–99; Magnus J. Kryński, "Politics and Poetry: The Case of Julian Tuwim," *Polish Review*, no. 4 (1974): 11–14; and Antony Polonsky, "Why Did They Hate Tuwim and Boy So Much? Jews and 'Artificial Jews' in the Literary Polemics in the Second Polish Republic," in Robert Blobaum, ed., *Anti-Semitism and Its Opponents in Poland* (Ithaca, 2005).

138. The issue of ethno-nationalist attacks on Marceli Hendelsman is discussed in Monika Natkowska, *Numerus clausus, getto ławkowe, numerus nullus, paragraf aryjski. Antysemityzm na Uniwersytecie Warszawskim, 1931–1939* (Warsaw, 1999), 59–74.

139. Czerwiński, *Pamiętnik I Konferencji Żydoznawczej*, 56 (voice of the editor, Mieczysław Czerwiński).

140. *Kurier Warszawski*, 13 Mar. 1921, 9.

141. On the project of the cultural purification of the nation by ethno-nationalists, see Smith, "Ethnic Nationalism," 191–92.

142. See, e.g., the article by Stefan Kaczorowski in *Pro Christo*, no. 7 (July 1933): 4.

143. Reverent Stanisław Trzeciak, *Pornografia narzędziem obcych agentur* (Warsaw, 1929), 45.

144. "O unarodowienie życia polskiego," *Mały Dziennik*, 13–14 Nov. 1938, 5. The same issue includes an article explaining why the nationalization of all forms of social, cultural,

and economic life was urgently needed in Poland: J. Z., "Dlaczego rozpisujemy ankietę p.t. 'Jak unarodowić życie w Polsce!' " 4.

145. Adam Heydel, *Myśli o kulturze* (Warsaw, 1936), 39.

146. Cała, *The Image*, 39–41.

147. This slogan was promulgated by the writer and critic Karol Hubert Rostworowski. Cited in Tadeusz Bielecki, *Zarys idei społeczno-politycznych* (Warsaw, 1938), 15.

148. This slogan is cited in Landau-Czajka, *W jednym*, 219–20.

149. *Mały Dziennik*, 26 Oct. 1935, 4.

150. On the prominence of the extreme ethno-nationalist position in professional organizations, see Jan Józef Lipski, *Katolickie Państwo Narodu Polskiego* (London, 1994), 139–40.

151. Ludwik Jaxa-Bykowski, "Poziom intelektualny młodzieży polskiej i żydowskiej w naszych gimnazjach," *Psychometria*, no. 1 (1933): 1–27. On Professor Ludwik Jaxa-Bykowski, see Tadeusz Bartoszewski, *Warto być przyzwoitym człowiekiem* (Warsaw, 1990), 184.

152. Partia Pracy, 1938 program, cited in Olaf and Pasternak, *Programy*, 190.

153. Trzeciak, "W obliczu," 7.

154. For a detailed description of the emigration programs advocated by various political parties, see Laudau-Czajka, *W jednym*, 240–68; Mich, *Obcy*, 55–67; and Paruch, *Od konsolidacji*, 231–46, 283–360.

155. See Lipski, *Katolickie*, 138–42.

156. ONR program, in Olaf and Pasternak, *Programy*, 49.

157. See Steinlauf, *Bondage*, 16–17.

158. See Studnicki, *Sprawa*, 4–5.

159. On the way ethnic nationalists exclude minority groups from membership within a nation, see Brubaker, "Nationalizing," 430; and Smith, "Ethnic Nationalism," 193.

160. The two most striking examples of works representing opposing points of view on the subject are Celia Heller, *On the Edge of Destruction: Jews of Poland between the Two World Wars* (New York, 1977); and Joseph Marcus, *Social and Political History of the Jews in Poland, 1919–1939* (Berlin, New York, and Amsterdam, 1983).

161. Hagen, "Before," 352.

4. The Myth and Anti-Jewish Violence

1. On exclusivist ethno-nationalism and antiminority hostilities, see Smith, "Ethnic Nationalism," 196–98; and Kecmanovic, *Mass Psychology*, 132–50. There is a vast literature on riots and pogroms. For an important analysis of various approaches to the subject, see Paul R. Brass, "Introduction: Discourse of Ethnicity, Communalism and Violence," in Paul R. Brass, *Riots and Pogroms* (New York, 1996), 1–55. On the importance of emotions and symbols in riots and ethnic violence, see Stuart J. Kaufman, *Modern Hatreds: The Symbolic Politics of Ethnic War* (Ithaca and London, 2001); and Roger D. Petersen, *Understanding Ethnic Violence: Fear, Hatred and Resentment in Twentieth-Century Eastern Europe* (Cambridge, 2002). The historical use of emotions

and symbols in anti-Jewish violence in Poland has not been discussed, except in Joanna Michlic-Coren, "Anti-Jewish Violence in Poland, 1918–1939 and 1945–1947," *Polin* 13 (2000): 34–61. This chapter is an expanded version of this article.

2. See Michlic-Coren, "Anti-Jewish," 34, 44.

3. See Jerzy Tomaszewski, "Pińsk, Saturday 5 April 1919," *Polin* 1 (1986): 227–51; and Sarunas Liekes, Lidia Miliakova, and Antony Polonsky, "Three Documents on Anti-Jewish Violence in the Eastern Kresy during the Polish-Soviet Conflict," *Polin* 14 (2001): 116–49.

4. See Jerzy Tomaszewski, "Trzeci maja 1919 roku w Rzeszowie," *Almanach Żydowski*, 1996–97, 7–16; and Adam Penkalla, "The Przytyk Incidents of 9 March 1936 from Archival Documents," *Polin* 5 (1990): 327–59.

5. On anti-Jewish hostilities, see Melzer, *No Way Out*, 53–80, 131–53; Modras, *The Catholic*, 301–23; Jolanta Żyndul, *Zajścia antyżydowskie w Polsce w latach 1935–1937* (Warsaw, 1994); Joshua Rothenberg, "The Przytyk Pogrom," *Soviet Jewish Affairs* 16, no. 2 (1986): 40. On anti-Jewish hostilities at universities, see Natkowska, *Numerus clausus*; and Rudnicki, *Obóz*. On attitudes toward Jews in the Polish Army, see Józef Lewandowski, "History and Myth: Pińsk, April 1919," *Polin* 2 (1987): 50–72.

6. See Golczewski, *Polnisch-Jüdische*, 181–245.

7. William Hagen, "The Moral Economy of Popular Violence: The Pogrom in Lwów, November 1918," in Blobaum, *Anti-Semitism*. I would like to thank Professor Hagen for giving me permission to cite the article. See also an article by the same author on German-Jewish reactions to anti-Jewish violence in Poland: William W. Hagen, "Murder in the East: German-Jewish Liberal Reactions to anti-Jewish Violence in Poland and Other East European Lands, 1918–1920," *Central European History* 34, no. 1 (2001): 1–30.

8. Józef Lewandowski was perhaps the first scholar to discuss Polish historians' partisan approach toward anti-Jewish riots conducted by the Polish Army between 1918 and 1920. He argues that "historians become the high priests of the nation's memory and memory itself acquires the characteristics of a cult; it becomes something one believes in." See Lewandowski, "History," 64–69. Hagen also makes brief remarks on the nationalistic approach of historians whose work contains anti-Semitic rhetoric. See Hagen, "The Moral," 7, 32.

9. Piotr Gontarczyk, *Pogrom? Zajścia polsko-żydowskie w Przytyku 9 marca 1936 r. Mity, Fakty, Dokumenty* (Biala Podlaska-Pruszkow, 2000), 132–37. Documents constitute half of this book. For critical essays on this book, see Jolanta Żyndul, "If Not a Pogrom, Then What?" and "It Was No Ordinary Fight," *Polin* 17 (2004): 385–91. These articles were first published in *Gazeta Wyborcza* on 8 and 28 Mar. 2001.

10. See Michlic-Coren, "Anti-Jewish," 35.

11. On the pogrom in Lwów, see Golczewski, *Polnisch-Jüdische*, 185–205; and Hagen, "The Moral."

12. On the Pińsk riot, see Golczewski, *Polnisch-Jüdische*, 219–29; and A. Shohat, "Parashat

hapogrom bepinsk behamishah be'april 1919," *Gal-Ed* 1 (1973): 135–73. See also Jerzy Tomaszewski, "Polskie formacje zbrojne wobec Żydow 1918–1920," in Tomaszewski, *Żydzi w obronie Rzeczypospolitej*, 97–111; and Żyndul, *Zajścia antyżydowskie*, 9.

13. On the hostilities in Lida and Wilno, see Golczewski, *Polnisch-Jüdische*, 229–33.

14. See Witold Stankiewicz, *Konflikty społeczne na wsi polskiej 1918–1920* (Warsaw, 1963), 159–63; Tomaszewski, "Trzeci maja," 7–16.

15. The data is cited in Stankiewicz, *Konflikty*, 162.

16. See reports on student anti-Jewish demonstrations in *Sprawy Narodowościowe*, no. 6 (1931): 644–54, and no. 6 (1932): 698–703.

17. On the issue of the linking anti-Jewish and antigovernment actions by National Democracy in the early 1930s, see Rudnicki, *Obóz*, 58–59.

18. The owp (1926–33) was an umbrella organization of various right-wing and center political parties, unified in order to fight the Sanacja government. Its leadership was in the hands of the "younger" generation of the National Democracy movement, which enjoyed the full support of Dmowski. The owp was a fast-growing political movement, gaining popularity not only among students but also among workers and the lower middle class. In Jan. 1930 the owp numbered 35,000 individuals, by May 1932 its membership had increased to 120,000, and by early 1933 it had reached almost a quarter million. On the development of the owp and structural changes within Endecja, see Grott, *Nacjonalizm*, 80–85.

19. On the participation of various student organizations in anti-Jewish violence, see Rudnicki, *Obóz*, 72–75; and Szymon Rudnicki, "From 'Numerus Clausus' To 'Numerus Nullus,'" *Polin* 2 (1987): 246–68.

20. See Rudnicki, *Obóz*, 73.

21. Rudnicki, *Obóz*, 70–75.

22. On Jewish student reactions condemning the "numerus clausus" policy, see, e.g., Rabinowicz, *The Legacy*, 104–6.

23. On the anti-Jewish hostilities of the onr in the late spring and early summer of 1934, see the report "Żydzi," *Sprawy Narodowościowe*, no. 4 (1934): 474.

24. See the report "Żydzi," 286.

25. See Melzer, "Anti-Semitism," 126–37.

26. See mp Izaak Rubinsztein, speech, *Sprawozdanie stenograficzne z 14 posiedzenia z dnia 21 lutego 1936 Kadencja IV Sesja zwyczajna* (1935–36): 60–61.

27. On the policy of "ghetto benches," see Melzer, *No Way*, 71–80. At the Lwów Polytechnic the "ghetto benches" system was introduced by the dean's council in two departments in Dec. 1935, two years before the government officially granted universities power to regulate the seating of students. However, violence continued at the polytechnic between Jan. and Mar. 1936, and therefore this regulation was abolished the same year. See "Wystąpienia żydowskie i ich echa," *Sprawy Narodowościowe*, nos. 1–2 (1936): 107.

28. For a list of foreign and Polish organizations and individuals protesting the policy of

"ghetto benches" and anti-Jewish campus violence, see *Memorandum on Anti-Jewish Excesses* (London, 1938), 1–3. Also see the writings of Polish authors condemning campus violence, such as Ryszard Ganszyniec, *Ghetto Ławkowe* (L'viv, 1937); and Antoni Gronowicz, *Antysemityzm rujnuje moją ojczyznę* (L'viv, 1938).

29. See Jolanta Żyndul, "Zajścia antyżydowskie 1935–1937. Geografia i formy," *BZIH*, no. 3 (1991): 69.

30. The article from the *Warszawski Dziennik Narodowy* is cited in the report "Żydzi," *Sprawy Narodowościowe*, no. 5 (1935): 481. On the problem of anti-Jewish terror between 1935 and 1937, see also Mich, *Obcy*, 84–89.

31. Jewish sources in Palestine presented higher figures of injured and killed than did Polish sources. For a discussion of these figures, see Żyndul, "Zajścia," 70–71.

32. See Żyndul, "Zajścia," 58.

33. A faction within the National Democracy movement objected to the bombing of synagogues on the grounds that they were not fighting against Judaism as a religion but against the "judaization" of Poland. See Żyndul, "Zajścia," 58.

34. St. P., "W szrankach polemiki," *Alma Mater*, no. 3 (1939): 6–7.

35. Zbigniew Dymecki, "W obliczu czerwonego niebezpieczeństwa. Agentury komunizmu w Polsce," *Alma Mater*, nos. 6–7 (1938): 4.

36. Adolf Reutt, speech, "Rola Polski wśród innych narodów wielkich," published in *Pro Christo*, no. 11 (Nov. 1936): 10–12.

37. See Żyndul, *Zajścia antyżydowskie*, 67–68.

38. For a discussion of the circulation and readership of various ethno-nationalist journals, both the official press of the National Democracy movement and newspapers that expressed ideological positions similar to those of National Democracy, see Paczkowski, *Prasa*, 275–90.

39. For a discussion of the radical tabloid press, see Paczkowski, *Prasa*, 291–92. I would like to thank Professor Paczkowski for discussing this subject with me in detail.

40. On the elite of the ONR, see Lipski, "Antysemityzm," 96–97.

41. This case was reported in *Warszawski Dziennik Narodowy*, no. 31 (1937), cited in Żyndul, *Zajścia antyżydowskie*, 92.

42. Stanley Cohen was the first sociologist to use the term *moral panic* and to note the collective behavior–like quality of this phenomenon. On the subject of "moral panic" and its elements, see Erich Goode and Nachman Ben-Yehuda, *Moral Panics: The Social Construction of Deviance* (Oxford and Cambridge MA, 1994), 31–53.

43. On the portrayal of Jews as Bolsheviks between 1918 and 1920, see Golczewski, *Polnisch-Jüdische*, 233–40.

44. See the document on the events that took place in the town of Lida after the entry of the Polish Legion, in the Collection of the Supreme Command of the Polish Army, Moscow Center for the Preservation of Historical Documents. This document was published in Liekes, Miliakova, and Polonsky, "Three Documents," 131.

45. On the importance of war as a factor in an increase of aggression and hostility toward

ethnic minorities, see Panikos Panayi, "Dominant Societies and Minorities in the Two World Wars," in Panikos Panayi, ed., *Minorities in Wartime* (Oxford and Providence, 1993), 3–23.

46. Arthur L. Goodhart, *Poland and the Minority Races* (London, 1920), 95.

47. For excerpts of Daszyński's speech, and also of Piłsudski's and other PPS politicians' condemnations of anti-Jewish violence, see *Evidence of Pogroms in Poland and Ukraine: Documents, Accounts of Eye-witnesses, Proceedings in Polish Parliament, Local Press Reports, Etc.* (New York, 1919?), 163–66. This book was issued by the Committee for the Defense of Jews in Poland and other East European Countries, affiliated with the American Jewish Committee. It was one of the first popular publications in English presenting a whole spectrum of views and history of, and Jewish responses to, the riots and pogroms.

48. See the statement of General Józef Leśniewski, cited at length in the introduction to Liekes, Miliakova, and Polonsky, "Three Documents," 120.

49. Tomaszewski, "Polskie," 100. On attitudes among the Polish military elite toward the Jewish community, see Lewandowski, "History," 50–72.

50. Roman Halny, "Ze Lwowa," *Robotnik*, 19 Dec. 1918, 1.

51. See the statement of Ignacy Dzaszyński, from *La Situation des Juifs en Pologne: Rapport de la commission d'étude dèsignèe par la Conférence Socialiste Internationale de Lucerne* (1920), cited in the introduction to Liekes, Miliakova, and Polonsky, "Three Documents," 118.

52. Goodhart, *Poland*, 21.

53. On the importance of the notion of national honor and reputation in Polish national discourse, see Iwona Irwin-Zarecka, *Frames of Remembrance* (New Brunswick and London, 1994), 81–82.

54. On German-Jewish liberals' responses to anti-Jewish hostilities in Poland, see Hagen, "Murder." The article also briefly examines the responses of other European and American Jewish communities.

55. See the statement of Dezydery Ostrowski, published in Tomaszewski, "Trzeci maja," 14.

56. This is from the political debate on student anti-Jewish riots in the autumn of 1931, reported in *Sprawy Narodowościowe*, no. 6 (1931): 651.

57. Andrzej Paczkowski, *Zdobycie władzy 1945–1947* (Warsaw, 1993), 64.

58. See Rothenberg, "Przytyk Pogrom," 40.

59. Rothenberg, "Przytyk Pogrom," 39–43.

60. See Żyndul, "Zajścia," 92.

61. "Dalszy ciąg procesu grodzieńskiego. Przemówienia stron," *Mały Dziennik*, 14 Nov. 1935, 4.

62. The pastoral letters of Hlond and Sapieha were published in the report on anti-Jewish riots found in *Sprawy Narodowościowe*, nos. 1–2 (1936): 107–8. The pastoral letter of Sapieha was also published in *Tygodnik Polski*, 5 Apr. 1936, 2.

63. The response of the Catholic Press Agency to the Przytyk pogrom was published in *Sprawy Narodowościowe*, no. 4 (1934): 474–75.

64. The report of the visit of a delegation of the Union of Rabbis of the Polish Republic to Cardinal Kakowski was published in *Sprawy Narodowościowe*, nos. 2–3 (1934): 285–86. In the aftermath of the meeting the Jewish community expressed shock and disillusionment with the cardinal's statement, whereas Zionists condemned the rabbis' visit to Kakowski as inappropriate.

65. The pattern of the Church's attitudes toward Jews from the earliest councils and popes focused on condemnation of violence against Jews (who had, after all, to be preserved as "witnesses to the true faith"), mixed with condemnation of the perfidy of Jews. On the pattern of the Church's attitudes toward Jews in the premodern and modern periods, see two classic studies: Moore, *The Formation*, 35–39; and Leon Poliakov, *The Aryan Myth* (London, 1974), 326–28.

66. For a detailed discussion of the ozn's political programs and policies toward Jews, see Paruch, *Od konsolidacji*, 283–319. See also Andrzej Chojnowski, *Koncepcje polityki narodowściowej rządów polskich w latach 1921–1939* (Wroclaw, 1979).

67. Wiktor Alter, *Antysemityzm gospodarczy w świetle cyfr* (Warsaw, 1937), 4. Leon Kruczkowski (1900–1962), a Polish left-wing writer and Communist, also wrote critical articles on cultural anti-Semites. See Leon Kruczkowski, "Antysemityzm kulturalny," in *Polacy*, 28–35.

68. For a summary of Świętochowski's position toward Jews, a subject of discussion in *Wiadomości Literackie* in Apr. 1937, see Modras, *The Catholic*, 372.

69. Aleksander Świętochowski, "Antysemityzm," *Wiadomości Literackie*, 16 Apr. 1937, 3.

70. On active condemnation of anti-Jewish violence by Polish political organizations and members of the cultural elite, see, e.g., Melzer, *No Way Out*, 64, 71–80.

71. On the presidential election of Dec. 1922 and the assassination of Gabriel Narutowicz, see Leslie et al., *The History*, 155; and Wandycz, *The Price*, 223–24.

72. "Po wyborze," *Gazeta Warszawska*, 11 Dec. 1922, 1.

73. "Tragiczny konflikt," *Gazeta Warszawska*, 17 Dec. 1922, 1.

74. For a description of this event, see Rudnicki, "From 'Numerus,'" 246–68.

75. To prevent further fighting the rector closed down the university and issued a statement condemning anti-Jewish violence, according to the report "Zajścia antyżydowskie," *Sprawy Narodowościowe*, no. 6 (1931): 647.

76. See the report "Zajścia antyżydowskie," 647.

77. See the report "Zajścia antyżydowskie," 646.

78. The data are based on the report "Akademickie wystąpienia antyżydowskie," *Sprawy Narodowościowe*, no. 6 (1932): 698–700.

79. Such references to Wacławski appeared in leaflets and brochures. The abovementioned onr leaflet was published in *Czas*, 2 Nov. 1936, cited in Rudnicki, "From 'Numerus,'" 266.

80. Melzer, "Anti-Semitism," 129.

81. See the report on Grotkowski's death and student anti-Jewish demonstrations in *Sprawy Narodowościowe*, no. 6 (1932): 700–703.
82. Rothenberg, "Przytyk Pogrom," 37.
83. See the document "Conclusions of the Investigation Signed by the Public Prosecutor S. Dotkiewicz," in Penkalla, "The Przytyk," 349.
84. Andrzej Penkalla, "Zajścia przytyckie 9 marca 1936 roku," *Kultura*, no. 9 (1989): 10.
85. Żyndul, "Zajścia," 66.
86. Rudnicki, *Obóz*, 295.
87. On the impact of anti-Jewish hostilities on interethnic relations between Poles and Jews, and on the decision-making process regarding emigration from Poland within the Jewish community, see Melzer, *No Way Out*, 53–80, 131–53. See also excerpts of testimonies of Jewish youth published by Alina Cała, "The Social Consciousness of Young Jews," *Polin* 8 (1994): 42–65.

5. Perceptions during the German Occupation

1. I view my analysis in this chapter as a point of departure for deeper analysis of certain subjects under discussion. A large body of primary sources crucial for an analysis of Polish attitudes toward Jews in WWII has been published in the last decade. See, e.g., Paweł Szapiro, ed., *Wojna żydowsko-niemiecka. Polska prasa konspiracyjna 1943–1944 o powstaniu w getcie Warszawy* (London, 1992); Kazimierz Przybysz, ed., *Wizje Polski. Programy polityczne lat wojny i okupacji 1939–1944* (Warsaw, 1992); and Wojciech Rojek and Andrzej Suchcitz, eds., *Protokoły Posiedzień Rady Ministrów Rzeczypospolitej Polskiej*, vols. 1–4 (Cracow, 1994–98). I base my analysis in this chapter on these published sources and on primary sources from the collections of the Yad Vashem Archives (YVA), the Archives of the Polish Institute, the Sikorski Museum, and the Jewish Historical Institute (ZIH).
2. On the subject of hostile perceptions by dominant nations of ethnic minorities in wartime, see Panayi, "Dominant," 3–23.
3. On the subject of the strengthening of ethnic self-consciousness and imagery in wartime in multinational societies, see Smith, "Warfare," 390.
4. The expression the "universe of national obligation" is a paraphrase of the "universe of human obligations," introduced by Helen Fein in *Accounting for Genocide: National Responses and Jewish Victimization during the Holocaust* (Chicago and London, 1984).
5. The subject of the exploitation of Polish domestic anti-Semitism by the Nazi regime still awaits a separate monograph. On the Polish-language Nazi press in Nazi-occupied Poland, see Lucjan Dobroszycki, *Journalism: The Official Polish-Language Press under the Nazis 1939–1945* (New Haven and London, 1994), 140–49.
6. Although there is vast literature on the Soviet occupation of eastern Poland, the subject of domestic Polish anti-Semitism and its exploitation by the Soviets has not been discussed in depth, neither the interplay between the two phenomena nor their impact on the situation of Jews. For the most extensive bibliography of secondary sources on the history of the Soviet occupation of Poland, see Jasiewicz, *Pierwsi*, 1243–

56. For a short discussion of the Soviet negotiations with Western powers over western Belarus and western Ukraine, see Piotr Wróbel, *The Devil's Playground: Poland in World War II*, published as *The Wanda Muszyński Lecture in Polish Studies* (Montreal: n.d.), 9–30; and Leslie et al., *The History*, 218–20.

7. Tomasz Gąsowski, *Pod sztandarami orła białego* (Cracow, 2002), 134–76 .

8. The 10 Sept. 1943 statement of PPS politician Józef Beloński condemning anti-Jewish attitudes and behavior among soldiers and officers of the Anders Army can be found in the YVA, Collection of Dr. Ignacy Schwarzbart, M2/152, 2–8. Beloński disputes the notion of "unique Jewish desertion" from the Polish Army by citing the official figures provided by the government-in-exile in the second half of 1943. The total official number of desertions from the army was cited as 1,368, with Jewish desertions at 621. Therefore ethnic Poles committed 724 desertions.

9. Only in the post-2000 period did Polish historians begin to address the subject of negative ideas about Jews in Polish society in WWII with rigorous historical analysis. The best and most important example of this is Dariusz Libionka, "Polska ludność chrześcijańska wobec eksterminacji Żydów—dystrykt lubelski," in Dariusz Libionka, ed., *Akcja Reinhard. Zagłada Żydów w Generalnym Gubernatorstwie* (Warsaw, 2004), 306–33. See also Barbara Engelking, *"Szanowny panie gistapo": Donosy do władz niemieckich w Warszawie i okolicach w latach 1940–1941* (Warsaw, 2003).

10. Shmuel Krakowski, "The Polish Underground and the Extermination of the Jews," *Polin* 9 (1996): 138.

11. See Gutman and Krakowski, *Unequal Victims*; Engel, *In the Shadow*; and Engel, *Facing the Holocaust*.

12. See, e.g., Tadeusz Bór-Komorowski, *The Secret Army* (New York, 1951); Kazimierz Iranek-Osmecki, *He Who Saves One Life* (New York, 1971); and Stefan Korboński, *The Jews and the Poles in World War II* (New York, 1989). See also Czesław Madajczyk's two-volume *Polityka III Rzeszy w okupowanej Polsce* (Warsaw, 1970), which is one of the main historical works on the Nazi occupation of Poland. It also contains some narratives regarding the self-defensive approach toward the treatment of Jews in Polish society in WWII. A good example of a historical study in English representing such a trend, although more aggressive and elaborated, is Richard C. Lukas, *The Forgotten Holocaust: The Poles under German Occupation, 1939–1944* (Lexington KY, 1986). Also see Jerzy Śląski, *Polska Walcząca*, vols. 1–6 (Warsaw, 1985–86).

13. For a discussion of apologetics, see Antony Polonsky, "Beyond Condemnation, Apologetics and Apologies: On the Complexity of Polish Behavior toward the Jews during the Second World War," in Jonathan Frankel, ed., *Studies in Contemporary Jewry* (Jerusalem, 1998), 13: 190–224. See also Polonsky's introduction to the volume *My Brother's Keeper? Recent Polish Debates on the Holocaust* (London, 1990); and Michlic-Coren, "The Troubling Past," 75–84. For the most recent discussion of the subject, see the main introduction in Polonsky and Michlic, *The Neighbors Respond*, 1–43. On the problem of apologetics in Polish historiography of the Holo-

caust, interesting observations are made by Jerzy Tomaszewski in the article "Polish Historiography on the Holocaust," in David Bankier and Israel Gutman, eds., *Nazi Europe and the Final Solution* (Jerusalem, 2003), 111–36. On the narrative of denial of any wrongdoings, see Michlic-Coren, "The Troubling Past," 75–84.

14. Michlic-Coren, "The Troubling Past," 81.

15. Israel Gutman, "The Attitude of the Poles to the Mass Deportations of Jews from the Warsaw Ghetto in the Summer of 1942," in Israel Gutman and Efraim Zuroff, eds., *Rescue Attempts during the Holocaust: Proceedings of the Second Yad Vashem International Historical Conference, Jerusalem, April 8–11, 1977* (Jerusalem, 1977), 399.

16. Alexander Donat, *The Holocaust Kingdom* (New York, 1965), 542.

17. Mordekhai Tenenbaum-Tamaroff, *Dapim min hadelakah* (Tel Aviv, 1947), 49–50.

18. Testimony of Sonia Orbach, YVA, 03/5268 (in Polish).

19. Emanuel Ringelblum, *Polish-Jewish Relations during the Second World War* (Evanston IL, 1992), 7–8. The work was written in the Warsaw Ghetto in the Polish language.

20. David Blatman, "The Past Refuses to Vanish," *East European Jewish Affairs* 27, no. 1 (1997): 57–60. For a discussion of the prewar school of history writing advocated by Jewish historians, see, e.g., Ruta Sakowska's introduction in Ruta Sakowska, ed., *Archiwum Ringelbluma. Konspiracyjne Archiwum Getta Warszawy*, vol. 1, *Listy o Zagładzie* (Warsaw, 1997), 11–13.

21. Ludwig Landau, a social historian, created this data, which is considered to be the most accurate for the first two years of WWII. In the aftermath of the German invasion of the Soviet Union, on 22 June 1941, the entire territory of prewar Poland came under German occupation. In Jan. 1944 the Red Army reentered the prewar Polish territory. See Bardach, Leśnodorski, and Pietrzak, *Historia*, 584; and Władysław Bartoszewski, "Polish-Jewish Relations, 1939–1945," in Abramsky, Jachimczyk, and Polonsky, *The Jews*, 149.

22. German occupation policies during WWII have given rise to a vast literature. Among the most important historical studies on the subject are Jan Tomasz Gross, *Polish Society under German Occupation: The General Government, 1939–1944*, 1st ed. (Princeton NJ, 1979); Martin Broszat, *Nationalsozialistische Polenpolitik 1939–1945* (Munich, 1963); Eugeniusz Duraczyński, *Wojna i okupacja* (Warsaw, 1974); and Madajczyk, *Polityka III Rzeszy*. For a concise history of Poland in WWII, see Leslie et al., *The History*, 209–80.

23. On the "Germanization" of the areas incorporated into the Reich, see Leslie et al., *The History*, 214–15.

24. Duraczyński, *Wojna*, 57–59. On Nazi racial perceptions and treatment of the Slavs, see John Connelly, "Nazis and Slavs: From Racial Theory to Racial Practice," *Central European History* 32, no. 1 (1999): 1–33.

25. See Durewicz, *Wojna*, 57–58; Władysław Bartoszewski, "Polish-Jewish Relations," 150; and Michael Burleigh and Wolfgang Wippermann, *The Racial State: Germany 1933–1945* (Cambridge, 1998), 72.

26. Władysław Bartoszewski, "Polish-Jewish Relations," 149–50.

27. Jerzy Stempowski, Letter to the Ministry of Information in the Polish Government-in-Exile, written in Lisbon, Portugal. The letter was received in London on 24 Oct. 1940. Stempowski's letter is in the archival collection of the Polish Institute in London, PRM-K-96, file no. 13, 144–45. Polish historiography incorporated wartime reflections about the similarity of the Nazi treatment of Jews and Poles in the first two years of the occupation. Some historians, e.g., Władysław Bartoszewski, argued that until the end of 1941 the overall German oppression of Polish and Jewish population "was separate but equal." See Bartoszewski, "Polish-Jewish Relations," 149–50.

28. Data cited in Lucy Dawidowicz, *A Holocaust Reader* (New York, 1976), 65–66.

29. Fein, *Accounting*, 213.

30. According to the historian Tomasz Szarota, the Warsaw municipal authorities distributed the same rationing coupons to the Jewish and Christian populations until Feb. 1940, when the Nazi authorities took over the rationing process. In July of the same year the difference between food rationing for ethnic Poles and Polish Jews increased drastically—698 and 331 calories per day, respectively. At the same time the German allocation of food was 2,310 calories per day. See Tomasz Szarota, *Okupowanej Warszawy Dzień Powszedni* (Warsaw, 1973), 180–81.

31. On the history of the Warsaw Ghetto, see Israel Gutman, *The Jews of Warsaw, 1939–1943: Ghetto, Underground, Revolt* (Brighton and Sussex, 1982); and one of the pioneering studies of the subject, Philip Friedman, ed., *Martyrs and Fighters: The Epic of the Warsaw Ghetto* (New York, 1954).

32. There is vast literature on the Holocaust. Among the most important studies on the mechanism of the Nazi genocidal program are the following: Omer Bartov, ed., *Holocaust: Origins, Implementation, Aftermath* (London and New York, 2000); Christopher R. Browning, *The Path to Genocide: Essays on Launching the Final Solution* (Cambridge, 1992); Christopher R. Browning, *The Origins of the Final Solution: The Evolution of Nazi Jewish Policy, September 1939–March 1 1942* (Lincoln, 2004); Raul Hilberg, *The Destruction of the European Jews*, 3d ed. (New Haven, 2003); and Leni Yahil, *The Holocaust: The Fate of European Jewry, 1932–1945* (New York and Oxford, 1990). The latter was originally published in 1987 in Hebrew as *Ha-Shoah: Goral Yehude Europah, 1932–1945*.

33. At the beginning of 1942 the Germans built three death camps in Bełzec, Sobibór, and Treblinka. Auschwitz started to operate as the combined labor camp Auschwitz I and the death camp Auschwitz II–Birkenau in May of the same year. The first death camp was built in Chełmno in late 1941. Polish Jews from the Warta region were murdered there. For the history and historiography of the death camps, see Jeremy Noakes and Geoffrey Pridham, eds., *Nazism 1919–1945*, vol. 3, *Foreign Policy, War and Racial Extermination* (Exeter, 1988), 1137–68.

34. Leslie et al., *The History*, 217–18.

35. See Gross, *Polish Society*, 259–91.

36. Bardach, Leśnodorski, and Pietrzak, *Historia*, 615.

37. On the general history of the government-in-exile and its institutions, see Eugeniusz Duraczyński, *O Polsce na uchodźstwie: Rada Narodowa Rzeczypospolitej Polskiej, 1939–1945* (Warsaw, 1997).

38. See Steinlauf, *Bondage*, 26–27.

39. On the importance of the patriotic "Decalogue" in the life of the underground state, see Szarota, *Okupowanej Warszawy*, 436–37.

40. For a more detailed discussion of this subject, see Engel, *Facing the Holocaust*, 17–23; see also David Engel, "Possibilities of Rescuing Polish Jewry under German Occupation and the Influence of the Polish Government-in-Exile," in Bankier and Gutman, *Nazi Europe*, 136–48.

41. See the minutes of the National Council, 9 Jan. 1940, Angers, in Rojek and Suchcitz, *Protokoły*, 1: 154–55.

42. Rojek and Suchcitz, *Protokoły*, 1: 155.

43. Rojek and Suchcitz, *Protokoły*, 1: 154.

44. For a list of Jewish officers in the Polish armed forces, see a work written by one such officer: Benjamin Meirtchak, *Jew-Officers in the Polish Armed Forces, 1939–1945* (Tel Aviv, 2001).

45. On the situation of the Anders Army in the Soviet Union, see Wróbel, *Devil's Playground*, 21–22.

46. Beloński, statement, 10 Sept. 1943, YVA, Schwarzbart Collection, M-2.152, 7; Władysław Anders, secret memo, 30 Nov. 1941, file no. 138/237, Collection of Lieutenant Wincenty Bąkiewicz, deposited in the Polish Institute and Sikorski Museum, London.

47. See the minutes of the National Council, 9 Jan. 1940, in Rojek and Suchcitz, *Protokoły*, 1: 154.

48. See David Engel, "Lwów, 1918: The Transmutation of a Symbol and its Legacy in the Holocaust," in Zimmerman, *Contested Memories*, 32–44. In this article Engel demonstrates how a particular perception of Jews as "a neutral and thus unsupportive group for the Polish cause," common among Polish politicians in 1918, reemerged as a premise in political discussions with the representatives of Polish Jewry in WWII. This is the first article in which Engel discusses symbols and ideas, not policies and practices.

49. For a good summary of Polish-Soviet relations in the second half of 1941, see Wróbel, *Devil's Playground*, 22–25; and Leslie et al., *The History*, 225–26.

50. See the minutes of the session of parliament, 15 Jan. 1942, in Rojek and Suchcitz, *Protokoły*, 4: 104.

51. On the issue of Jewish representatives in the government-in-exile, see Gutman and Krakowski, *Unequal Victims*, 58–65. For a polemical position, see Dariusz Stola, *Nadzieja i zagłada: Ignacy Szwarzbart—żydowski przedstawiciel w Radzie Narodowej RP: 1940–1945* (Warsaw, 1995). Stola's impressive historical account of the activities of Ignacy Schwarzbart, the Zionist representative to the National Council, emphasizes Schwarzbart's links with Poland and his commitment to the "Polish cause." How-

ever, in his historical narrative Stola does not seem to pay much attention to the "drama" of Schwarzbart as a Zionist representative of Polish Jews and Polish citizens—to the frustrations and disappointments borne out of his political discussions with various politicians in the government-in-exile, who advocated an exclusivist ethnonationalist model of Poland. These frustrations are pronounced in Schwarzbart's wartime communications with various representatives of the government-in-exile. On the relationship between the Bund and the Polish underground state, especially the pps, see Daniel Blatman, "A Hesitant Partnership: The Bund and Polish Socialists during the Holocaust," in Bankier and Gutman, *Nazi Europe*, 199–214.

52. On Marian Seyda and Tadeusz Bielecki, see Jerzy Janusz Terej, *Rzeczywistość i polityka. Ze studiów nad dziejami najnowszymi Narodowej Demokracji* (Warsaw, 1979), 270–300. In contrast to Seyda, Bielecki enjoyed popularity in National Democratic circles in Nazi-occupied Poland.

53. In the minutes of the National Council, 9 Jan. 1940, it is stated that "Minister Seyda, zgadzając się z tym, ze uprawianie antysemityzmu w obecnej chwili jest niepożądane, zwrócił uwagę na konieczność zachowania umiaru w tej sprawie" (Minister Seyda agreed that the use of anti-Semitism is an undesirable strategy at the present time and advised members to be cautious in this matter). See Rojek and Suchcitz, *Protokoły*, 1: 157.

54. Rojek and Suchcitz, *Protokoły*, 1: 157–158.

55. Karol Estreicher, review of *Alarm*, by Antoni Słonimski, *Dziennik Polski*, 17 Aug. 1940, 3.

56. Tadeusz Gajcy (pseud. Karol Topornicki), "Już nie potrzebujemy," *Sztuka i Naród*, Sept.–Oct. 1943, 10–15. The writings of Gajcy and his colleague-writers from *Sztuka i Naród* about Jews still await a detailed analysis. The literary critic Sandauer, who briefly discusses Gajcy's article, sees his statement not as anti-Semitic but as a pronouncement of indifference toward the Holocaust. See Sandauer, *Pisma*, 3: 479–80.

57. See the minutes of the National Council, 26 and 28 Aug. 1940, London, in Rojek and Suchcitz, *Protokoły*, 2: 95–114. Vol. 2 of Rojek and Suchcitz's work covers the period between June 1940 and June 1941.

58. On the subject of the policies of the government-in-exile toward Jews, see Engel's *In the Shadow* and *Facing the Holocaust*.

59. Engel, *In the Shadow*, 80.

60. See the declaration presented on behalf of the government-in-exile by Minister of Labor and Social Welfare Jan Stańczyk to the Council of the Jewish Labor Committee, Dec. 1941, New York, in Manfred Kridl, Józef Wittlin, and Władysław Malinowski, eds., *The Democratic Heritage of Poland* (London, 1944), 197–98.

61. Between Mar. 1938 and June 1939 88 percent of all persons dispossessed of Polish citizenship were Polish Jews. See Jerzy Tomaszewski, "Wokół obywatelstwa Żydów polskich", in Marcin Kula, ed., *Narody. Jak powstawały i jak wybijały się na niepodległość* (Warsaw, 1989), 512.

62. The more radical faction of the National Democrats, headed by Tadeusz Bielecki, remained in opposition. According to the historian Jerzy Janusz Terej, Bielecki's faction was more popular among supporters of the National Democrats in Nazi-occupied Poland. See Jerzy Janusz Terej, *Rzeczywistość*.

63. Declaration, Stańczyk, Dec. 1941, in Kridl, Wittlin, and Malinowski, *The Democratic*, 198.

64. S. Brodetzky, *From Ghetto to Israel: Memoirs* (London, 1960), 198. Confirmation of Raczyński's and Kot's statements can be found in official Polish letters; see Stola, *Nadzieja*, 73–74.

65. See the minutes of the session of parliament, 11 June 1941, in Rojek and Suchcitz, *Protokoły*, 2: 375

66. This is described in Stola, *Nadzieja*, 77.

67. See the minutes of the session of parliament, 11 July 1940, in Rojek and Suchcitz, *Protokoły*, 2: 44.

68. "General Sikorski and the Jews," *East London Observer*, 9 Mar. 1942, 1.

69. See *Sprawozdanie z działalności w latach 1940–1945* (Tel Aviv, 1995), 127–29 (issued by Reprezentacja Żydostwa Polskiego). Excerpts from the reports are cited in Gutman, "The Attitude," 410; and in Engel, "Possibilities," 137–39. The Representation of Polish Jewry comprised Zionist and Orthodox members, its headquarters located in Tel Aviv. There was also a branch in the United States.

70. *Sprawozdanie z działalności w latach 1940–1945*, 410.

71. See Andrzej Friszke, "Publicystyka Polski podziemnej wobec zagłady Żydów," in Wojciech Wrzesiński, ed., *Polska-Polacy-mniejszości narodowe* (Wroclaw, 1992), 193–213. This was perhaps the first article by a Polish historian in which a critical albeit cautious stance toward the historical material is advocated. See also Andrzej Friszke's more recent article, which critically discusses the issue of attitudes toward Jews in the press in the GG: "Attitudes toward the Jews in the Polish Underground Press, 1939–1944," in Bankier and Gutman, *Nazi Europe*, 163–74.

72. Declaration of Jan Banaczyk, member of the Polish National Council, presented on behalf of the Peasant Party at a session of the parliament, 26 Mar. 1941, YVA, Schwarzbart Collection, M2/149.

73. Ignacy Schwarzbart, report from the conference held with the leaders of the émigré Peasant Party, 20 Feb. 1941, London, YVA, M2/149.

74. Schwarzbart, report, YVA, Schwarzbart Collection, 6.

75. Delegate's Bureau: Department of Interior Affairs, Local Reports, 1940–42, YVA 02–25, 202/II-11.

76. A representative record of the PPS position on Jews can be found in YVA, Schwarzbart Collection, M2/152.

77. See the testimony of Chil Cejlon, YVA, M-1/E 815/685. On this subject, see the historical discussion "Polish-Jewish Relations during the Second World War," *Polin* 2 (1987): 351–53.

78. Stefan Grot Rowecki, dispatch, 25 Sept. 1941. The text is cited in full in Gross, *Upiorna*, 46. On Rowecki, see the following important political biography: Tomasz Szarota, *Stefan Rowecki "Grott"* (Warsaw, 1983). This book does not discuss the anti-Jewish prejudices of General Rowecki.

79. Gross, *Upiorna*, 47.

80. On criticism of the government-in-exile and left-wing political organizations, see, e.g., excerpts from the radical nationalist papers in Szapiro, *Wojna*, 317–27.

81. The issue of a "distant detached reaction" toward Jews in the underground Polish state was first raised in Engel, *In the Shadow*, 190–91.

82. Delegate's Bureau, Presidential Bureau, Local Reports, YVA, 02–25, file no. 202/I-29.

83. Delegate's Bureau, Department of Internal Affairs, Reports on the Situation, 1941–42, YVA, 0–25, file no. 202/II-6.

84. Memoranda on the Situation in Poland, 11 Oct.–15 Nov. 1942, "The Jewish Population in Poland: Overview," YVA, 02–25, file no. 202/I/31.

85. General Stefan Grot-Rowecki, report, 10 Nov. 1942. The text is cited in full in Gutman and Krakowski, *Unequal Victims*, 74–75.

86. On the reactions of the chief of staff of the AK and the Delegate's Bureau toward the deportations of Jews, see Andrzej Bryk, "The Hidden Complex of the Polish Mind: Polish-Jewish Relations during the Holocaust," in Polonsky, *My Brother's Keeper?* 71–73. On the reactions of the government-in-exile toward the news of the deportation, see Engel, *In the Shadow*, 185–97.

87. Delegate's Bureau, Department of Internal Affairs, Local Reports, 1940–42, YVA, 02–25, file no. 202/II-11.

88. There is agreement between some Polish and Jewish historians on the late issuing of appeals by the Delegate's Bureau against blackmailers; see Joseph Kermish, "The Activities of the Council for Aid to Jews ('Żegota') in Occupied Poland," in Gutman and Zuroff, *Rescue Attempts*, 383; and Teresa Prekerowa, "Relief Council for Jews, 1942–1945," in Abramsky, Jachimczyk, and Polonsky, *The Jews*, 170–72. For a detailed analysis of blackmailers in wartime Warsaw, see Jan Grabowski, *Szantażowanie Żydów w Warszawie, 1939–1943* (Warsaw, 2004).

89. Council for Aid to the Jews: Minutes I/2, 3, YVA 06/82.

90. Council for Aid to the Jews, Minutes I/1–34, 6, YVA 06/82.

91. Council for Aid to the Jews, letter to the head of the Delegate's Bureau, 30 June 1944, signed by Łukowski and Sławiński, 1–4 (49–52), YVA 06/82. In "Activities" Kermish mentions the anti-Semitic publications of *Nowy Wspólny Dom* but does not cite the reaction of PPS members of Żegota toward this document. See Kermish, "Activities," 388.

92. Prekerowa, "Relief Council," 173. See also her main study about Żegota: Teresa Prekerowa, *Konspiracyjna Rada Pomocy Żydom w Warszawie 1942–1945* (Warsaw, 1982). On Żegota, also see Kermish, "Activities," 367–98; and Engel, *Facing the Holocaust,*

138–55. Further historical study of the relationship between various factions of Żegota and the Delegate's Bureau in various regions is necessary.

93. My differentiation of three groups within the underground press is based on readings of the *Biuletyn Informacyjny, Do Broni, Nowa Polska,* and *Sztuka i Naród*—published collections of writings of the underground press about the Warsaw Ghetto Uprising. See Szapiro, *Wojna.* I also examined other published press material, as well as secondary sources. Given the fact that this examination represents only a section of this chapter, most of the primary material is not discussed in detail.

94. For a general history of the Polish press in WWII, see Stanisława Lewandowska, *Polska konspiracyjna prasa informacyjno-polityczna 1939–1945* (Warsaw, 1982). On the subject of democratic clandestine organizations and their underground press, see Lucjan Dobroszycki, "The Jews in the Polish Clandestine Press," in Paluch, *The Jews,* 289–96. On two underground papers, *Dzieci Warszawy* and *Biuletyn Informacyjny,* see Friszke, "Publicystyka," 193–214; and Paweł Szapiro, "Problem pomocy dla walczącego getta," in Daniel Grinberg and Paweł Szapiro, eds., *Holocaust z perspektywy półwiecza. Materiały z konferencji zorganizowanej przez ŻIH w dniach 29–31 Marca 1993* (Warsaw, 1993), 291–322. For critical descriptions of the underground press, also see Friszke, "Attitudes"; and Klaus Peter Friedrich, "Polskie reakcje na powstanie," *Midrasz,* no. 4 (2003): 18–19. Friedrich is also the author of a dissertation dedicated to this subject: "Der nationalsozialistische Judenmord in polnischen Angen: Einstel-lungen in der polnischen Presse 1944–1946/47," University of Köln, 2002, http://kups.ub.uni-koeln.de/volltexte/2003/952/. For a brief discussion of anti-Jewish perceptions in the Polish underground press, see also Andrzej Żbikowski's epilogue to Samuel Willenberg's *Bund w Treblince* (Warsaw, 2004), 189–90.

95. Excerpt from *Nowe Drogi,* 7 Feb. 1944, in Szapiro, *Wojna,* 342–43.

96. Delegate's Bureau, Department of Information and Press, Weekly Reports of the Chairman, YVA, 0–25, file no. 202/III/80.

97. The leaflet was published in *Wolność,* 1 May 1940, and included in the report *Uwagi o sytuacji w Wilnie i na Wilenszczyźnie,* written by a PPS member of the underground state. See the Archive of New Acts, HI-MID, 122, 34. I would like to thank Professor Krzysztof Jasiewicz for sharing this document with me. In Polish historiography of the Wilno region six occupations are differentiated: the first Soviet occupation (17 Sept. 1939–28 Oct. 1939); the second Lithuanian occupation (Oct. 1939–June 1940); the third Soviet occupation (June 1940–22 June 1941); the fourth German occupation (June 1941–44); the fifth Soviet occupation (1944–45); and the sixth Soviet occupation (1945–91). Nineteen ninety-one was the year of the proclamation of Lithuanian sovereignty. See Jasiewicz, *Pierwsi,* 32–33.

98. See Friszke, "Publicystyka," 193–214.

99. On ambivalent attitudes expressed in *Racławice,* see Friszke, "Attitudes," 169–70.

100. Excerpt from *Naród,* 15 Aug. 1942, cited in Polonsky, "Beyond," 214.

101. Excerpt from *Polska,* Jan. 1943, cited in Gutman and Krakowski, *Unequal Victims,* 115.

102. Excerpt from *Młoda Polska*, 13 Oct. 1943, in Szapiro, *Wojna*, 315.

103. YVA, O–25, file no. 202/III/81.

104. Prekerowa, "Relief Council," 161.

105. See Gutman and Krakowski, *Unequal Victims*, 107.

106. Program of the ZSP, July 1940, in Przybysz, *Wizje*, 43.

107. Excerpt from *Iskra*, 28 Apr. 1943, in Szapiro, *Wojna*, 58.

108. According to Dobraczyński's own recollections, he was a member of the National Military Organization and the Propaganda Section of the National Democrats in WWII. See his preface to Roman Dmowski's *Myśli nowoczesnego Polaka* (Warsaw, 1989), 5.

109. On the subject of Kossak-Szczucka's participation in Żegota, see Nechama Tec, *When Light Pierced the Darkness: Christian Rescue of Jews in Nazi-Occupied Poland* (New York, 1986), 107. For an interesting account of Kossak-Szczucka's activities, see the article by her grandson Francois Rosset: "Zofia Kossak i kultura konfrontacji," *Gazeta Wyborcza*, 28 Nov. 2003, http://ww1.gazeta.pl/wyborcza/1093892,34591,1801477 .htm1?as=1&ias=2.

110. Michał Głowiński, "Tajemnica Dobraczyńskiego", *Gazeta Wyborcza*, 3–4 July 1999, 22–23. According to Głowiński, who was one of the Jewish children who found shelter in the Roman Catholic monastery in Turkowice, Dobraczyński most likely supplied him with false papers. On Głowiński's wartime experiences, see one of his memoirs: Michał Głowiński, *Czarne sezony* (Warsaw, 1999). This book was translated into English by Marci Shore. See Michal Glowinski, *The Black Seasons* (Evanston IL, 2005).

111. See Przybysz, *Wizje*, 149.

112. Program of the FOP, Sept. 1942, in Przybysz, *Wizje*, 143–44.

113. "Komu pomagamy," *Prawda*, Aug. 1943, cited in Tec, *When Light*, 107.

114. Zofia Kossak-Szczucka, *Protest*, Aug. 1942. The full text is cited in Polonsky, "Beyond," 212.

115. Excerpt from *Prawda dnia*, May 1944, in Szapiro, *Wojna*, 380.

116. Excerpt from *Prawda*, Apr.–May 1943, in Szapiro, *Wojna*, 218.

117. See Władysław Bartoszewski, *The Warsaw Ghetto* (Boston, 1987), 30–31. For a contesting position, see Tec, *When Light*, 52–69.

118. One of the most recent examples of such a position is Gunnar S. Paulsson, *Secret City: The Hidden Jews of Warsaw 1940–1945* (New Haven and London, 2002). Although Paulsson's work introduces a neglected dimension to the study of the Holocaust, his work fails to consistently address certain major interpretive problems. For example, his comparative analysis with other European countries such as the Netherlands— an approach that is badly needed in Holocaust studies—is unfortunately shallow. Paulsson does not seem to be interested in describing or explaining similarities and differences in the dynamics of rescue activities in the Netherlands and Poland, where the survival rates of Jews were similar. On the issue of anti-Semitism, Paulsson draws

upon both the old apologetic Polish narrative and the new critical Polish scholarship, mutually exclusive positions that create certain major inconsistencies in his position. See Joanna B. Michlic, review of "Secret City," by Gunnar S. Paulsson, *Holocaust and Genocide Studies* 19, no. 3 (2005).

119. In her work Nechama Tec convincingly argues that such a position was represented by only a small section of Polish society. She also conducts an interesting analysis of members of the radical ethno-nationalist group as rescuers or helpers of Jews; see Tec, *When Light*, 99–104, 184.

120. For an approach that seems to make "exceptional heroes" out of the anti-Semitic members of the radical right-wing groups who were involved in various rescue activities, see Paulsson, *Secret City*, 161–62.

121. For a discussion of individuals who were anti-Semites yet were involved in rescue activities of Jews in Belgium, see Dan Michman, "Problematic National Identity, Outsiders and Persecution: Impact of the Gentile Population's Attitude in Belgium on the Fate of the Jews in 1940–1944," in Bankier and Gutman, *Nazi Europe*, 469–90.

122. Steinlauf, *Bondage*, 40.

123. Polish scholars also agree that Polish society as a whole was indifferent toward the fate of the Jews in the Holocaust; an active stance, whether helpful/positive or hostile/negative, was a marginal phenomenon. See Cała, *The Image*, 212; and Teresa Prekerowa, "The 'Just' and the 'Passive,'" in Polonsky, *My Brother's Keeper?* 76.

124. The most recent discussion of anti-Jewish violence based on the "rediscovery" of Jewish testimonies from small towns in Żółkiewka, in the region of Lublin in southeastern Poland, tentatively indicates that this was also a region in which one or more anti-Jewish riots occurred in Oct. 1939, albeit on a smaller scale than in the region of Łomża. Between Sept. and Oct. 1939 the area of Lublin was invaded first by the Germans, then by the Soviets, and then was reinvaded by the Germans. The anti-Jewish riot of 7–8 Oct. 1939 in Żółkiewka, in which approximately twenty-two Jewish men, women, and children were killed, was made public in Paweł Reszka, "Miejsce zbrodni Żółkiewka," *Gazeta Wyborcza*, 10 July 2004, *http://serwisy.gazeta.pl/wyborcza/2029020 ,34474,217657.html*.

125. For a description of anti-Jewish violence in the Łomża region, see Gross, *Neighbors*, 56–70; and Andrzej Żbikowski, "Pogromy i mordy ludności żydowskiej w Łomżyńskiem i na Białostocczyznie latem 1941 roku w świetle relacji ocalałych żydów i dokumentów sądowych," in Machcewicz and Persak, *Wokół*, 1: 159–273.

126. Jan Błoński, "Polish-Catholics and Catholic Poles: The Gospel, National Interest, Civic Solidarity and the Destruction of the Warsaw Ghetto," *Yad Vashem Studies* (Jerusalem) 25 (1996): 184.

127. For an interesting analysis of Polish and Jewish diaries, showing that the notion of Jewish and Polish truths is false, see Feliks Tych, "Witnessing the Holocaust: Polish Diaries, Memoirs and Reminiscences," in Bankier and Gutman, *Nazi Europe*, 175–98.

128. See introduction and conclusion in Tec, *When Light*.

129. See Zofia Kossak-Szczucka, *Z otchłani* (Rzym, 1946), 99–111, 129–31. In the recent edition of this book published by the Auschwitz Museum the most damaging passages containing anti-Jewish pronouncements about Jewish women are omitted. See Zofia Kossak-Szczucka, *Z otchłani* (Oswiecim and Warsaw, 2002).

130. On elements of the Nazi conceptualization of German Jewry as the enemy of the German polity and its people, see Bartov, "Defining," 779–85. See also Bartov, *Mirrors*, 91–142.

131. On the failure of collaboration between German and Polish fascist groups, see Tomasz Szarota, "Zajścia anty-żydowskie i pogromy w okupowanej Europie," in Grinberg and Szapiro, *Holocaust*, 153–75. For similar views on the same subject, see Tomasz Szarota, *U progu zagłady: zajścia antyżydowskie i pogromy w okupowanej Europie: Warszawa, Paryż, Antwerpia, Kowno* (Warsaw, 2000).

132. "Endecja's Attitude toward Jews," Archives of Emanuel Ringelblum, no. I/91, cited in Joseph Kermish, ed., *To Live with Honor and Die with Honor! Selected Documents from the Warsaw Ghetto Underground Archives "O.S"* (Jerusalem, 1986), 614.

133. See "Inny świat," *Do broni*, 11 Aug. 1942, 1–2. See also "Likwidacja Żydów," *Nowa Polska*, 12 Aug. 1942, 1–3. *Do broni* and *Nowa Polska* were the two main papers of the Konfederacja Narodu.

134. L. Rościszewski, "No Second Troy," *Times* (Czas), 21 Mar. 1938, cited in Mich, *Problem*, 261.

135. Hertz, "Swoi," 159.

136. On the prevalence of a lack of objectivity in intellectual discourse on the "Jewish question," even in the 1980s, see Irwin-Zarecka, *Neutralizing*, 165.

137. See Kopstein and Wittenberg, "Who Voted Communist?" 107.

138. See Paweł Korzec and Jean-Charles Szurek, "Jews and Poles under Soviet Occupation (1939–1941): Conflicting Interests," *Polin* 4 (1989): 204–25; and Krystyna Kersten, *Polacy Żydzi Komunizm. Anatomia półprawd 1939–68* (Warsaw, 1992), 30–31.

139. Schatz, *The Generation*, 152.

140. Ben-Cion Pinchuk, "Facing Hitler and Stalin: On the Subject of Jewish 'Collaboration' in Soviet-Occupied Eastern Poland, 1939–1941," in Zimmerman, *Contested Memories*, 61.

141. On the subject of the behavior of Jews under Soviet occupation and their relations with the Soviet regime, and the Soviet purge of Jewish communal culture, see Ben-Cion Pinchuk, *Shtetl Jews under Soviet Rule: Eastern Poland on the Eve of the Holocaust* (London, 1990), 21–38; Pinchuk, "Facing Hitler," 65–66; Gross, *Polish Society*, 20, 185; Gross, "The Jewish," 155–71; and Jasiewicz, *Pierwsi*, 39–56, 157–206.

142. On the varied treatment of Jews by the Soviets and varied reactions of Jews toward the Soviet Union, see a collection of Jewish testimonies from the eastern territories: Andrzej Żbikowski, ed., *Archiwum Ringelbluma. Konspiracyjne Archiwum Getta Warszawy. Relacje z Kresów*, vol. 3 (Warsaw, 2000). Many secret reports and memos are deposited in the Polish Institute–Sikorski Museum in London. The archival collection

of the Polish National Council (PRM) contains a large number. See, e.g., PRM no. 96, file no. 33, 1–6; PRM no. 96, file no. 28, 1–8; and PRM no. 99, file no. 2, 3–5. What is characteristic about these reports is that those written by ethno-nationalists contain anti-Jewish prejudices, whereas those written by believers in inclusive civic nationalism are free of anti-Jewish prejudices and anti-Jewish evaluations of historical events in the eastern territories. Further research is needed to examine the entire range of perspectives on Jews in this material.

143. Cited in David Engel, "The Polish Government-in-Exile and the Holocaust," *Polin* 2 (1989): 280.

144. Terej, *Rzeczywistość*, 310–18.

145. On the development of the PPR in WWII, see a good overview in Schatz, *The Generation*, 179–89.

146. There is a new growing literature on Soviet crimes committed against ethnic Poles and other Polish citizens. See, e.g., Stanisław Ciesielski et al., *Represje sowieckie wobec Polaków i obywateli polskich* (Warsaw, 2000); Dariusz Baliszewski and Andrzej K. Kunert, *Prawdziwa historia Polaków*, vol. 2 (Warsaw, 1990).

147. See Łepkowski, *Myśli*, 37.

148. Home Army: The Headquarters—section II, Report from the Trip to Eastern Poland, 20 Nov. 1941, YVA, O2–25, file no. 203/III-55.

149. Delegate's Bureau: The Presidential Office, Correspondence with the Government-in-Exile, YVA, O–25, file no. 202/I-35.

150. Delegate's Bureau: The Department of Internal Affairs, YVA, O–25, file no. 202/II-25.

151. Report by Kreton, 28 Jan. 1942, YVA, O–25, file no. 202/III/28.

152. Polonsky, "Beyond," 219.

153. Order of General Tadeusz Bór-Komorowski, 31 Aug. 1943, cited in Polonsky, "Beyond," 219.

154. Polonsky, "Beyond," 219.

155. For a revisionist position on the attitudes of right-wing military units toward Jews, see Marek J. Chodakiewicz, Piotr Gontarczyk, and Leszek Żebrowski, *Tajne oblicze* GL-AL *i* PPR, 3 vols. (Warsaw, 1997). This book is based on the premise of a "zero-sum game" between Poles and Jews and is strongly anti-Communist. In fact, the authors portray the Communist military units that emerged in WWII as those that were involved in killing Jews and the right-wing military units as those that provided shelter to Jews. See, in particular, vol. 2.

156. Gutman and Krakowski, *Unequal Victims*, 80–97.

157. See Tomasz Szarota, *Życie codzienne w stolicach okupowanej Europy* (Warsaw, 1995), 179–80. Nazis announced the discovery of mass graves of Polish officers on Berlin radio on 13 Apr. 1943. Moscow called this news a "fabrication by Goebbels's slanderers." For documents on the massacre of Polish officers in Katyń, see Wojciech Materski and Natalia S. Liebiediewa, eds., *Katyń. Dokumenty Zbrodni. Losy ocalałych, Lipiec 1940–Marzec 1943*, vol. 3 (Warsaw, 2001). The data for all murdered Polish officers

and other members of the Polish state apparatus by the Soviets is still uncomplete. According to the most reliable estimates, 21,763 Polish officers were murdered by the Soviets: 4,410 in Katyń; 3,739 in Charków; and 6,314 in Twer. In addition 7,300 Polish prisoners of war were murdered in Mińsk, Belorussia, and parts of the Ukraine. See *Indeks Represjonowanych*, vols. 1–3 (Warsaw, 1995). The full list of all the victims of the Katyń massacre is in the process of being prepared by Professor Anna Cienciała, whom I would like to thank for discussing with me Soviet crimes against Polish society.

158. Excerpt from Nurt Młodych, 30 Apr. 1943, cited in Szapiro, *Wojna*, 76.

159. Department of Information and Press, weekly reports, YVA, 0–25, file no. 202/III/80.

160. On Feliks Koneczny, see a short article by S. L. Shneiderman, "'High' Anti-Semitism Revived," *Midstream*, Aug.–Sept. 1973, 76–81. National Democracy in London published several of Koneczny's works in the 1980s. In post-1989 Poland there is a noticeable revival of interest in Koneczny's books in right-wing cultural circles.

161. Feliks Koneczny, *Cywilizacja żydowska* (London, 1974), 389–94.

162. The notion of Judeo-Bolshevism also has to be considered one of the main causes of anti-Jewish riots that were conducted on a smaller scale in the town of Żółkiewka, near Lublin, in Oct. 1939; see Reszka, "Miejsce." The theme of Judeo-Bolshevism and Judeo-Communism was not only characteristic of the right-wing nationalistic discourse in Poland in WWII but was also present in political discourse in other East and Southeast European countries. In countries like the Ukraine and Romania the theme of Judeo-Communism played a role in the inciting and development of anti-Jewish violence in the summer of 1941. See, e.g., Leon Volovici, "Judeo-Bolshevism and the Efficiency of Anti-Semitic Propaganda," paper presented at the Conference on the Holocaust in Romania, Apr. 2004, U.S. Holocaust Memorial Museum, Washington DC. I would like to express my gratitude to Dr. Leon Volovici for sharing his paper with me.

163. For an analysis of perceptions of Jews as Communists and the actual participation of Jews in the Communist regime, see Gross, "The Jewish," 168–70; and Gross, *Neighbors*, 21–29.

164. Gross, *Neighbors*, 61–63.

165. Jasiewicz, *Pierwsi*, 27–138.

166. See, e.g., "Ochrona Nazwisk Polskich," *Myśl Narodowa*, no. 32 (1922): 6–7.

167. Excerpt from *Kierownik*, 16 May 1943, in Szapiro, *Wojna*, 179–80.

168. On the notion of national honor and reputation in Polish national discourse in the post-1945 period, see Irwin-Zarecka, *Frames*, 81–82.

169. Cited in Engel, *In the Shadow*, 80.

170. Delegate's Bureau: The Department of Internal Affairs, Reports on the Situation, 1941–42, YVA, 02-25/6.

171. Memorandum by Roman Knoll, head of the Foreign Affairs Commission in the Office of the Delegate's Bureau. The whole text is reprinted in Ringelblum, *Polish-Jewish*, 257.

172. Delegate's Bureau: The Information and Press Bureau, Collection of Reports, YVA, 02-25/22.

173. Kersten, *Polacy*, 3.

174. On the subject of the increased influence of the National Democrats in the underground state and the population at large in the GG, see Terej, *Rzeczywistość*, 108–9.

175. On the issue of the identification of Poles in WWII, see Antonina Kłoskowska, *Kultury narodowe u korzeni* (Warsaw, 1996), 299–321.

176. All Polish political parties that went underground had clandestine press. The numbers of such publications increased vastly, from forty titles at the end of 1939 to six hundred titles by 1944. See Lucjan Dobroszycki, ed., *Centralny katalog polskiej prasy konspiracyjnej 1939–1945* (Warsaw, 1962), 11–12. See also Lewandowska, *Polska*, 97–100.

177. Jerzy Jarowiecki, Jerzy Myśliński, and Andrzej Notkowski, *Prasa polska w latach 1939–1945* (Warsaw, 1980), 96–101.

178. David Engel, "An Early Account of Polish Jewry under Nazi and Soviet Occupation Presented to the Polish Government-in-Exile, February 1940," in Norman Davies and Antony Polonsky, eds., *Jews in Eastern Poland and the USSR, 1939–46* (London, 1991), 259.

179. This is from Jan Karski's report: "The Jewish Problem in the Homeland." The entire document is cited in Davies and Polonsky, *Jews*, 269. John E. Mack introduced the notion of the "egoism of victimization." This was cited by Vamik D. Volkan in "The Need to Have Enemies and Allies: A Developmental Approach," *Political Psychology* 6, no. 2 (1985): 222.

180. Archives of Emanuel Ringelblum, no. I/91, Polish-Jewish Relations, cited in Kermish, *To Live*, 615–16.

181. See, e.g., Miriam Peleg-Mariańska and Mordechai Peleg, *Witnesses: Life in Occupied Cracow* (London and New York, 1991), 97–101; and Antoni Marianowicz, *Life Strictly Forbidden*, trans. Alicja Nitecki (London and Portland OR, 2004), 73–75, 80–87.

182. Edmund Wierciński, "Gałązki Akacji," *Twórczość*, no. 1 (1947): 47.

183. Israel Gutman, *Resistance: The Warsaw Ghetto Uprising* (Boston and New York, 1994), 228–35.

184. For historical descriptions of Polish reactions (military and civil) toward the Warsaw Ghetto Uprising, see Gutman, *Resistance*, 228–35; and Szapiro, "Problem."

185. Barbara Engelking, *Zagłada i pamięć* (Warsaw, 1994), 55–56. On Nazi legislation against Poles rescuing Jews, see Ruta Sakowska, *Ludzie z dzielnicy zamkniętej* (Warsaw, 1993), 235–36.

186. Janina Walewska, "In a Sense I Am an Antisemite," cited in Shmuel Krakowski, "Jews and Poles in Polish Historiography," *Yad Vashem Studies* 19 (1998): 321.

187. For the first discussion by a Polish intellectual of the merry-go-round at Krasiński Square in the context of the destruction of the Warsaw Jewry, see Jan Błoński, "The Poor Poles Look at the Ghetto," *Polin* 1 (1986): 322. The first reflection about the lonely dying of Warsaw Jews in which the image of merry-go-round features is the well-

known poem by Czesław Miłosz, "Campo dei Fiori," written in Warsaw in 1943. See Czesław Miłosz, "Campo dei Fiori," in *New and Collected Poems 1931–2001* (New York, 2003), 33–35. For a recent discussion of the merry-go-round that reveals contemporary questioning of its use, see Ryszard Matuszewski, "Nieruchoma karuzela na Placu Krasińskich," *Rzeczpospolita*, 10 May 2003, 4. Also see Miłosz's response: Czesław Miłosz, "Karuzela," *Tygodnik Powszechny*, htpp:tygodnik.onet.pl/1572,1134902 ,felieton.html.

188. This problem is briefly discussed in Tych, "Witnessing," 176–79.

189. Ringelblum, *Polish-Jewish*, 141.

190. Edward Reicher, manuscript, *"Za niepopełnione winy,"* YVA, Memoirs, no. 033/2824, 178.

191. Interview with H. M., cited in Engelking, *Zagłada*, 58.

192. On the reactions of the Warsaw population to children from the Zamość region, see Szarota, *Okupowanej Warszawy*, 485–87.

193. See Gross, *Upiorna*, 25–60; and Steinlauf, *Bondage*, 30–42.

194. On the frequency of announcements of the Nazi decree of death for sheltering Jews, see, e.g., Sakowska, *Ludzie*, 235.

195. Steinlauf, *Bondage*, 41–42.

196. Emanuel Tanay, "Passport to Life," in Marian Turski, ed., *Losy żydowskie. Świadectwo żywych* (Warsaw, 1996), 66.

197. See Engelking, *Zagłada*, 51–52.

198. Maria Hochberg-Mariańska, introduction to Maria Hochberg-Mariańska and Noe Grüss, eds., *The Children Accuse* (London, 1996), 24.

199. Michał Borwicz, "Polish-Jewish Relations, 1944–1947," in Abramsky, Jachimczyk, and Polonsky, *The Jews*, 193.

200. Discussion of the problem is based on my reading of sixty-four early postwar testimonies of Jewish children and their rescuers that are held in the collection of the Jewish Historical Institute of Warsaw. It is also based on my reading of Hochberg-Mariańska's and Grüss's published collection of Jewish children's testimonies, *The Children Accuse*. Since the subject of the relations between low societal approval of rescue actions and the legacy of exclusivist ethno-nationalism constitutes just a small section of this chapter, I provide only a small sample of illustrations. The subject deserves a separate monograph.

201. See, e.g., "The Diary of Adela Domanus (Historia jednej dziewczynki z czasów hitlerowskiej okupacji Warszawy)," YVA, no. 06/546, 42 (in Polish).

202. Testimony of Wanda Chrzanowska, 9 Aug. 1945, ZIH, file no. 301/5127.

203. Statement of Józefa Krawczyk, ZIH, no. 301/4200 (in Polish).

204. Statement of A. Konarska, ZIH, no. 301/5284 (in Polish).

205. Statement of Felicja Bolak, ZIH, no. 301/5119, (in Polish).

206. Statement of Zygmunt Assman, ZIH, no. 301/4437 (in Polish).

207. Statement of Sabina Kryszak, ZIH, no. 301/1424 (in Polish).

208. Memoirs of Szlama Kutnowski (n.d., written approximately one or two years after the end of WWII), YVA, no. M-49/273–279.
209. Julian Tuwim, "Kwiaty Polskie," in Adam Gillon, ed., *The Dancing Socrates and Other Poems* (New York, 1968), 52–53. Tuwim was also the author of the powerful long poem *My, Żydzi Polscy* . . . , written in 1944. See Julian Tuwim, *My, Żydzi Polscy . . . We, Polish Jews* (Warsaw, 1993).

6. Old Wine in a New Bottle

1. The approximate total number of Jewish survivors is estimated at three hundred thousand. By June 1945 the Central Committee of Jews in Poland, the main Jewish institution, had registered seventy-four thousand. On the history of the reemergence of Jewish community and organizations in Poland in the early postwar period, see Lucjan Dobroszycki, "Re-emergence and Decline of a Community: The Numerical Size of the Jewish Population in Poland, 1944–47," YIVO *Annual* 21 (1993): 3–32; and Józef Andelson, "W Polsce Zwanej Ludową", in Jerzy Tomaszewski, ed., *Najnowsze dzieje Żydow w Polsce (w zarysie do 1950 roku)* (Warsaw, 1993), 395–404.
2. The estimated figure of Poles murdered in WWII varies according to the inclusion or exclusion of some of the still-unverified data on the victims of the Soviet terror. On the problematics of the subject, see a short statement by the historian Andrzej Paczkowski in the section about WWII in Janusz Tazbir, ed., *Polska na przestrzeni wieków* (Warsaw, 1995), 635.
3. On the Warsaw Uprising, see the classic historical study by Andrzej Ciechanowski, *The Warsaw Rising of 1944* (Cambridge, 1974); and the latest book by Norman Davis, *Rising '44: The Battle for Warsaw* (Pan, 2004), which is an impressive volume, although not free of errors and unsatisfactory discussions, including one on the subject of Polish-Jewish relations in WWII. For a historical summary and literature on Operation Tempest and the Warsaw Uprising of 1944, see Leslie et al., *The History*, 264–75.
4. On the human and material losses suffered by Poland in WWII, and on territorial and ethnic changes, see Andrzej Paczkowski, *Pół wieku dziejów Polski* (Warsaw, 1995), chap. 1. The book appeared in English under the title *The Spring Will Be Ours: Poland and the Poles from Occupation to Freedom* (University Park PA, 2003); Andrzej Paczkowski, *Zdobycie*, 10–15; and Bardach, Leśnodorski, and Pietrzak, *Historia*, 632–35.
5. For a general historical discussion of the negotiations that led to the establishment of the new Polish borders and literature, see Leslie et al., *The History*, 257–64, 275–79.
6. One of the most useful collections of essays on the subject in English, including history and literature, is Phillip Ther and Ana Siljak, eds., *Redrawing Nations: Ethnic Cleansing in East-Central Europe, 1944–1948* (Lanham MD and Oxford, 2001). The volume's opening essay on Poland is Krystyna Kersten, "Forced Migration and the Transformation of Polish Society in the Postwar Period," 75–86.

7. Winston Churchill, *Churchill Speaks: Winston S. Churchill in Peace and War, Complete Speeches, 1897–1963*, Vol. 7, *1943–1949* (New York, 1974), 7064 ff.

8. The highest estimated number of Germans transferred to Germany is 3.5 million. There is extensive literature on the subject in German, including documentation. See, e.g., the classic study Theodor Schieder, ed., *Documents on the Expulsion of the Germans from Eastern-Central Europe* (Bonn, 1961). See also the following articles, all in Ther and Siljak, *Redrawing Nations*: Stanisław Jankowiak, " 'Cleansing' Poland of Germans," 87–105; Claudia Kraft, "Who Is a Pole, and Who Is a German? The Province of Olsztyn in 1945," 107–20; and Bernard Linek, " 'De-Germanization' and 'Re-Polonization' in Upper Silesia 1945–1950," 121–34.

9. There is a vast growing literature on the subject in Ukrainian, Polish, and English. One of the most important works in English is Snyder, *The Reconstruction*, esp. 187–91. See also Igor Hałagida, *Ukraińcy na zachodnich i północnych ziemiach Polski 1947–1957* (Warsaw, 2003), 22–41; Orest Subtelny, "Expulsion, Resettlement, Civil Strife: The Fate of Poland's Ukrainians, 1944–1947," in Ther and Siljak, *Redrawing Nations*, 155–72; and Jan Pisuliński, "Przesiedlenia Ukraińców do ZSRR w latach 1944–1946," 37–42, and Grzegorz Motyka, "Łemkowie i Bojkowie," 43–54, both in *Biuletyn Instytutu Pamięci Narodowej*, no. 8 (2001). The Lemko ethnic group, which traditionally inhabited the Carpathian Mountains, was and still is divided about whether it belongs to the Ukrainian nation. Those who do not perceive themselves as part of the Ukrainian nation see themselves as part of the Russ-Carpathian community.

10. On the situation of Belorussians and Lithuanians in post-1945 Poland, see Jerzy Kulak, "Pacyfikacja wsi białoruskich w styczniu 1946 roku," 49–54, and Jan J. Milewski, "Litwini w Polsce Ludowej," 55–58, both in *Biuletyn Instytutu Pamięci Narodowej*, no. 8 (2001).

11. On the history and literature of the Action Vistula, see Snyder, *The Reconstruction*, 193–201; Hałagida, *Ukraincy*, 30–41; and Subtelny, "Expulsion," 166–68. On the latest historical interpretations of the Action Vistula by Ukrainian and Polish historians, see Jan Pisuliński, ed., *Konferencja IPN Akcja Wisła* (Warsaw, 2003). See also Grzegorz Motyka, *Tak było w Bieszczadach: Walki polsko-ukraińskie* (Warsaw, 1999); Grzegorz Motyka and Dariusz Libionka, eds., *Antypolska akcja OUN-UPA 1943–1944: Fakty i interpretacje* (Warsaw, 2002); and Grzegorz Motyka and Piotr Kosiewski, eds., *Historycy polscy: Ukrainscy wobec problemów XX wieku* (Cracow, 2002).

12. The number of repatriates from the Soviet Union to Poland in the years 1945–47 is estimated at more than 1.2 million. See Kersten, "Forced Migration," 82. See also Jerzy Kochanowski, "Gathering Poles into Poland: Forced Migration from Poland's Former Eastern Territories," in Ther and Siljak, *Redrawing Nations*, 135–54.

13. The number of 140,000 Jews includes just the individuals who emigrated from Poland with the help of Zionist organizations. See Andelson, "W Polsce," 414.

14. See Andelson, "W Polsce," 388–89; and Arieh Joseph Kochavi, "Britain and the Jewish Exodus from Poland following the Second World War," *Polin* 7 (1992): 162.

15. On PPR methods of consolidating power, see Paczkowski, *The Spring*, chaps. 1 and 2; Paczkowski, *Zdobycie*, 28–33; Krystyna Kersten, *Między wyzwoleniem a zniewoleniem: Polska 1944–1956* (London, 1993); Krystyna Kersten, *Narodziny systemu władzy. Polska 1943–1948* (Poznan, 1990), published in English as *The Establishment of Communist Rule in Poland, 1943–1948* (Berkeley, 1991). For a concise overview of the history of the PKWN, see Bardach, Leśnodorski, and Pietrzak, *Historia*, 623–33.

16. Archives of the Workers' Movement, vol. 9, 110. Gomułka's well-known statement of June 1945 is cited in Paczkowski, *Zdobycie*, 5.

17. On the constitutional opposition, see Andrzej Friszke, *Opozycja polityczna w* PRL (London, 1994), 23–44.

18. Leaders of the PPS, such as Kazimierz Pużak and Tadeusz Szturm de Szterm, were arrested, while others, such as Zygmunt Zaremba, left Poland for the United Kingdom. See Friszke, *Opozycja*, 25–26.

19. On the illegal opposition, see Friszke, *Opozycja*, 45–66; and Kersten, *Między wyzwoleniem*, 28–36.

20. See Paczkowski, *Zdobycie*, 58; Friszke, *Opozycja*, 62; and Kersten, *Między wyzwoleniem*, 37–46. An interesting detailed analysis of the theme of Judeo-Communism in the press of WiN in the region of Lublin is presented by Rafał Wnuk, *Lubelski Okręg* AK DSZ *I WiN 1944–1947* (Warsaw, 2002), 199–219. Wnuk makes a distinction between the theme of Judeo-Communism and the representation of the Jew as the other in Polish society, viewing the image of Judeo-Communism as separate from the image of the Jew as the other. His work is perhaps the first in which a Polish author discusses the theme of Judeo-Communism as anti-Semitic and attempts to analyze it within the context of anti-Semitic discourse.

21. YVA, Collection of Anti-Semitic Leaflets in Poland 1945–1946, no. 06/91, WiN's publications, 2.

22. Feliks Koneczny made this statement in Oct. 1945. Cited in Giertych, *Polski*, 34.

23. Vestiges of this way of thinking were clearly evident in the right-wing nationalist press during the debate about Jedwabne. See Michlic, "Coming to Terms," 15–17. In this debate some professional historians, like the late Tomasz Strzembosz and Bogdan Musiał, also referred to the realization of Judeo-Communism in the early postwar period. For analysis and excerpts of their positions, see Michlic, "Coming to Terms," 16–17; and Polonsky and Michlic, *The Neighbors Respond*, 311–12.

24. For an analysis of Jewish Communists and the patterns of their positions and careers, see Schatz, *The Generation*, 211–30; and August Grabski's recent political study of Communist Jews in the early postwar period, *Działalność komunistów wśród Żydów w Polsce (1944–1949)* (Warsaw, 2004).

25. Israeli historian Ben-Cion Pinchuk introduced the phrase "the reversal of natural order" in "Facing Hitler." For a detailed statistical study of the participation of Jews and other ethnic national groups in the Soviet state apparatus and the NKWD in western Belarus during the Soviet occupation, between 1939 and 1941, see Jasiewicz,

Pierwsi. In this book Jasiewicz demonstrates that collaboration with the Soviet regime in this region was cross-ethnic and included not only Jewish and Slavic minorities but also ethnic Poles.

26. See a popular historical biography of Anatol Muelstein by Robert Jarocki entitled *Żyd Piłsudskiego* (Warsaw, 1997).

27. See Jacek Majchrowski, ed., *Kto był kim w Drugiej Rzeczypospolitej* (Warsaw, 1994), 225.

28. For analysis of the concerns of Soviet intelligence regarding the perception of Communist Jews as enemies of Poland in early postwar Polish society, see Norman M. Naimark, "Gomułka and Stalin: The Antisemtic Factor in Postwar Polish Politics" (working paper). I would like to thank Professor Naimark for giving me permission to cite his work.

29. Statement by Andrzej Łobodowski, cited in Barbara Toporska, "Wybieram wątek najmniej popularny," *Wiadomości*, no. 47 (1970), rpt. in Józef Mackiewicz and Barbara Toporska, *Droga Pani* (London, 1984), 121.

30. Message written on the back of an illegal leaflet circulated in Kielce in Aug. 1945, published in Danuta Blus-Węgrowska, "Atmosfera pogromowa," *Karta*, no. 18 (1996): 101.

31. See Kersten, *Polacy*, 78, 80.

32. See Paczkowski, *Zdobycie*, 44, 74.

33. This illegal leaflet was published in the bulletin of the Ministry of Public Security, no. 17 (1947). See the published collection of these bulletins: *Biuletyny Informacyjne Ministerstwa Bezpieczeństwa Publicznego 1947. Źródła do Historii Polski XX Wieku—ze Zbiorów Centralnego Archiwum Ministerstwa Spraw Wewnętrznych*, series C, vol. 1 (Warsaw, 1990), 182–83.

34. The program of National Democracy, written in late autumn 1944 or winter 1945. This program was found in the archives of the Ministry of Interior Affairs in the Collection on National Democracy, vol. 103, and was published in the selection of early postwar National Democratic programs by Lucyna Kulińska, Mirosław Orłowski, and Rafał Sierchuła. The authors, particularly Kulińska, do not have a critical approach to the position of National Democracy on Jews or other matters and therefore repeat National Democratic points of views as objective statements. Thus, as in some other cases, the vision of National Democracy enters the realm of post-1989 Polish historiography. See Lucyna Kulińska, Mirosław Orłowski, and Rafał Sierchuła, eds., *Narodowcy. Myśl polityczna i społeczna obozu narodowego w Polsce w latach 1944–1947* (Warsaw andCracow, 2001), 54–55.

35. See the program of National Democracy, 10 Sept. 1945, written by Władysław Jaworski, in Kulińska, Orłowski, and Sierchuła, *Narodowcy*, 60–61.

36. Anti-Jewish Propaganda within psl, yva, no. 06/91, 5.

37. Anti-Jewish Propaganda within psl, yva, no. 06/91, 5.

38. "Jews and Polish Government: Vicious Campaign of Slander," *Jewish Chronicle*, 1 Mar. 1946, 1.

39. See the secret protocol of the meeting of the Central Committee of the PPR, 11 Aug. 1945, in Aleksander Kochański, ed., *Protokoły posiedzeń Sekretariatu KC PPR 1945–1946* (Warsaw, 2001), 89.

40. See the secret protocol of the meeting of the Central Committee of the PPR, 16 Aug. 1945, in Kochański, *Protokoły*, 92.

41. On the history and literature of, and Communist documents about, the UB, see Andrzej Paczkowski, "Żydzi w UB próba weryfikacji stereotypu," in Tomasz Szarota, ed., *Komunizm. Ideologia, System, Ludzie* (Warsaw, 2001), 192–204. This article makes an interesting comparison with the number of Jews and members of other nationalities, such as Poles and Latvians, in the Soviet state apparatus in the 1920s. It appeared in English in *Polin* 16 (2003): 453–64. See also Lech Głuchowski, letters to the *Times Literary Supplement*, 29 Mar. 1997.

42. See Paczkowski, "Żydzi," 197–98. The data cited by Paczkowski is accepted as the most reliable and is cited widely by historians: see, e.g., Kersten, *Polacy*, 83–84; and Polonsky and Michlic, *The Neighbors Respond*, 17. In his analysis Paczkowski takes into account the fact that some available Soviet and Polish documents give contradictory data and that some available data might not be wholly satisfactory because it was prepared by the Ministry of Internal Affairs in the 1970s.

43. See Wnuk, *Lubelski Okręg*, 205.

44. On the subject of the demography of the Polish-Jewish community in the early postwar period, see Andelson, "W Polsce," 389–90, 417–20.

45. See the documents about the UB in Andrzej Paczkowski, *Aparat bezpieczeństwa w Polsce w latach 1953–1954: Taktyka, strategia, metody* (Warsaw, 2004). Paczkowski's documentation of the number of employees in the UB is based on archival materials from the Bureau of State Defense (UOP).

46. On the scope and activities of the Jewish section of the PPR, see Grabski, *Działalność*, 67–100.

47. On the activities of various Jewish political parties and organizations and their membership, see Andelson, "W Polsce," 433–50. On the Zionist movement in early postwar Poland, see Natalia Aleksiun, *Dokąd dalej? Ruch syjonistyczny w Polsce (1944–1950)* (Warsaw, 2002).

48. On the self-identification of Polish-Jewish Communists and various perceptions of them within the Jewish community, see Schatz, *The Generation*, 236–42; and Teresa Torańska's interviews with prominent Jewish Communists in the PPR/PZPR: *Them: Stalin's Polish Puppets* (New York, 1987).

49. See Percy S. Cohen, *Jewish Radicals and Radical Jews* (London, New York, and Toronto, 1980), 85–88.

50. Concerning PPR membership in the early postwar period, see, e.g., Paczkowski, *Zdobycie*, 34, 79.

51. For a highly problematic account claiming that Communist military forces were responsible for the mistreatment of Jews in WWII, see *Tajne oblicze* GL-AL *i* PPR, a three-volume book published in Warsaw in 1997 by right-wing nationalistic historians Marek J. Chodakiewicz, Piotr Gontarczyk, and Leszek Żebrowski.

52. See *Manifest lipcowy* PKWN *i Deklaracja* PPR (Warsaw, 1982), 33.

53. For accounts of contradictory statements on equal rights made by PPR leaders, see Kersten, *Między Wyzwoleniem*, 11–12; and Marcin Zaremba, *Komunizm, legitymizacja, nacjonalizm. Nacjonalistyczna legitymizacja władzy komunistycznej w Polsce* (Warsaw, 2001), 125–28. Zaremba's *Komunizm* is an impressive account of the ethnonationalization of the PPR and the PZPR. The author not only conducts an impressive sociohistorical analysis but also cites Western literature on nationalism, including theoretical studies.

54. PKWN Manifesto of 22 July 1944, in *Manifest*, 2. The same sections of the PKWN Manifesto are cited in English in Bernard D. Weinryb, "Poland," in Paul Meyer et al., *The Jews in the Soviet Satellites* (Syracuse, 1953), 258.

55. For the use of national and religious ceremonies and the emphasis on creating a homogenized Polish nation-state in PPR propaganda, see Zaremba, *Komunizm*, 121–74; Marcin Zaremba, "Partia i naród. PRL: internacjonalizm w cudzysłowie," *Polityka*, no. 48 (1995): 72; Kersten, *Między Wyzwoleniem*, 12–13.

56. In his detailed analysis of Communist propaganda, Zaremba states that the language and arguments of the PPR were closer to those of Roman Dmowski than to the language and arguments of the Communist Rosa Luxemburg. See Zaremba, *Komunizm*, 140.

57. See Zaremba, *Komunizm*, 139–41, 145–47.

58. See Norman Davies, *The Heart of Europe: A Short History of Poland* (Oxford, 1986), 325–26; Jerzy Jedlicki, "Nationalism and State Formation," in Gerrits and Adler, *Vampires Unstaked*, 130; Łepkowski, *Uparte*; and Steinlauf, *Bondage*, 43. By contrast, Andrzej Walicki opposes making close links between the vision of Poland proclaimed by the National Democrats and the vision of Poland proclaimed by the Communists. Walicki argues that this position obscures understanding of the nature of Polish integral nationalism and its nation-building project. See Walicki, "Naród," 22–23.

59. Krystyna Kersten briefly discusses the problem of the critical reactions of the Jewish section of the PPR toward advocacy of a homogenized Polish nation-state for Poles and the negative effects of this idea on minorities. See Krystyna Kersten, "The Polish Stalinism and the Jewish Question," in Leonid Luks, ed., *Der spatstalinismus und die "jüdische Frage": Zur antisemitischen Wendung des Kommunismus* (Weimar, 1998), 222–23; and Maciej Pisarski, "W Nowej Polsce," *Karta*, no. 18 (1996): 114.

60. Marek Bitter, statement made at a session of the Jewish faction of the PPR, autumn 1945, cited in Kersten, "The Polish," 222.

61. Stanisław Ossowski, "Na tle wydarzeń kieleckich," *Kuźnica*, no. 38 (1946): 123–25.

62. For a detailed analysis of PPR propaganda about the Germans, see Zaremba, *Komunizm*, 141–42, 157–62.

63. Władysław Gomułka, speech, minutes of the plenum of the PPR Central Committee, 20–21 May 1944. Large sections of this document have been published in a collection of Communist documents: Antony Polonsky and Bolesław Drukier, eds., *The Beginnings of Communist Rule in Poland* (London, Boston, and Henley, 1980), 440–41. This is the first important collection of PPR documents of the early postwar period published in English.

64. There is a vast literature in Polish and Ukrainian on the anti-Polish violence in Wołyń and the activities of the Ukrainian nationalists in WWII and the early postwar period. Ukrainian nationalist authors maintain that the actions against Poles in Wołyń were a retaliation for Polish attacks on Ukrainian villages and political activities. See, e.g., Petro R. Sodol, *UPA, They Fought Hitler and Stalin: A Brief Overview of Military Aspects from the History of the Ukrainian Insurgent Army, 1942–1949* (New York, 1987). Some Polish sources portray Ukrainian aspirants as "hirelings" of Nazi Germany, using this interpretation as an explanation of the Action Vistula. See, e.g., Edward Prus, *Atamania* UPA*: Tragedia kresów* (Warsaw, 1985). For a balanced overview of anti-Polish violence by Ukrainian nationalists in Wołyń in 1943, see Snyder, *The Reconstruction*, 168–72. For an overview of historical literature on the subject, see Bogumiła Berdychowska, "Ukraińcy wobec Wołynia," *Zeszyty Historyczne* 146 (2004): 65–104.

65. See Hałagida, *Ukraińcy*, 34; and Timothy Snyder, " 'To Resolve the Ukrainian Problem Once and for All,' The Ethnic Cleansing of Ukrainians in Poland 1943–1947," *Journal of Cold War Studies* 1, no. 2 (1999): 114–15.

66. Historians vary in their interpretation of the PPR's commitment to combating anti-Semitism. For example, Grzegorz Berent claims that during the first fifteen years of Communist Poland the ruling elites were committed to combating anti-Semitism. See Grzegorz Berent, "Polacy-Żydzi, 1918–1945-1989," in Roman Wapiński, ed., *U progu niepodległości* (Gdansk, 1999), 189. In *Działalność* Grabski, who seems to agree with Berent's thesis, at the same time notes that contradictions in regard to Jews were transparent within the Party and were manifested in different forms. See Grabski, *Działalność*, 30. I argue that contradictions and ambivalence played a much more important role within the ethnic Polish section of the PPR in the lower and higher ranks of the Party. This problem needs further investigation.

67. See Andelson, "W Polsce," 400–403; Cała and Datner-Śpiewak, *Dzieje*, 16–18; and Blus-Węgrowska, "Atmosfera," 87–99.

68. Central Archives for the History of the Jewish People (CAJP), Jerusalem, HM 2/8112–8134, no. 2, letter, 23 Feb. 1945, Voivode of Kielce Province, signed by M. Lewaniewski.

69. Minutes of the Meeting of the Jewish Committee of Kielce Province, 14 May 1945, CAJP, HM 2/8112–8134.

70. See Blus-Węgrowska, "Atmosfera," 87–88, 98–99.

71. Roman Zambrowski, speech at the plenum of the Central Committee of the PPR, 3–4 July 1945, in Kochański, *Protokoły*, 78.

72. Ostap Dłuski (Adolf Langer), speech at the plenum of the Central Committee of the PPR, 29 July 1946, in Kochański, *Protokoły*, 280.

73. On this issue, see Naimark, "Gomułka and Stalin," 12.

74. Records of anti-Jewish attitudes among the PPR leadership can be found in the Bolesław Bierut Archives, held in the Archives of New Documents (ANN) in Warsaw. I express my gratitude to Professor Andrzej Paczkowski of the Institute of Political Studies of the Polish Academy of Sciences for providing me with access to a sample of Bierut's notes. Historians gained access to these archives only after the political changes of 1989.

75. Ignacy Loga Sowiński, speech, minutes of the plenum of the Central Committee of the PPR, 20–21 May 1944, in Polonsky and Drukier, *The Beginnings*, 435.

76. Władysław Gomułka, speech, minutes of the plenum of the Central Committee of the PPR, 20–21 May 1944, in Polonsky and Drukier, *The Beginnings*, 441.

77. See the novel by Julian Stryjkowski, *Wielki Strach* (Warsaw, 1980), 124 (samizdat edition). *Wielki Strach* was republished in a legal edition in 1989. Also see the memoirs of Hersz Smolar, *Ojf der lecter pozicje mit der lecter hofenung, in Pojln noch der cwejter welt milchome* (Tel Aviv, 1982), 30, 31.

78. Norman Naimark views Gomułka's position on Jews expressed in this letter to Stalin as a manifestation of his anti-Jewish prejudices. See Naimark, "Gomułka and Stalin," 15–16. In *Działalność* Grabski interprets the same letter as a sign that Gomułka had succumbed to anti-Semitic propaganda. See Grabski, *Działalność*, 36–37.

79. On the historical background to the conversation between Stalin and Gomułka, see Zaremba, *Komunizm*, 183–84; and Lech W. Głuchowski, "Gomułka Writes to Stalin in 1948: Introduction," *Polin* 17 (2004): 365–75. Głuchowski's article is the most thorough exploration of the myth of Judeo-Communism among the leaders of PPR.

80. Bolesław Bierut, speech, minutes of the plenum of the Central Committee of the PPR, 31 Aug.–3 Sept. 1948, in Aleksander Kochański, ed., *Posiedzienie Komitetu Centralnego Polskiej Partii Robotniczej 31 sierpnia–3 września 1948 r* (Pultusk and Warsaw, 1998), 19–45.

81. Gomułka to Stalin, 14 Dec. 1948, in *Dziś*, no. 6 (1993): 108–9 (with an introduction by Andrzej Werblan). This letter recently appeared in English, translated by Lech W. Głuchowski, in *Polin* 17 (2004): 376–81.

82. For an overview of anti-Jewish policies in the Soviet Union, see, e.g., Jonathan Frankel, "The Soviet Regime and Anti-Zionism," in Mendelsohn, *Essential Papers*, 449–51. In this article Frankel discusses the general pattern of replacing Jewish Communists with members of (territorially based) majority nations during the period of Communist consolidation of power in the Soviet Union. It is worth mentioning here that some historians argue that Stalin, in the Sovietization of Poland, used Jewish Communists to reinforce, qualitatively and numerically, the meager PPR cadre avail-

able to him in 1944. See Davies and Polonsky, *Jews*, 51–52; and Schatz, *The Generation*, 180–81.

83. In Polish historiography there has been a tendency to portray the working class and peasants as passive victims of the Communist regime. For a more complex social history of the working class and the relationship between the workers and the regime in early postwar Poland, see Padraic Kenney, *Rebuilding Poland: Workers and Communists, 1945–1950* (Ithaca and London, 1997). On the relationship between peasants and the Communist regime, see Dariusz Jarosz, *Polityka władz komunistycznych w latach 1948–1956 a chłopi* (Warsaw, 1998); and Dariusz Jarosz, *Polacy a stalinizm* (Warsaw, 2000).

84. On Gomułka's sensitivities about the national cause and his insistence that the PPR was a Polish Communist party, see Zaremba, *Komunizm*, 172–73.

85. Naimark discusses the opposition of Gomułka to the repatriation of Polish Jews from Russia in "Gomułka and Stalin," 14.

86. Excerpt of an anti-Communist leaflet, May 1947, cited in Zaremba, *Komunizm*, 173.

87. On the subject of the links between Communism and nationalism/ethno-nationalism, see the introduction in Klein and Reban, *The Politics*, 1–7.

88. Minutes of the meeting of the Jewish Committee of Kielce Province, 14 May 1945, CAJP, HM 2/8112–8134.

89. This leaflet is cited in Blus-Węgrowska, "Atmosfera," 98.

90. Leaflet to the Jewish community of Jedlińsk, 29 July 1945, CAJP, HM 2/8112–8134, no. 5, 11.

91. It is estimated that among 214,210 repatriates from the Soviet Union who returned between 8 Feb. and 31 July 1946, 136,579 were Jews. See Andelson, "W Polsce," 397–98.

92. According to Blus-Węgrowska, the new influx of Polish-Jewish repatriates from the Soviet Union contributed to the spread of anti-Jewish propaganda in Lower Silesia and Pomerania in the spring of 1946. See Blus-Węgrowska, "Atmosfera," 97–98. On the anti-Jewish atmosphere in the western territories, see Albert Stankowski, "Emigracja Żydów z Pomorza Zachodniego w latach 1945–1960," in Jerzy Tomaszewski, ed., *Studia z dziejów i kultury Żydów w Polsce po 1945 roku* (Warsaw, 1997), 83–102.

93. Ossowski, "Na tle," 124–25.

94. See Cała and Datner-Śpiewak, *Dzieje*, 15; Steinlauf, *Bondage*, 51; and Kersten, *Polacy*, 135. Waves of anti-Jewish violence also broke out in Hungary and Slovakia during this period.

95. The figures on Jewish casualties vary in different sources. The highest figure, of almost three thousand dead, is cited by Israel Gutman in *Hayehudim bepolin ahari milhemet haolam hashniyah* (Jerusalem, 1985), whereas David Engel, in his "Patterns of Anti-Jewish Violence in Poland 1944–1946," *Yad Vashem Studies* 26 (1998): 43–86, assesses the number of casualties at between five hundred and six hundred. Other cited figures for casualties vary from thirteen hundred to fifteen hundred. See Cała and Datner-Śpiewak, *Dzieje*, 15.

96. See Blus-Węgrowska, "Atmosfera," 93, 95.

97. For a detailed historical description of the Kielce pogrom, see Bożena Szaynok, *Pogrom w Kielcach 4 Lipca 1946* (Wroclaw, 1992). Another individual case is the Cracow pogrom of 11 Aug. 1945. See Anna Cichopek, *Pogrom Żydów w Krakowie 11 sierpnia 1945 r* (Warsaw, 2000). Cichopek's book contains a large selection of documents from the pogrom (129–234). Although Cichopek's book, like Szaynok's, is a well-researched and solid study, neither work provides a broader historical contextualization of these pogroms.

98. On the subject of different approaches to the anti-Jewish violence of 1945 and 1947 in Polish and Jewish historiography, see Daniel Blatman, "Polish Antisemitism and 'Judeo-Communism,'" *East European Jewish Affairs* 27, no. 1 (1997): 35–41.

99. For example, Krystyna Kersten presents a thesis about a possible masterminding of the pogrom by Soviet security forces. See Krystyna Kersten, "Pogrom kielecki-znaki zapytania," in Wrzesiński, *Polska-Polacy*, 158–59.

100. For a thesis positing the spontaneous nature of the Kielce pogrom, see Andelson, "W Polsce," 400–404.

101. In the short article "Dom na Plantach" Polish historian Andrzej Garlicki presents a conclusion similar to Paczkowski's about the lack of research into the role of the population at large in the Kielce pogrom. See Andrzej Garlicki, "Dom na Plantach," *Polityka*, no. 27 (2001): 60–62.

102. See Andrzej Paczkowski's introduction to the first edition of special Communist reports on the Kielce pogrom, in Andrzej Paczkowski, ed., "Raporty o pogromie", *Puls*, no. 50 (1991): 109–10. The English translation of some of these reports, with a new introduction by Joanna Michlic-Coren, was published in *Polin* 13 (2000): 253–67. These reports were prepared only for very limited circulation among the top leadership of the PPR.

103. See Marek J. Chodakiewicz, *After the Holocaust: Polish-Jewish Conflict in the Wake of World War II* (New York, 2003). Chodakiewicz's thesis about early postwar violence is based on a premise identical to that of Piotr Gontarczyk regarding interwar anti-Jewish violence. See Gontarczyk, *Pogrom?* chap. 4.

104. See Józef Orlicki, *Szkice z dziejów i stosunków polsko-żydowskich 1918–1949* (Szczecin, 1983). I would like to express my gratitude to Professor Jerzy Tomaszewski for pointing out to me that Orlicki was a member of the UB in postwar Poland. In fact, Orlicki's book provides an example of the anti-Semitic attitudes present among UB forces.

105. For a comparison of anti-Jewish violence between 1945–47 and 1918–39, see Michlic-Coren, "Anti-Jewish."

106. See Engel, "Patterns," 84–86.

107. For the most useful definitions and analyses of the project of ethnic cleansing, see Norman M. Naimark's introduction to his *Fires of Hatred: Ethnic Cleansing in Twentieth-Century Europe* (Cambridge MA and London, 2001), 1–16.

108. Other reasons for the emigration of Jews from Poland in the early postwar years were

desire to join families living abroad, Zionist ideology, and strong negative attitudes toward Communism. On this subject, see Schatz, *The Generation*, 203–4; and Borwicz, "Polish-Jewish," 190.

109. For figures on the emigration of Jews from Poland in 1945–47, see Yehuda Bauer, *Flight and Rescue: Brichah* (New York, 1970), 7–10.

110. On the hostilities of the NSZ toward Belorussians, see Kulak, "Pacyfikacja," 51–53.

111. Blus-Węgrowska, "Atmosfera," 98.

112. Stefan Tomaszewski, head of the Warsaw Department of Communication, report, 10–11 July 1946, Dęblin. See Paczkowski, "Raporty," 109–10.

113. On the subject of "moral panic," see chap. 4.

114. The ritual-murder allegation (blood libel) was a medieval religious belief that claimed that Jews were required by their religion to murder Christian children in order to use their blood to bake the Passover bread (matzo). The subject of ritual murder in Poland during the first three decades of the twentieth century has not been widely researched.

115. On fears in Polish society, see Andrzej Paczkowski, *Pół wieku* (Warsaw, 1996), 149. On the subject of rumors circulating in the early postwar period, see Dariusz Jarosz and Maria Pasztor, *W krzywym zwierciadle. Polityka władz komunistycznych w świetle plotek i pogłosek z lat 1949–1956* (Warsaw, 1995), 132–35. On the psychological need to search for "the guilty" responsible for social and political crises in early postwar society, see Alina Cała, "Kształtowanie się polskiej i żydowskiej wizji martyrologicznej po II wojnie światowej," *Przegląd socjologiczny* 2 (2000): 167–80.

116. See *Biuletyny*, 135.

117. *Biuletyny*, 144.

118. According to a survey conducted by Alina Cała, belief in ritual murder persisted among peasants even into the 1970s. Among sixty peasants she interviewed during her fieldwork only twelve firmly rejected the concept of ritual murder. See Cała, *The Image*, 3–5.

119. Bishop Teodor Kubina, appeal, 9 July 1946. The appeal was aired in Polish by Warsaw Radio. See Poland's Radio for Overseas, Archives of the Wiener Library, PC, 8189, 22, A.

120. For an overview of ritual murder in the Roman Catholic Church in Poland from the sixteenth century until 1939, see Modras, *The Catholic*, 194–98, 203–7.

121. Ambassador Victor Cavendish-Bentinck, telegram, 28 Aug. 1946, in Aryeh Joseph Kochavi, "The Catholic Church and Antisemitism in Poland Following World War II as Reflected in British Diplomatic Documents," *Gal-Ed* 11 (1989): 123.

122. Three documents about the anti-Jewish artifacts in the church in Łęczyca were published by Danuta Blus-Węgrowska in *Karta*, no. 18 (1996): 120.

123. *Biuletyny*, 30.

124. *Biuletyny*, 135.

125. *Biuletyny*, 183.

126. The Cracow pogrom was the first major anti-Jewish riot of the postwar era. See Cichopek, *Pogrom*, 67–93; Tomasz Polański, "Pogrom Żydów w Krakowie," *Echo Krakowa*, Aug. 1990, 2. The Stalin files also contain information about the Cracow pogrom. See Siergiej Kriwienko, "Raporty z Polski," *Karta*, no. 15 (1995): 30–32.

127. Mojżesz Cukier, eyewitness account, cited in Stanisław Meducki and Zenon Wrona, eds., *Antyżydowskie wydarzenia kieleckie 4 Lipca 1946 roku* (Kielce, 1992), 113.

128. Itzhak Cukierman, statement, minutes of the CKZP, 10 July 1946, published in Marian Turski, "Pogrom kielecki w protokołach Centralnego Komitetu Żydów w Polsce," *Almanach Żydowski* (1996–97), 57.

129. Paczkowski, "Raporty," 107.

130. See Dariusz Jarosz, "Problem antysemityzmu w Polsce w latach 1949–1956 w świetle akt niektórych centralnych instytucji państwowych i partyjnych," *BZIH*, no. 2 (1997): 49–52.

131. For the records of the trial of 11 July 1946, see Meducki and Wrona, *Antyżydowskie*, 192–205.

132. Meducki and Wrona, *Antyżydowskie*, 200–205.

133. An American journalist of Polish-Jewish origin, Shmuel L. Shneiderman, raised this issue in his popular book *Between Fear and Hope* (New York, 1947), 118.

134. This anonymous letter is cited but not analyzed in Kersten, *Polacy*, 113.

135. Comrades Doliński, Domagała, Krych, and Fir, report, published in Paczkowski, "Raporty," 111.

136. The issue of Bishop Wyszyński's position on the anti-Jewish violence of 1945 to 1947 was first raised by Michał Borwicz. See Borwicz, "Polish-Jewish," 195.

137. Archives of the Jewish Historical Institute in Warsaw, file no. 248, CKZP, Legal Department, Sprawozdanie z audiencji u Jego Ekscelencji księdza biskupa Wyszyńskiego delegacji wojewódzkiego Komitetu Żydów w Polsce w Lublinie, 1.

138. Cardinal August Hlond's statement from W. H. Lawrence, Press Archives of the Wiener Library, no. 2B, 208; "Cardinal Puts Blame on Some Jews for Pogrom" and "Poles to Be Hanged," *New York Times*, 12 July 1946. See also "Cardinal Hlond," *Manchester Guardian*, 17 July 1946.

139. See Engel, "Patterns," 69–70.

140. Four documents were found in the offices of Kielce Cathedral on 12 Jan. 1952. According to Bożena Szaynok of the University of Wrocław, they all are deposited in private archives in Poland.

141. R. Zalek, "Uwagi i ostrzeżenia na temat zajść kieleckich z dnia 4 lipca," introduction and conclusion. I would like to express my gratitude to Dr. Bożena Szaynok for giving me a copy of this document.

142. Official appeal to the Kielce public, 4 July 1946, published in the appendix to Szaynok, *Pogrom*, 112.

143. See Jerzy Andrzejewski, "Zagadnienie polskiego antysemityzmu," *Odrodzenie*, no. 27 (1946): 4, and no. 28 (1946): 3. For an analysis of the reactions of left-wing Polish

intellectuals to the Holocaust and anti-Semitism in early postwar Poland. see Joanna Michlic, "The Holocaust and Its Aftermath as Perceived in Poland: Voices of Polish Intellectuals, 1945–1947," in David Bankier, ed., *"The Jews are Coming Back": The Return of Jews to Their Countries of Origin in Europe after WWII* (Jerusalem, 2005), 206–30. For an analysis of the reactions of various media toward the Holocaust and anti-Semitism, see Dariusz Libionka, "Antysemityzm i zagłada na łamach prasy w Polsce w latach 1945–46," *Polska 1944/45–1989: Studia i materiały* 2 (1996): 151–90.

144. See Blus-Węgrowska, "Atmosfera," 88.

145. See Szaynok, *Pogrom*, 90–93.

146. See Andrzej Rzepliński, "Ten jest z ojczyzny mojej? Sprawy karne oskarżonych o wymordowanie Żydów w Jedwabnem w świetle zasady rzetelnego procesu," in Machcewicz and Persak, *Wokół*, 1: 353–60; and Andrzej Rzepliński, "Jedwabne—Let Us Be Silent in the Face of This Crime: Piotr Lipiński Talks with Professor Andrzej Rzepliński," in Polonsky and Michlic, *The Neighbors Respond*, 137–44. (The original Polish version of this interview appeared in *Gazeta Wyborcza* on 22 July 2002.) Various documents of the post-1945 trials for the Jedwabne pogrom were well researched and well edited by Krzysztof Persak, appearing in Machcewicz and Persak, *Wokół*, 2: 375–414, 415–712, 713–816, 817–62.

147. On the reactions of the PSL to anti-Jewish violence, see Borwicz, "Polish-Jewish," 197; and Libionka, "Antysemityzm," 165–70.

148. On the referendum of 30 June 1946, see Kersten, *Narodziny*, 249.

149. "Kielce," *Honor i Ojczyzna*, Aug. 1946, cited in Kersten, "Pogrom," 158–59.

150. Letter published in the Bulletin of the Ministry of Public Security, 30 Mar. 1947, cited in *Biuletyny*, 16.

151. For an analysis of left-wing intellectuals' writing on anti-Semitism in the early postwar period, see Michlic, "The Holocaust," 206–30; and Libionka, "Antysemityzm," 157–65.

152. Witold Kula, "Our Role in It," *Gal-Ed* 18 (2002): 110. The article, with the introduction by Marcin Kula, the son of Witold, was first published in English in *Gal-Ed* 18 (2002): 101–17.

153. See Marcin Kula, *Uparta sprawa. Żydowska? Polska? Ludzka?* (Cracow, 2004), 154–68.

154. On the issue of Polish cultural elites opposing anti-Jewish actions and prejudice in the early postwar period, see Borwicz, "Polish-Jewish," 196.

155. There has been very little written in a scholarly fashion on the subject of the All-Polish Anti-Racist League. On the All-Polish Anti-Racist League and its activities and publications challenging anti-Jewish perspectives within Polish society, see the article by Władysław Bartoszewski, one of its prominent members, "The Founding of the All-Polish Anti-Racist League in 1946," *Polin* 4 (1989): 243–54.

7. The Communist Regime and the Myth

1. There is a vast growing body of literature on the links between Communism and nationalism. See, e.g., Benedict Anderson, *Imagined Communities: Reflections on the*

Origin and Spread of Nationalism (London and New York, 1990), 11–14; Roman
Szporluk, *Communism and Nationalism: Karl Marx versus Friedrich List* (New York
and Oxford, 1988), 223–24; the introduction in Klein and Reban, *The Politics*; Gerrits,
"Paradox of Freedom"; and Elemer Hankiss, "In Search of a Paradigm," *Daedalus*, no.
119 (1990): 183–214.

2. Gerrits, "Paradox of Freedom," 100.

3. See the BBC's Summary of World Broadcasts for Eastern Europe, 10 Mar. 1981, 4–5. A
short report about the events taking place at Warsaw University was published in
Życie Warszawy on 9 Mar. 1981.

4. On Aleksander Kwaśniewski's apology for Mar. 1968 and various reactions to it, see
Marek Beylin, "Narodowy Marzec," *Gazeta Wyborcza*, 5 Mar. 1998, 2; and Andrzej
Osęka," Orzeł i krzywe nosy," *Gazeta Wyborcza*, 14–15 May 1998. On the thirtieth
anniversary of Mar. 1968, also see articles published by various intellectuals, including
former victims of the Zionist purge of 1968: Leopold Unger, "Za duzo Żydów czy za
mało socjalizmu?" *Gazeta Wyborcza*, 10 Apr. 1998, 24–26; Marcin Król, "Podzwonne
dla Marca '68," *Tygodnik Powszechny*, 8 Mar. 1998, 9; Krzysztof T. Toeplitz, "Bierz karabelę, chamie bracie . . . ," *Gazeta Wyborcza*, 3 Mar. 1998, 19–21; *Życie Warszawy*, special
issue of *Ex Libris*, Mar. 1998, including articles by contributors Adam Bromberg, Jan
T. Gross, Józef Duriasz, and Michał Komar; and *Marzec hańby, 1968–1998*, special issue
of *Wprost*, 8 Mar. 1998, including Jacek Kurczewski's article "Rekolecje marcowe" and
interviews with the March émigrés.

5. On the subject of the recovery of Polish citizenship for victims of the anti-Zionist
purge, see, e.g., the editorial "Obywatelstwo polskie," *Gazeta Wyborcza*, 16 Mar. 1998,
2.

6. For works that were the outcome of special conferences dedicated to 1968, see, e.g.,
Marzec 68. Sesja na Uniwersytecie Warszawskim 1981 (Warsaw, 1981) (samizdat publication); and Marcin Kula, Piotr Osęka, and Marcin Zaremba, eds., *Marzec 1968.
Trzydzieści lat później*, vol. 1, *Referaty* (Warsaw, 1998). In vol. 2 important secret state
and police documents were published. See Marcin Zaremba, ed., *Marzec 1968. Trzydzieści lat później*, vol. 2, *Dzień po dniu w raportach* SB *oraz Wydziału Organizacyjnego*
KC PZPR (Warsaw, 1998). See also Grzegosz Sołtysiak and Józef Stępień, eds., *Marzec
'68. Między tragedią a podłością* (Warsaw, 1998); and Piotr Osęka, *Syjoniści, inspiratorzy,
wichrzyciele. Obraz wroga w propagandzie Marca 1968* (Warsaw, 1999).

7. Dariusz Stola, *Kampania antysyjonistyczna* (Warsaw, 2000). This important book
discusses some anti-Jewish images and contains a large selection of documents (270–
385). One of its reviews was published by Włodzimierz Rozenbaum in *Kwartalnik
Historii Żydów*, June 2001, 241–52. (In English the review was published in *Polin* 16
[2003]: 491–504.)

8. Jerzy Eisler, *Marzec 1968. Geneza, Przebieg, Konsekwencje* (Warsaw, 1991).

9. Michał Głowiński, *Nowomowa po polsku* (Warsaw, 1991), 63–67; and Michał Głowiński, *Pismak 1863 i inne szkice o różnych brzydkich rzeczach* (Warsaw, 1995), 60–94.

10. See Paul Lendvai, *Anti-Semitism in Eastern Europe* (London, 1971); Josef Banas, *The Scapegoats: The Exodus of the Remnants of Polish Jewry* (London, 1979); Łukasz Hirszowicz, "The Jewish Issue in Post-War Polish Communist Politics," in Abramsky, Jachimczyk, and Polonsky, *The Jews*, 199–208; Celia Stopnicka Heller, " 'Anti-Zionism' and the Political Struggle within the Elite of Poland," *Jewish Journal of Sociology*, no. 2 (1969): 133–50.

11. See, e.g., *Czas Zadymy*, special issue of *Krytyka Polityczna* (2004)

12. On the impact on Poland of the transformation of the Soviet regime after the death of Stalin, see Leon W. Głuchowski, "Poland, 1956: Krushchev, Gomułka, and the 'Polish October,' " see *http://www.gwu.edu/nsarchiv/CWIHP/BULLETINS/b5a2.htm*.

13. See Schatz, *The Generation*, 264–67.

14. On political, social, and economic changes brought about by the "political thaw" of Oct. 1956, see, e.g., Marian K. Dziewanowski, *The Communist Party of Poland: An Outline of History* (Cambridge MA and London, 1976), 282–93.

15. Głuchowski, "Poland, 1956," 9.

16. On the popularity of Władysław Gomułka in Oct. 1956, see, e.g., Dziewanowski, *The Communist Party*, 286; and Paweł Machcewicz, *Polski Rok 1956* (Warsaw, 1993), 184–91.

17. On anti-Jewish sentiments and attitudes within society at large and in the rank and file of the PZPR and the Party apparatus in 1956, see Machcewicz, *Polski*, 216–31. Machcewicz's findings about the scale of the anti-Jewish mood in society in 1956 challenge the popular proposition, which argues that such sentiments were confined only to some factions within the Party.

18. For a description of cases of anti-Jewish disturbances in 1956, see Machcewicz, *Polski*, 217–22; Schatz, *The Generation*, 273; and Jarosz, "Problem," 52–55. On anti-Jewish hostilities among youths, see Jadwiga Siekierska, "O sprawach draźliwych słów kilka," *Nowe Drogi*, no. 6 (1956): 3–4. On anti-Jewish attitudes among schoolchildren in early postwar Poland, see Stankiewicz, "Emigracja," 90. Stankiewicz cites results of a questionnaire conducted in primary schools in Szczecin in Apr. 1947, according to which 50 percent of interviewed pupils said no when asked if they would accept a Jewish child as a friend.

19. The article about the situation of Jewish children in schools written by Antoni Czałkowski was published in *Trybuna Ludu* on 6 June 1956. Konstanty Jeleński discussed Czałkowski's article in the émigré journal *Kultura* in 1956. See Jeleński, "Od Endeków," 13–14.

20. This case is described in documents held in the Archives of New Acts, VI-237/VII-3835. The document is cited in Machcewicz, *Polski*, 219.

21. See the Jewish Telegraphic Report sent to London on 7 Mar. 1975, "Jews in Poland Urged to Alert Parliament against Anti-Semitism," Archives of the Joint in Jerusalem, collection C 61.00.

22. See M. S. Handler, "Attacks on Jews in Poland Mount," *New York Times*, 9 Jan. 1957, 2.

23. This phenomenon is also shown in Machcewicz, *Polski*, 220–24.

24. See Leszek Kołakowski, "Antysemityzm—pięć tez nienowych i przestroga," in *Wybór artykułów, Po Prostu 1955–1956* (Warsaw, 1956), 160–67. Anti-Semitic attitudes were also condemned in the émigré journal *Kultura*. See Jeleński, "Od Endeków," 13–20.

25. Jerzy Turowicz, "Antysemityzm," *Tygodnik Powszechny*, 11 Mar. 1957. This article was noted by Western correspondents. See Sydney Gruson, "Church in Poland Denounces Bias," *New York Times*, 21 Mar. 1957, 2.

26. Tadeusz Mazowiecki, "Antysemityzm ludzi łagodnych i dobrych," *Under One Heaven: Poles and Jews*, special issue of *Więź* (1998): 30. This edition includes a short commentary by the author. The article was first published in *Więź* in 1960.

27. Mazowiecki, "Antysemityzm," 31.

28. On the history of these groups and their membership, see Eisler, *Marzec*, 22–30. See also Hirszowicz, "The Jewish Issue," 201–3; and Schatz, *The Generation*, 267–69.

29. Schatz, *The Generation*, 267.

30. Schatz, *The Generation*, 268.

31. See the conversation of Adam Bromberg with Tomasz Jastrun: "Encyklopedyści," *ExLibris/Życie Warszawy*, Mar. 1993, 6.

32. The terms *Chamy* and *Żydzi* were introduced in the pamphlet "Chamy i Żydy," by Witold Jedlicki. The pamphlet first appeared in the Paris-based *Kultura* in 1961 and was republished in Poland in samizdat publications such as Warsaw's *Krąg* in 1981.

33. Jerzy Eisler discusses the presence of former Stalinists within the Natolin and Puławska groups. See Eisler, *Marzec*, 25. See also Cała and Datner-Śpiewak, *Dzieje*, 91.

34. For excerpts of Nowak's speech, see Cała and Datner-Śpiewak, *Dzieje*, 145–47; and Zaremba, *Komunizm*, 236–37. On Nowak's speech, see Zaremba, *Komunizm*, 236–38. Zaremba recognizes the anti-Semitic nature of Nowak's speech. On the same subject, see also Schatz, *The Generation*, 268; and Lendvai, *Anti-Semitism*, 221.

35. Zenon Nowak's speech, cited in Zbysław Rykowski and Wiesław Władyka, *Polska próba Październik '56* (Cracow, 1989), 210, 211.

36. The Poznań demonstrations were conducted under the slogans of "More bread," "More freedom and Catholic religion in public life," and "Let's get rid of the Communists and the Russians." On the Poznań demonstrations, see Machcewicz, *Polski*, 77–111; and Rykowski and Władyka, *Polska próba*. The estimated number of individuals killed in the Poznań demonstration varies from fifty-three to seventy.

37. Schatz, *The Generation*, 273.

38. For data concerning the size of the Jewish community in the 1950s and 1960s, see Cała and Datner-Śpiewak, *Dzieje*, 175–76; and Schatz, *The Generation*, 273.

39. See Eisler, *Marzec*, 83–85; and Schatz, *The Generation*, 283–86.

40. For data on membership in the PZPR, see Feliks Tych, *Długi cień zagłady* (Warsaw, 1999). Tych cites the number of newcomers to the PZPR, published in 1968 in the Party's statistical documents for internal use. Similar figures are cited in Schatz, *The Generation*, 286.

41. See Lendvai, *Anti-Semitism*, 226.

42. See Mieczysław F. Rakowski, *Dzienniki polityczne 1958–1962* (Warsaw, 1998), 252, 253.

43. On this problem in the Soviet Union, see Frankel, "The Soviet," 441.

44. For an overview of Schaff's arguments and responses to Schaff's *Marksizm a jednostka ludzka*, see Zaremba, *Komunizm*, 298–301.

45. Andrzej Werblan, discussing Schaff's *Marxism and the Human Individual*, in *Nowe Drogi*, no. 12 (1965): 59.

46. Wincenty Kraśko, discussing Schaff's *Marxism and the Human Individual*, in *Nowe Drogi*, no. 12 (1965): 76.

47. According to Schatz, the process of collecting data about prominent Jewish members of the PZPR, the government, state institutions, and the army had been completed by 1964. See Schatz, *The Generation*, 290. The historian Dariusz Stola cites Tadeusz Walichnowski's comments about the greatly advanced collection of data on Zionists by 1967. In 1967 Walichnowski became deputy director at the Ministry of Interior Affairs, Department 3, which specialized in collecting such data. This is evidence that the collection of index cards about "Zionists" was indeed advanced by the second half of the 1960s. See Stola, *Kampania*, 64–65.

48. On the discreet and unpublicized removal of Jewish personnel from the Ministry of Interior Affairs and the army, see Schatz, *The Generation*, 289–94; and Tadeusz Pióro, "Czystki w Wojsku Polskim," *BZIH*, no. 2 (1997): 61–63. See also Stola, *Kampania*, 58–64.

49. Soviet leaders' encouragement of the policy of the "dejudaization" of the PZPR, the state apparatus, and the army is briefly discussed in Schatz, *The Generation*, 290; Pióro, "Czystki," 64; and Dziewanowski, *The Communist Party*, 298–99. This issue requires a separate treatment.

50. Lendvai, *Anti-Semitism*, 226.

51. On Mieczysław Moczar, see Krzysztof Lesiakowski, *Mieczysław Moczar "Mietek." Biografia polityczna* (Warsaw, 1998). See also Stola, *Kampania*, 246–47; Zaremba, *Komunizm*, 285–86, 287–92; Eisler, *Marzec*, 39–70; and Lendvai, *Anti-Semitism*, 227–30. For Moczar's statement of 28 June 1967, see Stola, *Kampania*, 293–95.

52. Mieczysław Moczar, speech at the executive meeting of ZBOWiD, 4 May 1968, *Za Wolność i Lud*, 16–31 May 1968, 4, cited in Osęka, *Syjoniści*, 46.

53. Dziewanowski, *The Communist Party*, 291.

54. Moczar's 1948 saying that "a good AK member is a dead one" is not verified. It is cited in Eisler, *Marzec*, 44. By the 1960s Moczar had totally changed his tune about the AK. In 1966, at the news of the death of one of the former heads of the AK, General Bór-Komorowski, Moczar supposedly sent a wreath with a card attached that stated: "Sleep my colleague in a dark grave and have dreams about Poland." Toeplitz cites the latter information in "Bierz karabelę," 21.

55. Dziewanowski, *The Communist Party*, 291.

56. Steinlauf, *Bondage*, 79.

57. On Bolesław Piasecki's prewar and postwar political affiliations and activities, see the political biography by Antoni Dudek and Grzegosz Pytel, *Bolesław Piasecki. Próba biografii politycznej* (London, 1990).

58. Dudek and Pytel, *Bolesław Piasecki*, 158–89.

59. See Łukasz Hirszowicz and Tadeusz Szafer, "The Jewish Scapegoat in Eastern Europe," *Patterns of Prejudice* 11, no. 5 (1997): 8.

60. On Czesław Pilichowski as director of the Commission to Investigate Crimes against the Polish Nation, see Steinlauf, *Bondage*, 82–83.

61. For other political slogans of the late 1960s, see *The Anti-Jewish Campaign in Present-Day Poland: Facts, Documents, Press Reports* (London, 1968), 21 (published by the Institute of Jewish Affairs). See also Zaremba, *Komunizm*, 348.

62. Michał Głowiński first raised this point in *Pismak*, 76–78.

63. For the differentiation among the various meanings of *Zionism*, I draw on an important analysis of uses of the term within official Soviet propaganda. See Frankel, "The Soviet," 440–41.

64. In agreement with the historian Michael Steinlauf, I reject the proposition that the anti-Jewish campaign of 1967–68 in Poland was organized by the Soviets. This proposition was put forward by some Polish historians such as Dziewanowski; see Dziewanowski, *The Communist Party*, 296–98. For a critical analysis of this thesis, see Steinlauf, *Bondage*, 78.

65. See Jerzy Jedlicki, *Źle urodzeni czyli o doświadczeniu historycznym. Scripta i postscripta* (London and Warsaw, 1983), 65–72.

66. Gomułka's speech of 19 Mar. 1968 is published in English in *The Anti-Jewish Campaign*, 30–32. For a detailed description of this speech, see Zaremba, *Komunizm*, 342–46.

67. See the song "Open Letter to Comrade First Secretary of the Central Committee of the PZPR," in *Folklor marca '68* (Warsaw, 1981) (samizdat publication).

68. Various anonymous letters were sent to the leadership of the PZPR asking that all Zionists be banished, constituting proof of such a trend within society at large. Stola published a small sample of such letters in *Kampania*, 322, 323.

69. Special Report of the Ministry of Internal Affairs, addition to the Biuletyn Wewnętrzny, nos. 68–69, Warsaw, 21 Mar. 1968. The document is published in Sołtysiak and Stępień, *Między tragedią*, 252.

70. Sołtysiak and Stępień, *Między tragedią*, 254. Records of negative reactions to Gomułka's speech of 19 Mar. can also be found in other secret Party reports. See Zaremba, *Dzień*, 175–79. On this subject, see also Mieczysław Rakowski, "Cała władza w ręce," *Gazeta Wyborcza*, 6 Mar. 1998, 20–21; and Marcin Zaremba, "Biedni Polacy 68. Społeczeństwo polskie wobec wydarzeń marcowych w świetle raportów KW i MSW dla kierownictwa PZPR," in Marcin Kula, Osęka, and Zaremba, *Referaty*, 144–82. These reports have to be treated with caution because the members of the Partisan group, which at this time dominated the Ministry of Internal Affairs, prepared them. How-

ever, the fact that they were prepared for internal circulation among PZPR leadership may also indicate that the information presented in these reports is most likely not false or exaggerated.

71. Franciszek Całka, director of the Predom factory, report, Apr. 1968, published in Stola, *Kampania*, 331–32.

72. Beata Dąbrowska, undated letter to Władysław Gomułka, first secretary of the Central Committee of the PZPR. This letter, together with an anonymous response of 2 May 1968 threatening that Dąbrowska would not be allowed to complete her studies if she continued to write such letters, was published in Sołtysiak and Stępień, *Między tragedią*, 360–62, 363. Dąbrowska's other letter to Gomułka, of 23 Feb. 1968, was published in Stola, *Kampania*, 317–18.

73. Józef Ledwoń, letter to the editors of *Polityka*, 8 May 1968, published in Stola, *Kampania*, 348.

74. Kliszko's speech was in accord with Gomułka's thesis circulated at the conference.

75. Zenon Kliszko, speech, 8 July 1968, Twelfth Conference of the Central Committee of the PZPR, 8, Archives of the Jewish Institute for Policy Research (AIJPR), file no. 323 0 (180).

76. Zaremba also notes the use of the expression "Fifth Column" in Gomułka's speech and its spread and impact in the anti-Jewish campaign of 1968. See Zaremba, *Komunizm*, 333.

77. Władysław Gomułka, speech, 19 July 1968, Sixth Congress of the Polish Trade Union, in *Anti-Jewish Campaign*, 11. On the historical background to this speech, see, e.g., Eisler, *Marzec*, 134–36; and *Anti-Jewish Campaign*, 10–12.

78. See *Anti-Jewish Campaign*, 12.

79. See Anna Barbara Jarosz, "Marzec w prasie," in Marcin Kula, Osęka, and Zaremba, *Referaty*, 99–125.

80. See Głowiński, *Nowomowa*, 63.

81. In Dec. 1970, in the treaty signed with Poland, West Germany officially recognized the post-1945 western Polish borders. See Dziewanowski, *The Communist Party*, 303–4.

82. On the issue of insecurity over the western Polish border and anti–West German propaganda in Communist Poland of the 1960s, see Zaremba, *Komunizm*, 278–79, 312–13.

83. The Situation in Poland: "Who Are You?" *Trybuna Mazowiecka*, 25 Mar. 1968, 3, AIJPR, file no. 323 0 (180). The concept of slandering the "good name of Poland" here refers to the Western media's portrayal of Polish attitudes toward Jews in WWII and during the Holocaust. On this particular subject and the reactions of official Polish historiography of this time, see Steinlauf, *Bondage*, 75–88.

84. On the presentation of Marxist revisionism as Zionist activity, see *Anti-Jewish Campaign*, 42–44. At the conference of the Central Committee of 9 July 1968 Gomułka himself admitted that the equation between Zionism and Revisionism was made in

the PZPR's leadership. See Polish Facts and Figures, Gomułka's Thesis, 4, AIJPR, file no. 323 0 (180).

85. On the student demonstrations, see Eisler, *Marzec*, 224–320; and Banas, *Scapegoats*, 123–32.

86. I would like to thank Professor Irena Grudzińska-Gross, a former participant in the student events of 1968 and a victim of the 1968 anti-Zionist purge, for discussing the demonstrations with me in great detail.

87. See Stola, *Kampania*, 111–12.

88. Excerpt from Ryszard Gontarz, "Shut Up or Lie," *Prawo i Życie*, Nov. 1968, 1, AIJPR, file no. 323 0 (180).

89. Excerpt from Alina Reutt and Zbigniew Andruszkiewicz, "Alliance of Hatred," *Walka Młodych*, Nov. 1968, 12, AIJPR, file no. 323 0 (180).

90. The Technocrat group, like the Partisan group, emerged in the early 1960s. It was characterized by its advocacy of professionalism, its pragmatism over ideological zeal, and its stress on middle-class values and attitudes. See Schatz, *The Generation*, 227.

91. Situation in Poland: Edward Gierek, speech, 14 Mar. 1968, AIJPR, file no. 323 0 (180). This speech was published in *Trybuna Ludu*, 15 Mar. 1968.

92. Statement by ZBOWiD on student demonstrations; see *Trybuna Ludu*, 13 Mar. 1968, 2.

93. Antoni Słonimski, minutes of the Executive Meeting of the Warsaw Section of the Union of Polish Writers, 29 Feb. 1968. The document is published in Sołtysik and Stępień, *Między tragedią*, 99.

94. Mieczysław Moczar, interview, 12 Apr. 1968. For an excerpt of this interview in English, see *Anti-Jewish Campaign*, 39.

95. Andrzej Werblan, "Przyczynek do genezy konfliktu," *Miesiecznik Literacki*, June 1968, 4–5. A large excerpt from this article is published in English in *Anti-Jewish Campaign*, 40–51. For an interesting analysis of Werblan's article, see Adam Ciołkosz, "Anti-Zionism in Polish Communist Party Politics," in Robert S. Wistrich, ed., *The Left against Zion Communism, Israel and the Middle East* (London, 1979), 145–47.

96. Andrzej Werblan, "Przyczynek do genezy konfliktu," *Miesięcznik Literacki*, June 1968, 3–4. For excerpts in English, see *Anti-Jewish Campaign*, 47–48.

97. See *Research Report* (London, Aug. 1981), 3–4 (published by the Institute of Jewish Affairs). The report gives a variety of other examples of the accusation of only Communist Jews for Stalinist crimes.

98. On the interpretation of Stalinist crimes as only Jewish in origin among some segments of the anti-Communist political elite in the 1970s and 1980s, and in intellectual discourse, see Irwin-Zarecka, *Neutralizing*, 172.

99. A good example of this position can be found in the writings of the respectable, popular, right-wing Catholic historian Andrzej Micewski. See Andrzej Micewski, *Między dwiema orientacjami* (Warsaw, 1990), 11–28. For a recent interesting view

opposing the concept of Judeo-Stalinism as a biased social construction, see Henryk Grynberg, "Żydzi pod flagą biało-czerwoną," *Wprost*, 1 Feb. 2004, 30.

100. For examples of such an interpretation of Mar. 1968, see excerpts from the extreme right-wing press of 2001, published in the collection of press cuttings by Sergiusz Kowalski and Magdalena Tulli, *Zamiast Procesu. Raport o mowie nienawiści* (Warsaw, 2003), 230, 337.

101. For a detailed description of images of the immoral, cosmopolitan, and anti-Polish nature of Polish-Jewish artists and their works, which appeared in the Communist press in the late 1960s, see Osęka, *Syjoniści*, 47–51.

102. Situation in Poland: Resolution of Polish Journalists, 16 Mar. 1968, 28, AIJPR, file no. 380 o (180).

103. Tadeusz Gajcy, "Już nie potrzebujeme," *Poezja*, no. 8 (1969): 5–9 (orig. pub. 1943).

104. Julian Przyboś, "W sprawie Gajcego," *Współczesność*, Dec. 1969, 7.

105. On cases of protests against dismissal of Jewish colleagues, see Eisler, *Marzec*, 378–90.

106. On the instrumental use of the anti-Jewish purge to advance social mobility, see Stola, *Kampania*, 199–202.

107. See Lendvai, *Anti-Semitism*, 3. For literature and a brief discussion of the sociological status of Polish-Jewish emigrants of 1968, see Banas, *Scapegoats*, 122–23, 163–65; and Stola, *Kampania*, 230–33. On the more general problem of the sociological position of Polish Jewry in post-1945 Poland, see the important study by Irena Hurwic-Nowakowska, *A Social Analysis of Post-War Polish Jewry* (Jerusalem, 1986) (based on interviews with Polish Jews conducted in the early postwar period).

108. On the self-identification of the young generation of Polish Jews in the 1960s, see a series of interviews by Joanna Wiszniewicz, "Dzieci i młodzież pochodzenia żydowskiego w szkołach śródmiejskich Warszawy lat sześćdziesiątych," *Respublica Nowa*, 2004, http://respublica.onet.pl/1145735.2artykul.html, accessed Sept. 2005.

109. On the purge of Polish Jews from the state, and the ways in which the policy of emigration was conducted and enforced, see Stola, *Kampania*, 207–28. See also Banas, *Scapegoats*, 133–50; and *Anti-Jewish Campaign*, 59–69.

110. See Eisler, *Marzec*, 389–99.

111. See Zaremba, "Biedni Polacy 68," 144–70.

112. See Eisler, *Marzec*, 398.

113. Although there is scattered material on the subject, the issue of opposition to the anti-Jewish aspect of Mar. 1968 in Polish society awaits a separate scholarly monograph.

114. On the opposition of members of the small group Koło Posłów Znaku, representing the progressive Catholic intelligentsia in the Polish parliament, see Andrzej Friszke, "Trudny egzamin. Koło Posłów Znak w okresie Marca 68," in Marcin Kula, Osęka, and Zaremba, *Referaty*, 183–205. Koło Posłów Znaku emerged during the political thaw of 1956 and included five parliamentary representatives by 1961. Among its members, committed to opposing anti-Semitism, were Tadeusz Mazowiecki and Stanisław Stomma.

115. The demonstrations were brutally suppressed by the police and the army. Five hundred people lost their lives between 14 and 19 Dec. 1970.
116. On Gierek as the new leader of the PZPR, see Zaremba, *Komunizm*, 362–64. On Poland under Gierek's regime, see Neal Ascherson, *The Polish August: The Self-Limited Revolution* (New York, 1982), 106–32.
117. Zaremba, *Komunizm*, 364.
118. For a general discussion of anti-Jewish attitudes in the Communist press in the second half of the 1970s, see Hirszowicz and Szafer, "The Jewish Scapegoat," 7–9.
119. On the history and leaders of the KOR, see Jan Józef Lipski, KOR: *A History of the Workers' Defense Committee in Poland, 1976–1981* (Berkeley, Los Angeles, and London, 1985), 9–79.
120. Hirszowicz and Szafer, "The Jewish Scapegoat," 8–9; and Hirszowicz, "The Jewish Issue," 206–7.
121. On the rise of the Solidarity movement and the events of Aug. 1980, see Lipski, KOR, 331–30. See also Timothy Garton Ash, *The Polish Revolution: Solidarity* (New Haven and London, 2002), 3–72; and Ascherson, *The Polish August*, 229–81.
122. On the Communist regime's 1980 portrayal of Solidarity as Jewish and therefore anti-Polish, see Hirszowicz, "The Jewish Issue," 206–7; and "Poland's Jewish Policies under Martial Law," *Research Report* (London, May 1982) (published by the Institute of Jewish Affairs).
123. See "The Current Polish Crisis and the 1968 Anti-Semitic Campaign," *Research Report* (London, Dec. 1980), 5–6 (published by the Institute of Jewish Affairs).
124. A fabricated Solidarity leaflet, published in *Dziennik Bałtycki*, 10 Mar. 1982, 1, cited in "Poland's Jewish Policies," 10.
125. Bronisław Geremek, fabricated interview with Hanna Krall, *Żołnierz Wolności*, 15 Jan. 1982, 2. This interview was published as a "true interview" in Canada's *Gazeta Polska* in 1996 and is also available on the Web sites of some extreme right-wing ethnonationalistic Polish groups. See, e.g., http://www2.usenetarchive.org/Dir30/File154.html and http://www.polandonline.com/news/pol_Olzima.html, accessed Sept. 2005.
126. See Lipski, KOR, 432–46.
127. Ash, *The Polish Revolution*, 84.
128. For a discussion of the political and social goals of Solidarity, see Ash, *The Polish Revolution*, 216–43.
129. Solidarity's program, 16 Oct. 1981, published in the following collection of documents: Gale Stokes, ed., *From Stalinism to Pluralism: A Documentary History of Eastern Europe since 1945* (New York and Oxford, 1996), 210.
130. On the imposition of martial law, see Ash, *The Polish Revolution*, 273–83.
131. For an overview of the historical background to a "round table," see Jerzy Łukowski and Hubert Zawadzki, *A Concise History of Poland* (Cambridge, 2003), 278–79.

8. Conclusion

1. The legal provisions against discrimination were introduced into the new constitution of Poland, which came into force in Oct. 1997; into the new criminal code (articles 118, 119, 256, and 257); and into the labor code (article 11.3). On the new post-1989 legislation and regulations about the communal rights of minorities, see, e.g., Bogumiła Berdychowska, "Polska polityka narodowościowa, *Kultura*, no. 5 (1995): 89–93; and Zbigniew Łentowicz, "Mniejszości narodowe pokazują języki," published in *Nasza Europa*, an insert in the daily *Rzeczpospolita*, 23 June 2003, 5. For a critical report on the implementation of minority rights in Poland in the late 1990s, visit the Web site of the Council of Europe and see the "Report on Poland 1997," http://www.coe.int/T/E/human_rights/Ecri/5-Archives/Poland/, accessed 2004.

2. On the spread of anti-Jewish and xenophobic perspectives in the aftermath of the political transformation of 1989, see Marcin Kula, "Problem," 23; Kinga Dunin-Horkawicz and Małgorzata Melchior, "Żyd i antysemita," in Marek Czyżewski, Kinga Dunin, and Andrzej Piotrowski, eds., *Cudze problemy: O ważności tego, co nieważne: Analiza dyskursu publicznego w Polsce* (Warsaw, 1991), 37–78; and Kinga Dunin-Horkawicz, "Jak nie być antysemitą w Polsce? Antysemityzm w dyskursie publicznym", *Studia Socjologiczne*, nos. 3–4 (1991): 125–41.

3. For a discussion of the treatment of Mazowiecki by right-wing groups in the first presidential election, see Marcin Kula, "Problem," 23. See also Konstanty Gebert, "Anti-Semitism in the 1990 Polish Presidential Election," *Social Research* 58, no. 4 (1991): 723–55.

4. Wałęsa's demand that individuals disclose their Jewish background was originally made at a press conference on 29 July 1990 and was reported in *Tygodnik Solidarność*, 26 Oct. 1990, 1.

5. See various short reports of Wałęsa's innuendoes in *Gazeta Wyborcza*, 19, 23, 28, and 31 Oct. 1990.

6. See the Internet site of the organization Nigdy więcej: http://www.free.ngo.pl/nw/.

7. See Gebert, "Anti-Semitism," 727.

8. The poll conducted in three Warsaw schools is discussed in Agata Tuszyńska, "Nie jestem rasistką," *Kultura*, no. 513 (June 1990): 3–26. For similar opinions among 138 college students and secondary school pupils, based on research conducted in 1988, see Krystyna Daniel, "The Schools, the Church and Anti-Semitism among Polish Youth," in Paluch, *The Jews*, 429–34.

9. See Marcin Kula, "Problem," 45–49.

10. See Steinlauf, *Bondage*, 76–88. On attitudes toward Jews in the 1980s in Solidarity circles, see also Irwin-Zarecka, *Neutralizing*.

11. See Stefan Amsterdamski and Tadeusz Kowalik, *O czym myśleć nie lubimy czyli o niektórych dylematach zasady narodowej* (Warsaw, 1980), 11–18.

12. Amsterdamski and Kowalik, *O czym*, 11.

13. Jerzy Jedlicki, "Heritage and Collective Responsibility," in Ian Maclean, Alan Mon-

tefiore, and Peter Winch, eds., *The Political Responsibility of Intellectuals* (Cambridge, 1990), 57–58.

14. See Łepkowski, *Myśli*, 35–39.

15. See Krzemiński, introduction, in Krzemiński, *Czy Polacy są antysemitami?* 23.

16. On the issue of "low internal tolerance of others," see Nowicka, "Wprowadzenie," 23–25. For a detailed discussion of anti-Jewish and ethno-nationalist slogans, see Marcin Kula, "Polska 1993–1995: Motywy społeczne i narodowe," *Kultura*, nos. 7–8 (1995): 5–6, 14–15.

17. See Grzegosz Janusz, *Report on the Situation of Persons Belonging to National and Ethnic Minorities in Poland* (Warsaw, 1994), 17 (sponsored by the Phare Program of the European Communities and the Open Society Institute).

18. On the publications of the Antyk bookshop, see, e.g., the following critical essays: Maciej Geller and Jerzy Jedlicki, "Z nadzieją—mimo wszystko," *Tygodnik Powszechny*, 6 Apr. 2004, 5; letters to the editor, *Tygodnik Powszechny*, 13 Apr. 2004, 6; and Zuzanna Radzik, "Piwnice wciąż gniją," *Tygodnik Powszechny*, 30 Mar. 2003, 3.

19. See the report by Krzysztof Burnetko, "Antyk- ciąg dalszy nastąpił," *Tygodnik Powszechny*, 30 Nov. 2001, 11.

20. On anti-Ukrainian and anti-Roma attitudes and actions, see Berdychowska, "Polska polityka," 94–95. See also Marcin Kula, "Polska 1993–1995," 5–6, 14–15. On the situation of the Greek Catholic minority in Poland, see Christopher Hann, "The Development of Polish Civil Society and the Experience of the Greek Catholic Minority in Eastern Europe," in Peter G. Danchin and Elizabeth A. Cole, eds., *Protecting the Human Rights of Religious Minorities in Eastern Europe* (New York, 2002), 437–54.

21. See Marcin Kula, "Polska 1993–1995," 14; and Krzysztof Burnetko, "Ideowi faszyści czy zwykła żulia, czyli o podszewce polskiego skinheada," *Tygodnik Powszechny*, 7 Mar. 1993, 4.

22. See Hanna Świda-Ziemba, "Krótkowzroczność 'kulturalnych,'" *Gazeta Wyborcza*, 7–8 Apr. 2001, 18–19. For an English version of this article, see Polonsky and Michlic, *The Neighbors Respond*, 103–13.

23. See Ewa Nowicka, "Polak-Katolik. O związkach polskości z Katolicyzmem w społecznej świadomości Polaków," in Nowicka, *Religia*, 117–23. The strong connection between Catholic and ethno-national identity is also discussed in Lucjan Adamczuk and Witold Zdaniewicz, eds., *Religiousness of the Polish People 1991* (Warsaw, 1993), 49.

24. Mazowiecki, "Questions," 13.

25. On the development of the Roman Catholic Church in post-1989 Poland, see Jarosław Gowin, *Kościół w czasach wolności, 1989–1999* (Cracow, 1999); and Jarosław Gowin, *Kościół po komunizmie* (Cracow, 1995).

26. See Gowin, *Kościół w czasach wolności*, 344–50.

27. For an analysis of anti-Jewish publications and individuals belonging to the Closed Church, see Joanna Michlic, "The Open Church," 466–70.

28. On the Rydzyk television station, see, e.g., Janina Blikowska and Agnieszka Pukniel, "Telewizja Maryja," *Wprost*, 27 Apr. 2004, 30.

29. For anti-Jewish and xenophobic statements by Bishop Józef Michalik, see *Gazeta Wyborcza*, 30 Sept. 1991, 2; and *Tygodnik Powszechny*, 10 Sept. 2000, 2. For commentaries on the appointment of Archbishop Józef Michalik as primate, see Mikołaj Lizut, "Abp Michalik następcą Glempa," *Gazeta Wyborcza*, 18 Mar. 2004; and Jan Turnau, "Szklanka nie jest pusta", *Gazeta Wyborcza*, 18 Mar. 2004, http:www2.gazeta.pl/info/elementy/druk.jsp?xx=1973969&plik=&tablica=DOCUMENT.

30. See the report by Tomasz Słonimski, "Radio Maryja źle uczy modlić," *Gazeta Wyborcza*, 27 Feb. 2005, http://serwisy.gazeta.pl/kral/2029020,34474,257513.6.html, accessed Feb. 2005.

31. See Lech Wałęsa, letter addressed to bishops and the faithful of the Roman Catholic Church in Poland, 23 Feb. 2005. This letter was published in *Gazeta Wyborcza*, 23 Feb. 2005, http://wiadomosci.gazeta.pl/2029020,55670,2567403.html.

32. See Jan Turnau, "Najwyższa pora na ojca Rydzyka," *Gazeta Wyborcza*, 10 Mar. 2005, <http://serwisy.gazeta.pl/wyborcza/2029020,34474,2593456.html>; and Grzegorz Józefczyk, "Abp. Życiński o Radiu Maryja," *Gazeta Wyborcza*, 25 Feb. 2005, http://serwisy.gazeta.pl/kraj/2029020,34317,2571480.html.

33. See the manifesto of the new party of Radio Maryja, written by Hubert Joachim Bysławek, published in *Gazeta Wyborcza*, 16 Feb. 2005. See also Marcin Kowalski, "Powstaje Partia Maryja," *Gazeta Wyborcza*, 16 Feb. 2005, htpp://Serwisy.gazeta.pl/kraj/1,62905,2554555.html.

34. For an extensive report of Jankowski's anti-Jewish statements in the press, see Roman Daszczyński, "Skandalista Henryk Jankowski," *Gazeta Wyborcza*, 31 Oct. 1997, 4; and Grażyna Borkowska, "Obelgi ks. Jankowskiego," *Gazeta Wyborcza*, 29 July 1996, 2. On Father Rydzyk, see Cezary Gmyz, "Gdzie jest "Dwużydzian Polaków," *Wprost*, 1 Feb. 2004, 22–24.

35. The "storm" in the mass media around Jankowski's professional misconduct and corruption began in summer 2004. See, e.g., Roman Dzaszyński and Maciej Sandecki, "Prałat Jankowski na senatora," *Gazeta Wyborcza*, 25 Sept. 2004, http://serwisy.gazeta.pl/kral/2029020,34317,2304355.html; Marek Wąs and Marek Sterlingow, "Bunt księdza Jankowskiego," *Gazeta Wyborcza*, 26 Sept. 2004, http://serwisy.gazeta.pl/kraj/2029020,34308,2305822.html; and "LPR broni prałata Jankowskiego," http://serwisy.gazeta.pl/kraj/2029020,34308,2221698.html.

36. See Grzegorz Józefczuk and Paweł P. Reszka, "KUL w cieniu teczek," *Gazeta Wyborcza*, 18 Jan. 2005, http://serwisy.gazetapl/wyborcza/2029020,34474,2499778.html, accessed Jan. 2005; and Tomasz Niespial, "Porozumienie KIK-ów poparło abp. Józefa Życińskiego," *Gazeta Wyborcza*, 21 Feb. 2005, http://serwisy.gazeta.pl/kraj/2029020,34317,2562722.html.

37. See Nowicka, "Polak," 122.

38. See Ewa Nowicka and Magdalena Majewska, *Obcy u Siebie. Luteranie Warszawscy* (Warsaw, 1983), 151.

39. Jerzy Sławomir Mac introduced the phrase "anti-Semitism without anti-Semites" into the Polish lexicon in his article about the position of the Closed Church toward Jews; see Jerzy Sławomir Mac, "Antysemityzm bez antysemitów," *Wprost*, 27 Feb. 2000, 38–39.

40. For an insightful essay on the phenomenon of "anti-Semitism without anti-Semites," see Berel Lang, "Self-Description and the Anti-Semite," in Ron Rosenbaum, ed., *Those Who Forget the Past: The Questions of Anti-Semitism* (New York, 2004), 91–95.

41. Glemp issued this statement on 15 Apr. 1990; it was reported in *Gazeta Wyborcza*, 16 Apr. 1990, 2.

42. For a statement from Stanisław Obirek, see Michał Okoński, "Żeby istniał żal," *Tygodnik Powszechny*, 9 Apr. 2000, 3.

43. See Stefan Wilkanowicz, "Jego trudny testament," *Wprost*, 3 Apr. 2005, http://www .wprost.pl/drukuj/?O=75315.

44. For a general study of political parties in post-1989 Poland, see Hubert Tworzecki, *Parties and Politics in Post-1989 Poland* (Boulder co, 1996). For a study of extreme radical ethno-nationalist political parties, see Alina Cała, Dariusz Libionka, and Stefan Zgliszyński, "Monitoring Anti-Semitism in Poland, 1999–2001," *BZIH*, nos. 3– 4 (2002): 501–14. See also Marcin Kula, "Polska 1993–1995," 5–13; Maciej Łuczak, "Teraz Polska," *Wprost*, 23 Nov. 1997, 27–28; and Sławomir Jerzy Mac, "Hitlerjugend," *Wprost*, 16 July 2000, 21–23.

45. On the program of the Solidarity Electoral Alliance (aws), see Marian Krzaklewski, "21 punktów w XXI wiek," *Gazeta Wyborcza*, 10 Sept. 1997, 22. For an interesting analysis of mainstream right-wing political parties, see Artur Domosławski, "W okopach Św. Katarzyny. Z dziejów polskiej prawicy 1989–1997," *Gazeta Wyborcza*, 10 Sept. 1997, 18–21.

46. The Conservative Party of Aleksander Hall originated in the dissident political movement Ruch Młodej Polski. From its inception other right-wing ethno-nationalistic dissident organizations criticized this organization for being in contact with the left-wing kor and one of its leaders, Jacek Kuroń. See, e.g., "W sprawie "Polityki Polskiej," *Jestem Polakiem*, no. 10 (1987): 42, 51.

47. For an apologetic position on Roman Dmowski's anti-Semitism, see an interview with the mainstream right-wing politician Wiesław Chrzanowski, former chairman of the Christian-National Union, which is based on the ideological traditions of National Democracy. See Wiesław Chrzanowski, "Przyszedł lud do narodu", *Gazeta Wyborcza*, 14–16 Apr. 2001, 10–12.

48. See a report on the presidential election of 1995 in *The World Report of Anti-Semitism, 1996* (London, 1996).

49. *World Report of Anti-Semitism*.

50. On the annual Day of Judaism in the Roman Catholic Church in Poland, see Bishop Stanisław Gądecki's statement in *Tygodnik Powszechny*, 25 May 2000, 2.

51. See Shevah Eden, "Attempts to Use Historical and Literary Textbooks in Poland and Israel to Foster Mutual Understanding", *Polin* 14 (2001): 306–14.

52. See Andrzej Bryk, "Polish Society Today and the Memory of the Holocaust," in Yehuda Bauer et al., *Remembering for the Future: Working Papers and Addenda* (Oxford, 1989), 3: 2373. See also the report of a team of nine Polish scholars of the Jewish Historical Institute on how the Holocaust is presented in history textbooks, *BZIH*, nos. 3–4 (1997); and Hanna Węgrzynek, *The Treatment of Jewish Themes in Polish Schools* (New York, 1998).

53. See the report "Otwarta Rzeczpospolita," *Midrasz*, no. 6 (1999): 20. The organization published a collection of anti-Jewish excerpts from various radical ethno-nationalistic, conservative, and Catholic publications from 2001; see Kowalski and Tulli, *Zamiast*.

54. See Janion, *Do Europy*; Maria Janion, "Spór o antysemityzm," *Tygodnik Powszechny—Magazyn Kontrapunkt*, 22 Oct. 2000, 9–12; Stanisław Musiał, "Żydzi żądni krwi," *Gazeta Wyborcza*, 29–30 July 2000, 22; Stanisław Musiał, "Droga krzyżowa Żydów Sandomierskich," *Gazeta Wyborcza*, 5–6 Aug. 2000, 21–22; Stanisław Musiał, "Czarne jest czarne," *Tygodnik Powszechny-Magazyn Kontrapunkt*, 22 Oct. 2000, 12; Hanna Świda-Ziemba, "Rozbrajać własne mity," *Znak*, no. 6 (2000): 49–54.

55. See Świda-Ziemba, "Rozbrajać," 48.

56. See Gross, *Neighbors*, 94.

57. See Joanna Michlic, " 'The Heart of Darkness' in Polish-Jewish Relations: On the Study of Polish-Jewish Relations during the Second World War in the Aftermath of Jan Tomasz Gross's Sąsiedzi," *Gal-Ed* 19 (2004): 95–105 (in Hebrew).

58. For the history of the debate and various voices in the debate, see the main introduction by Polonsky and Michlic in *The Neighbors Respond*, 1–43; and Michlic, "Coming to Terms," 7–10.

59. The article by Jan Błoński (in English) appeared in *Polin* 1 (1986) and in Polonsky, *My Brother's Keeper?* 34–52. For a representative sample of the debate about Błoński's article see (in English) Aharon Weiss, ed., *Yad Vashem Studies* 19 (1997); and Polonsky, *My Brother's Keeper?* On the debate, see Steinlauf, *Bondage*, 89–121; Polonsky, "Beyond," 190–224; and Shmuel Krakowski, "Jews and Poles in Polish Historiography," *Yad Vashem Studies* 19 (1997): 317–40.

60. The debate, including a publication of letters and phone calls received by *Gazeta Wyborcza*, was published on 2, 3, 7, 11, and 12–13 Feb. 1994. The responses by historians Andrzej Friszke, Andrzej Paczkowski, Teresa Prekerowa, Włodzimierz Borodziej, Tomasz Strzembosz were published in *Gazeta Wyborcza*, 5–6 Feb. 1994. See *Intelligence Report—Article on Warsaw Uprising Touches Raw Nerve in Polish-Jewish Relations* (London, Apr. 1994), 1–2 (published by the Institute of Jewish Affairs). For a more detailed analysis of the debate about Cichy's article, see Polonsky and Michlic, *The Neighbors Respond*, 16; and Steinlauf, *Bondage*, 133–34.

61. See Polonsky, "Polish-Jewish," 231.

62. Jacek Kuroń, *Wiara i Wina. Do i od Komunizmu* (Warsaw, 1990), 18–27. The first edition was published by Aneks in London in 1989. For excerpts of Kuroń's memoirs in English, see Jacek Kuroń, "My First Encounter with Jews and Ukrainians," *Polin* 14 (2001): 237–48.

63. See Kuroń, *Wiara i Wina*, 246.

64. See Polonsky's introduction to *My Brother's Keeper?* 14.

65. See Dariusz Czaja, "To nie 'oni' niestety," *Gazeta Wyborcza*, 16–17 Dec. 2000, 21–22; Jacek Kurczewski, "Mord Rytualny," *Gazeta Wyborcza*, 10 Dec. 2000, 36–37; Krystyna Skarzyńska, "Zbiorowa wyobraźnia, wspólna wina," *Gazeta Wyborcza*, 25–26 Nov. 2000; Dawid Warszawski, "Odpowiedzialność i jej brak," *Gazeta Wyborcza*, 9–10 Dec. 2000, 20–21; Dawid Warszawski, "Trupi uścisk," *Wprost*, 15 July 2001, 24; Dawid Warszawski, "Mowa pokutna. Bez także," *Gazeta Wyborcza*, 9 Mar. 2001, 18; Dawid Warszawski, "Dwie Polski w Jedwabnem," *Wprost*, 21 July 2002, 24–26; and Joanna Tokarska-Bakir, "Nasz człowiek w Pieczarach. Jedwabne; pamięć nieodzyskana," *Tygodnik Powszechny*, 31 Mar. 2001, 1, 4. For other voices supporting Gross's stance, see Michlic, "Coming to Terms," 12–18.

66. See, e.g., Józef Życiński, "The Banalization of Barbarity," in *Thou Shalt Not Kill* (Warsaw, 2002), 257; Henryk Muszyński, "Biedny chrześcijanin patrzy na Jedwabne," *Tygodnik Powszechny—Magazyn Kontrapunkt*, 25 Mar. 2001, 13; and Michał Czajkowski, "Czysta nierządnica", *Tygodnik Powszechny*, 27 May 2001, 1.

67. See Jacek Kuroń, "Nienawiść do ofiary," *Gazeta Wyborcza*, 17–18 Feb. 2001, 23; Waldemar Kuczyński, "Płonąca stodoła i ja," *Gazeta Wyborcza*, 24–25 Mar. 2001, 21; Aleksander Kwaśniewski, "Polska szlachetność i polska hańba. Z prezydentem Aleksandrem Kwaśniewskim rozmawiają ks. Adam Boniecki i Krzysztof Burnetko," *Tygodnik Powszechny*, 15 Apr. 2001, 8–9; Aleksander Kwaśniewski, "Co to znaczy przepraszam," *Polityka*, no. 28 (2001): 13. See also the appeal of Jacek Kuroń, Henryk Wujec, Father Michał Czajkowski, and the well-known courier of the underground Polish state Jan Nowak-Jeziorański. The appeal was published in *Tygodnik Powszechny*, 22 Apr. 2001, 5.

68. See the interview with Leon Kieres in *Dziennik Bałtycki*, 15 June 2001, in which he states: "I treat 'Polishness' as a civic category and thus treat Jews of Jedwabne as my copatriots." Cited in *Polityka*, no. 22 (2001): 88.

69. See Michlic, "Coming to Terms," 11.

70. The League of Polish Families, a Catholic nationalist party, is currently one of the strongest radical right-wing nationalistic parties in Poland, similar to France's Front Nationale. It was formed just before the 2001 general parliamentary election, in which it won 7.87 percent of vote, giving it thirty-eight deputies in the parliament and two in the Senate House. Its spiritual authority is Father Tadeusz Rydzyk of Radio Maryja. Antoni Macierewicz was one of the party's first leaders. The party uses nationalist, xenophobic, and anti-Semitic rhetoric. In the most recent parlia-

mentary election of 25 Sept. 2005 LPR gained a similar percentage of votes, giving it thirty-four deputies in the parliament. See the report "Sześć wspaniałych," *Wprost*, 27 Sept. 2005, http://www.wprost.pl/drukuj/?O=81360. For a detailed analysis of various voices using the representation of the Jew as the harmful other, see Michlic, "Coming to Terms," 15–19, 23, 30–31.

71. Tomasz Strzembosz, "Przemilczana kolaboracja," *Rzeczpospolita*, 27–28 Jan. 2001, A6– A7. This article was a critical response to the positive review of *Neighbors* by historian Andrzej Żbikowski of the Jewish Historical Institute in Warsaw, who had argued that the accusation of Jewish collaboration with the Soviet regime was commonly manipulated in order to initiate anti-Jewish massacres. See Andrzej Żbikowski, "Nie było rozkazu," *Rzeczpospolita*, 4 Jan. 2001, A6–A7.

72. Strzembosz, "Przemilczana," A6.

73. Tomasz Strzembosz, "Inny obraz sąsiadów," *Rzeczpospolita*, 31 Mar.–1 Apr. 2001, A6– A7.

74. See Marek Jan Chodakiewicz, "Kłopoty z kuracją szokową," *Rzeczpospolita*, 5 Jan. 2001, A6. Chodakiewicz's new book on Jedwabne has also been published. See also Bogdan Musiał, "Historiografia mityczna," *Rzeczpospolita*, 24–25 Feb. 2001, A6; Piotr Gontarczyk, "Gross kontra fakty," *Życie*, 31 Jan. 2001, 4; and Leszek Żebrowski, "Jedwabnym szlakiem kłamstw," http://www.geocities.com/jedwabne/english/wywiad_z _leszkiem_zebrowskim_2.htm.

75. See, e.g., Lech Stępniewski, "Krew ich na nas i na dzieci nasze . . . ," *Najwyższy Czas*, 12 Mar. 2001; Lech Stępniewski, "Cud Purymowy i inne historie," *Najwyższy Czas*, 14 Mar. 2001; Lech Stępniewski, "Prolegomena do matematyki narodowej," *Najwyższy Czas*, 25–26 Apr. 2001; Lech Stępniewski, "O kanalizacjii," *Najwyższy Czas*, 29–30 Apr. 2001.

76. See Witold Starnawski, "Jak IPN chroni narodową pamięć," *Tygodnik Głos*, 26 Jan. 2002, http://www.glos.com.pl/archiwum/2002/004/06publ/publ.htm, accessed Feb. 2002.

77. For an anti-Kieres report, see Maciej Walaszczyk, "Kieres w naróżniku," *Nasz Dziennik*, 1 Mar. 2002, http://www.naszdziennik.pl/stcodz/polska/20020301/p032.shtml, accessed Mar. 2002. One of the first attacks against Kieres took place in June 2001. Andrzej Reymann, editor-in-chief of the extreme bimonthly *Najjaśniejsza Rzeczpospolita*, asked Lech Kaczyński, the chief prosecutor of Poland, to begin an investigation of Leon Kieres and Radosław Ignatiew; see Iwona Boratyń, "Prokurator Tuszował?" *Słowo Ludu*, 17 May 2002, 2.

78. On this event and the reactions of political and cultural elites to the criticism of Kieres, see Michlic, "Coming to Terms," 30–31.

79. See Ewa K. Czaczkowska, "Byłem sam, będą nas setki," *Rzeczpospolita*, 10 July 2001.

80. For opinion polls of the younger generations on the debate about Jedwabne, see Michlic, "Coming to Terms," 27.

81. See Antoni Sułek, "Władza Żydów i władza stereotypu," and Agnieszka Kublik,

"Polska wiara w Żydów—badania TNS OBOP dla *Gazety Wyborczej*," both in *Gazeta Wyborcza*, 24 July 2002, http://wyborcza.gazeta.pl/info/artykul.jsp?xx=947114&dzial= 0110198 and http://wyborcza.gazeta.pl/info/artykul.jsp?xx=947112&dzial=0110198.

82. On the links between the LPR and All-Polish Youth see, e.g., Wojciech Szacki, "Szkoła wszechpolaków; kup sobie Wrzodaka," *Gazeta Wyborcza*, 5 Jan. 2005, http://serwisy .gazeta.pl/kraj/2029020,62665,2477005.html. For anti-Semitic statements, see also the Web sites of All-Polish Youth, at http://www.wszechpolacy.pl, and the LPR, at http://www/super24.pl.

83. On the contemporary political scene in Poland, see Mirosława Grabowska, *Podział postkomunistyczny. Społeczne podstawy polityki w Polsce po 1989 roku* (Warsaw, 2004). For a review of this book, see Teresa Bogucka, "Pęknieta Polska," *Gazeta Wyborcza*, 28 Jan. 2005, http://serwisy.gazeta.pl/wyborcza/202902020,34474,25118948.html, accessed Jan. 2005. On the eve of the ensuing presidential and parliamentary elections in 2005 major newspapers such as *Gazeta Wyborcza* dedicated much space to discussion of current politics, including interviews with leading politicians on the left and on the right, opinion polls, and critical reports. One development was the announcement of the establishment of a new political party representing liberals and the liberal center, Partia Demokratyczna, in Apr. 2005. The emergence of this party in May 2005 marks the end of Unia Wolności, which was totally incorporated into it. In the parliamentary election of 25 Sept. 2005 the new Partia Demokratyczna failed to gain a sufficient number of votes to have representatives in the new parliament.

Index

Ingram Content Group UK Ltd.
Milton Keynes UK
UKHW010659250423
420618UK00011B/167